JUDGES, ADMINISTRATORS AND THE
COMMON LAW IN ANGEVIN ENGLAND

JUDGES, ADMINISTRATORS
AND THE COMMON LAW
IN ANGEVIN ENGLAND

RALPH. V. TURNER

THE HAMBLEDON PRESS
LONDON AND RIO GRANDE

Published by The Hambledon Press 1994

102 Gloucester Avenue, London NW1 8HX (U.K.)
P.O. Box 162, Rio Grande, Ohio 45674 (U.S.A.)

ISBN 1 85285 104 X

© R.V. Turner 1994

A description of this book is available from
the British Library and from the Library of Congress

Printed on acid-free paper and bound in Great Britain by
Cambridge University Press

Contents

Acknowledgements	vii
Reflections and Reconsiderations	ix
1 Henry II's Aims in Reforming England's Land Law: Feudal or Royalist?	1
2 The Origins of Common Pleas and King's Bench	17
3 The Origins of the Medieval English Jury: Frankish, English, or Scandinavian	35
4 Roman Law in England before the Time of Bracton	45
5 Who was the Author of *Glanvill*? Reflections on the Education of Henry II's Common Lawyers	71
6 The Reputation of Royal Judges under the Angevin Kings	103
7 The *Miles Literatus* in Twelfth- and Thirteenth-Century England: How Rare a Phenomenon?	119
8 Religious Patronage of Angevin Royal Administrators, *c.* 1170–1239	137
9 Clerical Judges in English Secular Courts: The Ideal Versus the Reality	159
10 Richard Barre and Michael Belet: Two Angevin Civil Servants	181
11 Simon of Pattishall, Early Common Law Judge from Northamptonshire	199

12 Roger Huscarl, Professional Lawyer in England and Royal Justice in Ireland, *c.* 1199–1230	215
13 Changing Perceptions of the New Administrative Class in Anglo-Norman and Angevin England: The *Curiales* and their Conservative Critics	225
14 The Royal Courts Treat Disseizin by the King: John and Henry III, 1199–1240	251
15 Exercise of the King's Will in Inheritance of Baronies: The Example of King John and William Briwerre	269
16 The Mandeville Inheritance, 1189–1236: Its Legal, Political and Social Context	289
Index	307

Acknowledgements

The essays reprinted below are reproduced by the kind permission of the original publishers

1   *Law in Medieval Life and Thought*, ed. Edward B. King and Susan J. Ridyard, *Sewanee Medieval Studies*, 5 (1990), pp. 121–35.

2   *American Journal of Legal History*, 21 (1977), pp. 238–54.

3   *Journal of British Studies*, 7 (1968), pp. 1–10.

4   *Journal of British Studies*, 15 (1975), pp. 1–25.

5   *Law and History Review*, 8 (1990), pp. 97–127.

6   *Albion*, 11 (1979), pp. 301–16.

7   *American Historical Review*, 83 (1978), pp. 928–65.

8   *Albion*, 18 (1986), pp. 1–21.

9   *Medievalia et Humanistica*, new series, 3 (1972), p. 75–98.

10 *Medieval Prosopography*, 6 (1985), pp. 25–48.

11 *Northamptonshire Past and Present*, 6 (1978), pp. 5–14.

12 *Irish Jurist*, new series, 16 (1981), pp. 290–98.

13 *Journal of British Studies*, 29 (1990), pp. 93–117.

14 *American Journal of Legal History*, 12 (1968), pp. 1–18.

15 *Albion*, 22 (1990), pp. 383–401.

16 *Haskins Society Journal*, 1 (1989), pp. 148–72.

Reflections and Reconsiderations

The essays reprinted here, all dealing in some fashion with the growth of administrative monarchy in England, were written over the past twenty-five years. The bulk of these papers began as inquiries into questions that struck me as needing answers in the course of writing two books, *The King and His Courts: The Role of King John and Henry III in the Administration of Justice, 1199–1240* and *The English Judiciary in the Age of Glanvill and Bracton, c. 1179–1239*.[1] They are published here largely unaltered, although reflection and reconsideration since their publication have resulted in some alterations in my views, which I present in this introductory essay. My debt to other scholars working on the common law and the royal administration in Angevin England in reshaping my views will be evident from the references to their works.

My essays fall into three categories. First are some general considerations of the early common law and institutions for justice in the Angevin period, including the central courts, juries, and the lawbook *Glanvill*. Second are those concerned with the personnel of the royal courts and with other royal servants as a new administrative class conducting the king's business by written documents. This section includes some individual biographies of second-level royal agents that grew out of my study of the careers of the royal justices. Third are essays concentrating on the functioning of the law in the Angevin period, especially the royal courts' treatment of cases touching the king as feudal lord. This last group derives from a desire to reconsider my earlier findings on the king's role in justice, especially the impact of his will on cases involving succession to baronial landholdings.

When engaged in writing my doctoral thesis on the role of the king in the work of the royal courts of justice in Angevin England, I did not realize that I was working in legal history. My original aim had been to investigate how theories of kingship worked in practice, how the king as the "fount of justice" took responsibility for the work of his judges and what role the royal will played in operations of the courts, a study that I viewed as belonging to political and institutional history. Only later did it dawn on me that my

---

[1] Cornell University Press, 1968; Cambridge University Press, 1985.

examination of cases from the *curia regis* rolls made me a legal historian, and I strove to educate myself in the literature of English legal history. My aim was to look at the evolution of English common law in a broad context, connecting it to the intellectual currents of the twelfth and thirteenth centuries and to the biographies of the individuals who were shaping it.

Once my doctoral thesis was revised and published as *The King and his Courts*, I came to see that work as institutional history, written without much awareness of the individuals who were assisting the king in administering justice and neglecting the impact of human personality on the law and the courts. I felt a need to learn much more about the chief justiciar and his justices, their origins, their preparation for their work, the paths they followed to the judiciary, their relationship with the king, and something of their attitude toward their work as judges. This quest took longer than I had anticipated, leading me into many byways before I published my second book, *The English Judiciary in the Age of Glanvill and Bracton*. A broader interest in the Angevins' royal servants, many of them ambitious "new men" capable of operating the new machinery of government, resulted in another book, *Men Raised from the Dust: Administrative Service and Upward Mobility in Angevin England*.[2]

I place first in this collection an essay, "Henry II's Aims in Reforming England's Land Law: Feudal or Royalist?" that places that monarch's legal reforms in a broad context. It seeks to shed some light on the vexed question of the aims behind his innovations. After writing this piece and reflecting on it, I remain convinced that the Angevin reforms in English law were basically "royalist" in nature and intent and that characterizations of Anglo-Norman and Angevin England as a "feudal monarchy" or searches for purely feudal sources of the legal innovations contribute little to historical understanding. R.C. van Caenegem's recent edition of *English Lawsuits from William I to Richard I* reveals that pleas concerning knights' quotas of military service first appeared under Henry I and that they did not become frequent until Henry II's time. He concludes that the Norman conquest "in no way destroyed everything the Old-English monarchy had built".[3] As noted in my article, doctrines of royal authority descending from the Anglo-Saxon period permitted frequent interventions by twelfth-century monarchs, with the possible exception of Stephen of Blois, in the fiefs of their tenants-in-chief, "overturning the principles and the functioning of a feudal regime of the classic type".[4]

Modern study of Henry II's revolution in land law began with F.W. Maitland. In his view, feudal ties of personal loyalty and performance of

---

[2] University of Pennsylvania Press, 1988.

[3] Selden Society, 106 (London, 1990), p. xiv.

[4] Jacques Boussard, "Aspects particuliers de la féodalité dans l'empire Plantagenêt", *Bulletin de la Société des Antiquaires de l'Ouest*, 4th series, 7 (1963): 34.

military services had rapidly lost their significance after their introduction to England after 1066, and the property element in the feudal pattern of landholding quickly took on greater prominence than the personal aspect. Tenants began to regard their tenements as their own property; and they desired recognition of their sons' rights of hereditary succession to their tenements and the right to alienate portions of their holdings. Maitland and his followers concluded that proprietary right, the primary control over feudal tenements, was tending to pass from lords to tenants before 1154. In their view, Henry II and his justices recognized this and took steps to protect tenants' proprietary interest, providing procedures that reduced lords' jurisdictional rights over their feudal tenants, limited their power to dispossess their tenants, and strengthened tenants' ability to dispose of their lands as they wished. While later experts disagreed about details, most accepted this essentially royalist interpretation. R.C. van Caenegem found in his edition of *Royal Writs in England from the Conquest to Glanvill* that growth of the common law was an evolutionary process, with Norman kings' executive writs building upon Anglo-Saxon royal practice and evolving into Henry II's writs and assizes, while Doris M. Stenton recognized an "Angevin leap forward", propelled by Henry's conscious invention of new writs, in her *English Justice between the Norman Conquest and the Great Charter*.[5]

Maitland's view of the anti-feudal or anti-baronial character of Henry's legal reforms held sway until challenged by S.F.C. Milsom. While Milsom's analysis of feudal courts' inadequacies in settling disputes raised over lords' disciplining of their tenants by distraint of land displays great originality, my survey casts doubt upon the larger Milsomian construct of England before Henry II's reign as "a truly feudal society" and its placing of Henry's reforms in a totally feudal context. In the view of Milsom and his most ardent disciple, Robert C. Palmer, the property element in the feudal contract remained subordinate to the performance of services throughout much of the twelfth century. Questions raised about performance or non-performance of services constituted the chief issues between lords and tenants, not proprietary right over fiefs. Milsom and his followers see Henry II's imposition of the royal court's authority over the feudal courts as aimed simply at making them function more effectively, and they find that this royal regulation of the feudal courts had an unintended effect of undermining lords' authority over their tenants. As the king's justices hardened flexible feudal customs into rigid rules of law, they tipped the balance from a personal tie based on performance of services toward the property aspect.

---

[5] Van Canegem, *Royal Writs*, Selden Society, vol. 77 (London, 1959); Stenton, *English Justice*, American Philosophical Society (Philadelphia, 1964).

According to Milsom's followers, Henry II's common law created property when royal justices guaranteed feudal tenants secure possession of their lands, limiting their lords' power to dispossess them. In stating this view that legal protection for proprietary right to feudal tenures only appeared about 1200, they follow S.E. Thorne's late dating of rights of inheritance in his 1959 article, "English Feudalism and Estates in Land".[6] Numerous cases collected in Van Caenegem's *English Lawsuits from William I to Richard I*, however, record claims based on hereditary right; for example, a grant *c.* 1137–38 by Stephen of Blois to Walter Martel "and his heirs after him" of land *in feodum et hereditatem*.[7] For a useful discussion of this question, see John Hudson, "Life-Grants of Land and the Development of Inheritance in Anglo-Norman England".[8] He finds that much progress toward inheritance of feudal tenements, at least those held of ecclesiastical honors, had been made by 1135 in considerably more instances than allowed for by Thorne and Milsom. See also Joseph Biancalana, "For Want of Justice: Legal Reforms of Henry II"; he follows Sir James Holt in rejecting rigid distinctions between "mere customs and rules of law" governing succession to fiefs in the twelfth century, and he sees "strong norms of inheritance at work".[9]

Since publishing this piece, I have found reinforcement for my questioning of the Milsomian conclusion that the usurpation of the feudal courts' jurisdiction by Henry II's *curia regis* was unplanned and accidental. Work on the Anglo-Norman kings shows that they followed their Anglo-Saxon predecessors in accepting a royal responsibility to intervene in settling their subjects' quarrels, for example, channeling their quests for revenge into the royal court. Biancalana's lengthy overview of the Angevin monarch's legal innovations, "For Want of Justice", rejects both Maitland's view that Henry's legal reforms constituted "an unbridled attack on lords" and Milsom's view that they were "a series of unrelated experiments protective of a pre-existing feudal framework". Biancalana's analysis of Henry's writs and assizes leads him to assert that expanded royal jurisdiction rested on traditional grounds of failure of justice in lay lords' courts, with sources in both feudal tradition and concepts of public authority. In his view, Henry II and his counselors "imagined an organized central power" that could remedy failures of seignorial justice. He denies Milsom's contention that the assize of novel disseizin was "merely a well-intentioned though heavy-handed attempt to make seignorial courts work according to established custom".[10]

---

[6] *Cambridge Law Journal*, new series, 6 (1959); reprinted in S.E. Thorne, *Essays in Legal History* (Hambledon Press, 1985).
[7] *English Lawsuits*, 1, no. 294.
[8] *Anglo-Norman Studies*, 12 (1990): 67–80.
[9] *Columbia Law Review*, 88 (1988): 495.
[10] Biancalana, pp. 446, 534, and p. 483.

Paul A. Brand in "'Multis Vigiliis Excogitatam et Inventam': Henry II and the Creation of the English Common Law", comes to the conclusion that "Henry II and his advisers possessed a vision of a legal system they wished to create in England, a legal system that was radically different from the fragmented, localized and inefficient system they had inherited".[11] Brand rejects a "feudal" view that Henry II and his counselors were incapable of reaching out beyond their own feudal world; he sees them "consciously attempting to create something quite new and very significantly different from anything that had existed before".[12] See also David Crouch's warning against treating twelfth-century England as "a truly feudal world". He sees twelfth-century society as one of feudal honors, but also "a society in which public authority, whether stemming from the king or the concerns of the local community, underlay, or existed side-by-side with, such aristocratic groupings".[13]

In the essay, "The Origins of Common Pleas and King's Bench", I sought to delve more deeply into questions earlier considered in my first book, *The King and His Courts*. This examination of the earliest years of the Bench at Westminster and the court following the king reveals the expanded scope of royal justice under the Angevins; the king's court was no longer a feudal tribunal only for "the great men and the great causes".[14] Yet the development of two central royal courts with almost parallel jurisdictions and procedures seemed to call for explanation. I go over some of the same ground in my second book, *The English Judiciary in the Age of Glanvill and Bracton*, especially Chapter 3, part 2, "The Emergence of a Professional Judiciary", where I assert more strongly that 1194 was the date for the separation of the Bench from the Exchequer as one of Hubert Walter's innovations, based on identification of men who were specializing in the work of justice.

Likewise, an early essay of mine that took a historiographical approach, "The Origins of the Medieval English Jury: Frankish, English or Scandinavian?", indicates non-feudal sources for Henry II's legal reforms. It is a survey of different opinions on the sources of Henry's juries; my own contribution is a suggestion that the possessory assizes and the jury of presentment may have had different sources, allowing for more eclectic origins. Some work on jury origins since 1968 is worth noting. For a general overview of modes of proof, see R.C. van Caenegem, "Methods of Proof in Western Medieval Law", and also his "Public Prosecution of Crime in

---

[11] *Haskins Society Journal*, 2 (1990): 222.
[12] Brand, p. 271.
[13] "Debate: Bastard Feudalism Revised," *Past and Present*, no. 131 (1991): 166–67.
[14] Frederick Pollock and F. W. Maitland, *History of English Law* (Cambridge University Press, 1898), 1: 108.

Twelfth-century England".[15] He rejects Hurnard's finding of continuity between Æthelred's twelve thegns and Henry II's juries of presentment and suggests that under the Anglo-Norman kings the local justiciars initiated prosecutions of suspected criminals. Van Caenegem also suggests that collective accusations by synodal witnesses in the church courts may have contributed to the jury of presentment. Richard H. Helmholz takes up this suggestion in "The Early History of the Grand Jury and the Common Law". He finds that parallels between communal accusations by Angevin presenting juries and the church's collective synodal witnesses "make this influence likely. They do not prove it absolutely".[16]

As Van Caenegem's and Helmholz's comparisons of practice in the ecclesiastical courts with common law procedures indicate, some authorities still find Roman law making an impact on the common law. This is another area in which I find myself inclining toward a "royalist" view of English legal history rather than following current tendencies, which find the basis for the common law lying completely in English and western French feudal custom. Although my study, "Roman Law in England before the Time of Bracton", found evidence for considerable knowledge of Roman legal principles in twelfth-century England, I concluded that the civil law made little impact on the early common law. Since writing this article in 1968, I have modified this view, in large part due to a closer examination of the two legal treatises, *Glanvill* and *Bracton*. My article "Who was the Author of *Glanvill*? Reflections on the Education of Henry II's Common Lawyers", put forward Godfrey de Lucy as a candidate for authorship of the treatise, since he was one of justices active in Henry's last decade who is known to have been a graduate of the schools, acquainted with rules of logic and with Romano-canonical principles. Francis de Zulueta and Peter Stein, *The Teaching of Roman Law in England around 1200*, reinforce the likelihood that the author of *Glanvill* was a competent Romanist. They make plain that in the last quarter of the twelfth century, "all who aspired to be lawyers in England, canonists and secular lawyers alike", had access to competent instruction in Roman law.[17]

In my book, *The English Judiciary*, I took into account S.E. Thorne's dating of the treatise known as *Bracton* as early as the 1230s in his edition.[18] That lawbook shows clearly that judges and clerks of the *curia regis* in the early

---

[15] The first article is in *Academiae Analecta, Klasse der Letteren, Koninklijke Academie voorf Wetenschalppen, Letteren en Schone Kunsten van Belgie*, 45 (1983): 85–127; an English translation of his "La Preuve dans le droit du moyen âge occidental," *Recueils de la Société Jean Bodin*, 17, 2, *La Preuve: Moyen Age et Temps Modernes* (Brussels, 1965), pp. 691–753; and the second in *Church and Government in the Middle Ages: Essays presented to C.R. Cheney on his Seventieth Birthday*, ed. C.N.L. Brooke, D.E. Luscombe, G.H. Martin and Dorothy Owen (Cambridge University Press, 1976), pp. 41–75.

[16] *University of Chicago Law Review*, 50 (1983): 626.

[17] Selden Society, supplementary series, 8 (London, 1990), p. xxx.

[18] S.E. Thorne, ed., *Bracton on the Laws and Customs of England*, 4 vols., Selden Society (Harvard University Press, 1968–77).

thirteenth century were competent Romanists, who used their knowledge of Roman and canonist principles to shape the common law into a coherent system. See my *English Judiciary*, chapter 5, part 3, "Book-Learning in Thirteenth-century English Law", for evidence of a "school" at Westminster for clerks of the common law courts.

Much recent work makes it clear, then, that despite the insistence of some legal historians that Henry II's legal innovations were crafted entirely from feudal materials, important reforms were "suggested by Roman law notions mediated through the canon law", to cite Richard H. Helmholz.[19] Joseph Biancalana also finds that Henry II's legislation against disseizins "applied canon law principles".[20] See also Charles Donahue, Jr., "Proof by Witnesses in the Church Courts of Mediaeval England: An Imperfect Reception of the Learned Law".[21] He and Norma Adams conclude from their survey of thirteenth-century ecclesiastical cases from the province of Canterbury that England's church courts' reception of Romano-canonical procedure was "already well-advanced" in the time of Archbishop Hubert Walter, 1193–1205.[22]

Sir Richard Southern sought in his article, "Master Vacarius and the Beginning of an English Academic Tradition", to show that Vacarius could not have taught Roman law in England in an academic setting; and, in a chapter in the new *History of the University of Oxford*, he finds that until the 1180s the schools at Oxford were teaching no law, but the *trivium* only.[23] Yet his views have not gone unchallenged.[24] Francis de Zulueta and Peter Stein in *The Teaching of Roman Law in England around 1200* edit the text of a course of lectures on Justinian's Institutes, given in England in the last quarter of the twelfth century. While they agree with Southern that Vacarius's *Liber pauperum* may not have been taught at Oxford before the 1190s, they find evidence that Vacarius was engaged in formal teaching of the civil law somewhere in England, possibly at Lincoln or Northampton, in the 1170s and 1180s.

The article, "The Reputation of Royal Judges under the Angevin Kings", was a prepatory piece for my book, *The English Judiciary*; and much of the

---

[19] "The Early History of the Grand Jury and the Common Law," *University of Chicago Law Review*, 50 (1983).

[20] "For Want of Justice," *Columbia Law Review*, 88: 476.

[21] *On the Laws and Customs of England: Essays in Honor of Samuel E. Thorne*, ed. Morris S. Arnold, Thomas A Green, Sally A. Scully, and Stephen D. White (Chapel Hill: University of North Carolina Press, 1981), pp 127–58.

[22] *Select Cases from the Ecclesiastical Courts of the Province of Canterbury, c. 1200–1301*, Selden Society, vol. 95 (London, 1981), p. 12.

[23] *Medieval Learning and Literature: Essays Presented to Richard William Hunt*, ed. J.G. Alexander and M.T. Gibson (Oxford, 1976), pp 257–86; and "From Schools to University", in the *The Early Oxford Schools*, vol. 1 of *History of the University of Oxford*, ed. J.I. Catto, (Oxford, 1984).

[24] See Leonard E. Boyle, "Vacarius and the Beginnings of Legal Studies at Oxford," *Viator*, 14 (1983): 107–31.

material presented in the article is repeated in the introduction and the final chapter of the book. Since I first set forth my mildly positive views of the work of the royal justices, I have seen little reason for any major alteration in my views. Indeed, I have collected many additional examples of the venality of the ecclesiastical courts that contrast sharply with the high reputation of the English royal justices.[25] For confirmation of the popularity of royal courts in the Angevin period, see the chapter, "Justice and Jurisdiction", that Sir James Holt added to his new edition of his book *Magna Carta*. In it he states, "But, by and large, for the ordinary litigant, knight or freeman, it was an effective system, probably more so than anything else available in western Christendom."[26]

If I were to rewrite this piece, however, I should seek to separate the two levels of royal justice under Henry II and his sons. The bulk of business heard by the *curia regis* – that is, the common law courts staffed by professionals – centered on suits brought by knights and smaller freeholders, often against their lords, not touching the king's interest. The *curia regis* could take another form, however, as an ill-defined body of magnates, royal counselors, household knights and domestic officials functioning as the king's own honor court, that is, a feudal tribunal resolving disputes between him and his tenants-in-chief. Here litigants could not take advantage of the common law procedures against their lord, the monarch, that their own tenants had against them. Paul R. Hyams illuminates the fact of the *curia regis* operating on two levels, both as the king's own honor court and also as a public court. Hyams notes that "the supposedly archaic form of oral trial proceedings" continued to prevail in the king's court, when hearing cases involving royal vassals and matters concerning the royal honor; and he speculates, "Perhaps Henry II's legal reforms merely opened to a certain section of the lesser nobility and freeholders the facilities of his court and justices for certain purposes that suited him, on a basis that was never automatic."[27] These two levels of the *curia regis* explain why King John's barons could complain bitterly of their treatment in the royal court, while the mass of his subjects could remain well satisfied with the justice that they received in the common law courts.

Also I would follow Michael Clanchy's lead and take greater account of the conflict that itinerant justices faced between their judicial and financial responsibilities.[28] On the one hand, eyre justices were obliged to render justice impartially; and on the other, they were expected to raise considerable royal revenues. The general eyre was an important source of revenue with

---

[25] See Jane Sayers, *Papal Judges Delegate in the Province of Canterbury, 1198–1254* (Oxford University Press, 1971).
[26] *Magna Carta*, second edition (Cambridge University Press, 1992), chap. 5, p. 125.
[27] "Henry II and Ganelon", *The Syracuse Scholar* (1986), p. 35.
[28] *Journal of Legal History*, 8 (1988), p 377, book review.

the first one in Henry II's reign producing over £250 in amercements from only one county, Lincolnshire. Henry Summerson's edition of *Crown Pleas of the Devon Eyre of 1238* reveals Henry III's ruthless exploitation of pleas of the crown, producing over £1600 from Devonshire.[29] Robert C. Stacey calculates judicial revenues in the 1240s at figures ranging roughly between 8 per cent and 20 per cent of total royal income, with nearly all of it coming from the general eyres.[30] This emphasis on the fund-raising aspect of the justices' work could well have compromised their impartiality as judges. Resentment aroused by the exploitation of Henry III's general eyres led to the baronial reformers' demands that they be limited to once every seven years.

For a rather pessimistic view of royal justices' venality, see Michael Clanchy's essay, "Law and Love in the Middle Ages". He finds traditional informal means of settling disputes that aimed not so much at application of abstract law as at friendly resolution of quarrels between neighbors, settlements *per amorem potius quam per placitum*. He sees these negotiated compromises giving way to "an automated system of justice emphasizing speed and decisiveness" after Henry II's reforms that encouraged haggling and purchase of favors from judges.[31] Paul Hyams sees the continued importance of non-judicial dispute resolution; he finds that "clerical peacemaking and private mediation functioned unrecorded for us behind the screen of a royal system of justice that was relatively well documented".[32]

David A. Carpenter reaches a pessimistic finding on the royal justices in his article on Henry III's personal rule. He concludes that Henry III's judges could either be intimidated or bribed into denying justice to persons seeking redress against aliens, *curiales,* or magnates enjoying royal favor.[33] For a more positive revision of views on Edward I's judges, see Paul A. Brand, "Edward I and the Judges: The 'State Trials' of 1289–93". He rejects complaints of widespread judicial corruption as causing Edward I to appoint commissioners to investigate his judiciary on his return from the Continent. He denies widespread evidence for corrupt judges and finds that for those accused by the commissioners, "Convincing evidence of corrupt behaviour exists only for a handful of cases at the most, a minute proportion of the total number of cases which the justices had heard during these years [of Edward's absence]."[34]

[29] Devon & Cornwall Record Society, new series, 28 (1985).
[30] Stacey, *Politics, Policy and Finance under Henry III, 1216–1245* (Oxford University Press, 1987), pp 213–15.
[31] *Disputes and Settlements, Law and Human Relations in the West*, ed. John Bossy (Cambridge University Press, 1983), p. 33.
[32] Paul R. Hyams, "Feud in Medieval England", *Haskins Society Journal*, 3 (1991): 4.
[33] David A Carpenter, "King, Magnates, and Society: The Personal Rule of King Henry III", *Speculum*, 60 (1985): 39–70.
[34] *The Thirteenth Century: Proceedings of the Newcastle-upon-Tyne Conference, 1985*, ed. P.R. Coss and Simon Lloyd (Woodbridge, Suffolk, 1986), p. 37.

A second group of pieces resulted from my work on a collective biographical study of the Angevins' royal justices, c. 1179-1239, as I wrestled with questions of their mentality and their attitude toward their work as judges. While about half the justices were clerics, half were knights; and I felt that the question of the lay justices' educational background needed answering. The result was my article, "The *Miles Literatus* in Twelfth- and Thirteenth Century England: How Rare a Phenomenon?" At that time, it seemed that Michael Clanchy and I were pioneers in investigating lay literacy in the middle ages, but now a large literature exists treating the subject. See Clanchy's new edition of his *From Memory to Written Record, England, 1066–1307* for a complete bibliography.[35] I sought to gauge the royal judges' depth of religious sentiment from the limited evidence available, that is, records of their donations to religious houses, in the article, "Religious Patronage of Angevin Royal Administrators, c. 1170-1239".

An attempt to grasp how many clerics acting as royal justices reconciled their service on the bench with ecclesiastical condemnations of clerical participation in secular government, and especially in judgments of blood, led me to write "Clerical Judges in English Secular Courts: The Ideal versus the Reality". Opposition to clerics as secular judges is linked to opposition to clerical participation in the judicial duels and ordeals, and a large literature on this subject has appeared since John W. Baldwin wrote his piece, "The Intellectual Preparation for the Canon of 1215 against Ordeals".[36] Paul Hyams argues in his piece, "Trial by Ordeal: The Key to Proof in the Early Common Law", that popular preference for other means of dispute settlement was more important than theologians' and other academics' arguments in rejection of the ordeal.[37] Robert Bartlett in *Trial by Fire and Water: The Medieval Judicial Ordeal* presents a revisionist view that the ordeals were still flourishing in 1215;[38] his views are strongly rejected by R. C. van Caenegem in his "Reflexions on Rational and Irrational Modes of Proof in Medieval Europe".[39] Yet Van Caenegem's edition of *English Lawsuits* suggests that throughout the period 1066–1199 trial by combat and sworn inquests were seen as equally "reasonable" means of judgment.

Soon I discovered that my project of writing a collective biography of a category of royal officials fell within a specialized branch of history, prosopography; and I found support from others seeking to encourage studies in that field, particularly George Beech of Western Michigan University. He is a founder of the journal, *Medieval Prosopography*.[40] I

---

[35] Second edition (Oxford: Blackwell, 1993).
[36] *Speculum*, 36 (1961): 613–36.
[37] *On the Laws and Customs of England*, ed. Morris G. Arnold, Thomas A. Green, Sally A. Scully, and Stephen D. White, pp 90–126.
[38] Oxford University Press, 1986.
[39] *Tijdschrift voor Rechtsgeschiedenis*, 58 (1990): 263–79.
[40] Medieval Institute Publications, Western Michigan University, Kalamazoo, 1980–.

published one of my articles reprinted in this collection, "Richard Barre and Michael Belet: Two Angevin Civil Servants", in a volume of that journal. It compares the careers of two second-level royal servants under Henry II and Richard I – Barre, a cleric, and Belet, a knight – and it seeks to place them in the larger context of the professionalization that was underway in government by the late twelfth century. Their careers illustrate this process well, indicating the Angevin royal government's fluidity, as the two drifted back and forth between Henry II's household and other administrative spheres, and also increasing specialization, as they finally settled down at Westminster as royal justices under Richard I. Two other essays reprinted here are biographies of individual royal justices that grew out of my study of the judges as a group: "Simon of Pattishall", and "Roger Huscarl".

The work of piecing together the lives of such figures, who had previously earned no more than a brief entry in the *Dictionary of National Biography*, if that, and restoring to them a degree of individuality has given me much joy as a historian. These second-level government servants, derided by chroniclers and moralists as careerists, were responsible for putting into effect the reforms of the Angevin kings and ensuring their effectiveness. Later I published biographies of six more prominent royal servants in a book, *Men Raised from the Dust*. Those six, although similar in many ways to Barre, Belet, Pattishall, and Huscarl, achieved greater success in the king's service, rising to possess political clout, baronies or bishoprics, and greater wealth. Taken together, the ten biographies can provide a useful sample of career royal officials in the Angevin period and their varying degrees of success.

These biographies forced me to confront questions of social status in Angevin England, an age when greater self-consciousness about rank was arising. The place of patronage in social mobility appeared to me as central to understanding royal servants' activities at the royal court. The phenomenon of "new men" or *curiales* whose manipulation of patronage from the king or from great officers of state for material gain is one that has attracted the attention of many historians. One example is Emma Mason's "Magnates, Curiales and the Wheel of Fortune, 1066–1154";[41] another treating the French court is John W. Baldwin, "The Capetian Court under Philip Augustus". Baldwin finds "a crisis in the martial values of an aristocratic society confronted by a bureaucratic monarchy" in the France of Philip II.[42] Certainly, much of the aristocracy in Angevin England was descended from servants of Anglo-Norman kings who had obscure origins. Yet magnates by the end of the twelfth century were beginning to constitute a conscious nobility, proud of ancient lineage and of a military tradition,

[41] *Anglo-Norman Studies/Proceedings of the Battle Conference*, 2 (1979).
[42] *The Medieval Court in Europe*, ed. Edward Haymes (Munich, 1986), p. 81.

holding themselves to be repositories of traditional feudal values. Many participated in the continental campaigns against the Capetians, and they were mindful of their natural place as the king's companions, counselors, and generals. They shared an archaic view of monarchy, an ideal derived from romances of King Arthur and the knights of the Round Table when royal government could be conducted like a baronial honor court without permanent administrative mechanisms. As Scott L. Waugh points out, the increasing professionalism of royal government "may help explain the growing insistence by the barons on counsel and consent as their natural prerogative".[43]

The rapid rise of new men as royal intimates, *familiares regis*, aroused resentments. While most aristocrats were content to see lesser men staff the civil service, they were feeling themselves squeezed out of their proper place close to the king; they feared being replaced as royal counselors by *curiales*. Charlotte Newman in her book on Henry I's nobility points out that barons of the second generation after the Conquest felt that their noble rank alone entitled them to royal favors, while Henry I held a different view, convinced that royal patronage must be earned by performance of services.[44] The conflict between the point of view of third- and fourth-generation barons and the Angevin kings was even more pronounced. Marie Therese Flanagan in *Irish Society, Anglo-Norman Settlers, Angevin Kingship* finds anti-bureaucratic sentiments among the warrior aristocrats of Angevin England expanding into Ireland, who saw royal agents sent there as a hindrance to their creation of a truly feudal world for themselves and their retainers.[45] One of the essays reprinted here treats this problem, based on my examination of the royal justices as largely "new men" securing royal patronage through their skills as administrators: "Changing Perceptions of the New Administrative Class in Anglo-Norman and Angevin England: The *Curiales* and their Conservative Critics".

Medieval writers did not use terms such as *curialis, familiaris regis*, or *amicus regis* with any great precision; neither do many historians writing today. Proper understanding of the social dynamics at the royal court demands more precision than I may have given these terms in previous writings. The term *familiaris regis* means literally a member of the king's household. It is probably most applicable to no more than a dozen or two members of the *privata familia regis*. They were companions of the king of varied social standing, some holding posts in the royal household, others without specific office, whose names on the witness-lists of royal charters place them frequently in the king's presence. Once such royal *familiares*

---

[43] *Journal of British Studies*, 29 (1990), "Patronage, War, and Society in Medieval England": 389.
[44] Newman, *The Anglo-Norman Nobility in the Reign of Henry I: The Second Generation* (University of Pennsylvania Press, 1988).
[45] Oxford University Press, 1989.

obtained royal favor and office, they might leave the court for long periods to fulfill their responsibilities in the shires or abroad, returning only sporadically to the king's presence. In their frequent movement between the royal court, the Exchequer, the shires or the Angevins' overseas possessions, they formed useful links for the monarch between the organs of his government, central and local.

As John Gillingham points out, "Not all *curiales* were administrators, and not all administrators in royal service were *curiales*."[46] The literal translation of the Latin *curialis* is "courtier", yet it does seem to me that many contemporaries, especially moralists and satirists at Henry II's court, used the word in a pejorative sense of careerists that makes it particularly applicable to members of the new administrative class that was first making an appearance in Angevin England. Ambitious young knights and clerics could see the flow of wealth collected by a predatory government from the counties to the royal treasury, and common sense told them to follow the money there. Stephen Jaeger, in his book *The Origins of Courtliness*, comments: "The reality of the Renaissance courtier may not have been all that far from that of his medieval counterpart."[47] Like Renaissance courtiers, *curiales* at the Angevin kings' courts jostled against nobles of old family in seeking the king's favorable attention and his patronage in order to secure advancement; in short, they were seekers after lucrative appointments. In every period, the courtier's lack of independent resources and his ambition for higher rank set him apart from the aristocrats at court. Also, like Renaissance courtiers, dependence on their prince tempted them to flattery, fawning, and dissembling that earned them enemies. Again like Renaissance courtiers, some of the clerics among the *curiales* gloried in their urbanity, wit, and learning; and their sophistication could inspire contempt from conservatives who adhered to an older, simpler knightly ideal. Of course, ambitious young knights in the monarch's household might still win his favor through their military exploits instead of through administrative acumen. William Marshal's career is a reminder of the continued importance of this route to royal favor.

Historians today, myself included, often use *curialis* quite loosely to contrast with barons, magnates, or aristocrats. Frank Barlow, for example, termed the *curialis* "an upstart royal domestic".[48] Usage that contrasts the *curialis* with the baron must not convey an impression that great men were absent from the king's presence, however; they accompanied him on military campaigns, and royal charters always included some of them as witnesses, a few frequently enough to be counted among the *familiares regis*. Yet those barons present at court ought not be labelled *curiales* in the sense

---

[46] *Medieval Prosopography*, 12 (1991), book review, p. 131.
[47] University of Pennsylvania Press, 1985, p. 15.
[48] *William Rufus* (University of California Press, 1983), p. 159.

of courtiers. Their independent resources of vast estates, fighting men and other retainers of their own set them apart from the crowd of patronage seekers. They were present at court in the capacity of counselors or as military commanders, not as office-holders or as seekers after offices, even though they may have taken advantage of their place at the king's side to seek favors for themselves or for their followers. Another term should be coined for such men, possibly "court baron" or "court magnate".

Clearly, a significant category of civil servants was neither *curiales* nor *familiares regis*, rarely if ever in the king's presence and failing to climb much higher in rank. Some royal servants might be former *curiales* who had left the king's household to serve in posts elsewhere, for example, Richard Barre, who joined the Bench at Westminster under Richard I after having served as one of Henry II's household clerks. Others were primarily servants of the king's great officers rather than his own servants; for example, personal clerks of the royal justices who copied their plea rolls expected their patrons to win them favors, even eventual appointment to the Bench. Such second-level adminstrators were doubtless would-be *curiales*, hopeful of entering the king's household and attracting the king's favorable attention.

An important category of royal administrators consisted of local notables, sometimes knights of the counties, performing tasks of royal government in their locality only on a part-time basis for the power and prestige that it brought them. Others held greater responsibilities in the provinces; for example, my student Richard R. Heiser's doctoral thesis shows that two-thirds of Richard Lionheart's sheriffs were prominent local men who had little contact with the royal household.[49] One might borrow the term "field administrator" for such local officials from a historian of Capetian France.[50]

My study of justices and other royal officers has convinced me that the feudal tenurial tie had far less significance in Angevin England than it is traditionally assumed to have had. Ties of patronage were playing a much greater role in binding men together. The king and his officials were not choosing their servants from among their feudal vassals, and they did not always find it necessary to bind their servants to them with grants of feudal tenures. Although they in many instances did give them land in order to cement a feudal tie, this came *after* their employment in posts of some responsibility; and they clearly did not limit themselves to their own tenants when recruiting officials for their households or for great offices. My findings concerning royal servants conform closely to what David Crouch

---

[49] "The Sheriffs of Richard the Lionheart: A Prosopographical Survey of Appointments, Politics, and Patronage, 1189–1199," unpublished Ph.D. Dissertation (Florida State University, Tallahassee, 1993).

[50] James W. Fesler, "French Field Administrators," *Comparative Studies in Society and History*, 5 (1962): 75–111.

found from his study of William Marshal's retinue, indicating that lack of surplus land to enfeof these retainers resulted in something like late medieval "bastard feudalism" by the late twelfth century, co-existing with the "classical feudalism" of enfeoffed vassals.[51]

The final group of essays assembled here represents a return to one of the themes of my doctoral research: comparing and contrasting exercise of the royal will with application of common law procedures in disputes between the king and his tenants-in-chief. When gathering material for my study, *The King and his Courts*, I concentrated on the plea rolls as evidence and neglected suits that never went before the common law justices, yet many important cases involving earls and barons were concluded before the exchequer or in the king's presence, as he consulted with the *privata familia regis*. This latter body was still the *curia regis*, but its informal procedures did not make the common law's protections available to those complaining against disseizin by the king. Sir James Holt expresses this distinction in the second edition of his book, *Magna Carta*, where he notes that "the line between the immediate and supervisory jurisdiction of the king was drawn by tenure. His immediate jurisdiction was less fettered by procedure."[52] Such suits, combining legal, political, and financial considerations, give a new dimension to the question of the role of the king's will in the administration of justice.

In my essay, "The Royal Courts Treat Disseizin by the King: John and Henry III, 1199–1240," I tried to show how tenants-in-chief of the king, denied the common law remedies that their tenants had against their arbitrary disseizins, tried to deal with their lord's arbitrary acts. Like most young scholars' early publications, this drew heavily on material from my doctoral thesis; but the material took a different shape, as I sought to outline the dilemma faced by royal justices in confronting cases brought by royal tenants that questioned their master's wrongful acts. Also I wished to offer more comparison of medieval doctrines of kingship with the practice of the courts than I had in my thesis.

Two other pieces, "Exercise of the King's Will in Inheritance of Feudal Baronies" and "The Mandeville Inheritance" treat complicated questions of the descent of baronies. They show that in cases involving magnates the legal issues cannot be separated from political ones, and the litigants' position, their standing with the king, their ties of friendship within the royal household all played parts in settlement of their suits. While these two pieces cover much the same ground, together they make explicit the

---

[51] David Crouch, *William Marshal: Court, Career and Chivalry in the Angevin Empire, 1149–1219* (Longman, 1990). See also Crouch, David Carpenter, and Peter Coss, "Debate: Bastard Feudalism Revived," *Past and Present*, no. 131 (May 1991).
[52] Cambridge University Press, 1992, p. 127.

advantages that the *curiales* – namely William Briwerre and Geoffrey fitz Peter – enjoyed in the royal courts, their skills in manipulating the system for their own advancement. The case of Briwerre pointedly shows his initiation of pleas before the royal justices in favor of minors in his custody; and it shows also his use of his considerable wealth to finance their suits, advancing funds for fines and other court costs.

Recently Sir James Holt has also studied Geoffrey fitz Peter and the Mandeville inheritance in "The *Casus Regis*: the Law and Politics of Succession in the Plantagenet Dominions, 1185–1247".[53] He notes an unpublished charter by which Geoffrey fitz Peter established his wife, Beatrice de Say, as "the acknowledged representative claimant to the honor of Mandeville and the earldom of Essex", a final concord of 25 Jan. 1185, confirmed by Henry II's charter (P.R.O., DL 10/29). Holt argues that the claim of Geoffrey's wife, based on the representative principle – that is, a child representing a deceased parent's claim – explains the royal courts' hesitation in such cases. The justices feared confronting directly the conflicting bases for King John's claim to be heir to the English crown and the justiciar's claim to be heir to the earldom of Essex. Certainly all these cases demonstrate that lawsuits of the Angevin period cannot be understood by abstract analysis, in which the actual litigants are neglected in favor of accepting them as merely "tenant", "plaintiff", or "lord". The prominence of the opposing parties, their ties of patronage and kinship to other powerful persons, clearly could influence the judgment.

The common law of the twelfth and thirteenth centuries was about real people: the litigants making claims to land, the judges presiding over pleas, the *curiales* seeking to manipulate the judicial system for their own gain, and the king treating justice as a boon to grant to friends or to withhold from enemies. I hope that these essays breathe life into such individuals. In one of the pieces, I characterize the topic as "very Painteresque with its mixture of genealogy, feudal law, politics, and patronage". It is my hope that all the work gathered together here fits that definition and proves worthy of the Johns Hopkins University's tradition of medieval scholarship, which I inherited from my two mentors, Sidney Painter and his successor John W. Baldwin.

---

[53] *Law in Mediaeval Life and Thought*, ed. Edward B. King and Susan J. Ridyard, *Sewanee Mediaeval Studies*, 5 (The Press of the University of the South, Sewanee, Tenn., 1990).

1

Henry II's Aims in Reforming England's Land Law: Feudal or Royalist?

Henry II's legal reforms are credited with creating England's common law. By the time of his death in 1189, royal writs enabled litigants to remove suits easily from old local and feudal courts and to settle them before the king's agents by the rational process of juries. A new law common to all England resulted once litigation concerning landed property passed to the king's courts, which moved to the counties by means of itinerant justices. Substantive land law grew up once the new procedures for royal protection of seisin forced juries and justices to inquire into the facts underlying disputes over possession of land.

It is unfashionable today to see behind this shift in Henry II's time any deliberate plan by the king, any grand legislative vision, or any "conscious unfolding of principles of constitutional government." Instead, historians mostly see "self-interest and happenstance at work," as immediate solutions to concrete problems had long-range and often unintended consequences.[1] As S.F.C. Milsom wrote, "Great legal decisions are rare; but great consequences often follow from measures taken to meet immediate problems."[2] Why, then, did "the Angevin leap forward" in justice occur *c.* 1164-80?[3] Can we glimpse any purpose on Henry II's part? He may have had more conscious political aims with his writs, assizes, and itinerant judicature than some scholars today are willing to admit.

For simplicity's sake, we might label two opposed ways of viewing Henry II's aims "feudal" and "royalist." The traditional viewpoint sees Henry II's reforms as consciously anti-feudal, aimed at reducing lords' control over their tenants. It is succinctly stated in Bryce Lyon's review of Milsom's book. He writes: "To accelerate the disappearance of

---

1 The phrase is from Richard Helmholz's review of *On the Laws and Customs of England: Essays in Honor of Samuel E. Thorne*, ed. Morris S. Arnold *et al.* (Chapel Hill, NC, 1981) in *Harvard Law Rev.* 95 (1982) 724. See also S.F.C. Milsom, *The Legal Framework of English Feudalism* (Cambridge, 1976) 178, 186; R.C. van Caenegem, *The Birth of the English Common Law* (Cambridge, 1973) 33; Paul R. Hyams, "Warranty and Good Lordship in Twelfth-Century England," *Law and History Review* 5 (1987) 480-1.
2 Milsom, *Framework*, 178.
3 The phrase is Doris M. Stenton's, *English Justice between the Norman Conquest and the Great Charter 1066-1215* (Philadelphia, 1964), title of Chapter 2.

feudal law and the concomitant centralization of power in their hands, the kings and their counselors developed courts and procedures to adjudicate legal differences more rationally and efficiently. The more cases adjudicated in royal courts, the more revenues and power for the kings."[4]

S.F.C. Milsom, an English lawyer and legal scholar, set forth the feudal approach in several works, most notably his 1972 Maitland Lectures, *The Legal Framework of English Feudalism*. The Milsomian revision has had an impact on legal historians not yet felt among general historians of medieval England. Since he presented his ideas on the English common law's origins, legal scholars have taken them as their starting point, either confirming or challenging them.

Simply stated, Milsom's thesis concerning Henry II's land law is that the king did not intend to usurp feudal lords' jurisdiction. Instead, he wished "to make the seignorial structure work according to its own assumptions;"[5] that is, to guarantee to tenants due process of law by making their lords' courts follow their own custom. This royal control undermined the "conclusiveness" of lords' courts and of feudal custom. Supervision by the royal justices led to transfers of cases from feudal courts to the king's court. There flexible feudal custom was converted into hard and fast rules of law, protecting the tenant at the lord's expense. A "juristic accident," the work of royal judges "neither intended nor foreseen" by Henry II, was the creation of property rights for the tenant, which had not existed before Henry's reforms.[6] As one of Milsom's followers, Robert C. Palmer, states, "England was decisively feudal throughout the reign of Henry II."[7]

In Milsom's view, the feudal courts described by Sir Frank Stenton in his *First Century of English Feudalism* provided the only tribunals before 1166 for settling disputes about feudal services and tenures. Anglo-Norman England was truly a feudal world, where the personal tie of vassalage was paramount, and possession of land depended upon a lord's favor. He alone could make a tenant; no one became his tenant

---

4 Bryce Lyon, review of Milsom, *Framework*, in *Yale Law Journal* 86 (1977) 782-7.
5 Milsom, *Framework*, 186. For other presentations of Milsom's views, see *Historical Foundations of the Common Law*, 2nd edn (London, 1981); Introduction to F. Pollock and F.W. Maitland, *The History of English Law before the Time of Edward I*, 2nd edn (reprint, Cambridge, 1968). For a clear and sympathetic account of Milsom's thesis, see Robert C. Palmer, "The Feudal Framework of English Law," *Michigan Law Review* 79 (1981) 1142-5.
6 Milsom, *Framework*, 11, 36-8, 181, 186; *Foundations*, 123-4; Introduction to Pollock and Maitland, xxxiv.
7 See Robert C. Palmer, "The Origins of Property in England," *Law and History Review* 3 (1985) 1-50; and *idem*, "The Economic and Cultural Impact of the Origins of Property," *ibid.*, 375-96.

without first doing homage to him.⁸ Milsom emphasizes the contractual rather than the proprietary nature of feudal tenures. Lords' courts were the only tribunals for settling disputes about feudal services and tenures, determining succession to fiefs according to their own custom, and disciplining tenants who failed to fulfill their obligations.⁹

Milsom was challenging most historians who in his view, following F.W. Maitland, have found property rights in England earlier than they existed. Maitland, in Milsom's view, had tended to read back into the twelfth century the settled law he saw in the thirteenth-century collection of cases, *Bracton's Note Book*. He and his followers thus assumed that proprietary right to tenures had evolved soon after the Norman Conquest, and that Henry II's assizes regulated "a flat world in which equals dispute about title to property."¹⁰ Milsom found to the contrary that feudal tenants' heirs had no proprietary rights to inherit before 1166, although they may have had a customary claim on the lord to accept them as new tenants.¹¹ When a lord granted land to a tenant "and his heirs," he was assuming a customary obligation but not creating true property right for the heirs.¹² Milsom follows S.E. Thorne in finding that feudal tenures did not become fully heritable until *c.* 1200. Henry II's activist judges hardened a customary presumption in an heir's favor into firm law, making feudal tenures legally heritable *c.* 1200.¹³

Robert Palmer explains this more starkly. He argues that property only appeared around 1200, "when title is protected by a bureaucratic authority according to set rules. Property derives from the state; it cannot exist prior to the state." He criticizes other historians for failing to see the distinction between "social notions of inheritance" and rights to property that can be protected in the public courts.¹⁴ Palmer fails to find such protection until Henry II's legislation had given rise to a professional judiciary, enforcing rules of law that "separated title from lordly acceptance." Since landholding no longer depended on the personal relationship of lord and vassal, the feudal tenure had become

---

8 Milsom, *Framework*, 110, 171; *Foundations*, 102-5; F.M. Stenton, *The First Century of English Feudalism* (Oxford, 1932) 43-54.
9 Milsom, *Framework*, 39; *Foundations*, 20-1, 104-5.
10 Milsom, *Foundations*, vi, 122, 150; Introduction to Pollock and Maitland, xlvii-xlviii.
11 Milsom, *Framework*, 7-8.
12 Milsom, *Foundations*, 106-7, 121.
13 Milsom, Introduction to Pollock and Maitland, xxxiv; he follows S.E. Thorne, "Feudalism and Estates in Land," *Cambridge Law Journal*, New Series 6 (1959) 198-209. For historiography of this question, see J.C. Holt, "Politics and Property in Early Medieval England," *Past and Present* (1972) 3-5.
14 Palmer, "Origins of property," 4, n. 10.

the tenant's property, an economic resource that he could alienate as he saw fit.¹⁵

Milsom recognizes that many cases heard in the lords' courts raised the question: "Is one of the parties [would-be tenant] entitled to hold the land of the other [lord]?" The lord was a party to the suit at the same time that he was sitting in judgment, for he had placed the current tenant in seisin and had taken his homage. The sitting tenant was his man, and he was honor bound to protect him in his possession, to warrant (or guarantee) his right.¹⁶ If an excluded heir sought to be placed in seisin in his lord's court, he could hardly expect justice, for the lord would not allow his court to challenge a tenant whom he had already seised, whose homage he had already taken. The one claiming hereditary right, then, would have no choice but to turn to the king for a writ of right requiring the lord to entertain the plea. *Glanvill*'s maxim, "No one is to be impleaded concerning his free tenement without the king's writ," was thus a statement of fact before it became a rule of law, for no lord's court would have heard such a plea unless by the king's command.¹⁷ The writ of right was "the first and perhaps the decisive step in bringing down the seignorial world."¹⁸

This impossible situation made inevitable a default of justice and removal of the case to the royal court. The possessory assizes were not aimed against strangers who violently took land from peaceful landholders, but against lords who were alleged to be denying tenants or heirs their rightful holdings. Henry II's purpose was to regulate the feudal relationship, to provide justice that lords were failing to give in their courts. Would-be tenants sought a writ of right or one of the possessory assizes against a lord. *Mort d'ancestor* imposed on lords an obligation to accept without delay the heirs of their recently deceased tenants, and novel disseisin checked abuses of lords' power to discipline their tenants by dispossessing them. In Milsom's words, "All began as about the feudal relationship rather than about ownership and possession."¹⁹

---

15 *Ibid.*, 24; also Milsom, *Framework*, 183-6; and Palmer, 'The Economic and Cultural Impact of the Origins of Property," 341-2.
16 Milsom, *Framework*, 58; *Foundations*, 127; see also Hyams, "Warranty and Good Lordship," 453-4.
17 *The Treatise on the Laws and Customs of the Realm of England Commonly Called Glanvill*, ed. G.D.G. Hall, Medieval Texts (London, 1965) 13:3, p. 138; Milsom, *Foundations*, 134; *Framework*, 58.
18 Milsom, *Framework*, 178-9, 183.
19 Milsom, Introduction to Pollock and Maitland, xliv; also xxxvii; *Framework*, 177. For other views on the origins of the assizes, see *Royal Writs in England from the Conquest to Glanvill*, ed. R.C. van Caenegem, Selden Society 77 (London, 1958-9); Donald W. Sutherland, *The Assize of Novel Disseisin* (Oxford, 1973).

Henry II's writs and assizes converted what had been simply the lords' obligation to enfeoff heirs into proprietary right. Milsom writes, "Legally, [the tenant] became an owner because the jurisdiction of the lord's court was first controlled and then replaced by the king's court." Royal measures destroyed the link between seisin and homage; it became possible for one who had not done homage to be put into seisin by royal command.[20] Forcing lords to accept unwanted tenants meant that tenants were well on the way to becoming owners of their fees, and the feudal courts' decline followed. Once feudal courts lost their independence and had to operate according to royal rules, they proved useful to lords only for prestige and for collecting occasional income from the feudal incidents.[21]

What are we to make of Milsom's teaching that Henry II's reforms merely sought to make feudalism work according to its own assumptions? Certainly Milsom is correct to notice that Henry II's legal innovations concerned chiefly relations between feudal lords and their tenants, and that the king aimed at insuring due process for tenants. Although Milsom's chief concern was with the results of Henry's legal reforms and not his aims, certain assumptions about the king's aims lay behind his findings. For several reasons, his presentation of Henry II's aims appears inadequate.

Since Milsom first formulated his views, doubts have arisen about the "decisively feudal" character of the kingdom of England as he pictures it. The very word "feudalism" opens a Pandora's box, for the term means many different things to different people, and Milsom fails to supply his readers with his own definition.[22] He seems to define it as a confusion of government and property with lordships comprising both rights to land and rights to jurisdiction. More of the state and public authority may have survived after the Norman Conquest than he and Palmer are willing to recognize; kingship in post-Conquest England could be perceived in two ways, "as a lordship over vassals or as a sovereignty over all subjects."[23] We might ask, then, whether or not

20 Milsom, *Foundations*, 103, 143; *Framework* 110, 171; Introduction to Pollock and Maitland, xliv.
21 Milsom, Introduction to Pollock and Maitland, xxx; *Foundations*, 124. See also Sidney Painter, *Studies in the History of the English Feudal Barony* (Baltimore, 1943) 137-8.
22 Stephen D. White, review of Milsom, *Framework*, in *American Journal of Legal History* 21 (1977) 363. See Milsom, *Foundations*, 19, 99-101; Milsom seeks to avoid the terms "feudal" and "seignorial" in the 1981 edition, often substituting "lordship." W.L. Warren, *The Governance of Norman and Angevin England 1086-1272* (London, 1987) 12, eschews the word "feudalism" in favor of "lordship" or "vassalage." He adopts the term "fief-holding" for the pattern of dependent land tenure usually termed "feudal."
23 Warren, *Governance of Norman and Angevin England*, 15. See also his Introduction, xiii-xv.

English society and government in the mid twelfth century were as thoroughly feudal as Milsom pictures them? We may wonder whether Henry II, his advisers, and his barons all shared "an 'ancient' feudal mentality."[24]

The Milsomian portrait of Henry II as a monarch who functioned within "the truly feudal world" and who sought to protect "the accepted body of feudal custom" presents problems both of fact and of interpretation.[25] Is he attempting to force the king to fit into a feudal framework? Can he be sure that Henry had a preconceived notion of feudalism and of its proper functioning? Elizabeth A.R. Brown warned against this sort of thinking in her article, "The Tyranny of a Construct: Feudalism and Historians of Medieval Europe." She pointed out the dangers of historians creating some ideal or model feudalism to test kings and their policies, measuring their achievements by this standard. She cautioned against projecting into the minds of Henry II and his advisers "a degree of calculation, narrowness of vision, and rigidity that the surviving evidence does not suggest characterized them." This denies their true creativity and flexibility in adapting institutions and ideas to new situations.[26]

We might ask whether lords could or would protect their tenants in their courts. If the king was a great tyrant inspiring in great men fear of his *vis et malevolentia*, then many lords were petty tyrants inspiring similar fear in their humbler tenants.[27] Some scholars paint a very different picture of the feudal courts from Milsom's version of men of goodwill working together to resolve disputes, often through compromise. Instead, they find men seeking royal protection, when pleading against their lords. R.C. van Caenegem observes that a complainant would be "very wise to secure the king's support if he decided to implead some powerful local magnate."[28]

Many landholders, especially religious houses, sought confirmation of their right from Henry II. Since Henry could regard neither his mother nor Stephen of Blois as his lawful predecessor, but only his grandfather, his confirmations looked back to the last "time of peace," calling into question changes in possession that had occurred 1135-53. Obviously, these royal charters led to litigation, and pleas challenging

24 Emily Z. Tabuteau, *Transfers of Property in Eleventh-Century Norman Law* (Chapel Hill, NC, 1988) 2; *idem*, "Ownership and Tenure in Eleventh-Century Normandy," *American Journal of Legal History* 21 (1977) 99.
25 Milsom, *Framework*, 46, 52, 60; *Foundations*, 124; also "within the feudal dimension," *Framework*, 104.
26 Elizabeth A.R. Brown, "The Tyranny of a Construct: Feudalism and Historians of Medieval Europe," *American Historical Review* 79 (1974) 1077-8.
27 Hyams, "Warranty and Good Lordship," 464.
28 Van Caenegem (ed.), *Royal Writs*, 208.

their right fell under the king's jurisdiction, not the lords'. Paul R. Hyams observes that such pleas may have been "the major springboard for royal justice into the sphere of real property."[29]

Van Caenegem observes such dissatisfaction with lords' courts, their antiquated procedures, and interminable delays that men despaired of finding justice in them. In his view, the feudal courts' inadequacies caused men to flee them, seeking remedies from the king. What created the common law, in his view, was people's insistence on settling their disputes in royal courts by use of juries, coupled with the king's willingness to provide access to his courts in return for payments.[30] It is difficult to argue with his depiction of the feudal courts. The author of *Glanvill c.* 1187-9 dismissed lords' courts as unworthy of consideration, since the diversity of their customs made it impossible to reduce them to writing.[31] The standard of justice in many twelfth-century feudal courts cannot have been much higher than that in eighteenth-century country squires' courts.

The whole question of proprietary right within a system of dependent land tenures has engaged scholars since Milsom wrote. Clearly, the grant of property was replacing the personal tie of fealty as the most important aspect of feudalism by the mid twelfth century. Whether or not the law recognized a tenant's right, he clearly felt that he had a property right, and he confidently assumed that his son would succeed him as his lord's tenant. Tenants were treating their tenements as if they were heritable properties. Fathers sought to make provision for younger sons and for daughters, and husbands to provide for wives who might be left widows, out of their tenements that under feudal law did not belong to them.[32] Such grants, often to the detriment of the eldest son's and the lord's interests, resulted in landholding patterns that obscured the original direct and simple tie between lord and man. They created some of the uncertainties about feudal landholdings that brought cases into the royal courts.

Accompanying the tenants' growing desire to determine succession to their holdings was their insistence on freedom to alienate. With the growth of a commercial economy in the twelfth century, some tenants searched for ways to sell, lease, or mortgage land—to use their tenement as an economic resource—yet such transactions had to be disgui-

---

29 Hyams, "Warranty and Good Lordship," 477; Milsom, *Foundations*, 129.
30 Van Caenegem (ed.), *Royal Writs*, 46, 246; idem, *Birth of Common Law*, 17-19, 33-4; idem, *Judges, Legislators and Professors* (Cambridge, 1987) 116.
31 *Glanvill*, ed. Hall, 12:6-7, pp. 239-41.
32 J.C. Holt, "Feudal Society and the Family in Early Medieval England: I. The Revolution of 1066," *Transactions of the Royal Historical Society*, Fifth Series 32 (1982) 199-200; "Politics and Property," 5, 7-8.

sed with legal language placing them in a feudal form. Perhaps economic changes are more significant for converting the old pattern of obligations into a proprietary one than are judges' rigid applications of Henry II's assizes.[33]

Common sense has led some general historians to conclude that "property" did in fact exist before Henry II's reforms, even if the legal protections for true property rights, demanded by such legal historians as Robert Palmer, were not yet in place.[34] Paul R. Hyams, although a legal historian, tries to be conciliatory. He writes: "The advent of regular royal procedures can hardly have created 'ownership.' Rather, an existing tenuous customary ownership was brought under royal protection to be strengthened, defined, and formalized."[35]

Clearly, Milsom sees feudalism as a political pattern characterized by weakened public power, with justice chiefly left to private courts. He underestimated the survival of the state, of a strong sense of public authority. Henry II as king of England was not heir to feudal governmental traditions alone, but also to Anglo-Saxon traditions of sacred monarchy, and these traditions fused with continental concepts of royal power stretching back to imperial Rome and Constantinople. Doctrines of an authoritarian monarch, "to whom ... the general care of his subjects has been entrusted by God," were widely accepted in twelfth-century England.[36] The Becket conflict had caused the king's counselors to search for doctrines that supported royal supremacy.[37] Three of Henry's *familiares* who had advised him during the Becket controversy were among the most active justices during the king's last decade, and a fourth served as a justice frequently under Richard I.[38] Writers of Henry I's and Henry II's time still felt strongly the royal majesty's

---

33 The opposite of Palmer's view, "Economic and Cultural Impact of Property," 371-89.
34 E.g. J.C. Holt, "Feudal Society and the Family in Early Medieval England: II. Notions of Patrimony," *Transactions of the Royal Historical Society*, Fifth Series 33 (1983) 193-220; also "Politics and property;" and RaGena De Aragon, "The Growth of Secure Inheritance in Anglo-Norman England," *Journal of Medieval History* 8 (1982) 381-91.
35 Hyams, "Warranty and Good Lordship," 274; see also p. 454, where Hyams finds that the lord's obligation of warranty insured most tenants that they "already possessed a certain form of property right."
36 *Dialogus de Scaccario*, ed. Charles Johnson, Medieval Texts (London, 1950) 101; also *Glanvill*'s tutelary view of royal power, 2:7, p. 28.
37 Van Caenegem, *Birth of Common Law*, 8-12, 18; *Royal Writs*, 223. Paul Brand, in *Irish Jurist*, New Series 10 (1975) 366, review of Milsom, *Framework*, questions how Norman kings' jurisdiction over defaults of justice and false judgment can be reconciled with Milsom's picture of independent feudal lordships.
38 The bishops Geoffrey Ridel, John of Oxford, Richard of Ilchester, and Richard Barre, archdeacon of Ely; see Ralph V. Turner, *The English Judiciary in the Age of Glanvill and Bracton c. 1176-1239* (Cambridge, 1985) 19, 95-6.

aura, and the *Dialogus de Scaccario* and *Glanvill* show royal servants sharing this exalted view of the kingly office.[39]

According to J.E.A. Jolliffe, it was the king's feudal overlordship that gave him a general responsibility for justice, but Henry II knew other models of kingship besides the feudal one.[40] Surviving Anglo-Saxon traditions gave him wide authority in the sphere of justice, allowing him to intervene in instances of *defectus justitiae* or of *injustum judicium*. R.C. van Caenegem characterized the Norman and Angevin monarchs as "real busybodies" because of their zeal to right wrongs.[41] Even in the years before 1166, public courts provided an alternative to the feudal courts that Milsom neglects. Legacies from both Anglo-Saxon monarchy and the Normans' Frankish predecessors provided instruments for such royal interventions in lesser courts.

Some scholars follow van Caenegem's view that the assize of novel disseisin grew out of public prosecutions of disseisors brought before the itinerant justices in 1166. Milsom himself acknowledged the possibility that the assize had its origin in quasi-criminal inquiries by the 1166 itinerant justices.[42] Mary Cheney notes that English bishops after 1154 were busily disseising their tenants without judgment, leaving them no remedy under feudal custom. One of the most active disseisors was Thomas Becket, once he was installed at Canterbury; and among his victims was a prominent royal servant, John Marshal. She suggests that an aim of the assize of novel disseisin was to protect laymen from unlawful disseisin by their episcopal lords.[43] Although authorities disagree widely about novel disseisin's origin, the possibility that it grew out of royal concern for suppression of crime—prosecuting breaches of the king's peace and defaults of justice—raises doubts about its purely feudal context.

Evidence for frequent interventions by the Anglo-Norman kings in

---

39 *Ibid.*, 268-77.
40 J.E.A. Jolliffe, *Angevin Kingship* (London, 1955) 23-31.
41 Van Caenegem (ed.), *Royal Writs*, 18.
42 Milsom, Introduction to Pollock and Maitland, xxxviii; *Framework*, 11-18, 36; *Foundations*, 138-40. Also van Caenegem (ed.), *Royal Writs*, 121, 283-91; *idem, Birth of Common Law*, 40-6. W.L. Warren, *Henry II* (Berkeley, Calif., 1973) 336-7, follows van Caenegem. Lady Stenton, *English Justice*, 36-7, expresses doubts. She sees the eyre as "a means of promulgating information about the new civil action, not a means of initiating a new crown plea." Donald W. Sutherland, *Assize of Novel Disseisin*, 13-14, takes a middle ground, writing that "the assize in its original form probably directed some use of juries of presentment." He finds that it "somehow combined procedure by presentment with opportunity for private prosecution."
43 Mary Cheney, "The Litigation between John Marshal and Becket in 1164: a Pointer to the Origin of Novel Disseizin," in *Law and Social Change in British History*, ed. J.A. Guy and H.G. Beale, Royal Historical Society Studies in History 40 (London, 1984) 9-26.

their magnates' courts casts shadows on Milsom's picture of independent feudal lordships. Henry I decreed early in his reign that disputes between the vassals of two different lords (*inter vavasores duorum dominorum*) should be settled in the shire court.[44] The scattered pattern of English knightly landholdings meant that many pleas about property would have involved tenants of different lords. Over time, such situations would have grown even more likely with divisions of holdings into smaller and smaller plots, and they must have caused great uncertainty over whose feudal court could claim jurisdiction. For example, partition of an honor among daughters created several new feudal courts where only one had existed earlier.[45]

The *Leges Henrici Primi* provided that a complainant, alleging defect of justice, could seek removal of his plea from his lord's court.[46] Very early in his reign Henry II issued a decree with similar intent, by which cases alleging defect of justice could be withdrawn from their lords' courts.[47] The magnates saw the new decree as a threat to their jurisdiction, and, according to a contemporary account, "They lamented in secret about it."[48] Pleas also reached the royal courts through Anglo-Norman and Angevin kings' generosity in granting favored churchmen, courtiers, and others the privilege of being impleaded only before the *curia regis*.[49]

Indeed, there is some doubt about the originality of Henry II's legal changes compared with his Anglo-Norman predecessors. Henry's admiration for Henry I and his aim of imitating him are well known, but recent scholarship finds more precedents for Henry II's reforms in his grandfather's reign than previously recognized. Van Caenegem, in his study of royal writs, found antecedents to Henry II's assizes under the Anglo-Norman kings. He demonstrated that they issued executive orders to right wrongs, among them concessions to favored individuals allowing them to settle certain of their suits by means of juries, previously used mainly as administrative devices.[50] He found Henry

---

44 *Select Charters*, ed. William Stubbs, 9th edn (Oxford, 1913) 122; translation in *English Historical Documents*, II, *1042-1189*, ed. David C. Douglas and George W. Greenaway (London, 1968) 433-4; charter of Henry I, c. 1108/11.
45 Suggestion of J.C. Holt.
46 *Leges Henrici Primi*, ed. L.J. Downer (Oxford, 1972), p. 109, cap. 10, 1; p. 137, cap. 33, 1a.
47 Mary Cheney, "A Decree of Henry II on Defect of Justice," in *Tradition and Change: Essays in Honor of Marjorie Chibnall*, ed. Diana Greenway *et al.* (Cambridge, 1985) 183-93, whether for hearing in the overlord's court or the king's court is unclear.
48 Cheney, "A Decree of Henry II," 186, citing the biographer of Thomas Becket, Roger of Pontigny or Anonymous I.
49 Jolliffe, *Angevin Kingship*, 89-94.
50 Van Caenegem (ed.), *Royal Writs*, 83.

II's legal innovations—writs, juries, and itinerant justices—evolving from earlier concepts and practices.[51]

Recently Judith Green and Stephanie Mooers have re-examined Henry I's work of justice, and they conclude that he did more than previously thought to implement regular judicial procedures, and that he was particularly active in land actions. They find evidence that writs of right were issued frequently. From study of the pipe roll for 1130, Mooers concludes: "It seems likely that Henry I was as preoccupied with just tenure as was his grandson fifty years later. Clearly, the finely tuned machinery for obtaining possession was operative, although perhaps not perfect, in 1130." Green does not wish to challenge Milsom's thesis, and she finds that royal intervention in the lords' courts was "as yet too spasmodic and unsystematic to constitute a threat," while Mooers's count of payments for writs convinces her that "royal intervention in land pleas was not sporadic or unusual."[52]

Milsom's insistence that Henry II must not be depicted as anti-feudal has won wide acceptance, yet we find some points in favor of the more traditional royalist interpretation. He and his advisers seem to have had an anti-lord, or perhaps better a pro-tenant bias, if not an anti-feudal one. Clearly, he aimed to extend to tenants the royal courts' protection against their lords, providing them with security of possession. The tilt toward tenants cannot have been entirely a "juristic accident;" it must have been an aim consciously sought.[53] In other spheres of Henry II's government, we can observe a tendency toward centralization, toward the royal government's taking direct responsibility for government throughout the kingdom instead of leaving local authorities or feudal lords in charge. The Constitutions of Clarendon show Henry extending his centralization of authority even to the church.[54]

Henry II, in his relations with his own tenants—the magnates—did not show any great respect for feudal custom. Years ago, Jolliffe argued that the Angevin kings achieved their vast power by abusing their feudal position, "by arrogating to themselves a discretionary power which they denied their vassals." While Henry's magnates were losing their disciplinary powers to distrain and disinherit their tenants, he and his sons insisted on disciplining their own by disseisins without judg-

---

51 *Ibid.*, 18; idem, *Birth of Common Law*, 34-41. See also Richard H. Helmholz's review of *Birth of Common Law*, in *Speculum* 51 (1976) 364-5.
52 Stephanie L. Mooers, "A Reevaluation of Royal Justice under Henry I of England," *American Historical Review* 93 (1988) 345, 355-7; Judith A. Green, *The Government of England under Henry I* (Cambridge, 1986) 102-5.
53 See Hyams's review, in *English Historical Review* 93 (1978) 859; also Brand's in *Irish Jurist*.
54 Warren, *Governance of Norman and Angevin England*, 106; Cheney, "Litigation between John Marshal and Becket," 24-5.

ment.⁵⁵ They constantly pushed customary services and payments to their limit, exploiting every possible means of raising revenues from their tenants-in-chief. The feudal relationship between king and baronage was being converted more and more into a financial one, with many magnates deeply in debt to the crown.⁵⁶

Both Milsom and Palmer make much of the "bureaucratic" mentality of the royal justices, who changed flexible feudal custom into inflexible rules of law. But perhaps they do not make enough of it! An awareness of the character of the men who were implementing the king's legal reforms can contribute to the debate. Henry II drew his justices about equally from the clergy and from knights. Among the eight clerics most often on the bench 1179-89 were several archdeacons and bishops; they brought to the bench Roman and ecclesiastical notions of the public power.⁵⁷ Both the clerics and the laymen among the judges came largely from the tenant class, and they would have enthusiastically implemented Henry II's policy of protecting tenants against their lords. For example, Richard de Lucy (d. 1179/80), justiciar during the crucial years of legal innovations, built up his barony out of lands held mediately, not held in chief of the king. Since his approximately 30 fees belonged to at least three different honors, he would have had considerable experience with feudal courts.⁵⁸ A son and heir to part of the Lucy lands, Godfrey de Lucy, joined the judiciary at the time of his father's retirement and continued to serve as a royal justice throughout Richard I's reign.⁵⁹ Richard's successor as justiciar, Ranulf de Glanvill, also would have appreciated the tenant's point of view. He was the second son of an East Anglian subtenant, belonging to a family whose origins, "though not humble, were not exalted either." Through his long service to Henry II, he acquired much more land than he inherited.⁶⁰

A revolution in all aspects of government, not only the law, was

---

55 Jolliffe, *Angevin Kingship*, 33-4.
56 *Ibid.*, 51, 78-82.
57 Three bishops: Geoffrey Ridel, of Ely; John of Oxford, bishop of Norwich; Richard of Ilchester, bishop of Winchester. Other clerics were Richard fitz Neal, Master Godfrey de Lucy, Master Jocelin, archdeacon of Chichester; and two who joined the judiciary after 1185, Hubert Walter and Master Thomas of Hurstbourne. Six of the clerics were current or former archdeacons. See Turner, *English Judiciary*, 35.
58 Emily Amt, "Richard de Lucy, Henry II's Justiciar," *Medieval Prosopography* 9 (1988) 69-70.
59 Turner, *English Judiciary*, 22.
60 J.S. Falls, "Ranulf de Glanville's Formative Years c. 1120-79: the Family Background and his Ascent to the Justiciarship," *Mediaeval Studies* 40 (1978) 312-27; Richard Mortimer, "The Family of Rannulf de Glanville," *Bulletin of the Institute of Historical Research* 54 (1981) 1-16.

under way in twelfth-century England, and Henry II needed professionals with proven administrative ability. Since Henry clearly chose his own *familiares*, it was by his choice that masters of administrative skills were transforming English law. There can have been little difference in outlook between Henry's counselors devising and implementing his legal changes c. 1164-80 and Milsom's and Palmer's professional judges who were bureaucratizing the law a few years later. Three of the itinerant justices carrying out the Assize of Northampton in 1176 continued to be prominent in the judiciary until their deaths.[61] The royal justices of Henry II's last decade had close personal connections with him; six of the 13 most active royal judges in the period also appear among the 15 most frequent witnesses to royal charters.[62] Indeed, in many instances the justices remained the same in Richard I's time. Eight of 14 most often on the bench under Richard Lionheart had joined the bench during his father's last decade; all of these had been connected with Henry II's household or administration.[63]

A closer look at the justices confirms attitudes that might be termed bureaucratic, or possibly proto-*bourgeois*. Literate and numerate, they manifested in their work a more calculating and rational approach, less concerned about the traditional feudal military virtues praised in the romances. Their ambition alarmed conservative moralists and jealous courtiers, who saw them as "new men" threatening the traditional social order.[64] Often they were sons of knights or low-level royal servants, seeking their fortunes through service to the crown and improving their prospects through patronage rather than through vassalage.[65] None of the 13 justices most often on the bench during Henry II's last decade came from old aristocratic families, while eight came from families with a tradition of administrative service.[66]

Such men had a practical interest in promoting rules of inheritance that would make more likely succession of minors or heiresses. Some prominent justices had a personal stake in questions of inheritance,

61 William Basset (d. 1185), Michael Belet (d. 1201), Ranulf de Glanvill (d. 1190); see Turner, *English Judiciary*, 20.
62 Glanvill, Michael Belet, Hugh Bardolf, Richard of Ilchester, John of Oxford, and Geoffrey Ridel; see Ralph V. Turner, *Men Raised from the Dust: Adminsitrative Service and Upward Mobility in Angevin England* (Philadelphia, 1988) 16 and note 61, p. 159.
63 Turner, *English Judiciary*, 74-7. Hugh Bardolf, Michael Belet, Geoffrey fitz Peter, Master Ralf Foliot, Hubert Walter, Master Thomas of Hurstbourne, Godfrey de Lucy, and Richard fitz Neal. Two newcomers, Richard Barre and William de Sainte-Mère Eglise, had been Henry II's clerks.
64 Turner, *Men Raised from the Dust*, 1-13.
65 Turner, *English Judiciary*, 25-8.
66 *Ibid*. Only one of Richard I's frequently serving justices, William de Warenne of Wormegay, came from the baronage (p. 90).

such as the *casus regis* or representative principle and the partition of estates among daughters.[67] Royal patronage in the form of marriages to heiresses provided an easy means for them and their relatives to rise in social status and wealth, while custodies of minor heirs and marriages to widows with dower estates offered temporary control of wide lands, and they took full advantage of the opportunities presented to them.[68] Richard I's justiciar, Hubert Walter, whose uncle Glanvill had brought him into the judiciary a few years before Henry II's death, was notorious for profiting from wardships.[69]

Perhaps the question posed in this paper's title should be rephrased to read "Feudal and Royalist," deleting the question mark. In *The Legal Framework*, Milsom reminds us to place Henry II's contribution to the land law in a feudal context. He shows the gradual growth of feudal tenants' proprietary right, still incomplete by 1189. Milsom reasserts the significance of the feudal courts as centers for settlement of tenurial disputes throughout much of the twelfth century. He clarifies the contradictions in the lord—tenant relationship that made justice in lords' courts less and less likely for tenants, necessitating royal regulation. He makes clear that the possessory assizes mainly protected tenants from their lords, not from unknown occupiers of their land, and that they had altered the nature of the lord—tenant relationship by the end of the century, undermining lords' courts. These contributions to our understanding of the evolution of English land law are undoubted.

Milsom is unconvincing, however, when he argues that replacement of the feudal courts' jurisdiction by royal justice was unplanned and accidental. Henry II cannot have been too dismayed when his reforms let loose a flood of lawsuits flowing from his magnates' courts into his own. Traditions of the supremacy of royal jurisdiction were powerful in both Anglo-Norman and Angevin England, and Henry's much-admired grandfather had not hesitated to intervene in the lesser courts, often at the request of the litigants themselves. The tools that Henry II took up to regulate his barons' courts were not feudal, although adapted for the feudal end of enforcing his overlordship, but originated in Anglo-Saxon

---

67 E.g. Ranulf de Glanvill, who had only daughters; Geoffrey fitz Peter, whose claim to the Mandeville inheritance came from his wife and raised questions similar to the *casus regis*; Godfrey de Lucy, a younger brother with surviving nieces, a situation which again raised the issues of the *casus regis*; Michael Belet and others, who married co-heiresses; or William Briwerre, whose eldest son predeceased him and who had several daughters to provide for.
68 Turner, *English Judiciary*, 52-63, 112-16.
69 Charles R. Young, *Hubert Walter, Lord of Canterbury and Lord of England* (Durham, NC, 1968) 156-9.

and Frankish executive measures. Finally, the justices whose work caused the decline of the feudal courts were not on the bench by accident. They were royal appointees, removable by the king, owing their fortunes to his patronage, striving to do his will. If their zeal to apply the new assizes' protection to more and more tenants displeased him, he had only to dismiss them. It will not do to depict Henry II as a perfect feudal overlord, served by anti-feudal, royalist judges.

2

The Origins of Common Pleas and King's Bench

English common law is unlike continental law in many ways. The system of courts that grew up to administer English law also differs from others, for only in medieval England did two central law courts — common pleas or Bench at Westminster and *coram rege*, later king's bench — appear, both of them following the same procedures and performing much the same work. In the later Middle Ages and continuing into the Tudor period, monarchs created new courts that would be more closely controlled by them as older courts tended to become less flexible. The late medieval conciliar courts with their different procedures could be shaped to the king's will more readily than the old common law courts. Yet with the creation of the court *coram rege* first under John and revived by Henry III, we find a duplicate of the court of common pleas with little or no distinction in the work of the two courts. How did this unlikely situation arise? What did the two monarchs have in mind in creating a second common law court to sit in their presence? Did they feel that it was needed in order to impose their will upon the judges and juries?

For generations, answers to students' questions about the early growth of the royal courts came from two pioneers in English legal and constitutional history, Bishop William Stubbs and F. W. Maitland. In the twentieth century, however, historians have made important studies in medieval English history, using materials unavailable to Stubbs and Maitland in the nineteenth century.[1] Be-

---

1. E.g., Doris M. Stenton, ed., *The Earliest Lincolnshire Assize Rolls, A.D. 1202-1209* (Lincoln Record Society, 22; 1926); *The Earliest Northamptonshire Assize Rolls, A.D. 1202 and 1203* (Northampton Record Series, 5; (1930); *Rolls of the Justices in Eyre for Lincolnshire (1218-19) and Worcestershire (1221)* (Selden Society, 53; 1934); *Rolls of the Justices in Eyre for Yorkshire in 3 Henry III* (Selden Society, 56; 1937); *Rolls of the Justices in Eyre for Gloucestershire, Warwickshire and Staffordshire, 1221, 1222* (Selden Society, 59; 1940); *Pleas before the King or his Justices, 1198-1202*, (4 vols.; Selden Society, 67-68, 83-84; 1948-67); G. O. Sayles, *Select Cases in the Court of King's Bench under Edward I — Henry V* (7 vols.; Selden Society, 55, 57, 58, 74, 76, 82, 88; 1936-71); and with H. G. Richardson, *Select Cases of Procedure without Writ under Henry III* (Sel-

cause these new findings are hidden away in the introductions to editions of plea rolls and other royal records, they have not yet been revealed in the textbooks, which still follow the traditional accounts. Building upon their work, then, a re-examination of the whole question of the origin of common pleas and king's bench is now possible. Such an examination cannot be purely institutional, but must take into account personalities and politics.

The traditional view of the rise of common pleas and king's bench was that their creation was part of a centuries-long process of professionalization and specialization, during which many institutions, from the Exchequer, to the Chancery, to the common law courts, were spun off from the *curia regis*. Recent writing on common pleas and king's bench suggests, however, that the growth of institutions in medieval England was more complex. The appearance of these two courts illustrates two distinct trends in twelfth and thirteenth century English government that were often in tension. Growth of the court of common pleas can be explained in terms of increasing professionalization and specialization in government. Growth of king's bench, on the other hand, must be explained in terms of royal resistance to the tendency of offices to 'go out of court' and to a royal effort to preserve 'familiar' or 'household' government which would be more responsive to the king's will.[2]

At the outset, one must recognize that all the judicial branches of the royal court — itinerant justices, exchequer, common pleas, and king's bench — can be traced back to the *curia regis* of the Norman kings. This was an inchoate and constantly changing core of great officers of state, household servants and feudatories serving the Conqueror and his sons as advisers, administrators and judges, which expanded on special occasions to become the *magna curia regis*. But ordinarily it was a much smaller group of royal servants dubbed by historians the 'lesser *curia regis*'.

Under the Norman kings, the *curia regis* was the highest judicial body in the kingdom, but it was a court "only for the great men and the great causes."[3] There was no central court with its own staff, functioning regularly apart from the monarch. On great

---

den Society, 60; 1941). H. G. Richardson, *Memoranda Roll 1 John* (Pipe Roll Society, new series; 1943), Richardson and Sayles incorporated many of their findings in *The Governance of Mediaeval England* (1963). R. C. Van Caenegem, *Royal Writs in England from the Conquest to Glanvill* (Selden Society, 72; 1959). C. A. F. Meekings, author of introductions to *Curia Regis Rolls*, v. 11-15 (Public Record Office; 1954-61).

2. See the too-often overlooked work of J. E. A. Jolliffe, *Angevin Kingship* (1955).

3. Frederick Pollock and F. W. Maitland, *The History of English Law before the Time of Edward I* (2nd ed., 1898), v. 1, p. 108.

feast-days the *magna curia regis* rendered judgments in important cases; at other times the king's household officers acted as judges, and after the establishment of the Exchequer it sometimes sat as a court. Under Henry I, members of the *curia regis* went on circuits to the counties to hear pleas while carrying out other governmental tasks. Later, Henry II's system of writs and assizes vastly increased the number of legal proceedings coming before the *curia regis*. This necessitated machinery for the judgment of these new actions, and the king tinkered in experiment after experiment in an effort to construct some mechanism.

One experiment was the revival of the itinerant judicature in 1166. Another was the assignment of five members of the royal household — three laymen and two clerks — to the task of helping to handle this new litigation in 1178. This tribunal would accompany the king on his travels up and down the kingdom, but would only consult him about cases too important or too difficult to decide themselves.[4] Stubbs traced the court of king's bench to this measure,[5] but Maitland did not accept Stubbs' view. Instead, he traced to it the origin of the court of common pleas at Westminster. He explained that these judges traveling with the king failed to evolve into the permanent court *coram rege* because of Henry's long absences from England. During the years that Henry II and Richard I were abroad, the tribunal settled at Westminster, where it sat at the house of the Exchequer. The two bodies doubtlessly shared some of their personnel, although they were not identical.[6]

Maitland's version of the creation of the court of common pleas received endorsement from a number of legal historians, and it became almost the standard account.[7] But Richardson and Sayles attacked this interpretation of the ordinance of 1178; Sayles said, "This was but one among many schemes improvised by that king's fertile inventiveness . . ., it was short-lived, and we ought not to see in it the solemn foundation of a court of law simply because it

---

4. *Gesta Regis Henrici Secundi*, ed. William Stubbs (Rolls Series; 1867), v. 1, pp. 207-8.

5. William Stubbs, *Constitutional History of England* (1874-78), v. 1, p. 525. He is followed even today by Alan Harding, *The Law Courts of Medieval England* (Historical Problems: Studies and Documents 18; 1973), p. 54.

6. Pollock and Maitland, v. 1, pp. 153-55.

7. G. B. Adams, *Council and Courts in Anglo-Norman England* (Yale Historical Studies 5; 1926), pp. 217-19, 240-42; J. E. A. Jolliffe, *The Constitutional History of Medieval England* (3rd ed.; 1954), pp. 215-16; Bryce Lyon, *A Constitutional and Legal History of Medieval England* (1960), p. 282; Van Caenegem, *Royal Writs*, 30; W. L. Warren, *Henry II* (1973), p. 297.

chanced to be mentioned by a chronicler."[8] Others have agreed that this was only a temporary measure to relieve the burden upon the barons of the Exchequer.[9]

Richardson and Sayles followed Maitland in attributing the rise of a permanent tribunal at Westminster to the long absences of Henry II and Richard I; however, their view is that it grew, not from the five justices appointed in 1178, but from the Exchequer. They found the origin of the Bench at Westminster in the *curia regis ad scaccarium* — the justiciar's court — the first sedentary branch of royal government. They were convinced that the court of common pleas had its origin in an omni-competent Exchequer. They felt that only slowly, because of increased business by the time of King John, did the royal officers at Westminster come to make a distinction between their financial and judicial work.[10] Richardson's and Sayles' opinion of the Exchequer contrasts with traditional views, which can be summarized in the words of T. F. Tout. He describes the Exchequer as "primarily and essentially a 'segregated' revenue department, and its 'secretarial', nay, even its judicial aspects, were quite subordinate to its prime function."[11] Richardson and Sayles developed a number of ingenious arguments to support their view, including textual criticism of the twelfth-century lawbook attributed to Glanvill.[12]

A problem is that what such terms as *curia regis, bancus,*

---

8. Sayles, *Select Cases*, v. 4, p. xxvii.

9. S. B. Chrimes, *Introduction to the Administrative History of Medieval England* (revised ed.; 1958), p. 49, n. 1, "only one of a series of similar experiments." Similarly A. L. Poole, "From Domesday Book to Magna Carta", *Oxford History of England*, (2nd ed.; 1955) v. 3, p. 413; and Doris M. Stenton, *English Justice Between the Norman Conquest and Magna Carta, 1066-1215* (1965), pp. 75-76.

10. Richardson and Sayles, *op. cit. supra* note 1, 210-11.

11. T. F. Tout, *Collected Papers* (1932), v. 1, p. 193.

12. For example, they pointed out that the justices of the Bench also served as barons of the Exchequer, that the two groups were housed together at Westminster, and that the titles 'justices' and 'barons' were interchangeable in the late twelfth century, Richardson and Sayles, *op. cit. supra* note 1, p. 210. Turning to *Glanvill*, they note a passage where the law courts are enumerated: *curia regis ad scaccarium et coram justitiis ubicumque fuerint*. G. E. Woodbine, *Tractatus de Legibus et Consuetudinibus Regni Angliae* (1932), pp. 183-84, had placed a comma after *curia regis*, indicating two courts. Richardson, *Memoranda Roll 1 John*, [Pipe Roll Soc.], pp. xiii, xiv, argued that the phrase *curia regis ad scaccarium* denotes a single court — the Exchequer — and the most recent editor of Glanvill, G. D. G. Hall, *Tractatus de Legibus et Consuetudinibus Regni Angliae qui Glanvilla Vocatur* [Medieval Texts] (1965), p. xii, also omitted the comma.

justiciarii, meant to Richardson and Sayles may not be precisely what they meant to Glanvill and men of the twelfth century, who were maddeningly imprecise in their language. Brian Kemp has pointed out the varied ways in which Richard fitz Neal, author of the *Dialogus de Scaccario*, employed the term *curia regis*.[13] Exchequer clerks could even use it in a material sense, as in a pipe roll entry for repairs to the quay of the *curia regis* at Westminster.[14] In 1182, they described witnesses to a final concord made in the king's court as *baronibus et justiciariis domini regis*.[15] Did they mean a single group who were both barons of the Exchequer and justices? Or did they mean two distinct groups?

Brian Kemp's survey of the problem of the Exchequer and Bench in the twelfth century has brought him to share Richardson's and Sayles' view that there was only a single body. He notes the lack of precision in the language of the pipe rolls and final concords.[16] He then discusses a document which he feels illuminates the problem, the testimony of the treasurer of Salisbury concerning conveyance of land to Forde Abbey.[17] Kemp concludes, "It provides irresistable evidence that in the early 1190's there was as yet no separation into distinct institutions of the financial and general judicial aspects of the *curia regis* at Westminster.[18] Richardson's and Kemp's version of the text of Glanvill has not, however, gone unchallenged. For example, R. C. van Caenegem, citing an entry in the pipe roll for 1188 which records that a litigant offered one fine for having his plea *in curia regis*, and a second fine later to have it heard *in curia regis ad scaccarium*, concludes that "the difference between the *curia regis* as the highest law court, to become soon the common bench, and the exchequer as accounting office for royal debtors was clearly realized in the late twelfth century."[19]

---

13. "Exchequer and Bench in the later twelfth century — separate or identical tribunals?" 87 *Eng. Hist. Rev.* 563 (1973).
14. *Pipe Roll 30 Henry II* [Pipe Roll Society] (1912), p. 137.
15. *Pipe Roll 28 Henry II* [Pipe Roll Society] (1910), p. 107.
16. "Exchequer and Bench," 87 *Eng. Hist. Rev.* 565-66 (1973).
17. *Forde Abbey Cartulary*, pp. 418-19, text on p. 577, "Exchequer and Bench." Ranulf, treasurer of Salisbury and former notary of Ranulf Glanvill, used the terms *justiciarii scaccarii, justiciarii domini regis apud Westmonasterium, barones Scaccarii* and *curia domini regis* interchangeably.
18. "Exchequer and Bench," 87 *Eng. Hist. Rev.* 570 (1973).
19. *Royal Writs*, Van Caenegem, *op. cit. supra* note 1, p. 31. Kemp's response is that the former fine was for a plea before the itinerant justices, the later for moving it to the Exchequer, "Exchequer and Bench," 87 *Eng. Hist. Rev.* 565 (1937). But Lady Stenton noted that by the 1170's pipe roll

It is unclear, then, whether Glanvill was aware of a distinction between the *curia regis* and the *scaccarium*—whether or not he would have inserted a comma between them had he used modern punctuation. His term *curia regis ad scaccarium* could imply the place at which the king's court sat, 'the king's court at the house of the Exchequer'. This translation of the phrase makes sense in practically every instance, and the idea of the Exchequer as a place can be detected in late twelfth-century references.[20] Sometime between 1182 and 1185, the witness list for a deed recognized royal justices and barons of the Exchequer as two distinct groups even when jointly witnessing a document.[21] By the early thirteenth century, the *curia regis* rolls of John's reign make clear that the terms "barons" of the Exchequer and "justices" of the Bench were not being used interchangeably by the clerks who kept the plea rolls.[22] A monk's account of litigation involving his house in 1201 indicates that he saw the Bench and Exchequer as separate entities, for he described the justices as "rising from the bench" to take counsel with the "barons of the exchequer and lieges of the lord king."[23]

Since linguistic analysis of the Latin of the plea rolls, final concords, and legal treatises does not offer a fully satisfactory solution

---

clerks did distinguish between pleas *in curia regis* and pleas before justices *errantes,* Stenton, *op. cit. supra* note 1, p. 75.

20. Francis J. West, "The *Curia Regis* in the Late Twelfth and Early Thirteenth Centuries," *Historical Studies (Australia and New Zealand)*, v. 6 p. 173, n. 5 (1954). William fitz Stephen's life of Becket, written 1173-75, *Materials for the History of Thomas Becket*, ed. J. C. Robertson (Rolls Series; 1875-85), v. 3, p. 51, describes the Exchequer as "where the pleas of the king's crown are heard." *Adami de Domerham Historia de rebus gestis Glastoniensibus*, ed. Thomas Hearne (1727), v. 2, pp. 377-99, describing a disputed abbatial election in 1198, notes that the monks sent representatives to London *ad regis justiciarios*, and that the representatives then elected an abbot *in scaccario regis*.

21. David Douglas, ed., *Feudal Documents from the Abbey of Bury St. Edmunds* (British Academy Records of Social and Economic History; 1932), p. 181, no. 220: *coram justiciis domini regis Henrici secundi vidilicet Ricardo episc. Winton. et Ranulfo de Glanvilla Wmo. Basset et Rogero fitz Reinfrei et coram Ricardo thesaurario et baronibus de scaccario apud Westmonasterium . . .*

22. Stenton, *Pleas before the king or his Justices* (Selden Soc. 67) v. 1, pp. 60-61, the barons of the Exchequer heard pleas, Feb.-Mar. 1200, while the justices were with King John. See references to *banco* in *Curia Regis Rolls*, v. 3, p. 274; v. 5, p. 119; v. 6, p. 66; v. 7, p. 113; references to *barones de scaccario*, v. 7, p. 33; v. 8, pp. 87, 309, 316.

23. Stenton, *op. cit. supra* note 9, p. 195, dispute between the abbey of Croyland and the priory of Spalding, 1189-1202.

to the problem, we must examine the personnel of the Exchequer and the Bench in our attempt to resolve the difficulty. Francis West made such an examination, compiling lists of the judges of Richard I and John, and his study enabled him to detect a change about 1196.[24] Before then, the men who composed the *curia regis* "were not professional justices, but well-known figures in the financial administration, or even in politics;" after 1196, they were a smaller, more stable group of men, "who look like professional justices, whose main duties were judicial. . . in sharp contrast to the larger and more diffuse group of the previous reigns."[25] Actually, a look at the lists of justices reveals that more 'professionals' joined the Bench in 1194 than in 1196.[26] The earlier date is more likely, for in the autumn of 1194 the justiciar, Hubert Walter, introduced a number of administrative reforms. He undertook a reform of the office of sheriff, replacing a number of *curiales,* and he issued new sets of instructions for the itinerant justices which led to creation of the offices of coroner and Exchequer of the Jews.[27]

It is almost impossible to identify the barons of the Exchequer. Madox did manage to make sketchy lists of them in the eighteenth century, even though they are named only rarely in the charters or final concords.[28] If one compares lists of justices at Westminster with Madox's list of barons of the Exchequer, then a larger degree of specialization can be seen under Richard I than under Henry II: of forty-eight justices named in the last ten years of Henry's reign, eighteen were also barons of the Exchequer; for Richard's reign, the figures are ten of sixty-two. Biographical study of King John's judges indicates an even greater degree of specialization, for it becomes clear that he had a core of royal servants concentrating on judicial affairs apart from the barons of the Exchequer.[29] As justices they carried out financial tasks from time to time, and many of them may have begun their careers as royal servants at the Exchequer; but from the middle 1190's at the latest, there were two

---

24. West, *op. cit. supra* note 20, The work of identifying the early royal justices is easier with Lady Stenton's list, "The Development of the Judiciary 1100-1215," *Pleas before the King,* v. 3, (Selden Soc. 83) pp. xlvii-ccxciv.

25. West, *op. cit. supra* note 20, pp. 174-75.

26. Richard Barre, Ralf Foliot, William de Ste. Mère Église, Richard of Herriard, all men who would serve at least ten terms on the Bench.

27. David A. Carpenter, "The Decline of the Curial Sheriff in England 1194-1258," 91 *Eng. Hist. Rev.* 6-7 *(1976).*

28. Thomas Madox, *The History and Antiquities of the Exchequer of the Kings of England* (2nd ed., 1769), v. 2, pp. 312-19.

29. West, *op. cit. supra* note 20.

distinct bodies. A process of professionalization and specialization had resulted in a new branch of government, the Bench at Westminster. The justices had their own rolls, known as the *rotuli curie domini regis de Westmonasterio,* clearly distinguished from the Exchequer records.[30]

With the appearance of the court of common pleas by the end of the twelfth century, the origin of the second central court, the king's bench, remains to be considered. The Anglo-Saxon kings had summoned their wise men to aid them in giving justice, and the Norman kings had called upon their tenants-in-chief for counsel. The court *coram rege* of the thirteenth century, however, was not the *magna curia regis.* It was a court composed of a few professional justices following the king, while the great council was more a deliberative body, composed of the king's ministers and magnates — the bishops, earls, and barons. When did this regularly constituted court with its own staff appear?

No court *coram rege* with a permanent staff, plea rolls, and procedures seems to have existed in the twelfth century. Yet the king judged important cases concerning persons of political importance, and this alone would have brought a number of actions into his court, for many persons and almost all religious houses had charters granting them the right to be tried only before the king or justiciar.[31] In addition, the king heard other cases which raised difficult questions, and he received petitions for justice in cases where there was no legal remedy. The number of pleas had grown great enough by 1178 for Henry II to make some provision for their hearing; but as has been seen, the king's prolonged absences from the kingdom prevented the growth of any permanent court following him. Indeed, Richardson and Sayles wrote that Henry II's court *coram rege* was not at all significant:

> If we may judge by "Glanville," lawyers in the closing decades of the twelfth century gave hardly a thought to the court *coram rege;* their attention was confined to the court at the exchequer and the courts of the itinerant justices. It was at Westminster that the common law of England was born and grew up.[32]

But whatever may have been the role of the court following the king under Henry II and Richard I, with John's accession to the

---

30. *Curia Regis Rolls,* v. 1, pp. 57, 123, 181, 408.
31. E.g. cases judged before Henry II in M. M. Bigelow, ed., *Placita Anglo-Normannica, Law Cases from William I to Richard I* (1881); or purchases of this privilege recorded in the pipe rolls, *Pipe Roll 2 John* (Pipe Roll Society, new series; 1934), pp. 47, 99, 109, 147, 207, 239.
32. Richardson and Sayles, *op. cit. supra* note 1, p. 172.

throne that court began to take on new importance. King John was no absentee monarch, for the loss of Normandy in 1204 forced him to spend most of his time in England. In addition, he took a very active part in the administrative work of his kingdom, although his motives remain hidden. He may well have been plotting the kind of "unrealized absolutism" which J. E. A. Jolliffe asserted to be the aim of the Angevin monarchs.[33] Certainly creation of his own court, staffed in part with his *familiares,* fitted in with plans for a government which was to be essentially household government.

In any case, his desire for close supervision did result in the creation of a new body of royal justices, and scholars have recognized this. Maitland took an uncharitable view of King John's interest in justice, although he was aware that the creation of the two central tribunals — one following the king and another resident at Westminster — dates from his reign.[34] Possibly John felt that he was merely reviving the custom of his father in hearing pleas as he moved about the land. But his almost continuous residence in England meant that in his reign the court *coram rege* would develop into an important part of the judicial system. More likely, John's plan was from the first to make it a permanent body; for almost at once the justices *coram rege* began to keep plea rolls, the first surviving one dating from John's visit to England in the spring of 1200.[35] Naturally, there could be no court *coram rege* when the monarch was overseas, and during King John's expeditions to Ireland or to the Continent, the Bench at Westminster regained its position as the only central court. King John's work in establishing a dual system of royal courts was a real contribution to the development of the English judicial system. Yet it is difficult to guess his motives. Lady Stenton accepted as his motive mainly a desire for more smoothly functioning machinery of justice. She wrote:

> What the king seems to have desired was what current practice provided — a flexible system with the king himself and his own court at its head, a small Bench sitting at Westminster as a clearing house for pleas, and a succession of eyres dispatched through the country as the pressure of local business and the need for local taxation required.[36]

---

33. Jolliffe, *op. cit. supra* note 2, 341.
34. Pollock and Maitland, v. 1, p. 170; see also Sayles, *Select Cases,* v. 1, p. xxii; and Stenton, *Pleas before the King,* v. 1, p. 86.
35. Feb.-April 1200, printed in Stenton, *Pleas before the King,* v. 1, pp. 296-310. Lady Stenton noted (p. 61), that possibly a roll of proceedings before the king was begun on John's visit to England in 1199, but if so it has not survived.
36. Stenton, *op. cit. supra* note 9, p. 99.

King John's motivation for creating a second common law court remains clouded, nonetheless. Certainly he had close enough control over the justices of the Bench at Westminster, for they were professional royal servants whose hopes for advancement in wealth, power and prestige depended upon the king's patronage. While many cases coming before them — possessory or proprietary actions involving minor landholders — held no interest for the king; others touched him in some way. Suits involving his barons or bishops, his *familiares*, or his enemies received his personal attention, as did pleas which touched on royal grants or charters. Either the justices at Westminster sought to consult him or he issued commands to them about such cases.[37] Sometimes he simply forbade them to hear pleas brought by persons who had incurred his displeasure.[38]

For some reason, John grew dissatisfied with the dual system of courts, and the Bench began to decline during the years 1207-9 when more and more cases were removed from its jurisdiction. That this resulted from a royal command is clear from the record of an assize brought before the justices of the Bench in 1209. The action was adjourned for hearing *coram rege* because one of the parties declared, "No plea ought to be held at Westminster, and he vouches the lord king to warranty concerning this."[39]

King John's command closing the court of common pleas was condemned by Richardson and Sayles, who termed it "one of those gratuitous acts of folly of which John, for all his cleverness, was capable in a blind access of resentment."[40] Yet it may not have been so much an "act of folly" as a carefully reasoned scheme by John to concentrate power in his hands. There is a rational explanation for his actions, if one turns to the political events of the years 1208 to 1212, keeping in mind at the same time the king's suspicious nature. This would have been a time of stress for any man, all the more for one of John's unstable temperament: he had recently suffered the loss of Normandy, now he faced another possible defeat in his struggle with the pope, and he felt increasing uncertainty about his vassals' loyalty. It may not have been simply blind anger, then, that made the king center all judicial activity at his own court where he could closely supervise it. By 1214 King John's attention had turned to preparations for his great expedition to recover Normandy, however, and the royal justices once again heard pleas at Westminster. The court of the Bench at Westminster revived from

---

37. Ralph V. Turner, *The King and His Courts: The Role of John and Henry III in the Administration of Justice, 1199-1240* (1968), 269-77.
38. *Ibid.*, pp. 57-68.
39. *Curia Regis Rolls*, v. 5, p. 327, Easter term 1209.
40. Richardson and Sayles, *op. cit. supra* note 1, p. 384.

Hilary term 1214 until Trinity term 1215, when the baronial rebellion began.[41]

The death of King John in 1216 and the accession of Henry III, a boy of nine, marked a return to the conditions that had prevailed under the absentee monarch Richard I. Once order was restored in the kingdom, the Bench at Westminster could resume its work. From 1218 until 1234 it remained the only central royal court. Pleas which required the king's participation either had to be referred to the council governing England during the minority or else postponed until his coming of age. The council had no court associated with it comparable to the court *coram rege;* its occasional judicial activities were noted on the plea rolls of the Bench at Westminster.[42] By January 1227, Henry III had declared himself of age,[43] but this brought no immediate change in the organization of the royal courts; there remained only one regular central court, the Bench at Westminster. Occasionally pleas coming before the justices at Westminster were postponed for hearing in the king's presence, beginning as early as 1221, but no plea rolls from a court following the king exist for the years before 1234.[44]

Most authorities maintain that a permanent court *coram rege* did not reappear before 1234, when it was re-established apparently as part of the administrative reforms made in the years 1232-1234. There was a long delay between the time Henry III officially came of age and the time he actually took command of his government. Hubert de Burgh, his justiciar, was more the governor of England than was the king for a number of years, 1219 to 1232; but then the powerful justiciar fell from favor, and a new group of royal favorites took control of the country until they too lost the king's favor in 1234. Henry then sought to bring all his officers and all branches of government more closely under his own supervision.[45] Maitland wrote that after the dismissal of Stephen de Segrave, Peter des Rivaux, and the Poitevins, "It looks as if the king had determined to get all the highest justice of the realm done under his own eye by professional judges who would not be too powerful, whom he could

---

41. *Curia Regis Rolls,* v. 7, 113. The editor's note describes this roll (Trinity 1214) as "a record of proceedings before the justices of the Bench." Richardson and Sayles, *op. cit. supra* note 1, p. 386, n. 1, cite letters close and patent to the justices of the Bench as late as April and July 1215.

42. Sayles, *Select Pleas,* v. 1, xxxiii-xxxiv; F. M. Powicke, *King Henry III and the Lord Edward* (1947), v. 1, pp. 38-40.

43. Powicke, *op. cit. supra* note 42, p. 44

44. The first roll, *Curia regis* roll 115B dates from 19 June 1234.

45. Chrimes, *op. cit. supra* note 9, pp. 86-87; Powicke, *op. cit. supra* note 42 chap. iii.

trust, whom at all events, he could watch."[46] Henry III need not have had any fear about being unable to watch over the Bench at Westminster. The two senior justices at Westminster after William de Raleigh left to head the court *coram rege* were Robert de Lexington and William de York, both career royal judges.[47] Once Henry took personal charge of his government, the practical need for a court accompanying him became greater, for the justices of the Bench had to consult him about more and more questions, making for delays in judgments. The solution was a return to two central law-courts, as there had been in the time of King John: one group of justices following the king, and another seated at Westminster.

The two scholars who have studied most closely the revival of a court *coram rege* under Henry III are G O. Sayles and C. A. F. Meekings.[48] They both link its revival to the reforms in government in the Spring of 1234, following the fall of Stephen de Segrave and the Poitevins. Among the changes were a number of new appointments in late May and early June, but no one was appointed to the post of justiciar. Also among the reforms was the creation by Henry III of a court of his own, the king's bench. In Sayles' view, this seemed a not unusual step, in spite of the seeming illogic of two central courts with parallel jurisdictions, because the royal household needed a court to settle domestic disputes, and the king's household stewards sometimes had taken on judicial tasks.[49] Yet Meekings points out that the immediate political situation had significance, for following the dismissal of Stephen de Segrave as justiciar, Henry III needed an experienced judge with him to preside over the important political cases that were coming before the council. For one reason or another, the office of justiciar was left vacant, an effect of which was to give the senior justice *coram rege* greater stature in judicial work and in the council.[50]

Neither Meekings nor Sayles assesses in full measure the part the political situation played in the revival of the court *coram rege*. The fall of Segrave was followed by a concentration of power in the

---

46. F. W. Maitland, ed., *Bracton's Note Book* (1887), v. 1, introduction, pp. 58-59.

47. C. A. F. Meekings, introduction to *Curia Regis Rolls*, v. 15, pp. xvi-xvii.

48. Sayles, *Select Pleas*, v. 1, pp. 4, 7; "The Court of King's Bench in Law and History," Selden Society Lecture (1959); Meekings, *Public Record Office Lists and Indexes*, Suppl. Series, No. 1, *List of Various Common-Law Records* (reprint; New York; 1970), pp. 36-39; and introduction to *Curia Regis Rolls*, v. 15.

49. Sayles, *Select Cases*, v. 15, pp. xxvii-xxviii.

50. *Curia Regis Rolls*, v. 15, pp. xxvii-xxviii.

hands of household officials, and a household court to rival common pleas in much the same way that the Wardrobe rivalled the Exchequer was not to be unexpected. Henry III had managed to rid himself of two troublesome and ambitious justiciars within only a few years, and since the justiciar dominated the Bench at Westminster, he may have felt that another court, in effect a household court, directly dependent upon the king, would be a useful counterweight to the justiciar. He could not have known that he would be successful in leaving the office of justiciar vacant. He may have feared that he might have to fill the office once again with someone who might hedge his power or give him evil counsel. He may even have felt that the barons and bishops who had sympathized with Hubert de Burgh and with the young earl marshal might force him to fill the post with someone from the baronial ranks.

Henry III's court *coram rege* was not at first the equal of common pleas. Most of the business of the newly created court was "small and miscellaneous" in the summer of 1234, but much of it involved persons associated with the court or the Chancery.[51] Some of the court's business had, indeed, a wider importance: a number of actions were brought against Peter des Rivaux, Stephen de Segrave, and their followers, men whom Henry III resented for having led him into a crisis in their years of power, 1232-1234.[52] Another sign of inequality was that in its early days the court *coram rege* was something of a vacation court active between terms of common pleas, or when it adjourned for an eyre. Its rolls did not begin to approach the size of the Bench rolls in their bulk. *Coram rege* rolls for several terms bound together only approached the roll of one term of common pleas in number of membranes.[53] For another thing, king's bench did not yet possess the professional character of the group of judges who had followed King John; in fact, until 1240, the court consisted of only one career justice, William de Raleigh, sitting with one or more of the household stewards.[54]

But in 1236 the court *coram rege* began to regain the status of equality with common pleas that it had enjoyed in the years 1204-1209. First, it took steps in Easter term of 1236 to correct a pro-

---

51. *Ibid.*, p. xxxi.
52. Listed on p. xxxii. On Henry's turning against his former advisers, see Powicke, *op. cit. supra* note 42, pp. 135-37.
53. Curia Regis Roll 115B consists of 35 membranes for Trinity and Michaelmas terms 1234 and Hilary and Easter terms 1235. Rolls of the justices of common pleas in the years before the revival of king's bench, ca. 1230-1234, range from 33 to 7 membranes a term.
54. *Curia Regis Rolls*, v. 15, p. xxii; names given, pp. xxxviii-xxxix.

cedural mistake made by the Bench the previous term.[55] It also began, in the words of Meekings, to take "steps to control, where necessary, cases pending before the Bench or assize commissioners in ways which had not been explicit before under Henry III."[56]

This raises an important question: What distinction was there in the work of the early courts of common pleas and king's bench? A cause for confusion is the uncertain meaning of the term *communia placita*. As Sayles said, "The 'commonness' does not relate to the case at all, but to the litigants."[57] That is, common pleas were those brought by private persons, where the king was not one of the parties to the action. Chapter eleven of *Magna Carta* (1225) stated that common pleas should not follow the king, but should be held in some fixed place. Complaints by some suitors that their 'common pleas' were being heard *coram rege* indicate that Sayles caught the thirteenth century meaning of the term.[58] Criminal cases could be common pleas if they were brought by an individual's accusation and not by a jury of presentment. It is incorrect, then, to state that the court of common pleas heard civil suits and that the court of king's bench heard criminal cases. It was not until 1323 that an involvement with criminal work came to set king's bench apart from common pleas.[59]

No noticeable differences in procedure distinguish the two courts, for both followed that pattern that had developed from the writs, plaints and juries of the twelfth century. Yet some scholars have professed to see a distinction based on procedure.[60] G. O. Sayles pointed out that cases heard by the Bench at Westminster were chiefly proprietary and possessory actions, those with "a system of procedure that precluded haste and were conveniently heard in a sedentary court."[61] In his view, the court *coram rege* had a higher jurisdiction, reviewing miscarriages of justice and unlawful proceedings. Actually, the apportionment of tasks was not so logical, for the plea rolls reveal innumerable possessory assizes heard *coram rege*. Sayles suggests that often the only factor determining where a plea should be heard was the relative importance it had in the king's eyes.[62]

---

55. Maitland *Bracton's Note Book*, v. 3, pp. 179-80, no. 1166.
56. *Curia Regis Rolls*, v. 15, pp. xxxv.
57. Sayles, Selden Society Lecture (1959), 5.
58. Faith Thompson, *The First Century of Magna Carta* (1925), 44.
59. Sayles, Selden Society Lecture (1959), 12-14.
60. James F. Baldwin, *The King's Council in England during the Middle Ages* (1913), 40; to some extent also the view of C. T. Flower, *Introduction to the Curia Regis Rolls* [Selden Society 62] (1944), 25.
61. Sayles, *Select Cases, op. cit. supra* note 1, v. 4, pp. xxxii-xxxiii.
62. *Ibid.*, v. 1, p. xxxviii; v. 4, pp. xxxi-xxxii.

Not even this was always the determining factor, for litigants often offered fines to bring common pleas before king's bench. Lady Stenton, in her work of editing the pipe rolls for King John's reign, encountered numbers of these oblations; and she compared the fines recorded in the pipe rolls for one term with the pleas for which they were offered, recorded in the *curia regis* rolls.[63] She found that in several suits unusual circumstances accounted for these fines — some difficult point of law or some politically potent issue — but in other cases there was no ready explanation. Her conclusion was that John had embarked on a new policy of encouraging litigants to bring their actions directly to his court, and that his reason was a genuine interest in the work of justice. She summarized her findings:

> The king seems to have been less interested in the trickle of new income which might come to the Exchequer than in the cases themselves. Indeed, many cases came into his court for which there is no evidence that any special payment was made. The lists of points, or the single points, which the judges both *coram rege* and of the bench, refer to the king merely indicate the inclusive character of the king's interest and the close attention which he wished to give to the work of his courts.[64]

King John's true reason for encouraging litigants to remove their suits from other branches of the *curia regis* to the court accompanying him cannot be known. Perhaps the answer is his genuine interest in hearing pleas, as Lady Stenton indicated; but a darker side to his character makes it difficult to accept this as the sole explanation. One reason for his close watch over his courts was his fear and suspicion which made him seek to concentrate all power in his hands. Then financial motives undoubtedly played some part, for the fines offered for adjournments of pleas to the court *coram rege* aided John in his search for new revenues.

G.O. Sayles wrote that when the court following the king was reconstituted in 1234 jurisdiction was to be reserved to the common bench in actions concerning "ownership or possession of land and the personal actions of debt, detinue, convenant, and account."[65] The king's own court would then concentrate on pleas in which he had a personal interest. Sayles had to admit, however, that this seemingly logical apportionment of spheres sometimes broke down,

---

63. *Pipe Roll 6 John* [Pipe Roll Society, new series] (1940), Michaelmas 1204, pp. xi-xx. Most of the cases are found in *Curia Regis Rolls*, v. 3, pleas *coram rege*, Easter term 1204.

64. Stenton, *op. cit. supra* note 9, p. 95

65. Sayles *Select Cases, op. cit. supra* note 1, v. 4, xxxii-xxxiii.

for he noted that "inasmuch as private parties might decide to settle disagreements in the king's bench, it was a court of common pleas as much as the common bench."[66] Perhaps C. A. F. Meekings has most precisely defined the work of Henry III's court *coram rege*. He found seven categories of pleas heard there:

1. Pleas touching the king, those involving royal grants or charters, or his interests as feudal lord.

2. Suits in which one party had the privilege of being impleaded only before the king, a privilege often granted to heads of religious houses.

3. Pleas removed from another court because of some difficult or new question, or because of a miscarriage of justice in a lower court, even though king's bench was not technically a court of appeal.

4. Cases in which the complainant had offered a fine to have his complaint heard *coram rege*, which he might seek for various reasons, including simple convenience, should the king be passing through his county.

5. Actions *quare contra pacem nostram, quare vi et armis,* that is, actions of trespass committed against the king's peace.

6. Suits brought by barons, bishops, royal officials, or other prominent persons in the kingdom.

7. Proceedings that might be termed 'state trials', brought against individuals who had incurred the king's displeasure.[67]

A survey of cases from one term of King John's court *coram rege* shows that Meekings' categories apply to John's court as well. Cases from five of the seven classes of cases can be found; the only two missing are state trials and actions of trespass.[68] There was no great difference, then, in the work of Henry III's court of king's bench and his father's. Neither ruler seems to have envisaged the two central tribunals as courts with sharply differentiated jurisdictions. This should not surprise us too much, for medieval men — in spite of their concern for logical categories in the sphere of philosophy — were never too logical about apportionment of governmental tasks. Responsibilities were shifted from one office to another as the king's interests or circumstances dictated.

Yet Henry's court *coram rege* was more a tribunal for pleas

---

66. *Ibid.*, p. xxxiv.
67. Meekings *List of Various Common-Law Records, op. cit. supra* note 48, pp. 47-48.
68. *Curia Regis Rolls,* v. 3, cases of Easter term 1204, analyzed in Turner, *op. cit. supra* note 37, p. 37.

touching the king than was John's; it did devote a larger share of its work to royal matters. More questions of royal rights, prosecution of fallen royal favorites, and challenges to royal acts by his subjects came before the king's bench under Henry III. It is surprising that justices *coram rege* were sometimes willing to hear pleas that indirectly questioned royal acts, such as disseisin *per voluntatem regis*. Doubtlessly, such cases proceeded only with Henry III's permission, and the justices protected his interests, refusing to allow the king to be vouched to warranty and consulting him before passing judgment.[69] Another surprise in the *coram rege* rolls of Henry's reign is the state trials, showing his use of king's bench as an instrument for pursuit of royal servants who had lost his favor.[70]

It seems clear that the two central tribunals of thirteenth-century England were the result of two divergent tendencies in Angevin government. In the case of common pleas, it was a simple process of specialization and professionalization as a body of professional royal servants specializing in justice took shape. But the desire of the monarchs — John and Henry III — for personal supervision of justice cannot be neglected. Certainly the creation of the court *coram rege* by King John and, perhaps even more so, its revival by his son represent efforts to keep justice close to the king, to preserve 'familiar' government, or to concentrate power in the royal household.

In spite of the growth of a new court under the king's personal supervision, neither John nor Henry III made any move to devise new methods for the court *coram rege*. Putting questions to juries remained the basis for its proceedings. Resort to the inquisitorial methods of Roman law was never felt to be necessary in the early thirteenth-century royal courts. Only much later in English history, with the Chancery court and with the Tudor prerogative courts, did Roman law make much impact.

Note

For an examination of Hubert Walter's financial and judicial officials, see Richard Heiser, 'The Households of the Justiciars of Richard I: An Inquiry into the Second Level of Medieval English Government', *Haskins Society Journal*, 2 (1990), pp. 223-35.

---

69. Ralph V. Turner, "The Royal Courts Treat Disseizin by the King: John and Henry III, 1199-1240," below, pp. 264-68.

70. See the analysis of cases from Trinity term 1234 in Turner, *op. cit. supra* note 37, p. 47; *Curia Regis Rolls*, v. 15, pp. 231-392, nos. 1023-1516.

3

The Origins of the Medieval English Jury: Frankish, English, or Scandinavian?

Serious study of the origins of the jury began in the time of William Stubbs and F. W. Maitland, when the work of the German historical school of jurisprudence reached England. Until then knowledge of the medieval English jury before the time of Henry II had been more legendary than real. William Blackstone had traced the common law to a compilation that King Alfred supposedly commanded to be made.[1] Blackstone had written in his *Commentaries on the Laws of England,* "Some authors have endeavoured to trace the original of juries up as high as the Britons themselves, the first inhabitants of our island; but certain it is that they were in use among the earliest Saxon colonies."[2]

In the mid-nineteenth century the Anglo-Saxon origin of the jury was still a popular legend in England, but the German school of legal history sought a more scientific study of the problem. A representative of that group, Heinrich Brunner, in his book, *Die Entstehung der Schwurgerichte,* rejected the traditional teaching that the jury was Germanic and popular in origin.[3] Instead, he believed it to be royal in origin, an authoritarian means of gathering information, particularly information of a financial nature. It first appeared as the inquest of the Frankish kings, inherited from the imperial Roman fisc.[4] It passed from them to the Norman dukes and then was introduced to England with William. According to Brunner the Norman kings reserved this fact-finding technique for themselves, extending it to their subjects in only a few cases. He recognized Henry II as the originator of the jury as a regular judicial instrument, first in Normandy and later in England. It was only after Henry came to the English throne that what had been a royal monopoly came to be a part of the common law.

Brunner's thesis gained acceptance as the authoritative statement on the origin of the jury, even though most German and English historians in the nineteenth century preferred to find the origin of

---

1. William Blackstone, *Commentaries on the Laws of England* (London, 1823), I, 67-70: Introduction, sec. iii.
2. *Ibid.,* III, 381: Bk. III, ch. xxiii.
3. Heinrich Brunner, *Die Entstehung der Schwurgerichte* (Berlin, 1872).
4. *Ibid.,* p. 87.

all free institutions among the Germanic tribes. Stubbs held this preference; yet he surrendered to the Brunner thesis. In his *Constitutional History of England*, he admitted that the Norman inquest by sworn witnesses "forms an important link in the history of the jury."[5] Maitland accepted the new view more wholeheartedly, for he was less committed to a search for Germanic sources for English institutions and more concerned with the concrete work of the medieval monarchs. In a series of lectures in 1887-88, he said that the germ of trial by jury must be found in "the prerogative procedure of the court of the Frankish kings."[6] Later he incorporated this thesis in his *History of English Law*: the origin of the jury is "not English but Frankish, not popular but royal."[7] C. H. Haskins supported this interpretation in his *Norman Institutions*, which first appeared in 1918.[8]

A theory that gains such wide acceptance as Brunner's about the origins of the jury is bound to attract criticism from historians seeking sacred cows to slaughter. Attacks on Brunner's thesis have taken two approaches: (1) They have pointed to the existence of the jury in England before the Norman Conquest, demonstrating an Anglo-Saxon or a Scandinavian origin. (2) They have denied the existence of the jury in pre-Conquest Normandy, making impossible its introduction to England by the Normans.

The first line of attack was followed cautiously by Stubbs. He accepted Brunner's views, but not willingly, for he believed in the Germanic origin of most English institutions. He knew one Anglo-Saxon institution that had presented difficulties for Brunner: the twelve thegns from each wapentake mentioned in Ethelred II's code enacted at Wantage in 997.[9] They seemed to act as an accusing

---

5. William Stubbs, *Constitutional History of England* (Oxford, 1874-78), I, 246. For an analysis of Stubbs's point of view, see Norman F. Cantor (ed.), *William Stubbs on the English Constitution* (New York, 1966), Introduction.
6. Printed as F. W. Maitland, *The Constitutional History of England* (Cambridge, 1908, reprinted 1961), p. 120.
7. Sir Frederick Pollock and F. W. Maitland, *The History of English Law* (2nd ed.; Cambridge, 1895), I, 140-42.
8. C. H. Haskins, *Norman Institutions* [Harvard Historical Studies, XXIV] (Cambridge, Mass., 1918), ch. vi, "The Early Norman Jury," pp. 196-238; C. H. Haskins, "The Early Norman Jury," *A.H.R.*, VIII (1903), 613-40. The Brunner thesis has continued to find acceptance in English constitutional and legal histories. E.g., W. S. Holdsworth, *A History of English Law* (London, 1903), I, 145; T. F. T. Plucknett, *A Concise History of the Common Law* (5th rev. ed.; London, 1956), pp. 107-12; G. B. Adams, *Constitutional History of England* (rev. ed.; New York, 1934), p. 86; J. E. A. Jolliffe, *The Constitutional History of Medieval England* (3rd ed.; London, 1954), pp. 207-09; Bryce Lyon, *A Constitutional and Legal History of Medieval England* (New York, 1960), pp. 183-84.
9. Dorothy Whitelock (ed.), *English Historical Documents, c. 500-1042* (Oxford, 1955), p. 7.

jury much like Henry II's juries of presentment. Brunner, though aware of the existence of the twelve thegns, interpreted their duties narrowly. In his view they merely decided whether the accused was of good or bad reputation in order to determine the severity of the ordeal he must undergo.[10] Stubbs felt that there might have been some connection between Ethelred's twelve thegns and Henry II's jury of presentment. He suggested that juries of accusation may have continued after the Conquest but was unable to connect them directly to Henry II's accusing juries. He concluded cautiously, "And thus the growth of the jury in criminal matters may have kept pace with its development in civil affairs."[11] Elsewhere he was even more cautious, stating that the Wantage code "seems to imply no more than that the English were not far in arrears of the Frankish jurisprudence."[12]

Maitland also considered the possibility that Ethelred's twelve thegns constituted England's first accusing jury, but he rejected any connection with the twelfth-century jury of presentment. He dismissed the Wantage code as insignificant because it applied only to the Danish district, not to the whole kingdom.[13] William Holdsworth and other historians followed Maitland, so that rejection of an Anglo-Saxon origin for the jury of accusation became the orthodox view. Holdsworth wrote, "We cannot say that this institution has, like the fyrd, a continuous history which can be traced from Saxon to Norman times."[14]

Maitland's thoughts on the accusing jury of the Danelaw led him to propose the possibility that the Scandinavians came independently to something close to the jury.[15] Sir Paul Vinogradoff, a friend of Maitland's, developed this idea further. He was more willing than English scholars to see Scandinavian influences on Anglo-Saxon law, and he viewed Ethelred II's thegns as "another Scandinavian institution of considerable interest."[16] He accepted Brunner's views on the connection between the Frankish inquest and Henry II's possessory assizes, but he added:

---

10. Brunner, *Schwurgerichte*, pp. 402-04; Paul Vinogradoff, *English Society in the Eleventh Century* (Oxford, 1908), p. 7.
11. Stubbs, *Constitutional History*, I, 427.
12. *Ibid.*, I, 655.
13. Pollock and Maitland, *History of English Law*, I, 142. Naomi D. Hurnard, "The Jury of Presentment and the Assize of Clarendon," *E.H.R.*, LVI (1941), 374-410. Hurnard took issue with Maitland and wrote that there was no reason why the Danish example should not have been followed in Saxon areas, even though the Wantage code did not apply to them directly. *Ibid.*, LVI, 376-77.
14. Holdsworth, *History of English Law*, I, 147.
15. Pollock and Maitland, *History of English Law*, I, 143.
16. Vinogradoff, *English Society*, p. 6.

But this does not preclude that in preconquestual England itself there had existed legal customs which prepared the way for the indictment jury of the twelfth century. The leading men of the wapentake, to judge by the Wantage enactment, were called up to point out persons who had to be accused of crimes, and to settle the conditions under which they might purge themselves of the accusation.[17]

Not many scholars were won over to Vinogradoff's view. In 1941 Naomi D. Hurnard reviewed the evidence and found little to support the Scandinavian origin of the accusing jury. She concluded, "It is not necessary, therefore, to assume that communal accusation was a purely Danish institution: it may have been a native English growth or it may have been borrowed from Francia."[18] H. G. Richardson and G. O. Sayles have joined her in rejecting Vinogradoff's suggestion. In their recent book, *Law and Legislation from Aethelberht to Magna Carta,* they picture Ethelred's legislation as the introduction of a Wessex custom to the Danelaw rather than the introduction of a Danish custom to Wessex.[19]

Though Vinogradoff's views failed to win followers for a long time, today scholars are looking at them more sympathetically. R. C. Van Caenegem, a Belgian scholar, wrote recently that the jury or some similar institution could be found in the Scandinavian countries, where there could have been no Frankish influence.[20] He also followed Vinogradoff's interpretation of the function of the twelve thegns of Ethelred's code, stating that it was "clearly a jury of presentment."[21]

Another scholar in sympathy with Vinogradoff is Lady Doris M. Stenton, who has edited many of the plea rolls and pipe rolls. In a series of lectures on the growth of English law, she said, "Vinogradoff knew more than Maitland of the Scandinavian element in English law and was less ready than most of their contemporaries to write it off because there was little evidence about it coming from an early date."[22] She agreed with Vinogradoff and Van Caenegem that the twelve thegns were a jury of presentment, but she went further, connecting their criminal presentments with

---

17. *Ibid.,* p. 7.
18. Hurnard, "Jury of Presentment," *E.H.R.,* LVI, 378.
19. H. G. Richardson and G. O. Sayles, *Law and Legislation from Aethelberht to Magna Carta* (Edinburgh, 1966), p. 25.
20. R. C. Van Caenegem, *Royal Writs in England from the Conquest to Glanvill* [Selden Society, LXXVII] (London, 1959), p. 58 and n. 3.
21. *Ibid.,* p. 59.
22. Lady Doris M. Stenton, *English Justice between the Norman Conquest and the Great Charter 1066-1215* [Memoirs of Amer. Phil. Soc., LX] (Philadelphia, 1964), p. 17.

the inquests held in civil cases.²³ Lady Stenton's husband, Sir F. M. Stenton, acknowledged Scandinavian influence on early English law in his book *Anglo-Saxon England,* when he wrote that the sworn jury was not known in Anglo-Saxon law and that the accusing jury of the Wantage code was derived from Scandinavian practice.²⁴ In his discussion of the introduction of the sworn inquest to England by William the Conqueror, he took a moderate stand, refusing to support a single source: "The trend of the evidence suggests that the Anglo-Norman jury may well have owed as much to English practice as to Carolingian reminiscence."²⁵

The second line of attack on Brunner's thesis is a demonstration that there was no jury in Normandy in the years before 1066, for if it did not exist there, it could not have passed from the Frankish kingdom through the Normans. A number of English scholars have recently turned their attention to the slender supply of documents surviving from early Normandy. No references have been found to sworn inquests of the Frankish type.²⁶ Neither does the recent French edition of the ducal charters issued from 911 to 1066 contain any suggestion of sworn inquests.²⁷ Indeed, the latest French scholarship finds little continuity between the institutions of Carolingian Neustria and ducal Normandy.²⁸ One French scholar has suggested that the Norman jury developed in the twelfth century under the influence of English practice.²⁹ Hurnard came to a similar conclusion in her study of the jury of presentment: "On the evidence, it is far more reasonable to conclude that William

---

23. *Ibid.*, pp. 15-16.
24. Sir F. M. Stenton, *Anglo-Saxon England* [*Oxford History of England*] (2nd ed.; Oxford, 1947), p. 503.
25. *Ibid.*, p. 643.
26. Doris M. Stenton, *English Justice*, p. 15; F. M. Stenton, *Anglo-Saxon England*, p. 643, n. 2; H. G. Richardson and G. O. Sayles, *The Governance of Mediaeval England from the Conquest to Magna Carta* (Edinburgh, 1963), p. 205; David Douglas, *William the Conqueror* (Berkeley and Los Angeles, 1964), p. 309. Van Caenegem, *Royal Writs*, p. 57, n. 2, admits the lack of documentary evidence, but he does not conclude from this that there could not have been inquests under the Normans.
27. Marie Fauroux (ed.), *Recueil des Actes des Ducs de Normandie (911-1066)* [Mémoires de la Société des Antiquaires de Normandie] (Caen, 1961).
28. Michel Bouard, "De la Neustrie Carolingienne à la Normandie féodale: continuité ou discontinuité?" *Bull. Inst. Hist. Res.*, XXVIII (1955), 1-14. Neither does David Douglas, "The Rise of Normandy," *Proc. Br. Academy*, XXXIII (1947), 101-31, find much continuity. Jacques Boussard, *Le Gouvernement d'Henri II Plantagenêt* (Paris, 1956), pp. 292-93, acknowledges the survival of the Carolingian inquest in Flanders and Normandy, but he finds it surviving too in the feudal procedure of Aquitaine, which he feels may be the source of Henry II's juries.
29. Yvonne Bongert, *Recherches sur les cours laïques du X° au XIII° siècle* (Paris, 1946), pp. 262-65.

found the system at work in England than that he brought it with him from Normandy."[30]

Haskins was a great admirer of the Normans and a strong supporter of Brunner's theory of the Norman origin of the jury. Yet not even he could cite any evidence for its regular use in the courts there before the time of the Angevin dukes, Geoffrey and Henry Plantagenet.[31] Indeed, the earliest Norman cases that anyone can cite in which there were juries date from the years just following the Conquest, 1070-79.[32] In her 1963 lectures Lady Stenton noted the resemblance of these cases to some in pre-Conquest England, and she asked the question, "Is it not possible that King William was introducing to his duchy a procedure which he found worked well in his new kingdom?"[33] Richardson and Sayles date the first Norman jury even later — in 1133.[34] Since this case was heard before a Norman noble, who was also an English earl and had been active in the English administration, they give an affirmative answer to Lady Stenton's question: "We can no longer believe that our jury had Roman or Frankish ancestors, who left descendants in Gaul, where they passed to Normandy and thence to our own island."[35] But a current English expert on early Normandy, David Douglas, refuses to give an answer to this question. In his study of William the Conqueror, he simply says of the jury, "The matter may, therefore, be left in suspense."[36]

Perhaps Douglas is right, and the question must be left in suspense. But there is another question concerning the origin of the jury: the question of Henry II's role in making it into a regular judicial instrument. How much of a novelty were his assizes? The sworn inquest was widely used as an instrument for gathering information by the Norman kings. The best known example is the compilation of Domesday Book from statements of sworn bodies of men.[37] In the reign of William I a great trial was held that seems to have made use of the jury, an inquiry into the claims of the

---

30. Hurnard, "Jury of Presentment," *E.H.R.*, LVI, 395-96.
31. Haskins, *Norman Institutions*, pp. 237-38.
32. Lechaude d'Anisy, *Grands Rôles des Échiquiers de Normandie* (Caen, 1846), pp. 196-97, case concerning the priory of Bellême. *Gallia Christiana*, XI (Paris, 1759), cols. 61-65, case concerning the abbey of Fontenay.
33. Doris M. Stenton, *English Justice*, p. 15.
34. Richardson and Sayles, *Governance of Mediaeval England*, p. 205; Richardson and Sayles, *Law and Legislation*, p. 117, an inquest into the fiefs of the Bishop of Bayeux.
35. Richardson and Sayles, *Law and Legislation*, p. 117.
36. Douglas, *William the Conqueror*, p. 309.
37. F. M. Stenton, *Anglo-Saxon England*, pp. 644-49, summarizes what may be considered the standard account of the method of compiling Domesday Book.

Bishop of Rochester, Gundulf, to land in Cambridgeshire held by the King.[38] In the reign of Henry I juries continued to be used for inquiries into royal rights and into the possessions and liberties of religious houses. Occasionally inquests into the rights of private persons were authorized by royal writs. For example, as early as 1101 a writ was issued for a jury in a plea of land between Rualon of Avranches and the Abbot of Abingdon.[39] Thus juries were occasionally allowed in proceedings under the Norman kings, although they were not made available to all the king's subjects until Henry II's assizes.

According to Brunner juries were first introduced as regular procedures by Henry in his duchy of Normandy and only later in England.[40] Maitland accepted Brunner's theory, but Haskins gave credit to Henry's father, Geoffrey Plantagenet. In his view Henry II's assizes were simply an extension to England of a procedure earlier employed in Normandy.[41] Haskins felt that he had evidence that something much like the assize of novel disseizin was available in Normandy in 1159, five years before the first of the English possessory assizes, the assize *utrum*, was made available.[42] His theory was that the jury first became a regular instrument of justice in the ecclesiastical courts and that the Angevins then adopted it for their own courts.[43] Sayles has suggested that the reverse was more likely, that the church courts borrowed the jury from the secular courts.[44]

In addition to the possessory assizes, Henry II authorized the jury of presentment with the Assize of Clarendon in 1166. The existence of a similar institution, the twelve thegns of Ethelred II, raises some question of the novelty of Henry's innovation. Maitland was convinced that the first general use of the accusing jury in England dated from Henry II's time, and most authorities have

---

38. Melville Madison Bigelow, *Placita Anglo-Normannica* (London, 1879), pp. 34-36. The case is discussed in Richardson and Sayles, *Governance of Mediaeval England*, pp. 207-08, and in Van Caenegem, *Royal Writs*, pp. 62-63.
39. H. W. C. Davis (ed.), *Regesta Regum Anglo-Normannorum* (Oxford, 1913), I, No. 528; Van Caenegem, *Royal Writs*, p. 83.
40. Brunner, *Schwurgerichte*, pp. 465-66; Pollock and Maitland, *History of English Law*, I, 144.
41. Haskins, *Norman Institutions*, p. 215; Haskins, "The Early Norman Jury," *A.H.R.*, VIII, 618.
42. Haskins, *Norman Institutions*, pp. 196-238, suit brought by Osmund Vasce and suit between William Fitz Thetion and the church of St.-Etienne.
43. *Ibid.*, p. 226.
44. G. O. Sayles, *The Medieval Foundations of England* (London, 1948), p. 336. Haskins's theory about the church courts is also rejected by Hurnard, "Jury of Presentment," *E.H.R.*, LVI, 395.

accepted his conclusion.⁴⁵ Hurnard, however, having investigated the origins of the jury of presentment, came to a different conclusion. She found in the pipe roll for 1130, the only surviving roll from Henry I's reign, numerous references to men called *juratores*, whom she believed to be the predecessors of Henry II's juries of presentment.⁴⁶ She felt that Maitland connected the juries of presentment too closely with the eyres of the itinerant justices, and that he overlooked the *juratores* or *judices* because they were a part of the machinery of the old community courts continuing from Anglo-Saxon days.⁴⁷ In her opinion these local accusing juries continued in Henry II's early years, since she found a pipe roll entry for 1158 *pro placito celato*, a phrase which she interpreted as meaning crimes for which the jurors had failed to accuse suspects and for which they were fined.⁴⁸

Hurnard cited in support of her thesis a statement by Ronald Stewart-Brown, in which he rejected the view that the jury of presentment began only in 1166:

> In spite of the views of legal historians there seems great unlikelihood that before 1166 the criminal cases classed as pleas of the Crown, which date back before the Conquest, were left to be dealt with by contests of 'appeal' between the parties concerned, initiated by the action of the aggrieved person alone. There was money to be made by the Crown out of the punishment of crime . . . Is it likely that it would be left to private initiative whether or not a criminal was put on his trial?⁴⁹

Sayles shared a similar opinion. He found it hard to believe that accusation by the victim was the only way of prosecuting criminals before the Assize of Clarendon. Pointing to the duties in the field of justice that were assigned to the local communities by the Anglo-Saxon and Norman kings, he could not see why there should not have been among these duties an obligation by the community "to voice suspicions, tell tales, inform against the criminal."⁵⁰

Sayles and his colleague, Richardson, sought an answer to this question of accusations made by the community. They found the community's spokesmen in the *judices, judicatores*, or *juratores* of

---

45. Pollock and Maitland, *History of English Law*, I, 42-43, 151-53.
46. Hurnard, "Jury of Presentment," *E.H.R.*, LVI, 378; *Pipe Roll 31 Henry I*, pp. 28, 34, 69, 103.
47. Hurnard, "Jury of Presentment," *E.H.R.*, LVI, 378-79, 382-83.
48. *Ibid.*, LVI, 383; *Pipe Roll 2-4 Henry II*, p. 127.
49. Ronald Stewart-Brown, *The Serjeants of the Peace in Medieval England and Wales* (Manchester, 1936), p. 79.
50. Sayles, *Medieval Foundations*, p. 335.

Henry I and Hurnard. Calling these men "the forerunners of the juries of presentment" and also "old English lawmen," they connected them with both Henry II's accusing juries and the Anglo-Saxon doomsmen. Although they did not elaborate on this theory, they clearly meant that these representatives of the community who declared the law were assigned the additional task of presenting criminals.[51]

Now that historians' interpretations of both the remote and the recent origins of Henry II's juries have been surveyed, some attempt at a synthesis of their ideas must be made. The orthodox view since the late nineteenth century — the opinion of Brunner, Maitland, and Haskins — is that the juries in both possessory actions and criminal accusations had their origin in the administrative inquest, introduced to England from the Continent following the Norman Conquest. Strong blows have been dealt this thesis in recent years, so that some rethinking is necessary. Van Caenegem has presented a synthesis, a dual theory which tries to accommodate both Frankish and Norman origins and an Anglo-Saxon origin for the use of recognitors in pleas of land. He finds one source of the jury in the Frankish inquest, originally an executive instrument that could be allowed in private pleas as a royal boon.[52]

But Van Caenegem maintains that this is only half the story. He finds another source of the jury in the popular recognitions of the Anglo-Saxon local courts and offers evidence previously overlooked in support of this theory: a plea between Thorney and Ramsey abbeys which took place in 1053-55.[53] In his opinion this plea represents "at least one clear instance of the use of a free inquiry by a body of sworn neighbours to solve litigation on land in Anglo-Saxon times."[54] He cites other cases from the years 1092-1175 in which there were similar sworn inquests of neighbors.[55] Since no royal writs give evidence of the king's authorization, he classes them as popular juries. In his view then Henry II's possessory assizes were not so new, but simply a combination of these

---

51. Richardson and Sayles, *Governance of Mediaeval England*, pp. 182-84. Helen Cam, *Liberties and Communities in Medieval England* (Cambridge, 1944), ch. iv, "Suitors and *Scabini*," p. 52, also thought that the twelve thegns were doomsmen, much like the *scabini* of the Carolingian courts.

52. Van Caenegem, *Royal Writs*, pp. 60-61.

53. *Ibid.*, pp. 69-71. Two versions of the dispute survive: W. H. Hart and P. A. Lyons (eds.), *Cartularium Monasterii de Rameseia* [Rolls Series] (London, 1884-93), I, 188, No. 115, and III, 38-39, No. 544. Cambridge University Library, Red Book of Thorney, II, fol. 372.

54. Van Caenegem, *Royal Writs*, p. 59.

55. *Ibid.*, pp. 72-76.

popular recognitions and royal inquests; nevertheless, he gives Henry credit for making the jury a part of the ordinary procedure of the English courts. Lady Stenton, in summarizing Van Caenegem's findings in her 1963 lectures, indicates general sympathy with his approach. She is willing to give the Anglo-Saxons more credit for legal inventiveness than they have been given by others:

> For my own part, I believe that the rich stream of English case-law flowing through the Anglo-Saxon period reflects the minds and spirits of a people responsive to reason, ready to welcome a generous settlement of a plea, with a clear understanding of the sacral virtue of an oath. It was in this atmosphere that the seeds of the English jury grew and flourished.[56]

Van Caenegem's synthesis provides both Anglo-Saxon and Norman sources for the civil jury, but it leaves unanswered the question of the source of the accusing jury. Perhaps in accounting for the origins of the jury, it is best to look separately at the two types of juries, criminal and civil. Richardson and Sayles refuse to believe that Henry II and his contemporaries recognized any difference between one type of jury and another,[57] but possibly Henry was inspired by two different institutions. Hurnard's examination of the jury of presentment apart from the possessory assizes enabled her to make a convincing case for its Anglo-Saxon origin and survival in the Anglo-Norman period. Its source may lie in Scandinavian or early English institutions, while the source of the possessory assizes and the grand assize may lie in others, either Frankish inquests into royal rights continued by the dukes of Normandy or popular recognitions among the Anglo-Saxons. Whatever the origins of the jury, Brunner's account can no longer be accepted as the authoritative answer to the question. But no matter how early the origins of the jury and no matter where they lie, there is no reduction in the honor due to Henry II for making it into a regular instrument of justice, both civil and criminal. His inventive mind seized upon the possibilities that he found in these earlier instruments and shaped them into something new.

Note

See Constance I. Smith's letter in the same volume of *Journal of British Studies*, pp. 171-73, with references to procedures elsewhere that parallel the jury of presentment.

---

56. Doris M. Stenton, *English Justice*, p. 17.
57. Richardson and Sayles, *Law and Legislation*, p. 118.

4

Roman Law in England before the Time of Bracton

In Maitland's words, "Of all the centuries the twelfth was the most legal."[1] It was a time of growth for the great legal systems in the West: English common law, revived Roman law, and canon law. Students of medieval England have rarely concerned themselves with the question of the connection between these legal systems. For six centuries, from *Bracton* until the rise of modern legal history with Maitland, the study of English law was insular, ignoring the continental legal systems. When a seventeenth-century civilian wrote that "our common law, as we call it, is nothing else than a mixture of the Roman and the feudal," he aroused the anger of Coke and the common lawyers.[2] Recently scholars have taken such a view more seriously, and a number of studies have sought Roman or canonistic influences on English law. It might be useful, then, to reconsider the matter of the impact of Rome on English law in the light of recent scholarship, asking three questions: To what extent was Roman law known and studied in England before the time of Bracton? What influences, if any, do scholars find that it had on the legal innovations of Henry II and his sons? Why did the English fail to 'receive' Roman law in the way that countries on the Continent did?

Any influence of Roman law in England during the centuries after the withdrawal of Roman legions and before the Norman Conquest can be dismissed quickly. Once Christianity was re-introduced to the island, the revival of Roman Law, or at least of some notion of Roman legal concepts, was possible.[3] Scholars have long looked at the Anglo-Saxon law codes for some sign of Roman influence, but they have found little beyond the impetus to write down the laws. T. F. T. Plucknett found that a look at these codes makes it clear that their compilers had not learned the greatest lesson that Roman law has to teach, that is, the ability to arrange the material sys-

---

1. Frederick Pollock and F. W. Maitland, *The History of English Law before the Time of Edward I* (2nd ed.; Cambridge, 1898) (hereafter, *HEL*), I, 111.
2. C. H. McIlwain, "Our Heritage from the Laws of Rome," *Foreign Affairs*, XIX (1941), 598.
3. W. Senior traced this process in an article, "Roman Law in England before Vacarius," *Law Quarterly Review* (hereafter, *LQR*), XLVI (1930), 191-206.

tematically.⁴ When W. Senior examined the Anglo-Saxon codes, he could find few traces of Roman influence either.⁵

Also to be dismissed quickly is any Roman influence coming to England with the Normans. Plucknett found no possibility of this because, "As late as the twelfth century, the custom of Normandy was the least Romanized of the French *coutumes*."⁶ Mlle. Raymonde Foreville has examined the work of William of Poitiers, the first biographer of the Conqueror, seeking to show his knowledge of classical legal principles. She must admit, however, that any knowledge he had of Roman law came "by the intermediary of Latin philosophers, of Cicero principally," not from law collections.⁷

The Norman Conquest did, of course, bring England into closer contact with the intellectual life of the Continent; and clearly, an important aspect of that was the revival of Roman and canon law studies which had begun in eleventh-century Italy. A figure long supposed to have linked Normandy and England to the Italian legal revival is Lanfranc, who migrated first from Pavia to the abbey of Bec, then across the Channel to Canterbury. Pavia, the old capital of the Lombard kingdom, retained a group of lawyers in the Dark Ages who would make the city one of the earliest Italian centers of legal studies. One of the "lawmen" there at the beginning of the eleventh century was Lanfranc's father. Lanfranc was to follow his father's profession, and in his youth he gained some familiarity with Lombard law; but at an early age, he turned away from legal studies and left Pavia in order to study letters and dialectic.⁸ R. W. Southern and other scholars have shown that the evidence will not support

---

4. T. F. T. Plucknett, *Edward I and Criminal Law* (New York, 1960), pp. 6-7. For similar dubious views of Roman influence, see Alberto Alberti, *Scuole Italiane e Giuristi Italiani nel Sviluppo storico del Diritto Inglese, Biblioteca della rivista di storia de diritto Italiano* (Bologna, 1937, p. 42); J. M. Wallace-Hadrill, *Early Germanic Kingship in England and on the Continent* (Oxford, 1971), p. 33.

5. "Roman Law . . .", *LQR*, XLVI, 197, an apparent imitation of the *lex Julia majestatis* in Alfred's laws concerning treason. Similarly Pollock and Maitland, *HEL*, I, 51; II, 503. Senior also thought that the Anglo-Saxon *landboc* or charter indicated Roman influence, "Roman Law . . .", *LQR*, XLVI, 197.

6. "The Relations between Roman Law and English Common Law down to the Sixteenth Century: A General Survey," *University of Toronto Law Journal* (hereafter, *UTLJ*), III (1939-40), 27, following Génestal, "La Formation de la Coutume de Normandie," *Travaux de la semaine d'histoire du droit normand* (1927), p. 53.

7. "Aux origines de la renaissance juridique. Concepts juridiques et influences romanisantes chez Guillaume de Poitiers, biographe du conquérant," *Moyen Age*, LVIII (1952), 77.

8. R. W. Southern, "Lanfranc of Bec and Berengar of Tours," *Studies in Medieval History presented to F. M. Powicke* (Oxford, 1948), p. 29; Frank Barlow, "A view of Archbishop Lanfranc," *Journal of Ecclesiastical History*, XVI (1965), 166.

the tradition that Lanfranc was learned in the law. The tradition originated with the Norman chronicler Ordericus Vitalis, writing a generation after Lanfranc's death;[9] and it gained scholarly respectability in the nineteenth century, when Lanfranc was mistakenly identified with another Lombard lawyer of the same name.[10] In any case, the law taught at Pavia in Lanfranc's youth was Lombard, not classical Roman law. Lanfranc's significance for Anglo-Norman legal studies lies not in secular law, but in his canonical collection brought from Bec, which became the basic source-book of canon law in early twelfth-century England.[11]

Also cited as evidence of a revival of Roman law in Norman England is William of Malmesbury's work. He appended to one of his books a selection of extracts from the *Breviarium Alaricanum* and from some other collections.[12] This does not indicate the presence of any new legal texts in England, since William was using a seventh-century manuscript which had belonged to Aldhelm. Neither is there any indication that these extracts were studied as legal texts.[13] Norman Cantor cites William of Malmesbury's collection, along with the description of Henry I as *gloriosus Caesar Henricus* in the *Leges Henrici Primi* and the employment of similar phrases by others as evidence that Roman legal concepts were current in the early twelfth century.[14] Cantor's view is that Roman imperialist doctrines were being borrowed to enhance the status of the English monarch at the time of the investiture contest. Actually, similar grandiose terms had been applied to the Anglo-Saxon kings.[15] Both the Anglo-Saxon and Anglo-Norman writers had no doubt

---

9. Southern, "Lanfranc of Bec . . .", *Studies in Medieval History*, p. 29.

10. Pollock and Maitland *HEL*, I, 77-78; Maitland doubts the identification, but accepts Lanfranc's legal learning. William Holdsworth, *A History of English Law* (London, 1903-), II, 147, and J. H. Wigmore, "Lanfranc, the Prime Minister of William the Conqueror; Was He once an Italian Professor of Law?" *LQR*, LVIII (1942), 61-81, accept unreservedly the identification. Senior, "Roman Law . . .", *LQR*, XLVI, 199-200, dismisses any doubt about the correctness of the identification, following Tamassia, "Lanfranco, Arcivescovo di Canterbury e la scuola pavese," *Mélanges Fitting* (1908), II, 201. David Knowles, *The Monastic Order in England, 943-1216* (2nd ed.; Cambridge, 1963), p. 107, and Southern, "Lanfranc of Bec . . .", *Studies in Medieval History*, pp. 36ff, show that the identification is incorrect.

11. Z. N. Brooke, *The English Church and the Papacy from the Conquest to the Reign of John* (Cambridge, 1931), chap. V, pp. 56-83; and Alberti, *Scuole Italiane e Giuristi Italiani* . . ., p. 94.

12. His epitome of Hamo of Fleury's *Lives of the Emperors*; Senior, *LQR*, XLVI, 204-5; Norman F. Cantor, *Church, Kingship, and Lay Investiture in England 1081-1135* (Princeton, 1958), p. 280.

13. H. G. Richardson and G. O. Sayles, *Law and Legislation from Aethelberht to Magna Carta* (Edinburgh, 1966), p. 71.

14. Cantor, *Lay Investiture*, pp. 80, 280.

15. Senior, *LQR*, XLVI, 198.

borrowed them from the late classical rhetoricians, not from legal texts.

After the Conquest, the Norman kings, faced with the task of administering an alien law for their new subjects, needed codifications of the old English law. Some of the attempts to supply such codifications survive, but none of them sought the guidance of Roman law for organizing principles. This should not be surprising, since the systematic study of Roman law at Bologna only began after 1100 with the lectures of Irnerius. It took a number of years for the new discipline to drift north of the Alps and across the Channel to England.

One of the earliest of the Anglo-Norman lawbooks was the *Liber Quadripartitus,* an anonymous treatise from about 1114.[16] The author was, according to Plucknett, "a decidedly royalist cleric," whose goal was far too lofty for his limited education. He was incapable of achieving his plan of summarizing the English law of his day, and he managed to complete only two of the four books originally planned. They amount to little more than a disorderly translation of Anglo-Saxon laws, some of the legislation of William I, and a preface. The author knew Old English inadequately, and he wrote a "barely comprehensible" Latin, in spite of attempts to display his learning with quotations from classical authors.[17] Clearly, he lacked familiarity with Roman law which might have equipped him to carry out his plans. H. G. Richardson and G. O. Sayles have written that the author "shows no trace of legal training or understanding of the requirements of the most humble of lawyers."[18]

A second early twelfth-century work, which takes the place of the missing third and fourth books of the *Quadripartitus,* is the *Leges Henrici Primi,* available in a new edition and translation by L. J. Downer.[19] He dates its composition sometime between 1113 and 1118.[20] Most authorities, including the latest editor, accept a common authorship for the two works;[21] and certainly it shares the bad Latin, the "wonderful confusion," and other faults of the

---

16. T. F. T. Plucknett, *Early English Legal Literature* (Cambridge, 1958), p. 25. Maitland dated it between 1113 and 1118, Pollock and Maitland, *HEL,* I, 99.
17. *Early Eng. Legal Lit.,* pp. 25, 27.
18. *Law and Legislation,* p. 43.
19. (Oxford, 1972). Hereafter cited as *LHP.*
20. *Ibid.,* p. 36.
21. Felix Liebermann, *Über das Englische Rechtsbuch Leges Henrici* (Halle, 1901); Pollock and Maitland, *HEL,* I, 100; Plucknett, *Early Eng. Legal Lit.,* p. 27; Downer, *LHP,* p. 27; Richardson and Sayles disagree, *Law and Legislation,* p. 43.

Quadripartitus.²² A single borrowing from Roman law in the *Leges* leads some to conclude that the author had some knowledge of Roman legal science. The author refers in one passage to "the book of the Theodosian law,"²³ but in fact he was borrowing from an epitome of Roman law from the Dark Ages borrowed from an earlier barbarian code which was itself borrowed from the Theodosian Code.²⁴ Plucknett pointed out that he took as his chief guide not some text of Roman or canon law but Isidore of Seville's *Etymologiae*, and the passages that he chose to guide him "were not so much legal as poor specimens of decadent rhetoric."²⁵ Recent scholarship fails to find any Roman legal influences on the *Leges*. Downer cautiously concludes: "To Roman law as a source the author's debt is small;"²⁶ while Richardson and Sayles state strongly: "Above all we must not . . . credit him with a knowledge of Roman law or see any such influence in his work."²⁷

A third work, the *Leis Willelme*, is usually dated from the time of William Rufus or Henry I, although Richardson and Sayles date it much later.²⁸ They regard the work as a French translation of a lost *Leges Willelmi*, first written in Latin in the period 1150-1170, and subsequently translated into French. This is the reverse of Liebermann's view that it was written in French sometime between 1090 and 1135, and then translated into Latin.²⁹ Numerous scholars have noted that the middle section of the *Leis* contains six articles clearly revealing the influence of Roman law, among them an article on the jettisoning of cargo which follows the Rhodian sea law.³⁰ Richardson and Sayles believe that the author's knowledge of the Digest is evidence that he could not have written before the mid-twelfth century.³¹ Regardless of the date of the *Leis Willelme*, it does not indicate any depth of Roman influence on English law. As Richardson and Sayles write, "Its distinguishing mark is a

---

22. Pollock and Maitland, *HEL*, I, 100.
23. *LHP*, C. 33, 4, p. 137; Senior, "Roman Law . . .", *LQR*, XLVI, 202.
24. Downer, *LHP*, commentary, p. 344.
25. *Early Eng. Legal Lit.*, p. 29.
26. *Ibid.*, p. 31.
27. *Law and Legislation*, p. 44.
28. Felix Liebermann, "Über die leis Willelme," *Archiv für das Studium der Neueren Sprachen und Letteraturen* (Brunswick, 1901), CVI, 118-30, dated it 1090-1135. Richardson and Sayles, *Law and Legislation*, p. 121, and Appendix II.
29. "Über die Leis Willelme," pp. 118-30; *Die Gesetze der Angelsachsen* (Halle, 1903-16), III, 283-84. Pollock and Maitland, *HEL*, I, 102, follows Liebermann; Richardson and Sayles, *Law and Legislation*, pp. 121-22.
30. Chaps. 29-38; Pollock and Maitland, *HEL*, I, 102-3, note 1; Plucknett, "Roman and English Law", *UTLJ*, III, 26, note 6; Senior, "Roman Law . . .", *LQR*, XLVI, 202; Richardson and Sayles, *Law and Legislation*, p. 123.
31. *Ibid.*, p. 122.

small, and not altogether relevant, admixture of Roman legal learning."[32]

According to John of Salisbury, Roman law was "received into Britain through the household of the venerable father Theobald."[33] He was referring to the arrival of Vacarius in the mid-1140s. A Lombard scholar, Vacarius had studied at Bologna in the time of the Four Doctors.[34] Sometime about 1145, he was brought to England to join the Archbishop of Canterbury as a legal adviser, perhaps to aid in litigation against the powerful Bishop of Winchester.[35] It cannot be shown with any certainty that Vacarius conducted a school for members of the Archbishop's household, but he assuredly did arouse an interest in Roman law among its members. For example, he seems to have been the one who introduced John of Salisbury to the study of Roman law.[36] Vacarius soon began teaching at Oxford, where under his influence a center of legal studies arose that would endure well into the thirteenth century. About 1152 King Stephen banned the study of Roman law, not because Vacarius's teachings were seen as any threat to native English law, but probably because they were strengthening the Archbishop's hand at a time of conflict between Church and crown.[37] Since a teaching career was closed to him, Vacarius took orders, sought a clerical career, and entered the service of the Archbishop of York sometime before 1165. He may have taught some of the cathedral clerics at York, but it seems unlikely, for he was then busy with ecclesiastical matters.

Vacarius's most important contribution to Roman legal studies in England was his authorship of the *Liber Pauperum*, a manual of the Digest and Code for students too poor to purchase their own copies. As Maitland pointed out, it is "a thoroughly academic book," containing no comments on contemporary English law.[38] Numerous manuscripts of the *Liber Pauperum*, references to it,

---

32. *Ibid.*, p. 125.
33. *Policraticus*, viii, 22; trans., John Dickinson, *The Statesman's Book of John of Salisbury* (New York, 1927), p. 396.
34. For details of his life, see *Dictionary of National Biography*. ed. Sidney Lee (London, 1900-   ), XX, 80-81; F. de Zulueta, *Liber Pauperum* [Selden Society, 44] (London, 1927), introduction, pp. xxi-xxii.
35. Henry A. Cronne, *The Reign of Stephen 1135-54: Anarchy in England* (London, 1970), p. 280. He was at the papal *curia* in 1149-50, acting for the archbishop. W. H. Millor, Harold E. Butler, and C. N. L. Brooke (eds.), *The Letters of John of Salisbury* (London, 1955-   ), I, xxiii.
36. *Letters of John of Salisbury*, pp. xxii-xxiii.
37. *Policraticus*, viii, 22, p. 396; Cronne, *Reign of Stephen*, p. 280. Holdsworth, *History of English Law*, II, 148, states that the ban probably resulted from Stephen's fear that Vacarius was a supporter of Matilda.
38. Pollock and Maitland, *HEL*, I, 119.

and mention of law students known as *pauperistae* attest to the importance of Vacarius's work.³⁹ As late as 1190, students at Oxford were still copying it for use as a text.⁴⁰

By the time of Henry II, Roman law was making a powerful impact in England. More and more students were making the long journey to Bologna, and English schools were offering law courses. In the late twelfth century, conservative scholars throughout Europe were complaining that the law was driving out all other studies. Daniel of Morley told in his *Philosophia* that he left England in the 1170s to study at Paris and Toledo only to find, on his return, that the liberal arts had been abandoned nearly everywhere for Roman law. At Northampton alone did he find the teachings of the philosophers still flourishing.⁴¹ Later, that chronic malcontent Gerald of Wales complained of the desertion of the liberal arts at Oxford in favor of legal studies.⁴²

Ralph Niger, a master of arts and a theologian, complained of the popularity of Roman law in his *Moralia Regum*, a commentary on the Book of Kings written between 1179 and 1189.⁴³ He had been among the courtiers of Henry the young King, and at his court he had opportunity to observe the influence of the civil law. In his *Moralia* Ralph followed traditional rules for the moral interpretation of biblical passages, comparing Roman law to Absolom: "good in its nature, but liable to abuse."⁴⁴ He described the rise and triumph of Roman law studies, beginning with the Bolognese school; he lamented the pride and ambition of Roman lawyers; and he regretted the dissatisfaction they caused people to feel with their old customary law. Niger concluded by admitting, however, that mankind would benefit if the whole world lived under Roman law, provided that it would be administered religiously, by qualified persons.⁴⁵

Writers continued to complain about the selfish ambitions of students who turned to Roman law. Peter of Blois, who had much

---

39. Eleanor Rathbone, "Roman Law in the Anglo-Norman Realm," *Studia Gratiana*, XI (1967), 257-58.
40. Thomas E. Holland, "The Origin of the University of Oxford," *English Historical Review*, VI (1891), 247.
41. H. G. Richardson, "The Oxford Law School under John," *LQR*, LVII (1941), 323-24; R. W. Hunt, "English Learning in the Late Twelfth Century," *Trans. Royal Historical Society* (*TRHS*), XIX (1936), 24.
42. *Opera*, ed. J. S. Brewer *et al.* (Rolls Series; London, 1861-91), II, 318; LV, 3.
43. Herman Kantorowicz and Beryl Smalley, "An English Theologian's View of Roman Law; Pepo, Irnerius, Ralph Niger," *Medieval and Renaissance Studies* (hereafter, *MRS*),I, 245.
44. *Ibid.*, p. 247.
45. *Ibid.*, pp. 247-49.

contact with royal clerks after he came to England to seek his fortune, wrote to one of them, urging him to turn away from the study of law. He wrote: "There are two things which drive men strongly to the study of law, ambition for honors and vain appetite for glory."[46] He had studied civil and canon law himself after completing his arts studies at Paris.[47] Stephen Langton stated a similar opinion of civil law in one of his scriptural commentaries.[48]

Work by W. Senior, Neil Ker, and Pierre Legendre has shown how widespread were Roman law manuscripts in late twelfth-century England.[49] Legendre has found in British libraries copies of commentaries by Bolognese glossators and the work of a "flourishing school" of English glossators.[50] As early as 1160, copies of the Digest could be found in cathedral libraries at Hereford and Lincoln, secured by their bishops.[51] Even monastic libraries—Bury St. Edmunds, Christ Church, Canterbury, and Peterborough—had copies of the Institutes and other works of Roman legal science before the end of the twelfth century. The exact date that a complete copy of the *Corpus Juris Civilis* reached England cannot be pinpointed. The earliest certain point for the existence of a complete copy in England, however, is at the very end of the twelfth century, when Benedict, Abbot of Peterborough, left two copies to the abbey on his death.[52]

Many private individuals possessed legal treatises which they gave to monastic or cathedral libraries. For example, Thomas of Marlborough, a teacher of law at Exeter and Oxford, brought his books of civil and canon law with him when he entered the monastery of Evesham about 1200.[53] Ralph Foliot, a relative of Gilbert Foliot, a royal judge, and Archdeacon of Hereford, gave books to the Hereford cathedral library that included works by Bolognese glossators.[54] Since an obscure country parson, Master Peter of

---

46. Jacques Paul Migne (ed.), *Patrologia Latina, carsus completus* (Paris, 1844-64), CCVII, epistola cxl, col. 416.
47. Joseph Armitage Robinson, "Peter of Blois," *Somerset Historical Essays* (London, 1921), p. 102
48. Kantorowicz and Smalley, "Theologian's View", *MRS*, I, 246.
49. Senior, "Roman Law MSS. in England," *LQR*, XLVII (1931), 337-44; Ker, *Pastedowns in Oxford Bindings* (Oxford, 1954); Legendre, "Miscellanea Britannica," *Traditio*, XV (1959), 491-97.
50. *Ibid.*, p. 491.
51. Avrom Saltman, *Theobald, Archbishop of Canterbury* (London, 1956), p. 175; Adrian Morey and C. N. L. Brooke (eds.), *Letters and Charters of Gilbert Foliot* (Cambridge, 1967), no. 106.
52. Stephan Kuttner and Eleanor Rathbone, "Anglo-Norman Canonists of the Twelfth Century," *Traditio*, VII (1949-51), 281-82; Senior, "Roman Law MSS", *LQR*, XLVII, 337.
53. Hunt, "English Learning", *TRHS*, XIX, 28.
54. Rathbone, "Roman Law . . .", *Studia Gratiana*, XI, 259.

Paxton, possessed a complete set of civil and canon law treatises at the beginning of the thirteenth century,[55] it should be no surprise if books on Roman law were widespread before then.

By the mid-twelfth century, many Englishmen were being attracted to Bologna, the center of legal studies. English bishops were making it their practice to send promising young clerics to study law at Bologna.[56] Perhaps the most famous of all these young clerks was Thomas Becket, who spent a year at Bologna sometime in the 1140s, after receiving encouragement from his patron Archbishop Theobald.[57] Becket's later opponent among the English episcopate, Gilbert Foliot, may also have studied at Bologna. The editors of his letters find that "Roman law was a major part of the furniture of his mind," and they propose that the possibility of his having studied at Bologna is "tolerably strong."[58] Another English prelate of the same period, John de Bohun, Bishop of Salisbury, had studied at Bologna sometime in the 1130s.[59]

Other members of episcopal households who did not rise to such high rank were students in the Italian law schools. Gilbert Foliot, recognizing the need for lawyers in his household, sent two of his archdeacons, his nephew, and another protégé, Master David of London, to Bologna in the 1160s.[60] Master David later represented his patron and other English bishops at the papal *curia*.[61] Master Richard Barre, an agent of the King at the papal *curia* and occasional royal justice, also studied in Bologna.[62] Thomas of Marlborough, who lectured on law at Exeter and Oxford, went to Bologna in 1205 to perfect his knowledge of civil and canon law.[63] Hubert Walter continued the practice of seeking clerks for his household who were learned in the law. Among those he employed was Master Simon of Southwell, who had either studied or taught canon law in the Bolognese Schools.[64] Master Nicholas of Dunstable, a monk at Bury St. Edmunds in the time of King John and author of the history *Electio Hugonis*, quotes the Digest

---

55. Kuttner and Rathbone, "Anglo-Norman Canonists", *Traditio*, VII, 281.
56. *Ibid.*, pp. 280-81.
57. Adrian Morey and C. N. L. Brooke, *Gilbert Foliot and His Letters* (Cambridge, 1965), p. 62; Saltman, *Theobald*, p. 168.
58. Morey and Brooke, *Foliot*, pp. 63, 64, 68.
59. *Ibid.*, pp. 55-56.
60. Robert Bancaster and Richard Foliot. See *ibid.*, pp. 48, 62.
61. Kuttner and Rathbone, "Anglo-Norman Canonists", *Traditio*, VII, 286.
62. Rathbone, "Roman Law . . .", *Studia Gratiana*, XI, 260.
63. *DNB*, XII, 1063; Richardson and Sayles, *Law and Legislation*, pp. 74-75.
64. C. R. Cheney, *Hubert Walter* (London, 1967), pp. 165-66; Kuttner and Rathbone, "Anglo-Norman Canonists", *Traditio*, VII, 326-27.

in his work, and other statements indicate that he had received legal training, probably at Bologna.[65]

Many of the early English scholars at Bologna never achieved the fame that would imprint their names in historical accounts. These scholars were numerous enough, however, to dedicate an altar in the church of San Salvatore to Thomas Becket shortly after his canonization in 1173. A few years later, in the early thirteenth century, they built a chapel in honor of their patron saint.[66] Among records of the chapel is an obituary calendar of benefactors' names to include in prayers, which lists English scholars. For example, one of the earliest names is a certain Master William of London, who left his books and seventeen *solidi* to the chapel on his death.[67] The most famous name appearing on the list is Hubert Walter, lord of Canterbury. Any Englishman, of course, might make an offering to the chapel and be listed among its benefactors without his ever having enrolled in the Bolognese schools. C. R. Cheney argues this way in his biography of Hubert Walter; he rejects the inclusion of the Archbishop's name on the obituary list as evidence that he had studied at Bologna.[68] Certainly there is no indication in any source that Hubert Walter earned an academic degree anywhere, even though he did have a reputation for learning in the law and custom of England.

Canon law was the child of Roman law and, naturally, a close connection between the two continued. Bologna was the birthplace of Gratian's *Decretum*, and most clerical lawyers would have studied Roman law as a preparation for their canonical studies. An active school of Anglo-Norman canonists was working toward the close of the twelfth century; their work has become known largely through the studies of Stephen Kuttner and Eleanor Rathbone.[69] Also Charles Duggan writes of their work, describing "the formative role which English canonists played in decretal codification at its most creative period."[70] Several of these

---

65. R. M. Thomson (ed.), *The Chronicle of the Election of Hugh Abbot of Bury St. Edmunds and later Bishop of Ely* (Oxford Medieval Texts, Oxford, 1974), pp. xx, 46.
66. A. Allaria, "English Scholars at Bologna during the Middle Ages," *Dublin Review*, CXII (1893), 75.
67. The date is 1187. *Ibid.*, p. 79.
68. Cheney, *Hubert Walter*, p. 18. Richardson disagrees, *Law and Legislation*, p. 74; introduction to *Memoranda Roll I John* [Pipe Roll Society, n. s. 21] (London, 1943), p. lxii.
69. "Anglo-Norman Canonists," *Traditio*, VII, 279-358.
70. "The Reception of Canon Law in England in the Later Twelfth Century," *Proceedings of the Second International Congress of Medieval Canon Law*, eds.

Anglo-Normans were teachers in the schools in France, among them Gerard Pucelle, whom his friend John of Salisbury described as a lecturer in both laws.[71] In the late twelfth century centers for legal studies in England occupied some canonists, but by the turn of the century the best of them had abandoned England for Bologna.[72] One of them, Richard de Morins or *Ricardus Anglicus* wrote a number of canonistic works at Bologna in the 1190s.[73]

The increasing interest in civil and canon law led to the growth of schools in England, the first of which dates from Vacarius's days at Oxford. There is also evidence for the study of law at Exeter, Hereford, Lincoln, Northampton, and St. Albans Abbey in the twelfth century, and possibly at London and York.[74] The evidence consists chiefly of brief references in chronicles and letters to individual masters who were said to be "learned in the law." H. G. Richardson has sought evidence for the existence of a *studium* at Northhampton which offered legal studies in the late twelfth century. His evidence consists of fragments of an Oxford *ordo judiciarius* containing some mention of Northampton, which, he theorizes, a Northampton master brought with him during a migration to Oxford about 1192.[75] Most references to the school at Northampton, however, indicate that it was a center for the liberal arts, not the laws.[76]

Legal studies at these schools cannot have approached the level of the Vacarian school at Oxford, where texts were the Digest and Institutes or the Bolognese glosses.[77] Occasionally, some learned master may have lectured on these texts, but generally the texts were on a more elementary level, growing out of the study of rhetoric as part of the *trivium*. Rhetorical studies from the time of Cicero had included some legal teachings, and rhetorical schools at Bologna were the ground from which law studies there grew. The texts used in English schools resembled those of the early

---

Stephen Kuttner and J. Joseph Ryan, *Monumenta Iuris Canonica*, series C., Subsidia I (Vatican City, 1965), p. 366. H. G. Richardson takes a dimmer view of the Anglo-Norman canonists, writing that their work was "solid and substantial, even if none of it was specially distinguished," *LQR*, LVII, 322.

71. Kuttner and Rathbone, "Anglo-Norman Canonists", *Traditio*, VII, 296-97.
72. *Ibid.*, pp. 288-89, 321-33.
73. *Ibid.*, p. 338.
74. Kathleen Edwards, *The English Secular Cathedrals in the Middle Ages* (Manchester, 1949), pp. 188-90, 193; Kuttner and Rathbone, "Anglo-Norman Canonists", pp. 321-23; Pollock and Maitland, *HEL*, I, 122.
75. "The Schools of Northampton in the Twelfth Century," *EHR*, LVI (1941), 595-605.
76. Kuttner and Rathbone, "Anglo-Norman Canonists", *Traditio*, VII, 322, citing Daniel of Morley.
77. *Ibid.*, p. 323.

Bolognese schools. They were of two types: the *ordo judiciarius* and the formulary for the *ars notaria*.

The first, the *ordines judiciarii*, were primarily manuals of procedure attempting to remedy the deficiencies of contemporary law by reference to Roman law. Sometimes they took on the characteristics of formularies and *vice versa*.[78] Several *ordines* written in either England or Normandy survive, and Caillemar studied them in *Le Droit civil dans les provinces anglo-normandes*.[79] The best known of the *ordines* is the *Practica legum et decretorum*, a manual of both civil and ecclesiastical procedure for use in the continental possessions of the Angevin Kings. It was apparently written between 1181 and 1189 by William Longchamp.[80] Its author, Longchamp, was a Norman peasant who rose in the service of Henry II and Richard I to become Bishop of Ely, chancellor, and briefly justiciar.

Portions of another *ordo judiciarius*, produced in late twelfth or early thirteenth-century England, survive as part of an Oxford compilation, along with a collection of ecclesiastical and secular precedents. This manuscript, now at the Walters Art Gallery in Baltimore, has been studied by H. G. Richardson.[81] Its existence at Oxford proves that such manuals were known and studied in the schools of England, and it reveals that legal training at an elementary level formed part of the curriculum.

Another instrument for transmission of some elementary Roman law was the notarial formulary, which was the type of text studied in the schools of Bologna that trained future notaries. This course of study, the *ars notaria*, centered on models for notaries public to follow in framing legal documents. The *ars notaria* did not lead to any academic degree, but provided practical training for those who could not go on to law school. Portions of the Baltimore manuscript seem to represent an attempt by an English master, apparently a teacher of law in early thirteenth century Oxford, to compile a formulary similar to those of Italy for use in England.[82] The *ordines judiciarii* and the formularies indicate that it was possible for students who did not take university degrees to gain some smattering of Roman law.

---

78. Richardson, "Oxford Law School", *LQR*, LVII, 336.
79. *Mémoires de l'Académie de Caen* (Paris, 1883), pp. 157-226. Among them are Ulpianus de Edendo, written about 1150; *Summa Bellinesis; Ordo justiciarius Bambergensis*, written between 1181 and 1185; and *Summa Decreti Lipsiensis*, written about 1186.
80. Caillemar's dates.
81. Richardson, "Oxford Law School", *LQR*, LVII, 319-38.
82. *Ibid.*, pp. 325, 328.

The *ars notaria* developed into a formal discipline in Italy, passing on some principles of Roman law to notaries public, who might serve as secretaries to princes. That did not happen in England, and, as C. R. Cheney points out, notaries public were not found there before the mid-thirteenth century.[83] English common law failed to recognize the notarial instrument; and the seal remained the means of authentication for documents in England, even in the Church courts.[84] England offered some opportunity, nevertheless, for men with notarial training. Englishmen engaged in lawsuits before the papal *curia* found it necessary to use notarial instruments in the presentation of their cases.[85] A cleric with the training to draw up these documents might find advancement easier in the ecclesiastical hierarchy than his colleagues who had no training in civil or canon law.[86] Also, such training was useful for at least some of the king's chancery clerks; for the English monarch was also Duke of Aquitaine, a land of written law, and he used notarial instruments in his government there.[87] Furthermore, notarial training enhanced a clerk's usefulness in foreign affairs, enabling him to draw up diplomatic documents, and improving his skill as a negotiator with foreign princess.[88]

Few of the students who studied the *ordines judiciarii* and the notarial formularies at Oxford could have had such lofty ambitions as serving the king on foreign missions. H. G. Richardson has written that they were mainly young men, "who were seeking employment in the households of the larger landowners, where they would write their lord's letters, and keep his courts and his accounts, and draw up for him conveyances and leases and other instruments as occasion arose."[89] They might find a post with either a secular lord, perhaps a sheriff, or an ecclesiastical lord, an abbot or a bishop. They would find it useful to know a little of the procedure of the shire courts, common pleas, and lesser ecclesiastical tribunals, for they might be called to represent their masters as attorneys.

Clearly, as Eleanor Rathbone has written, we can assume "some degree of familiarity with the principles and doctrines of Roman law in a fairly wide stratum of the educated class in Eng-

---

83. *Notaries Public in England in the Thirteenth and Fourteenth Centuries* (Oxford, 1972).
84. *Ibid.*, pp. 12, 52.
85. *Ibid.*, p. 17.
86. Senior, "Roman Law MSS", *LQR*, XLVII, 343.
87. Cheney, *Notaries Public*, p. 23.
88. Senior, "Roman Law MSS", *LQR*, XLVII, 343.
89. "Oxford Law School," *LQR*, LVII, 334.

land about 1180."[90] A number of the servants of Henry II and his successors had academic training in Roman law either on the university level at Bologna or Oxford or on a lower level at other English schools. They range in rank from the chancellors Thomas Becket and William Longchamp down to obscure archdeacons who served only occasionally as itinerant justices.[91] John of Salisbury reveals the penetration of Roman legal doctrines into the court of Henry II. He complained that Henry's courtiers advocated such Roman legal concepts as "the prince is not subject to the laws, and what pleases the prince has the force of law," in support of royal supremacy.[92] Richard Fitz Neal, author of the *Dialogus de Scaccario*, had read the Institutes, although he seems to have known the Digest only indirectly.[93] The author of the treatise on English law known as *Glanvill* had some acquaintance with the Institutes also, for his prologue clearly is borrowed from it. Henry II himself acknowledged that he could lean upon the support of men learned in Roman and canon law. He told Thomas Becket during the quarrel over criminous clerks that he had advisers "sufficiently learned in both laws," who could refute the archbishop's arguments.[94]

Since Roman law did not become a basic part of the common law, a question arises about the effects, if any, which this wide knowledge of Roman law might have had on English law. Why did not England 'receive' Roman rules and doctrines of law as did the continental countries? Numerous scholars have looked at the legal reforms of Henry II in their search for possible influences from Roman law. Sometimes their examinations result in little more than speculation. Eleanor Rathbone speculates that canonically trained advisers may have influenced Henry II to seek a more rational alternative to trial by combat in pleas of land, leading him to the grand assize.[95] H. G. Richardson and G. O. Sayles presume

---

90. Rathbone, "Roman Law . . .", *Studia Gratiana*, XI, 263.
91. For example, John Kentish, a clerk of Hubert Walter who served in the royal chancery, and who possibly wrote a work on the Decretum. He was an itinerant justice in 1190. Kuttner and Rathbone, "Anglo-Norman Canonists", *Traditio*, VII, 320; Doris M. Stenton (ed.), *Pleas before the King or his Justices, 1198-1212*, III [Selden Society, 83] (London, 1966), Appendix I, "The Development of the Judiciary 1100-1215," p. lxxxi. Seffrid the archdeacon, a justice of the bench in 1190 and an itinerant justice in 1191, possibly studied at Bologna, since his name is on the *obit* list of the English scholars' chapel there. Rathbone, "Roman Law . . .", *Studia Gratiana*, XI, 261; Stenton, *Pleas before the King*, pp. lxxx, lxxxix.
92. *Policraticus*, vii, 20, pp. 307-8.
93. Charles Johnson (ed.), (London, 1950). Introduction, p. xvii.
94. W. L. Warren, *Henry II* (Berkeley and Los Angeles, 1973), p. 466.
95. Rathbone, "Roman Law . . .", *Studia Gratiana*, XI, 266.

that two men who had an important role in the legal reforms of Henry II — Richard of Ilchester and Geoffrey Ridel — were influenced by Roman law, although their only evidence is the fact that both were archdeacons.[96]

Perhaps the best way to assess the impact of Rome on the common law is to analyze the treatise on the laws of England known as *Glanvill*. This work was probably written between 1187 and 1189, and apparently not by Ranulf de Glanvill or Hubert Walter or any other candidate of historians, but by an unknown royal clerk.[97] Naturally, anyone who tried to write a legal treatise in Latin would absorb some Roman legal concepts simply from the vocabulary.[98] But *Glanvill's* author had gone far beyond the writers of the lawbooks of early twelfth-century England; his work resembles more the *ordines judiciarii* of the later twelfth century.[99] It differs from them and from any other twelfth-century legal treatise, however, in its exposition of the common law through comments on writs.

R. C. Van Caenegem, who has written the most widely accepted account of Roman elements in the treatise, asserts that its most direct model is not the *ordines judiciarii* but the *Dialogus de Scaccario*, another work of the late twelfth century, written by a civil servant to explain the workings of a branch of royal administration.[100] The origin of the common law as "the product of administrative process" tends to support Van Caenegem's view. Whether or not one supports Richardson's and Sayles' view that the Bench at Westminster evolved from the Exchequer, it is clear that the judges of Henry II and his sons were men "who approached their task from the point of view of the organizer, the higher civil servant," not from the viewpoint of the legal scholar.[101] A glance at the lists of justices compiled by Doris M. Stenton confirms this, for very few of them had the title 'master', and a surprising number were laymen.[102]

It has long been observed that the prologue to *Glanvill* is inspired by the Institutes, that some Roman legal terminology was borrowed, and that a number of distinctions came from Roman

---

96. *Law and Legislation*, p. 77.
97. G. D. Hall (ed.), (London, 1965), pp. xxx-xxxiii.
98. Plucknett, "Roman and English Law", *UTLJ*, III, 33.
99. Holdsworth, *History of English Law*, II, 176; Pollock and Maitland, *HEL*, I, 165; Richardson and Sayles, *Law and Legislation*, p. 78.
100. *Royal Writs in England from the Conquest to Glanvill* [Selden Society, 77] (London, 1959), p. 377.
101. Plucknett, "Roman and English Law", *UTLJ*, III, 32.
102. Stenton, *Pleas before the King*, Appendix I, pp. xlvii-ccxciv.

law: the basic division of pleas into civil and criminal, the differentiation between personal and real property, and the distinction between possession and property. R. C. Van Caenegem has analyzed the tract in detail, seeking Roman or canonical borrowings in terminology and acquaintance with rules of law, but finding few.[103] For example, he agrees with Frederic Joüon des Longrais's earlier discovery that the *saisina* and *rectum* or *jus* of twelfth-century England were not truly equivalent to the *possessio* and *proprietas* of classical Roman law, even though Glanvill and later Bracton did use them as equivalent terms.[104] Van Caenegem rejects the long-held view that the novel disseisin was derived from the Roman interdict *unde vi* by way of the canonical *actio spolii*. This was the thesis of such giants of English legal history as Maitland and Vinogradoff.[105] He points out the impossibility of such borrowing, proving it, as do Richardson and Sayles, on chronological grounds. The *actio spolii* could have had no influence on the novel disseisin in 1166, since it was developing at roughly the same time, during the second half of the twelfth century.[106] Van Caenegem goes on to suggest that both were the results of gradual processes of judicialization of what were originally executive measures for the protection of seisin, derived from the Germanic *Gewere*, that is, the primitive idea that evident possession of the land implies some right to it.[107] In a series of lectures recently published, he states his view of the origin of the novel disseisin more boldly: "There is no need to see influences of the *Corpus Juris Civilis* here, let alone of the canonistic *actio spolii*, which is of a later date, nor was novel disseisin conceived as a preliminary to a process on right."[108]

An authority who dissents strongly from the "insularity" of these views is the French scholar, Frederic Joüon des Longrais. In a 1961 lecture at Cambridge, Joüon des Longrais said, "There is no greater admirer of the Common law and of its originality than myself, but I maintain that if one takes the vocabulary of Glanvill and

---

103. *Royal Writs*, pp. 379-90.
104. *Ibid.*, p. 315; Frederic Joüon des Longrais, *La Conception anglaise de la saisine du XIIe au XIVe siècle* [Études de droit anglais, I] (Paris, 1925), pp. 45, 57.
105. Pollock and Maitland, *HEL*, II, 48; Paul Vinogradoff, *Roman Law in Medieval Europe* (2nd ed., Cambridge, 1968), p. 99; also Holdsworth, *History of English Law*, II, 204.
106. *Royal Writs*, p. 387; Richardson and Sayles, *Select Cases of Procedure without Writ under Henry III* [Selden Society, 60] (London, 1941), pp. cxviii-cxxxi; both of whom follow F. Ruffini, *L'Actio spolii, Studio giuridico* (Turin, 1889).
107. *Royal Writs*, p. 388; cf. Van Caenegem, *The Birth of the English Common Law* (Cambridge, 1973), p. 44.
108. *Birth of Common Law*, p. 44; cf. p. 123, note 61.

Bracton and their feelings about roman [sic] law for nothing, one cannot understand how later Common law could assert itself. The Roman influence was the drop which helped it to crystallise."[109] He sought to refute Van Caenegem's thesis that the assize of novel disseisin sprang from purely native sources without any watering from the well of Roman legal thought. He denied that the Norman kings' executive measures to restore seisin could have been sources for the assize of novel disseisin because they were summary acts, providing no possibility for subsequent action to determine proprietary right.[110]

Joüon des Longrais emphasizes "the principle of dual process," that is, settlement of seisin as a preliminary to determination of proprietary right. He pointed out that the canon lawyers of the Gregorian reform movement first made a distinction between *possessio* and *proprietas* and devised dual processes for these two rights.[111] He sought to show that the principle of dual process — first recovery of seisin, then a regular action for proprietary right— became known in Norman England through the example of canon law procedure.[112] He concluded, "Everywhere in the history of law the insistence on *possessio,* opposed to *proprietas* appears with the opposition of a new ambitious jurisdiction and of old decaying ones."[113] Joüon des Longrais complained that Van Caenegem fails to stress strongly enough the dual process. He feared that in neglecting the petitory (or proprietary) process before the traditional feudal courts Van Caenegem is blurring the distinction between seisin and proprietary right. Joüon des Longrais apparently forgot what he had written earlier: *"Jus et saisina sont également taillés dans une même étoffe et cette étoffe, c'est le droit réel antérieur s'exprimant surtout par la jouissance, la seule conception que le moyen âge entende pleinement."*[114] Seisin always contained greater elements of 'right' within it than did the Roman *possessio.*[115]

Donald W. Sutherland, author of a recent book on novel disseisin, has an eclectic approach which seems to solve the problem of the sources of the assize. In his view, Roman law, canon law, and

---
109. *Henry II and His Justiciars—Had They a Political Plan in their Reforms about Seisin?* Lecture delivered at Gonville and Caius College, 19th Sept. 1961 (Limoges, 1962), p. 10.
110. *Ibid.,* p. 13.
111. *Ibid.,* p. 5.
112. *Ibid.,* p. 13, citing *Leges Henrici Primi,* cap. 53, 3, p. 170 of Downer edition.
113. *Ibid.,* p. 12.
114. *La Conception anglaise de la saisine,* p. 57.
115. S. F. C. Milsom, *Historical Foundations of the Common Law* (London, 1969), pp. 103-4.

English administrative practice all played a part. He agrees with Joüon des Longrais that Henry II and his advisers knew the principle of canon law that any bishop deprived of his see must be put back in possession before legal proceedings could be brought against him, that is, the principle of dual process.[116] Sutherland suggests that both the ecclesiastical *actio spolii* and the assize of novel disseisin may have owed something to the Roman interdict *unde vi* as well.[117] He points out several similarities between the assize and the interdict, but he also notes a number of differences. He concludes, "The designers of the assize used Roman law as a source of suggestions but not as a model to be copied."[118] Sutherland follows Van Caenegem in citing informal executive measures for restoration of seisin, going all the way back to the Conquest. He notes that often such measures included the summoning of a jury to obtain the facts in the case.[119] It was Henry II's imaginative mind that converted the jury, originally an administrative tool, into a judicial instrument to settle disputes over seisin. The jury could often conclude cases without need for continuing to the second part of the dual process, a traditional action of right.

Richardson and Sayles have noted in their *Select Cases of Procedure without Writ* that *Glanvill* is an incomplete guide to English law. Not all cases in the royal courts originated with writs; some were begun by oral complaints known as plaints or *querelae*. Through the example of the Church courts, which in their turn had been influenced by Roman law, the plaints certainly came to be written down by the time of Henry III. They were drafted by clerks who had some experience in drawing up the libels of the ecclesiastical courts.[120] These clerks may have had some training in Roman law, although it might not have gone beyond elementary manuals of procedure or formularies.

Richardson and Sayles find another possible influence of Roman law not revealed in *Glanvill*: the action of trespass. Their explanation of its absence from the treatise is that it was begun by plaint, not by writ.[121] Their view is that the action of trespass had a dual origin: the appeal of felony, which came to England with the Conquest; and the *actio injuriarum*, which passed from Roman law by

---

116. Donald W. Sutherland, *The Assize of Novel Disseisin* (Oxford, 1973), pp. 20-21.
117. *Ibid.*, p. 22.
118. *Ibid.*, p. 24.
119. *Ibid.*, pp. 24-26.
120. *Procedure without Writ*, pp. lxv-lxvi.
121. *Law and Legislation*, pp. 80-81.

way of the canonists. Years earlier, Joüon des Longrais had hinted that the action of trespass owes something to the Roman interdicts.[122] It was the Roman source, in the view of Richardson and Sayles, that enabled the action of trespass to be separated from the appeal of felony.[123] Roman law exerted its influence through the use of written plaints in actions of trespass. Richardson and Sayles find a similarity between the words used in the plaints and the libels of the ecclesiastical courts, which indicates to them that professionals learned in canon law drew up the plaints.[124] They state that they do not find it difficult to see "the possibility of a distinct debt in this instance" to Roman law.[125]

Maitland's summary of the English situation — "As to Roman law, it led to nothing." — is much too sweeping. A more accurate statement is Van Caenegem's finding that there can be seen "a real but very limited and sometimes quite remote influence of the learned law of the day on the young common law, depicted in Glanvill's treatise, in certain points, none of which were of capital importance."[126] He finds that the author of *Glanvill* did have a knowledge of Roman law, "although not to any depth or width."[127] Neither do other modern authorities, such as Plucknett or Richardson and Sayles, quarrel with those scholars who earlier had found little trace of Roman law in *Glanvill*.[128] They agree that the major influence was simply the inspiration to write such a systematic work. Plucknett points out that the great lesson of Roman law for the author of *Glanvill* was the creation of an atmosphere which would convince him that "even a national law should be made the object of scientific study."[129] Richardson and Sayles note similarly that the lesson of Roman law for the writer was "the characteristic Roman virtue of order," inspiring him to shape the disorderly mass of royal writs into a rational system.[130]

Some fundamental features of English law do display sharp differences from canon law and the continental legal systems. One

---

122. *La Conception anglaise de la saisine*, p. 72.
123. *Procedure without Writ*, pp. cviii-cxvi.
124. *Law and Legislation*, p. 84; *Procedure without Writ*, p. cxi.
125. *Ibid.*, p. cxxxii.
126. *Royal Writs*, p. 386.
127. *Ibid.*, p. 376.
128. Van Caenegem surveys earlier literature in *ibid.*, pp. 363-64; Plucknett, "Roman and English Law", *UTLJ*, III, 33, 44; Richardson and Sayles, *Law and Legislation*, pp. 77-83. For views of some earlier scholars: Holdsworth, *History of English Law*, II, 204-205; Pollock and Maitland, *HEL*, I, 122.
129. "Roman and English Law", *UTLJ*, III, 35.
130. *Law and Legislation*, p. 79; cf. Plucknett, *Edward I and Criminal Law*, p. 6.

difference is the wide use of notarial instruments in the Church courts and in the secular courts on the Continent, the presentation of written claims and counter-claims by the parties to the suits. The English system with it emphasis on pleading and procedure placed less emphasis on written documents. The result was little employment in the English courts for notaries public, men who absorbed some Roman law through the formularies they studied. Slight opportunity was offered, then, for Roman legal principles to seep into English law through the notaries, as C. R. Cheney points out.[131] By the thirteenth century, the common lawyers had their own formularies, the registers of writs.

Other differences grew naturally out of the nature of the legal reforms of Henry II. As Plucknett writes, "The common law . . . crystallizes around procedures, for its growth is largely in response to the public's appreciation of the inquisition or jury as a mode of proof, a procedure in which the crown obtained a monopoly."[132] As a result, the judicial process in England would differ fundamentally from that of the continental courts. The English courts would be preoccupied with pleading and procedure.[133] Even *Glanvill* is in large part a book of procedure. Civilians and canonists with their reliance on written statements of the points at issue could easily separate substantive law from procedure, but English dependence upon the jury as both source of the evidence and its judge made such a separation impossible.[134] English process aimed at framing some question — either in the original writ or through a series of pleadings by the parties — to which a jury could give its collective answer. Its answer might bring the case to a conclusion without ever deciding the substantive issue.

Development of Romano-canonical procedure — the inquisitorial method — meant that the Church courts and those continental courts that adopted Roman law could ascertain the facts of a case through examination of individual witnesses on oath. The judge could then concentrate on deciding the case on the basis of the facts. In England, with the triumph of the jury system, the old Germanic notion survived, which left the judge as little more than a chairman of the assembled spokesman for the community, the jurors.[135] Even the task of bringing criminals to trial was left to a

---

131. *Notaries Public*, p. 52.
132. Plucknett, "Roman and English Law", *UTLJ*, III, 32.
133. *Early Eng. Legal Lit.*, p. 103.
134. John P. Dawson, *A History of Lay Judges* (Cambridge, Mass., 1960), p. 127.
135. R. C. Van Caenegem, "The Law of Evidence in the Twelfth Century," *Proceedings of the Second International Congress of Medieval Canon Law*, p. 299.

jury, the jury of presentment, while on the Continent it came to be the task of a single public prosecutor.[136] English judges knew nothing of a case except what the original writ told them, and the details came to light only through pleading. As Plucknett put it, "The facts of a case were a jealously guarded secret which was revealed to the court grudgingly and under pressure."[137] Further, the facts were provided by juries: groups of men who were expected to know the facts of the case and to give a unanimous verdict based on those facts, yet who could not be examined individually by the judges.[138] The result was that not even Bracton, writing at the height of Romanist influence, could successfully separate procedure from substantive law in England. This mingling made the common law of the later Middle Ages into a maze of technicalities that only the common lawyer trained in the Inns of Court could penetrate.

Why, then, did the English remain content with their native legal system, when the Church and the continental states chose Roman law? Many answers have been given to this question. The simplest one, however, is R. C. Van Caenegem's, which is based on chronology, ignored by some scholars who prefer to spin out more elaborate theses. Van Caenegem warns that historians ought not to become so preoccupied with large social, political, economic, or intellectual factors that they overlook "the chances of chronology."[139] He points out that the first strong government in medieval Europe, capable of creating effective judicial machinery for maintenance of order was Henry II's. His legal innovations began in 1166 with the Assize of Clarendon. At that time Romano-canonical procedure had not yet developed sufficiently to serve as a model for English law. It would not be until the end of the twelfth century that the ecclesiastical courts would devise the canonical inquest, and it would not be until the mid-thirteenth century, in the time of St. Louis, that the French royal courts would adopt the new procedure. Henry II and his advisers had to take native timbers — the writ and the jury — to carve into tools for strengthening royal justice.[140]

---

136. *Ibid.*, p. 300.
137. *Early Eng. Legal Lit.*, p. 103.
138. Dawson, *Lay Judges*, p. 126.
139. "L'histoire du droit et la chronologie. Réflexions sur la formation du 'Common Law' et la procédure romano-canonique," *Etudes d'Histoire du Droit canonique dédiés à Gabriel le Bras* (Paris, 1965), II, 1465. *Birth of Common Law*, pp. 90-108.
140. *Royal Writs*, p. 379.

A comprehensive listing of factors involved in the failure of Roman law to influence the common law is found in an article by Plucknett.[141] Although it is not one of his major points, he did recognize the chronological problem. He was aware that the early adoption of the jury fixed English procedure before Romano-canonical procedure was available as an alternative. He noted, too, that the common law grew into a settled system before the work of the Commentators in the late thirteenth century; their work of harmonizing customary law with Roman law would have facilitated the reconciliation of Roman and English laws.[142]

Plucknett concerned himself more with broader issues which could help account for England's failure to fall under the spell of Roman law. Looking far back to the Anglo-Saxon invasions, he emphasized their difference from the barbarian invasions of Gaul, Italy, or Spain. There would be no dual system of laws in England, for the Anglo-Saxons left no Romano-British population living under Roman law, not even a native British clergy.[143] A second factor was the thorough unification of England that came with the Norman Conquest, earlier than elsewhere in Europe. Unlike France, which had a multitude of regional customs, no strong provincial customs survived in England. Roman legal principles were not needed to harmonize conflicting customary laws into a single system, as on the Continent. Instead, English common law was a new creation, the rules of the king's court; the old local customs were not harmonized, but were simply ignored.[144]

A third factor centers about the careers of the judges in the English royal courts. Plucknett recognized that the common law sprang from administrative processes, first in the unspecialized *curia regis*, then at the Exchequer and only later in the courts of common pleas or king's bench. The key feature was the jury, basically a fact-finding device. The requirement of agreement among the jurors about the facts allowed judges to avoid the task of "the critical dissection of testimony."[145] This meant that the early justices did not need academic training in the law; they could come from other branches of the civil service.

Plucknett did not treat the topic of the justices and their training as fully as it merits in any account of the role of Roman law.

---

141. "Roman and English Law", *UTLJ*, III, 47-50.
142. *Ibid.*, p. 50.
143. *Ibid.*, p. 47.
144. *Ibid.*, pp. 47-48.
145. Pollock and Maitland, *HEL*, II, 627.

Roman Law in England before the Time of Bracton 67

Not even Maitland recognized how much a close look at the personnel of the courts could reveal. The justices's biographies reveal them to be men who had gained practical experience in other branches of royal administration, especially financial affairs, before their appointment to the bench. They often continued to hold other administrative posts while sitting at the bench. They cannot be considered 'learned', since their legal training was acquired largely through practical experience.

Few of the royal justices could have studied Roman or canon law at Bologna or Oxford, for from the first a surprising number of them were laymen. One of Henry II's judicial experiments, effected in 1178, was to assign five members of his household — two clerks and three laymen — to hear his people's pleas.[146] In the last years of Henry II, a number of pleas were heard at Westminster at the Exchequer. In the ten years before 1189, around forty-eight justices witnessed fines made at Westminster, and twenty of these were laymen.[147] By the reign of Richard I names of certain judges recur so often that they almost can be considered professionals. Five of the ten professionals who served Richard were laymen.[148] Under John, the proportion was higher: eleven of fifteen were laymen.[149] Some of these men may have studied the *ordines judiciarii*, although the education of the laity raises so many problems that speculation is pointless.

Of the clerical judges, few had the title of *magister* which would indicate an academic degree. A master of arts degree might have acquainted them with some principles of Roman law through their rhetorical studies. Only three of Henry II's justices at Westminster had that title. Some sixty men served Richard I as judge at one time or another at Westminster, and again three of them were called *magistri*. There were about ninety judges in John's reign, eight of whom were masters. One might safely assume that some of those clerical judges who were not masters had some slight acquaintance with Roman law from the schools, where they followed the course in *ars notaria*.

---

146. *Gesta Henrici Secundi*, ed. William Stubbs [Rolls Series] (London, 1867), I, 207-8.
147. Twenty were ecclesiastics, including eight bishops, while the status of eight is unknown. Calculations based on Lady Stenton's lists, *Pleas before the King*, Appendix I, and Edward Foss, *The Judges of England* (London, 1848), I.
148. Those who served at least ten terms at the Bench are counted as professionals.
149. More laymen partly because of the quarrel with Innocent III during John's middle years, for clerics could not serve an excommunicated king.

Several of the clerics were archdeacons, which would indicate that they had some practical knowledge of canon law, but not necessarily any advanced academic study. Some of these clerics came into the king's household from episcopal households — for example, Hubert Walter's clerks from Canterbury served interchangeably in the royal and archiepiscopal chanceries and in the royal and ecclesiastical courts.[150] Van Caenegem warns, however, that experience in the Church courts of late twelfth-century England would not necessarily mean much familiarity with Roman law, for he finds that the English ecclesiastical courts were slow to adopt Romano-canonical principles.[151]

Maitland stressed the ecclesiastical character of the English judiciary in the age of Glanvill, and he credited the clerical judges with rationalizing the common law.[152] Plucknett agreed that the English legal profession was largely clerical until 1300.[153] A look at the lists of judges under Henry II and his two sons, however, shows a large lay contingent a century earlier. Not even the clerics in the judiciary necessarily had advanced training in Roman law. Of the two dozen or so judges who might be termed professionals in the years 1189-1216 three can be connected definitely with the study of Roman law: Ralph Foliot, frequently a justice under Richard, gave some writings of the Bolognese glossators to Hereford Cathedral; Richard Fitz Neal, treasurer and judge at Westminster, shows in his treatise on the Exchequer that he had read the *Institutes*; Richard Barre, another of Richard's judges at Westminster, had studied at Bologna.

Clearly, Roman legal studies did flourish in late twelfth-century England, and Englishmen did have opportunities to gain at least some acquaintance with the law of Rome. Nevertheless, Roman law failed to make any deep dent in the shape of English common law. A crucial factor is the chronological one: Romano-canonical procedure was not yet available as an alternative to the jury at the time of Henry II's reforms. Another factor that has been largely neglected is the bureaucratic background of the judges of the Angevin kings. Since much of English common law

---

150. Cheney, *Hubert Walter*, pp. 164-65. Some of the archbishop's clerics were accomplished canonists, among them Master Honorius, Master Simon of Southwell, and Master John of Tynemouth; but none of these served as royal justices.
151. *Royal Writs*, p. 370.
152. Pollock and Maitland, *HEL*, I, 133-35, 205.
153. "The Place of the Legal Profession in the History of English Law," *LQR*, XLVIII (1932), 328-40.

grew out of native administrative traditions, such practical training was more useful than an academic degree. If the Angevin kings had needed scholars trained in the written law, they could have found them easily in England; but a degree in canon or civil law was not considered necessary for advancement in the king's service. The royal justices, half of whom were laymen, cannot be presumed to have been deeply learned in Roman legal principles.

Who was the Author of *Glanvill*? Reflections on the Education of Henry II's Common Lawyers

The legal treatise called *Glanvill* is proof that by the end of Henry II's reign men capable of shaping the custom of the English *curia regis* into a systematic law book were present at Westminster. *Glanvill* is "the first textbook of the English common law."[1] This treatise was written near the end of Henry II's reign and since the thirteenth century, it has borne the name of his justiciar, Ranulf de Glanvill, although not many scholars today accept his authorship. Why, then, should we raise once more the question: Who was the author of *Glanvill*? It remains a valid question because it affords an opportunity for reflection on questions concerning schools, learning, and twelfth-century English society. It forces us to consider the connections among the emerging English common law, the schools, the Scholastic method, and the study of Roman and canon law. It requires us to consider the contributions of Roman and eccesiastical law to Henry II's legal reforms.

A long debate has raged about the character of the common law: Was it an insular construction, built out of native administrative and feudal material? Or did it derive its structure from earlier continental practice? S. F. C. Milsom argues that Henry II and his lawyers lived in a feudal society, and that the aim of their innovations was to regulate how feudal lords disciplined their tenants, to require them to follow "due process." Milsom finds an unintended result was that bureaucratically minded judges turned a set of social conventions about feudal tenures into settled law, undermining the feudal courts. This hardening of feudal custom into law can be seen in *Glanvill,* Book Seven, where the author is wrestling with defining laws for inheritance of feudal

---

1. H. G. Richardson and G. O. Sayles, *Law and Legislation from Aethelberht to Magna Carta* (Edinburgh, 1966), 117; idem, *The Governance of Mediaeval England* (Edinburgh, 1963), 319.

tenures.² An older view than Milsom's sees Henry's aim as more consciously anti-feudal, intentionally undermining his magnates' feudal courts and inclining toward an absolutism that may have reflected Roman and canonical influences on the common law.³ Scholars today tend to see this question in either/or terms: either a common law growing out of feudal custom, or one reflecting Roman and canonical learning. A common law derived chiefly from native materials, however, need not imply its creators' ignorance of Roman and canon law.

This debate invites an evaluation of the learning of Henry II's lawyers, tumbling historians of English law into more disputes about links between the schools, the law courts, and the judges. One question involves the penetration of Romano-canonical principles into twelfth-century English law. Our knowledge of the impact of Roman and canon law on medieval England has increased enormously in recent years, yet uncertainties about the learned law's strength in the late twelfth century remain. For example, Sir Richard Southern, having demolished the theory that Chartres was a center of twelfth-century humanism, has trained his guns on the theory that Oxford was a center for twelfth-century Roman law.⁴ Another question involves changing views on lay literacy in the Middle Ages, for two prominent candidates for author of *Glanvill* were knights. What was their level of learning? What contributions could knights, who were a significant portion of the royal justices, have made to the shaping of the common law? Specifically, was a layman capable of writing a legal treatise? Another look at the treatise *Glanvill* and at the speculation about its author will afford an opportunity to confront some of these conflicting views.

Speculation centers chiefly on four possible authors: besides Ranulf de Glanvill, they include two other justiciars—his nephew Hubert Walter, who was also archbishop of Canterbury, 1193–1205, and Geoffrey fitz Peter, Hubert's successor—and Godfrey de Lucy, bishop of Winchester, 1189–1204, son of Glanvill's predecessor in the justiciarship. All four were active as royal justices during Henry II's last decade, and all except Ranulf remained in the judiciary under Richard I. Other

---

2. G. D. G. Hall, ed., *The Treatise on the Laws and Customs of the Realm of England commonly called Glanvill* (London, 1965), 69–91. Milsom's thesis is set forth in *The Legal Framework of English Feudalism* (Cambridge, 1976); also in his introduction to the reprint of Frederick Pollock and F. W. Maitland, *History of English Law* (1898; reprint Cambridge, 1965). See Robert C. Palmer, "The Feudal Framework of English Law," *University of Michigan Law Review* 79 (1981): 1130–64.

3. E.g., J. E. A. Jolliffe, *Angevin Kingship* (London, 1955).

4. R. W. Southern, "Master Vacarius and the Beginning of an English Academic Tradition," in *Medieval Learning and Literature*, ed. J. G. Alexander and M. T. Gibson (Oxford, 1976), 257–86; idem, "From Schools to University," in *The Early Oxford Schools*, ed. J. I. Catto, vol. 1 of *History of the University of Oxford* (Oxford, 1984), 9–10.

candidates could be nominated for the authorship of *Glanvill*, perhaps royal clerks who won appointment to the bench later,[5] but it is more likely that the author was one of the thirteen justices active in the curia regis in the decade spanning 1179-89. The probable author would not have been of the generation that introduced the great legal reforms of 1166-76, but he would have been closely connected to the innovators of that era. The treatise appears to be the work of someone active in the courts when the work of the justices and their clerks at Westminster was settling down into a routine, when it was becoming possible to impose some pattern on the writs and pleadings. The increasing litigation of this decade made necessary some handbook to guide newcomers to the bench. *Glanvill*'s author shows no interest in the origin of the rules he was writing down: His practical lawyer's approach does not read like the reminiscences of a retired statesman.

Because medieval thinking about authorship differs so much from our own, the possibility of a collective authorship for *Glanvill* must be considered. Modern emphasis on creativity, originality, and individuality can cause us to forget that these are not universal standards for authors. Medieval writers freely borrowed from other works, incorporating sizeable chunks into their own writings without attribution. *Glanvill* may be a weaving together of several shorter treatises. At the least, the author had discussions with colleagues who were longtime companions of Henry II. The two leaders of the first great eyre of 1166, which followed the Council of Clarendon, were long dead, but three justices from the eyre of 1176, which followed the Council of Northampton, remained on the bench during Henry II's last decade, 1179-89.[6] Three clerics who had been among the king's intimate counselors during the Becket conflict served frequently as royal judges in the years just before the treatise was composed.[7] Another colleague who could have taught the author much was Richard fitz Neal, treasurer since 1161 and author of the *Dialogus de Scaccario*.

Before discussing its authorship, it is necessary to take a look at the book itself. *Glanvill* was written between the autumn of 1187 and Henry II's death in July 1189, although the earliest surviving texts date from no earlier than 1200.[8] Some authorities, although not the treatise's most recent editor, G. D. G. Hall, surmise that the work survives as a draft left incomplete by its author. If such were the case, its abandonment

---

5. Hall, *Glanvill*, xxxiii.

6. Leaders of the 1166 circuits were Geoffrey de Mandeville (d. Oct. 1166) and Richard de Lucy (d. 1179). Those remaining from the 1176 eyres were Glanvill (d. 1190), William Basset (d. 1185), and Michael Belet (d. 1203).

7. Richard of Ilchester, bishop of Winchester (d. 1188); John of Oxford, bishop of Norwich (d. 1200); Geoffrey Ridel, bishop of Ely (d. 1189).

8. Hall, *Glanvill*, xxxi.

can lend support to three possible authors: The departure of both Glanvill and his nephew Hubert Walter in 1189 for Richard I's crusade would have turned them aside from the book, and Godfrey de Lucy's duties as newly elected bishop of Winchester would have led him to do the same.[9]

Incomplete draft or not, the book presents a summary of English common law as its first and most creative phase was ending. As the writer states clearly, his concern is only with the law and custom of the curia regis, not with shire courts or seignorial courts:[10] specifically, with "royal civil pleas concerning right," or the secure possession of feudal tenures. Debts and contracts concern *Glanvill* little; only Book Ten treats these topics. Neither do the criminal prosecutions that would have formed a large part of the itinerant justices' work much concern the author. Only Book Fourteen, the last one, treats criminal law. Years ago, G. E. Woodbine, the first twentieth-century editor of *Glanvill,* noted in Book Fourteen "a lack of enthusiasm which the writer shows in his treatment of criminal actions. He seems hardly interested in criminal matters."[11]

The author aimed at writing a book of instructions most useful to the judges and clerks working at Westminster, a practical guide much like the *Dialogus de Scaccario,* written about ten years earlier. F. W. Maitland used the word "dilemmatic" to describe the author's method, that is, a problem-solving approach.[12] The writer first shows which royal writ a complainant must procure to get his case into the king's court, then all the possibilities that can follow, from non-appearance of his opponent to the raising of various objections (*exceptiones*) to the suit. The work is largely based on the writs, some seventy of them, which began pleas in the king's court, ensured the parties' appearance, summoned juries, and enforced judgments. The work is preoccupied with procedure, although the author often drifts into discussions of substantive law. According to Hall, "These discussions lift the treatise from the level of clarity and competence to that of originality and distinction."[13]

Because the work occasionally wanders away from the writs, however, scholars have been able to point toward several types of law books as possible models for the treatise. Collections of old English laws were

---

9. Ibid., xxxiii n. 2.
10. Ibid. 12.23, 14.8.
11. Ibid., xxii, books 1–10; George E. Woodbine, ed., *Glanvill* (New Haven, 1932), 294.
12. Pollock and Maitland, *History of English Law* 1:166.
13. Hall, *Glanvill,* xxvii. Book 7 particularly moves away from writs.

still being circulated and recopied in *Glanvill*'s day, yet they offered little help to the author in summarizing the law of Henry II's curia regis.[14] These lawbooks dealt largely with criminal offenses, not with feudal custom concerning landholdings. They were relevant, if at all, only for local courts prosecuting the misdeeds of the peasantry. *Glanvill* was not a lawbook: its authors did not attempt to collect the legislative acts of Henry II, the assizes, although he undoubtedly had their texts at hand and referred to them while writing. For example, the passage on the grand assize reads like a paraphrase of a text of the assize, and references to the Constitutions of Clarendon show that he relied upon a text of it.[15]

A continental model was available for *Glanvill*'s author in the *ordines judiciarii,* collections of the forms used chiefly in the church courts. They too used a "dilemmatic" method.[16] Several Anglo-Norman *ordines* survive, the best known among them written *circa* 1181–89 by William Longchamp, Richard Lionheart's chancellor.[17] The *ordines* sometimes served as texts in English schools before the end of the twelfth century, and the author of *Glanvill* could easily have had some familiarity with them. *Glanvill,* however, does not greatly resemble the *ordines judiciarii,* which were primarily manuals of procedure with no attempt to summarize substantive law.[18]

Some scholars have found that *Glanvill* superficially resembles the glosses on papal decretals and have suggested that early decretal collections influenced the author.[19] Anglo-Norman canonists did play a formative role in making decretal collections in the late twelfth century,[20] but they depended heavily on written authorities, and the comments in their *summae* were little more than patchworks of

---

14. Hall, *Glanvill,* xxix–xxx; also J. C. Holt, "The Assizes of Henry II: The Texts," in *The Study of Medieval Records,* ed. D. A. Bullough and R. L. Storey (Oxford, 1971), 85–106.

15. Hall, *Glanvill,* xxxiv–xxxv; ibid. 4.13 and 10.12 are echoes of the Constitutions of Clarendon.

16. F. Donald Logan, "An Early Thirteenth-century Papal Judge-delegate Formulary of English Origin," *Studia Gratiana* 14, Collectanea Stephani Kuttner 4 (1967): 75–87.

17. M. Caillemer, "Le Droit civil dans les provinces anglo-normandes au XIIe siècle," *Memoires de l'Académie de Caen,* (1883): 157–226.

18. Chief supporters of the *ordines* as *Glanvill*'s model are Richardson and Sayles, *Governance,* 319; idem, *Law and Legislation,* 79, 105–7; a less enthusiastic supporter is Paul Hyams, "The Common Law and the French Connection," *Proceedings of the Battle Conference on Anglo-Norman Studies* 4 (1981): 80. Hyams's view is that *Glanvill* and the later French *coutumiers* share a common source. Hall rejects the *ordines* as a model. *Glanvill,* xxviii–xxix.

19. Hyams, "Common Law," 80.

20. Stephan Kuttner and Eleanor Rathbone, "Anglo-Norman Canonists of the Twelfth Century," *Traditio* 7 (1949–51): 279–339.

quotations from earlier writings.[21] The author of *Glavill* had no earlier authorities on whom he could rely, however, and his comments come from first-hand experience. Even when he had texts available, such as the Constitutions of Clarendon, he made no effort to incorporate them into his text.

The major raw materials for *Glanvill* were the writs, and the author had to have access to collections of them. It is uncertain that an official register of writs existed as early as the 1180s, perhaps not before 1210, when one was drafted to assist in the implementation of English law in Ireland.[22] Yet royal clerks and justices must have had some sample writs to guide them in their work. Did the author possess a register or did he make a collection himself preliminary to writing the treatise? T. F. T. Plucknett declared over thirty-five years ago that the problem of *Glanvill* and the register of writs is "an insoluble question."[23] It remains insoluble. If an authoritative register of writs did exist at the time of *Glanvill*'s composition, then it would have been quite natural to write an account of royal law based upon the writs.

Yet it is not certain that the author regarded writs as fixed and inflexible; he wrote of writs for the grand assize, "It is easy to formulate writs to fit the different circumstances."[24] Neither is it certain that *Glanvill* aimed at presenting a comprehensive collection of writs, for some writs in use at the time of its composition may have been omitted.[25] Books One through Three and Book Thirteen follow closest the pattern of writs with accompanying commentaries. *Glanvill*, then, is much more than a collection of writs and commentaries on them. The author had to impose upon the raw data—writs and unwritten custom—some logical organization. One expert calls the treatise "our first formulary of writs as well as our first treatise on the common law."[26]

The author of the treatise had no single model to imitate in his description of the workings of the curia regis as he observed it. His work is original, but the inspiration for it may well have been Richard

---

21. Hall, *Glanvill*, xxviii–xxix.
22. For the 1210 Register, see Paul Brand, "Ireland and the Literature of the Early Common Law," *Irish Jurist*, n.s., 16 (1981): 97, 112.
23. T. F. T. Plucknett, *Early English Legal Literature* (Cambridge, 1958), 33. See also Hall, *Glanvill*, xxxiii–xxxiv; Elsa de Haas and G. D. G. Hall, eds., *Early Registers of Writs* (Selden Society 86, 1970): cxix–cxxi.
24. Hall, *Glanvill* 2.13.
25. Paul Hyams, *Kings, Lords and Peasants in Medieval England* (Oxford, 1980), 166, finds two villeinage writs; *Glanvill* is silent on original warranty writs. Hyams, "Warranty and Good Lordship in Twelfth-Century England," *Law and History Review*, 5 (1987): 483–95 (Appendix I, "The Pre-history of the Action *De Warantia Carte*").
26. R. C. Van Caenegem, *Birth of Common Law* (Cambridge, 1973), 30.

fitz Neal's *Dialogus de Scaccario*. R. C. Van Caenegem writes, "What the *Dialogus* was to the exchequer, the *Tractatus* is to the central courts."[27] Both books have the same purpose, instructing the staff of a great office of government, and certain slight similarities point toward familiarity by the author of *Glanvill* with the work on the exchequer.[28] Besides differing in subject matter, however, the two works differ in form. Fitz Neal had greater literary pretensions than the author of *Glanvill*. He was freer with classical and biblical quotations, and he cast his treatise in dialogue form, a pattern for instructional works popular since Alcuin's day.

What does the treatise reveal about the author? What kind of man does it show him to have been? First, and above all, he was a loyal royal servant, taking pride in his work and admiring the monarch he served. Second, he possessed an orderly mind and had confidence in the powers of reason, a result of his study in the schools. Third, he had as much acquaintance with Roman and canon law as any royal servant might acquire in late twelfth-century England. Fourth, like many twelfth-century thinkers, he saw "the need for organizing knowledge in a comprehensive, rational manner."[29] Finally, he had a superb knowledge of the workings of the curia regis in the years since Henry II's assizes had so greatly increased its activity.

It is clear that the author was someone with "an intimate acquaintance with the practice of the courts."[30] Hall suggests that he may have been a royal clerk, not yet a judge, and "with his main career yet to come."[31] It is most likely, however, that he was a royal justice at the time of writing, active on the bench during Ranulf de Glanvill's justiciarship.

Whoever the author was, he had a high opinion of Henry II's justices. His work is full of praise for them, expressing confidence that the king appoints judges who do not show "favour or partiality," who are "most learned in the laws and customs of the realm," and who surpass other men in "sobriety, wisdom and eloquence."[32] Perhaps he knew the chronicle of Master Ralph de Diceto, dean of St. Paul's, which praised Henry II for appointing bishops as judges, men who "should neither oppress the poor in their judgments nor presume to favour the cause

---

27. R. C. Van Caenegem, *Royal Writs in England from the Conquest to Glanvill* (Selden Society 77, 1958-59), 377-78; Hall follows Van Caenegem. *Glanvill*, xxxvi.
28. Van Caenegem, *Royal Writs*, 377-78; Hall, *Glanvill*, xxxvi.
29. Stephan Kuttner, "The Revival of Jurisprudence," in *Renaissance and Renewal in the Twelfth Century*, ed. Robert L. Benson and Giles Constable (Cambridge, Mass., 1982), 310.
30. Richardson and Sayles, *Law and Legislation*, 106.
31. Hall, *Glanvill*, xxxiii.
32. Ibid., Prologue.

of the rich."[33] The writer of *Glanvill* trusts the justices to decide disputed points of law on the basis of utility and equity.[34] The work reflects the civil servant's pride in his craft.

The author was an admirer of Henry II and of the office of kingship. His Prologue proclaims Henry's fame as a warrior, but also praises his love of peace and his high standard of justice.[35] More than once he praises the king for his clemency.[36] Still, *Glanvill* presents as confused a picture of the royal office as any medieval writer. On the one hand, we read such statements as the Roman maxim, "What pleases the prince has the force of law," or "For the king can have no equal, much less a superior"; on the other hand, assertions are made that the king "does not scorn to be guided by the laws and customs of the realm," and that England's laws are made "on the advice of the magnates."[37] The author's description of the procedure for removing cases from the feudal courts to shire courts reveals his royalist bias. He remarks that the diversity of the customs in lords' courts makes it impossible to reduce them to writing, while his businesslike account makes transfers from feudal to royal or shrieval tribunals appear routine, giving no hint of the important implications such actions had for lords' power over their tenants.[38] The author's royalist attitude is also illustrated in his treatment of criminal law, where he chose as examples of criminal pleas for detailed discussion charges of *lèse majesté*.[39]

Glanvill does not go as far as the *Dialogus de Scaccario* in excusing the king's arbitrary acts, but the treatise does acknowledge that reliefs for baronies and royal serjeanties are set "at the mercy and will of the lord king."[40] *Glanvill* describes the grand assize as a royal favor to the people, "emanating from the clemency of the prince."[41] This implies the old "tutelary" notion of kingship, that justice was not the people's right but a favor for the king to give or to withhold as he saw fit.

Glanvill's author aimed to establish the English king's law as equal to the *jus scriptum* of Rome and the Church, taking pains to point

---

33. William Stubbs, ed., *Radulphi de Diceto opera historica*, 2 vols. (Rolls Series 68, 1876), 1:434–35; translated in *English Historical Documents*, ed. David C. Douglas and George W. Greenaway (London, 1968), 2:481–82.

34. E.g., Hall, *Glanvill* 2.12.

35. Hall, *Glanvill*, Prologue. Compare with Charles Johnson, ed., *Dialogus de scaccario* (London, 1950), 75–77.

36. Hall, *Glanvill* 2.7, 2.19, 7.17.

37. Ibid., Prologue; grand assize, 2.7.

38. Ibid. 12.6–7.

39. Ibid. 14.1–2, treason and fraudulent concealment of treasure trove.

40. Ibid. 9.4; Johnson, *Dialogus*, 120.

41. Hall, *Glanvill* 2.7.

out that the *leges anglicanae* were no less laws for not being written down.⁴² One reason may have been the Becket conflict and the contempt the archbishop's partisans showed for England's unwritten custom.⁴³ *Glanvill*'s author knew the Constitutions of Clarendon well enough to refer to several chapters, and he wholeheartedly accepted the Constitution's implications.⁴⁴ He saw clearly the competition between royal and ecclesiastical courts, and whenever he claimed a case for the king's court, he used the phrase *ad/contra coronem et dignitatem domini regis*.⁴⁵

From the mid-twelfth century on, more and more men educated in the schools were moving into the king's service, and the author's "precise and orderly mind," indicates that he was one of those with academic training.⁴⁶ His classification of writs may not be one which scholars today would adopt were they writing the book, but it is a well-reasoned plan based on the suits' connection to the curia regis that becomes clear to the reader. The book's organization reflects the concerns of the judges at Westminster and their clerks: first, traditional claims of right, and then, the newer possessory assizes. The first eleven books treat pleas of proprietary right beginning in curia regis; Book Twelve treats those pleas transferred to the curia regis from other jurisdictions; Book Thirteen, the longest, discusses the petty assizes, questions of possession rather than right, settled mostly by recognitions before itinerant justices. The order in which he treats the assizes might not seem logical, for the arrangement depends upon the number of essoins, excuses for non-appearance, allowed to the litigants. Yet there is a certain logic to this. First, he discussed the assizes that allowed two essoins and then the assize of *novel disseizin,* which allowed no essoin at all.⁴⁷ Essoins held such significance because the author explained legal proceedings step-by-step, and the necessary first step was securing the two opposing parties' presence in court. Book Fourteen, short and something of an afterthought, treats criminal procedure.

Throughout *Glanvill,* the author shows a clarity of thought that hints at formal study of dialectic, as he makes distinctions in a fashion familiar to readers of scholastic treatises. In Book One, he divides pleas into the two categories of civil and criminal, subdividing these categories

---

42. Ibid., Prologue.
43. Hyams, "Common Law and French Connection," 80.
44. Hall, *Glanvill,* xxxiv–xxxv; Plucknett, *Legal Literature,* 31n.
45. E.g., Hall, *Glanvill* 10.1, 12.21.
46. Richardson and Sayles, *Law and Legislation,* 106.
47. I follow Plucknett. *Legal Literature,* 36; and Van Caenegem, *Royal Writs,* 354. Cf. Donald W. Sutherland, *The Assize of Novel Disseizin* (Oxford, 1975), 16, where he sees the whole work arranged according to essoins, since proprietary causes—treated first—allowed three essoins.

into two classes, royal and shrieval.[48] He makes such distinctions throughout the book, showing the reader at each point in the proceedings the alternatives that are possible. Unlike students of the written law working with authoritative texts, the author rarely had to reconcile conflicting references. Yet he was familiar with their method, and in a few instances he cited judges' conflicting opinions. Some early manuscripts of *Glanvill* even match justices' names with the differing views.[49]

The author can see potential problems where no precedent provides him with answers. For example, when discussing the grand assize, he asks, "What if twelve knights from the neighborhood ... do not know the truth of the matter?" He asks whether it should then proceed to proof by battle.[50] Such questions again reveal his powers of reasoning. On the whole, however, the writing reveals his confidence in the law's certainty. Sometimes the law was actually less settled than he made it appear to be; he "described as the custom of England what he wanted to see as the custom of England."[51] For example, the account of partition of estates among heiresses in the absence of a male heir is presented as settled law, when in fact many uncertainties still surrounded such divisions.[52]

As royal finances grew more complex and the central government's control over local units expanded, royal households eagerly recruited men trained in mathematics, logic, and rhetoric.[53] This demand for trained officials was a powerful stimulus for growth of schools.[54] John W. Baldwin has shown that the Angevin kings made great use of *magistri* who had earned their degrees in France, and he concludes, "The high use of masters by the English monarchs contributed to their administrative success."[55] As Michael Clanchy writes, Henry and his advisers recognized that "subtle men, trained to think ingeniously in

---

48. The categories sometimes break down; e.g., the discussion of defaults in Book 1 includes defaults of appellors (accusers) and accused in breaches of the king's peace, Hall, *Glanvill* 1.32. This should have gone in Book 14.

49. Ibid. 1.32, 6.10, 6.17, 7.3, 10.5, 11.3.

50. Ibid. 2.21; also 4.9, the problem of clerks who cannot be constrained to appear in court because they possess no lay fee to be seized.

51. J. C. Holt, "Feudal Society and the Family in Early Medieval England: IV. The Heiress and the Alien," *Transactions of the Royal Historical Society,* 5th ser., 35 (1985): 19.

52. Ibid., 8–26.

53. The thesis of Alexander Murray, *Reason and Society in the Middle Ages* (Oxford, 1978).

54. Southern, "From Schools to University," 1.

55. John W. Baldwin, "*Studium et Regnum*: The Penetration of University Personnel into French and English Administration at the Turn of the Twelfth and Thirteenth Centuries," *Revue des études Islamiques* 44 (1976): 199–211.

the schools, could prove useful in worldly affairs."[56] Younger sons of knightly families, spurred by need and by ambition, sought an education that would equip them with these newly marketable skills.[57] In the late twelfth century, the distinction between academic and practical subjects was not yet as sharp as it would become in the thirteenth century. By then, schools teaching such practical subjects as accounting and the notarial arts had come to exist separately from the universities, which taught the liberal arts.[58] There is every reason to assume, then, that the author of *Glanvill*, like many twelfth-century royal clerks, had the equivalent of a university education.

Wide-ranging intellectual curiosity characterized Henry II's court. The king and his courtiers shared the confidence in human reason that the schoolmen were encouraging, and *Glanvill* too manifests this rational outlook. The Prologue states that the laws and customs of England "had their origin in reason,"[59] and the book frequently states that one party to a plea should "show reasonable cause" for his action or inaction.[60] In addition, the author shared the doubts of many of his contemporaries about the ordeal. Describing criminal proceedings, he admonishes the justices to discover the truth "by many and varied inquests and interrogations" and "by considering the probable facts and possible conjectures both for and against the accused."[61] Yet the author had not completely lost confidence in traditional modes of proof. His discussion of the grand assize acknowledges "the doubtful outcome of battle" and praises Henry II's clemency in granting the assize as an alternative mode of proof.[62] *Glanvill*'s other comments on battle, however, reveal that it remained for him a perfectly respectable method of proof in a number of disputes. In certain actions of debt, he found either combat or proof by written record equally acceptable: *scriptum vel duellum*.[63]

Another characteristic that a reading of the treatise reveals is the

---

56. M. T. Clanchy, "*Moderni* in Medieval Education and Government in England," *Speculum* 50 (1975): 679.

57. Walter Map, *De nugis curialium*, ed. and trans. M. R. James, revised by C. N. L. Brooke and R. A. B. Mynors (Oxford, 1983), 12–15; ibid., 1.10, claimed that villeins' sons were going off to school "so that they may win great riches."

58. Clanchy, "*Moderni* in Medieval Education," 685.

59. Hall, *Glanvill, De ratione introductis*.

60. Ibid., *Rationabilem causam ostendere*, e.g. 10.10, 10.14.

61. Hall, *Glanvill* 14.1. See Paul Hyams, "Trial by Ordeal: the Key to Proof in the Early Common Law," in *On the Laws and Customs of England*, ed. Morris S. Arnold et al. (Chapel Hill, N.C., 1981), 90–126.

62. Hall, *Glanvill* 2.7.

63. Ibid. 10.17. See also 5.4–5, 6.11, 10.12, 10.15.

author's acquaintance with Roman and canon law, doubtless acquired in the schools. A question remains: How extensive was his knowledge of Romano-canonical principles? Naturally, anyone writing a legal treatise in Latin would absorb some Roman legal concepts simply from the vocabulary. Woodbine believed that the alpha text, now held to be the oldest surviving text of the treatise, was an attempt by someone familiar with Roman law to express an earlier account of English law (beta text) in Romanist language.[64] Students of the treatise have long observed that its Prologue is inspired by the Prologue to Justinian's *Institutes*, that Roman legal terms are borrowed from the Roman texts, and that a number of distinctions came from Roman law, such as the division of pleas into civil and criminal categories or the distinction between possession and proprietary right.

Certainly *Glanvill*'s author knew Roman legal terms, and he could use them correctly when he chose.[65] He also assumed his readers' familiarity with the vocabulary of the written law, for example, his use of the terms *dos* or *infamia*. He noted that the term *dos* had different meanings in English and Roman law, but he did not bother to give its civilian or canonist definition; instead, he went ahead to describe its English usage, as if he assumed that his readers would already be familiar with its meaning in written law. Only in a later passage did he explain its civilian meaning.[66] Sometimes the author chose to usurp civilian terms for English legal practices that were not precisely parallel to Roman practices. In his discussion of the jury of presentment, he used the term *infamia*, borrowed from the Church's practice of prosecuting suspects on the basis of public ill-fame, to describe someone presented to the itinerant justices by a jury on the basis of public notoriety.[67] But the author could use *infamia* in its proper Roman legal sense, meaning the disabilities attached to persons who had been found guilty of crimes. He applied the term to convicted perjurers who had "lost their law," or their right to be witnesses or to swear oaths in the English law courts.[68] Book Ten of *Glanvill*, treating those pleas of debt that fall within the royal courts' jurisdiction, represents the author's most patent attempt to apply Roman legal language. His listing of four types of debts by their Roman names and his definitions of them

---

64. Woodbine, *Glanvill*, 187–88.
65. T. F. T. Plucknett, "The Relations between Roman Law and English Common Law Down to the Sixteenth Century," *University of Toronto Law Journal* 3 (1939–40): 33; Hall, *Glanvill*, xxxvii; Woodbine, *Glanvill*, 187–88; Sutherland, *Novel Disseizin*, 24, 27–28, nn. 2, 3.
66. Hall, *Glanvill* 6.1, 7.1. See Woodbine, *Glanvill*, 215.
67. Hall, *Glanvill* 14.1–2. See Richard Helmholz, "The Early History of the Grand Jury and the Canon Law," *University of Chicago Law Review* 50 (1983): 616.
68. Hall, *Glanvill* 2.19, 14.1.

clearly indicate familiarity with the *Institutes*' treatment of contracts.[69]

R. C. Van Caenegem has made a detailed analysis of the treatise seeking civilian borrowings in the common law, but finding few. He concludes that the author of *Glanvill* had some knowledge of Roman law, "although not to any depth or width."[70] Neither do other modern authorities find much Roman legal influence on the law set forth in the treatise.[71] That there is so little Roman law in the book is not because of the author's ignorance, but because it was irrelevant for him, since his main topic was feudal tenures and lord-tenant relationships. All authorities agree that the greatest lesson Roman law had to teach the author was how to arrange systematically the body of English law. One notes, for example, that the lesson that Roman law taught was "the characteristic Roman virtue of order," inspiring the author to shape sheaves of writs into an orderly system.[72]

Yet the author may have had a more intimate acquaintance with Romano-canonical teaching than some scholars are willing to admit; an absence of direct borrowing in the treatise does not necessarily imply his ignorance of the learned law. The question of Roman law's influence on *Glanvill* cannot be separated from another difficult question that has led to an endless debate: What role did Roman and canon law play in the shaping of Henry II's legal reforms?[73] Most scholars today find that because of its executive and feudal origins, English common law had little to borrow from Roman or canon law. It crystallized around pleading and procedures with the opposing parties seeking to frame some question that could be answered by a jury.[74] The common law grew out of administrative instruments as individual royal commands to feudal lords or sheriffs evolved into widely available authorizations for judicial inquiries, a process that Van Caenegem labels

---

69. Ibid., Book 10; Hall's discussion, xxxvi–xxxvii; Woodbine's notes, 206, 251. J. L. Barton, "The Study of Civil Law before 1380," in Catto, *Early Oxford Schools*, 520, notes that *Glanvill* treats Roman law "as an ideal to which the English law upon the subject [of debt] is to be deemed to approximate." Van Caenegem, *Royal Writs*, 380–82, finds that Book 10 is "remarkable for the purely formal, external indebtedness to Roman law." William S. Holdsworth, *A History of English Law*, 3d ed., 12 vols. (London, 1932), 2:191–92, found the Roman law in Book 10 "very much on the surface."

70. Van Caenegem, *Royal Writs*, 379–90.

71. For references, see Ralph V. Turner, "Roman Law in England before the Time of Bracton," above, p. 63.

72. Richardson and Sayles, *Law and Legislation*, 79; Van Caenegem, *Royal Writs*, 390.

73. E.g., the great debate over the relationship between the assize of novel disseizin and the Roman interdict *Unde vi*. For references, see Turner, "Roman Law before Bracton," above, pp. 60–63.

74. Plucknett, "Relations between Roman Law and English Common Law," 32; idem, *Legal Literature*, 103.

"judicialization" of royal writs.[75] Milsom stresses that the original aim of Henry II's writs was not to create a common law for England, but to ensure that feudal lords followed feudal custom in their dealings with their tenants.[76]

Chronology is crucial. England was precocious in its legal evolution. The legal procedure described in *Glanvill*—a pattern of writs and juries—developed before the canonical inquest had evolved sufficiently to serve as a model. When *Glanvill* was written, the church courts were moving toward new means of proof: reliance upon written documents and examination of individual witnesses, that is, the inquisitorial method. This procedure would not prevail in the ecclesiastical courts, however, until about 1200, and secular courts on the Continent would not adopt it until the mid-thirteenth century.[77]

A decade before *Glanvill* was written, a number of learned men in the English Church and curia regis were familiar with the outlines of Roman and canon law.[78] Of the thirteen royal agents most active in judicial work during Henry II's last decade, there were six clerics who doubtless had an acquaintance with Roman and canon law. Since three were bishops and the two others archdeacons, they combined their work as royal judges with work in the Church's tribunals.[79] Hubert Walter, who became a regular on the bench in 1185, sometimes heard ecclesiastical cases without leaving the house of the exchequer.[80]

Canon law studies flourished in late twelfth-century England. Gratian's *Decretum* was in use by the late 1150s, and Anglo-Norman scholars were soon active in making collections of papal decretals, many of which were housed in English monastic or episcopal libraries.[81] Students from England and Normandy flocked to Bologna, a center

---

75. Van Caenegem, *Birth of Common Law*, 38–41.

76. Milsom, *Legal Framework;* idem, Introduction, Pollock and Maitland, *History of English Law.*

77. Van Caenegem, "L'histoire du droit et la chronologie. Réflexions sur la formation du 'Common Law' et la procédure romano-canonique," in *Etudes d'histoire du Droit canonique dédiées à Gabriel le Bras*, 2 vols. (Paris, 1965), 2:1465; idem, *Birth of Common Law*, 92.

78. Eleanor Rathbone, "Roman Law in the Anglo-Norman Realm," *Studia Gratiana* 11 (1967): 263.

79. Ralph V. Turner, *The English Judiciary in the Age of Glanvill and Bracton c. 1176–1139* (Cambridge, 1985), 19, 37.

80. Adam of Domerham, *Historia de rebus gestis Glastoniensis,* ed. Thomas Hearne, 2 vols. (Oxford, 1727), 2:364. Once Hubert simply moved from the Exchequer to Westminster Abbey to hear a suit as papal judge-delegate, C. R. Cheney, *Hubert Walter* (London, 1967), 26.

81. Kuttner and Rathbone, "Ango-Norman Canonists," 292–339; Mary G. Cheney, *Bishop Roger of Worcester* (Oxford, 1982), 197–206. Several of them found posts on the Continent as lecturers, e.g., Gerard la Pucelle and Ricardus Anglicus.

for both Roman and canon law studies, throughout the late twelfth and early thirteenth centuries. Indeed, English bishops made it their practice to send promising young clerics to Bologna, who sometimes returned to England to win bishoprics for themselves.[82] Another sign of the spread of canon law is the famous Richard de Anesty series of lawsuits. These show that by 1160 professional advocates were assisting litigants in the ecclesiastical courts in preparing their cases.[83]

Canon and Roman law studies advanced simultaneously in England, for Roman law was a necessary preparation for canonical studies. Although the exact date that the complete *Corpus Iuris Civilis* reached England cannot be pinpointed, the *Digest* and the *Institutes* had certainly arrived by the third quarter of the twelfth century.[84] John of Salisbury complained at the time of the Becket conflict that Roman legal doctrines were circulating at Henry II's court.[85] In addition, England's first school for the learned law opened at Oxford about the time that *Glanvill* was being composed. According to long tradition, the Italian master Vacarius had begun lecturing on Roman law at Oxford in King Stephen's time, where he wrote his *Liber Pauperum* in 1149 and founded a law school that lasted into the thirteenth century. R. W. Southern, in a recent re-examination of that tradition, suggests, however, that Vacarius was too busy as legal adviser to the archbishops of Canterbury and York to have had time to give lessons at Oxford. Southern would date the founding of the Oxford law school much later in the twelfth century, after Vacarius had settled in the north of England. Southern concludes that if Master Vacarius taught in England, it was not at any organized school; rather, it would have been through informal lessons given in the archiepiscopal households to which he was at-

---

82. E.g., Gilbert Foliot of Hereford and later London, Adrian Morey and C. N. L. Brooke, *Gilbert Foliot and his Letters* (Cambridge, 1965), 63, 64, 68; John de Bohun of Salisbury, ibid., 55–56; Baldwin of Canterbury, Beryl Smalley, *The Becket Conflict and the Schools* (Oxford, 1972), 217; Seffrid II of Chichester, Henry Mayr-Harting, "The Bishops of Chichester 1075–1207," *The Chichester Papers* 40 (1963): 14–15; Roger of Worcester, Cheney, *Bishop Roger*; Gilbert de Glanvill of Rochester, Kuttner and Rathbone "Anglo-Norman Canonists," 289.

83. C. R. Cheney, *From Becket to Langton* (Manchester, 1956), 55; Patricia M. Barnes, "The Anesty Case," in *A Medieval Miscellany for Doris M. Stenton*, ed. P. M. Barnes and C. F. Slade (Pipe Roll Society, n.s., 36, 1960), 7. See also Eleanor Searle, ed., *The Chronicle of Battle Abbey* (Oxford, 1980), 324, where the abbot laments the lack of monks "knowledgeable in the law and the decretals" to advise in lawsuits.

84. See Turner, "Roman Law before Bracton," above, p. 52.

85. John of Salisbury, *Policraticus*, ed. C. C. J. Webb, 2 vols. (Oxford, 1909), 7.20. Thomas Becket complained that Henry II was seeking support from *sapientes Bononiae*. J. C. Robertson, ed., *Materials for the History of Thomas Becket*, 7 vols. (Rolls Series 67, 1875–85), 7:26, no. 538.

tached.⁸⁶ Stephan Kuttner, however, remains convinced that Vacarius did engage in some formal teaching somewhere in England. In his view, Southern underrated English glosses on the *Liber Pauperum* and other manuscripts that cite Vacarius's views. He finds that these writings "clearly indicate formal teaching, formal glosses ('notae') and formal discussions of the opinions of Bolognese masters. These are not the unstructured, leisurely observations of a country pastor."⁸⁷

Although Vacarius may not have founded a school at Oxford, evidence still exists for the study of Roman law at a number of cathedrals and other centers of learning after the mid-twelfth century. Studies at these other schools cannot have reached, however, a level equal to that achieved at Oxford by the end of the twelfth century. Oxford had become a center for ecclesiastical courts, attracting a number of clerics interested in the learned law. The connection between the Oxford schools and the church courts is so close that it is difficult to say which settled in the town first.⁸⁸ By the 1180s or 1190s, a law school was in operation at Oxford, using Vacarius's *Liber Pauperum* as text. This school began chiefly as a center for canon law studies, but both laws were taught there.⁸⁹ Clerics serving Henry II had ample opportunity to acquaint themselves with the written law.

The author of *Glanvill*, like other royal justices, needed some familiarity with the Church's law. Questions of marriage and legitimacy, mainly the concern of ecclesiastical courts, could sometimes arise in cases before the curia regis. The treatise contains an explicit reference to a decretal of Pope Alexander III on the legitimacy of children, with a comment that "the law and custom of the realm" differ from Roman and canon law on this point.⁹⁰ In *Glanvill*'s discussion of villeinage, the author rejects classical Roman law on the status of children born of a marriage between free and unfree persons in favor of a rule from vulgar Roman law that must have come to him by way of the canonists.⁹¹ The author knew well the procedures of the ecclesiastical courts, and

---

86. See Southern, "Master Vacarius," 9–10, and "From Schools to University" (cited *supra* n. 4), where he modifies these views. See also Peter Stein, "Vacarius and the Civil Law," in *Church and Government in the Middle Ages*, ed. C. N. L. Brooke (Cambridge, 1976), 121–36.

87. Stephan Kuttner, "Retractiones VIII," in *Gratian and the Schools of Law* (London, 1983), 26–27; Kuttner and Rathbone, "Anglo-Norman Canonists," 286–88, 288n. See also Barton, "The Study of Civil Law," 524.

88. Southern, "From Schools to University," 12–17.

89. Leonard E. Boyle, "Vacarius and the Beginnings of legal Studies at Oxford," *Viator* 14 (1983): 107–31; J. L. Barton, "Canon Law before 1380," in Catto, *Early Oxford Schools*, 531–64.

90. Hall, *Glanvill* 7.15.

91. Ibid. 5.6; Hyams, *Kings, Lords and Peasants*, 176; idem, "Proof of Villein Status in the Common Law," *English Historical Review* 86 (1974): 732–33.

he expected his readers to know them too. In his discussion of the grand assize, he notes that the grounds for challenging one of the jurors (*juratores*) were the same as those for witnesses (*testes*) in courts Christian.[92] The author did not think it necessary to discuss those grounds, assuming instead that his readers were familiar with them. Such points illustrate the author's acquaintance with Romano-canonical principles.

Examination of *Glanvill* seems to point to a product of the schools— a clerk—as author. Does the longtime link of laity with illiteracy eliminate the possibility of a layman as author? Much confusion on this subject arises from the changing meanings of the words *clericus* and *litteratus*. Since reading and writing were separate skills, these knightly civil servants were not literate in today's sense, but this need not suggest that they were ignorant and incapable of handling the business that came into their offices,[93] neither that they were literate in the eyes of some of their more learned contemporaries. Medieval usage limited the term *litteratus* to someone learned in Latin grammar and rhetoric, not to one capable only of reading simple Latin, and certainly not to one capable only of reading French or English. John of Salisbury wrote that those ignorant of grammar, poetry, history, or rhetoric are illiterate, even though they know their letters.[94] The growing use of written instruments in government, however, implies at least the "pragmatic literacy" of laymen working in royal administration by the late twelfth century.[95] The knights who held offices that required use of documents written in simple Latin, such as writs or charters, were able to read them.

The term *clericus* also could cause confusion, for it did not always mean someone in spiritual orders. It could simply refer to a scribe or secretary, or it could refer to a learned person, a scholar. The organization of the schools was not so rigid in the late twelfth century that students were automatically defined as *clerici* in the sense of belonging to the spiritual sphere and being subject to ecclesiastical jurisdiction. With the growing need for literate and numerate knights, opportunities for their schooling widened. Schools abounded in twelfth-century England, which were attended by lay youths as well as young clerics, and private

---

92. Hall, *Glanvill* 2.12.

93. M. T. Clanchy, *From Memory to Written Record: England 1066–1307* (2nd ed., Oxford, 1993), 232-33; see also Ralph V. Turner, "The *Miles Literatus* in Twelfth- and Thirteenth-Century England: How Rare a Phenomenon?" , below, p. 120.

94. John of Salisbury, *Metalogicon*, ed. C. C. J. Webb (Oxford, 1929), 1.24.

95. I borrow this phrase from M. B. Parkes, "Literacy of the Laity," in *The Medieval World*, ed. D. Daiches and A. Thorlby (London, 1972), 555–77.

tuition was also available to knights' children.[96] Yet somehow the words *litteratus/clericus* became linked together in medieval writers' minds, and their opposites *illitteratus/laicus* became similarly linked.[97] This usage has confused modern readers of medieval Latin, who define the terms anachronistically, drawing the conclusion that all laymen in the Middle Ages were incapable of reading even simple Latin.

It is unlikely that a layman who had not acquired at least "pragmatic literacy" would have served on the bench or in the exchequer at Westminster, and it is likely that anyone who attained the office of justiciar—a Ranulf de Glanvill or a Geoffrey fitz Peter—would have achieved a somewhat higher level of learning. Some noble youths growing up in the early twelfth century became remarkably learned. Two often-cited examples are the Beaumont twins, who received their schooling at Abingdon Abbey. As teenagers, their dialectical skills impressed the pope and his cardinals.[98] For most civil servants, however, advanced training was practical, consisting of the observation of experienced officials at work. Everyday experience under an expert's supervision was the preferred path to advancement in government posts. Indeed, Richard fitz Neal claimed that his *Dialogus* had more value than philosophy books for a beginner at the exchequer.[99]

The English common law was carved out of administrative materials and feudal custom, which meant that the laymen on the bench did not need to feel inferior to their clerical colleagues. Their knowledge of this material equalled or surpassed that of clerics, and seven of the thirteen justices who served most frequently in Henry II's last decade were laymen.[100] Knights in the twelfth-century Angevin domains had a tradition of eloquence and legal expertise in their honor courts and the public courts that was entirely unwritten. In addition, the French epics and romances that entertained Henry II's courtiers included dramatic trial scenes.[101] Attending the courts was both a duty and a diversion, a feudal obligation and an alternative to warfare. Knights on both sides of the Channel sharpened their skills in pleading through years of attending the courts, first as youthful observers, then as litigants, attorneys, and jurors. Ranulf de Glanvill's father declared that he had

---

96. See Turner, "The *Miles Literatus*," below, pp. 133-34.
97. Clanchy, *From Memory to Written Record,* 224-52 (chap. 7, "Literate and Illiterate"); Murray, *Reason and Society,* 263-70.
98. David Crouch, *The Beaumont Twins* (Cambridge, 1986), 7. For other examples, see Turner, "The *Miles Literatus,*" 127.
99. Johnson, *Dialogus,* 5.
100. Turner, *English Judiciary,* 31-32.
101. Paul Hyams, "Henry II and Ganelon," *Syracuse Scholar* (Syracuse, N.Y. 1986), 23-25.

attended the shire and hundred courts for fifty years, first doing so as a lad accompanying his father.[102] To defend their lands, knights had to have a thorough knowledge of the custom of the courts; as lords of lands or as their lords' stewards, they had to preside over seignorial courts.

Clerics among Henry II's justices would not have found their colleague's practical learning inferior to their own. Early manuscripts of *Glanvill* give the opinions of seven justices on disputed points, and among them only one cleric, Hubert Walter, is cited.[103] As for the discipline of rhetoric, both clergy and knights in the twelfth century regarded highly the art of speaking well. Not only did lay education rely heavily upon oral instruction, but the cathedral schools, with their lectures and disputations, also stressed oral presentation.[104] To call someone, knight or cleric, *vir eloquentiae* was a great compliment.

Some twelfth-century knights won such reputations for skill in pleading in the shire courts that they occasionally served as pleaders for others.[105] Monasteries often employed a tenant knight as pleader in their suits before the secular courts. The abbot of Battle, in a 1167 case, designated one of his monks and one of his knights to explain "the whole matter from the very beginning to the king and his justices."[106] It is likely that lay lords imitated the religious in employing their most eloquent knight to plead their causes. They had the feudal obligation of warranting their tenants' disputed lands in the courts, and great barons with many tenants would have found it useful to have knights who could plead for them. Such knights could also serve their lords as attorneys, authorized substitutes in their absence from proceedings.[107] By the time that the writ system described in *Glanvill* developed, these knights needed to be more than eloquent pleaders; they also needed to be experts on the selection of the correct writ.[108]

Such knights, however, are by no means evidence for a legal profes-

---

102. Helen Cam, "An East Anglian Shire-moot of Stephen's Reign," *English Historical Review* 39 (1924): 936.

103. Hall, *Glanvill*, xliv–xlv. The laymen are W.B., i.e., William Basset or possibly William Briwerre, Hugh Bardolf, Osbert fitz Hervey, Glanvill, Richard de Lucy, and Robert of Wheatfield.

104. Clanchy, *From Memory to Written Record*, 214–20.

105. Robert C. Palmer, "The Origins of the Legal Profession in England," *Irish Jurist*, n.s., 11 (1976): 126–35.

106. Searle, *Chronicle of Battle Abbey*, 214.

107. Bailiffs or stewards acted as their lords' attorneys, *Leges Henrici primi*, ed. L. J. Downer (Oxford, 1972), 7, 7a, pp. 100–101; Hall, *Glanvill* 11.1, 13.33; Johnson, *Dialogus*, 116–17.

108. Suggestion of Paul Hyams, review of *Legal Framework of English Law*, S. F. C. Milsom, *English Historical Review* 93 (1978): 860.

sion. If professional lawyers were practicing before the lay courts of mid-twelfth-century England, then surely Richard de Anesty would have sought their assistance, as he did professional pleaders practicing in the church courts. Professional pleaders practicing before the royal courts — legal experts whose income came chiefly from numerous clients in return for remuneration — appear only late in the third decade of the thirteenth century, after Henry III had come of age.[109] Nonetheless, these men do point out the high level of legal expertise among England's knightly class from whom the Angevin kings could draw their judges and jurors.

Who wrote *Glanvill*? Since the thirteenth century, the treatise has borne the name of the justiciar Ranulf de Glanvill. This title goes back to an *incipit,* added to some copies, which simply states that at the book's composition, "Justice was under the direction of the illustrious Rannulf de Glanville, the most learned of that time in the law and ancient custom of the realm."[110] The best text of Roger of Howden's *Chronica* includes texts of some early English laws, of *Glanvill,* and of some of Henry II's assizes.[111] When the chronicler recorded under the year 1180 Ranulf de Glanvill's appointment as justiciar, he added: *cuius sapientia conditae sunt leges subscriptae quas Anglicanas vocamus.*[112] To what laws was Howden referring? To the whole collection? Only to the old English laws? Only to the treatise? Most likely, Howden's phrase means that Glanvill inspired or sponsored the collecting of English laws, and possibly, that Glanvill encouraged the writing of the treatise that Howden inserted in his chronicle. Roger of Howden, "a retired administrator of the second class," who died *circa* 1201, was in a position to know whether or not the justiciar had actually written the treatise.[113] There is no reason why he should not have said so plainly, had Ranulf de Glanvill been the actual author. F. W. Maitland labelled Howden's phrase "obscure words," and he rejected both it and the *incipit* as evidence for the justiciar's authorship. Doris M. Stenton at one time took Howden's phrase more seriously. She wrote in 1926 that Ranulf's authorship is "most probable," and that if he did not

109. Paul Brand, "The Origins of the English Legal Profession," *Law and History Review* 5 (1987): 31–37.

110. Hall, *Glanvill,* xxxi. See Richardson and Sayles, *Law and Legislation,* 105–6.

111. Laws of William I, B.L. MS Royal 14.C.ii, fols. 214v–223v; glossary of English law terms, ibid., fol. 225; *Glanvill,* ibid., fols. 226–274v; Assizes of the Forest, ibid., fols. 274v–275; Assizes of Clarendon, ibid., fols. 275–76. See also *Chronica Rogeri de Hovedene,* ed. William Stubbs, 4 vols. (Rolls Series 51, 1868–71), 2:215–52.

112. Roger of Howden, B.L. MS Royal 14.C.ii, fol. 214v.

113. I owe this suggestion to J. C. Holt. See Frank Barlow, "Roger of Howden," *English Historical Review* 55 (1950): 308–11.

actually write it, then, "It was written at his inspiration and, in all probability, under his guidance."[114]

Maitland rejected Ranulf as author not because he believed him incapable of writing such a work, but because he would have lacked time for the task. Maitland acknowledged the justiciar's literacy, citing a comment Ranulf made to Walter Map critical of nobles who failed to educate their children in letters.[115] Another authority goes further in stressing Ranulf's literacy, suggesting that he was author of two other works: a crusading chronicle of the 1147 conquest of Lisbon and an account of an East Anglian shire court *circa* 1150.[116]

It is difficult to believe that the justiciar wrote one book, much less three. Very little is known about Ranulf's life before 1163, when he became a sheriff, and nothing at all about his education.[117] Certainly some noble youths growing up in the first half of the twelfth century excelled in learning, but the only ones this is known about with certainty were wards of King Henry I, reared in his household. One known fact about Ranulf's early life is the appearance of his name in connection with Richard de Anesty's case. In 1162 and 1163, Richard sought his presence at the hearing of his suit, but it is not clear whether he wanted Ranulf's legal advice or simply his presence to impress the court with the importance of his supporters.[118] If Ranulf de Glanvill possessed a reputation for legal learning at that early date, then his expertise had come through observation of court proceedings, not from books.

Ranulf would have read Latin less easily than Anglo-Norman, his everyday language and the speech most often heard in the courts. It is unlikely that his level of Latin advanced much higher than the pragmatic literacy attained by many knights by the late twelfth century, and it is less likely that he had the familiarity with Roman and canon law that the author of the book bearing his name must have possessed. Glanvill's knowledge of history seems to have come more from the *chansons de*

---

114. Pollock and Maitland, *History of English Law* 1:164–65; see also *Dictionary of National Biography,* s.n. "Glanville, Ranulf de"; D. M. Stenton, "England: Henry II," in *Contest of Empire and Papacy,* vol. 5 of *Cambridge Medieval History,* ed. J. R. Tanner, C. W. Prévite-Orton, and Z. N. Brooke, 2d ed., 8 vols. (Cambridge, 1924–36), 578–79.

115. Walter Map, *De nugis curialium* 1.10.

116. J. C. Russell, "Ranulf de Glanville," *Speculum* 45 (1950): 69–79. J. S. Falls, "Ranulf de Glanville's Formative Years *c.* 1120–79," *Mediaeval Studies* 40 (1978): 315n, finds Russell's arguments "difficult to accept."

117. The only evidence for his activity before *c.* 1160 is his name on some East Anglian charter witness-lists, Falls, "Glanville's Formative Years," 318.

118. Barnes, "Anesty Case," 13, 21; Brand, "Origins of the English Legal Profession," 32.

gestes than from Latin chronicles.[119]

Maitland's argument for rejecting Ranulf as author of the treatise, that his multiple responsibilities as justiciar would not have spared him the time, deserves attention. Maitland points out that in Henry II's harried last years, Ranulf would have had little leisure for writing; furthermore, he notes that the author writes "not as a statesman, but as a lawyer." For Maitland, the book does not read as it if were the work of a busy leader at the center of government, snatching spare moments for writing, but the result of reflection.[120] Centuries earlier, however, Alfred the Great had found time for writing in the midst of his kingly duties. Ranulf still has his partisans,[121] but arguments against his claim to authorship appear overpowering.

Maitland's own nominee for author was Ranulf's nephew Hubert Walter, who became justiciar in 1193.[122] Maitland's views are not be rejected lightly, and several scholars have seconded his suggestion.[123] Hubert Walter certainly earned a great reputation for knowledge of the common law and the courts. Roger of Howden wrote, "There was to be found no one like him who stored up the laws and customs of the kingdom," and other chroniclers echo Howden's view.[124] According to Hubert Walter's own words, it was his uncle Ranulf de Glanvill and his aunt who reared him.[125] The abbot of Reading, a longtime acquaintance of the archbishop, wrote in 1197 that he has been "trained from the cradle in secular studies [*secularibus disciplinis*]," and that he had come to the courts while still a youth, though one "of astonishing

---

119. *De Principis instructione liber,* ed. G. F. Warner, in *Giraldi Cambrensis opera,* 8 vols. (Rolls Series 21, 1861–91), 8: 257–59.

120. Pollock and Maitland, *History of English Law* 1:164.

121. Bryce Lyon, "Glanvill, Ranulf de," in *Dictionary of the Middle Ages,* ed. Joseph R. Strayer, 10 vols. (New York, 1982—), 5:544–45. Holt's study of division of inheritance among daughters lends some support to Glanvill's authorship. Holt, "Feudal Society," 19.

122. Pollock and Maitland, *History of English Law* 1:164. Maitland based his claim on Bracton's selection of the name "Hubertus Walteri" to use with his own name as examples. Maitland suggests that this was a subtle tribute by a later legal expert to a predecessor. G. E. Woodbine, ed., *Bracton de Legibus et Consuetudinibus Angliae,* trans. S. E. Thorne, 4 vols. (Cambridge, Mass., 1968–77), 3:79, fol. 188b.

123. E.g., Holdsworth, *History of English Law* 2:189–90; Stenton, "England: Henry II," 578, but she changed her mind; see idem, ed., *Pleas before the King or his Justices, 1198–1212,* 4 vols. (Selden Society 67–68, 83–84, 1948–66), 1:10; also Richardson and Sayles, *Governance,* 320 n. 2.

124. Roger of Howden, *Chronica* 4.12; William Stubbs, ed., *Gervase of Canterbury: Historical Works,* 2 vols. (Rolls Series 72, 73, 1879–80), 2:406.

125. William Dugdale, *Monasticon Anglicanum,* 6 vols., rev. ed. (London, 1846), 6(2):899.

wisdom."[126]

Yet neither of Hubert Walter's modern biographers accepts him as *Glanvill*'s author.[127] The evidence suggests that he spent little or no time in the schools. There is no doubt that Hubert received an education in Latin letters from clerks in his uncle's household, but he seems to have lacked the confidence in debate that scholastic disputations would have given him. Once he hesitated to involve himself in a dispute with Abbot Samson of Bury St. Edmunds, admitting his inferiority as a debator (*disputator*).[128] Several of the archbishop's acquaintances commented on his scholarly deficiencies: Gerald of Wales in particular was a harsh critic, fond of pointing out Hubert Walter's lack of academic attainment. He records three amusing anecdotes about grammatical mistakes the archbishop made while speaking Latin, the best known of which has Richard Lionheart correcting him.[129] In Gerald's view, Hubert's schooling consisted of practical experience at the exchequer, which he considered unworthy of a prelate. Gerald complained that the exchequer was no more than an accounting office, and he added, "This was the academy, this the school, in which he has already grown old, from which he was summoned to all the grades of his dignities."[130]

Gerald of Wales was correct, since Hubert Walter's preparation for his high offices was essentially a practical apprenticeship with his uncle's staff. He first appears as a royal justice in 1185, when Ranulf de Glanvill was beginning to bring his own *familiares* into the curia regis.[131] Hubert earned his knowledge of canon law and its procedures by experience, the same way that he mastered English law. This training must have resembled that of his contemporary, Abbot Samson of Bury St. Edmunds. According to the abbot's monastic biographer, when he was appointed a papal judge-delegate, he prepared himself in this way: "He called in two clerks learned in the law and associated them with himself, using their advice in ecclesiastical business, and he studied the decrees and decretals when he had an hour to spare." His biographer continues, "Soon, with reading and experience of cases, he gained the reputation of a wise judge."[132]

---

126. Giles Constable, "An unpublished Letter by Abbot Hugh II of Reading concerning Archbishop Hubert Walter," in *Essays Presented to Bertie Wilkinson*, ed. T. A. Sandquist and M. R. Powicke (Toronto, 1968), 16–17.

127. Cheney, *Hubert Walter*, 22; Charles R. Young, *Hubert Walter* (Durham, N.C., 1968), 16–17.

128. H. E. Butler, ed., *The Chronicle of Jocelin of Brakelond* (London, 1949), 84.

129. Giraldus Cambrensis, *Opera* (Rolls Series 3, 1863), ed. J. S. Brewer, 29–30, 254. See Young, *Hubert Walter*, 7–8, n. 10.

130. *Opera* 3:25; translation from H. E. Butler, ed. and trans., *The Autobiography of Giraldus Cambrensis* (London, 1937), 215.

131. Stenton, *Pleas* 3:lxix.

132. Butler, *Chronicle of Jocelin of Brakelond*, 33–34.

Some scholars maintain that Hubert Walter had studied Roman law at Bologna in his youth, but no strong evidence supports such speculation. The supposition rests on the slim evidence of an obituary calendar of benefactors for a chapel at Bologna, built by English students there to commemorate St. Thomas Becket. The name of Hubert Walter, lord of Canterbury, does appear on the list, but he could have made a contribution to the chapel without ever having enrolled in the Bolognese schools.[133]

It was Hubert Walter's intelligence, careful observation of the courts, and association with experts that gave him unequalled knowledge of exchequer procedures and English common law. Although the archbishop knew the common law better than anyone besides Ranulf de Glanvill, it is unlikely that he wrote the treatise bearing his uncle's name. He lacked the formal education and the familiarity with Roman law needed for such an effort, even though the book has no pretensions to literary grace. The author of *Glanvill* states that he writes intentionally in "a commonplace style [*stilus vulgarus*] and words used in court," so that learned persons unaccustomed to such "inelegant language" can gain knowledge of the royal courts' operations.[134] The implication is that he could have written elegantly, had he chosen to do so.

Having rejected the evidence for Hubert Walter, it is the turn of a third candidate, Geoffrey fitz Peter, to be considered. His strongest advocate was Lady Stenton, who took up his cause in her last years, and her views deserve respect. She wrote, "Though nothing stronger can be said, it is possible that the future justiciar was instructed or encouraged by his master, Glanvill, to write, or superintend the writing of this little book."[135] She found support for his authorship in an agreement made in Geoffrey fitz Peter's feudal court, which *Glanvill* gives as an example of a final concord. She argued that the copy of the chirograph came from Geoffrey himself, for at that time (November 1187) the royal court did not yet keep feet of fines, or copies of all such agreements.[136] J. C. Holt seconds her suggestion, basing his support for Geoffrey's authorship on *Glanvill*'s discussion of an eldest daughter's seniority among sisters sharing an inheritance due to lack of surviving sons. This problem had parallels with Geoffrey's wife's situation.[137]

Hall recognizes that Geoffrey fitz Peter had the required "ability,

---

133. Cheney, *Hubert Walter,* 18; idem, "Hubert Walter and Bologna," *Bulletin of Medieval Canon Law,* n.s., 2 (1972): 81–84. H. G. Richardson accepts Hubert's study in Bologna: *Memoranda Roll 1 John* (Pipe Roll Society, n.s., 21, 1943), lxii.
134. Hall, *Glanvill,* Prologue, 3.
135. Stenton, *Pleas* 1:10.
136. Ibid.: 9; Hall, *Glanvill,* 95–96.
137. Holt, "Feudal Society," 19.

authority and knowledge" to write the treatise, but he doubted that Geoffrey had the time to do so.[138] Whether or not Geoffrey had leisure for writing, it is unlikely that he wrote the treatise. Geoffrey fitz Peter resembles a number of Henry II's servants in his sudden appearance among the *familiares regis* from out of nowhere. Son of the forester of Ludgershall, Wiltshire, he is an almost invisible figure before he became sheriff and chief royal forester in 1184.[139] We know nothing of his education or earliest occupation, but we can assume that somehow he acquired administrative skills, the ability to keep accounts and to use written records. Even though Geoffrey would have been literate in Latin, he would have lacked the formal schooling needed to pen a treatise such as *Glanvill*. As an analysis of the treatise shows, its author had spent some time in the schools and had a more than nodding acquaintance with Roman and canon law. Nothing links Geoffrey fitz Peter with the intellectual curiosity of Henry II's *curiales*. While anecdotes depict Ranulf de Glanvill in conversation with writers, no similar stories point toward intellectual interest on Geoffrey's part.[140] His legal expertise, like his predecessors' in the justiciarship, was practical and not academic.

Chronology rules out Geoffrey fitz Peter as author, for he only began to acquire judicial experience in the royal courts toward the end of Henry II's reign, just at the time that *Glanvill* was written: The earliest he is recorded as being a royal justice is June 1188.[141] Before then, Geoffrey's experience had been as chief forester, hearing pleas of the forest. While foresters occasionally did double duty, hearing pleas of the crown and taking assizes while performing their forest duties, Geoffrey would not have had the same experience with the common law that other justices working at Westminster were gaining at the time of the treatise's composition. Furthermore, he won his reputation for learning in the law long after *Glanvill*'s composition, as King John's justiciar.[142]

The final candidate to consider is Master Godfrey de Lucy, son of the former justiciar Richard de Lucy. Hall guardedly supports his candidacy, mentioning him in a footnote as "an intriguing possibility."[143] Godfrey de Lucy had long experience in royal government, first appearing among the ranks of royal servants in 1169, when he joined

---

138. Hall, *Glanvill*, xxxii–xxxiii.
139. See Turner, *English Judiciary*, 93, 101, 104–5.
140. Russell, "Ranulf de Glanville," 75–76.
141. Stenton, *Pleas* 3:lxxiv; the second date is 29 Nov., ibid.: lxxv.
142. H. R. Luard, ed., *Matthaei Parisiensis Chronica majora*, 7 vols. (Rolls Series 57, 1872–84), 2:558–59.
143. Hall, *Glanvill*, n. 2.

several of them in witnessing a charter.[144] By the early 1170s, he was witnessing royal charters. Between then and the summer of 1188, he witnessed thirty of Henry II's charters, nine of them in France. He was also active in the 1180s, heading judicial eyres and hearing pleas at Westminster.[145]

A stronger case than Hall's can be made for Godfrey's authorship of the treatise. Of the thirteen justices most active between 1179 and 1189, he appears the strongest candidate. Godfrey first joined the judiciary about the time of his father's retirement, when he participated in the great eyre of 1179, heading the six justices on the northern circuit. He headed one of the three eyres of 1182, visiting the Midlands and the West. Godfrey then returned to northern England, leading eyres there in 1185, 1187, and 1188. He worked closely with his father's successor as justiciar, Ranulf de Granvill, who had earned his first experience in royal government in the North and who also led eyres to the northern shires. Glanvill joined Godfrey's northern eyre in August 1179, and the next year Godfrey joined his eyre. In 1188, he accompanied Glanville to Berkshire and Hampshire.[146]

It is more difficult to chart Godfrey's work on the bench at Westminster in the years before the feet of fines began to be kept. Surviving final concords enable us to locate him first witnessing agreements at Westminster during the Michaelmas Exchequer in 1182, and again in 1183 and 1185, witnessing fines at both exchequer sessions. On November 2, 1187, he was one of the justices present the day the chirograph from Geoffrey fitz Peter's feudal court was recorded. In January 1189, he was with the justiciar at Oxford acting as a justice.[147] All this activity means that Godfrey served on the bench through the last decade of Henry II's life, throughout Glanvill's justiciarship, and he remained on the bench for Richard I's entire reign, after he had become bishop of Winchester.

More is known of Godfrey de Lucy's schooling than of other judges in Henry II's time. He was one of only three with the title *magister*,

---

144. Stenton, *Pleas* 3:1v.
145. *Recueil des actes de Henri II*, ed. Léopold Delisle and Elie Berger, 3 vols. (Paris, 1909-27), 1:531, 2:165, 197, 207-8, 229, 369, 369, 387, 413; Robert W. Eyton, *Court, Household, and Itinerary of Henry II* (London, 1878), 228, 230, 242, 243, 245, 246, 247, 269, 287; *Calendar of Charter Rolls*, 6 vols. (Public Record Office, 1903-27), 3:405, 4:99, 131, 347, 5:110; J. C. Holt and Richard Mortimer, eds., *Acta of Henry II and Richard I* (List and Index Society, special series, 21, 1986), passim.
146. Senton, *Pleas* 3:lxi-lxxiv; Hall, *Glanvill*, 188n. *Early Yorkshire Charters*, ed. C. T. Clay, *The Honour of Richmond*, pt. 2 (Yorkshire Archaeological Society Record Series, extra series, 1936), 5:157, no. 263.
147. Stenton, *Pleas*, 3:lxvi-lxxvii.

which indicates advanced studies at a cathedral school or university.[148] It is known that he went to school at London in the early 1170s, studying under Master Henry of Northampton; one of his fellow students, Peter of Cornwall, dedicated a portion of his *Pantheologus* to him.[149] By 1176, Godfrey had gone abroad to continue his studies, for his attorney in a lawsuit against Battle Abbey stated, "He is studying at the schools far away beyond this realm."[150] Was he taking a master of arts at Paris or a law degree at Bologna?

Godfrey de Lucy held numerous ecclesiastical posts, some secured for him by his father. He became dean of St. Martin-le-Grand around 1170, a rich benefice that could support him while studying in London: He was a pluralist with prebends at Exeter, Lincoln, London, and York; he became archdeacon of Derby (Lichfield diocese) by 1174 and of Richmond (York) no later than 1184 and possibly as early as 1181.[151] His fellow canons at Exeter Cathedral thought highly enough of him to elect him bishop in 1186, but he refused the honor on grounds that Exeter's income was insufficient for the expenses he would have as bishop. He also won election to Lincoln, but the king preferred the saintly Hugh of Avalon.

Godfrey de Lucy also held parish churches. His father, when custodian of the abbacy at Battle in 1171, asked the monks to present Godfrey to half the church of Wye; soon he persuaded Henry II to present his son to the other half of the church, then in the king's hand. The king's half interest in the appointment of the parson of Wye inspired a lengthy lawsuit between the prior and monks of Battle and Godfrey.[152] Godfrey asked one of his colleagues in the Exeter chapter, Master Ivo of Cornwall,

---

148. I.e., out of 13 justices who served frequently in Henry's last decade and some 55 who served occasionally.

149. Alfred E. Emden, ed., *Biographical Register of the University of Oxford*, 3 vols. (Oxford, 1957–59), 3:2192; Richard W. Hunt, "The Disputation of Peter of Cornwall against Symon the Jew," in *Studies in Medieval History presented to F. M. Powicke*, ed. R. W. Hunt et al. (Oxford, 1948), 143. For the dedication, B.L. MS Royal 7.C.xiv, fol. 7.

150. Searle, *Chronicle of Battle Abbey*, 326.

151. Canon of Exeter, Lincoln, and London. Emden, *Biographical Register* 3:2192; J. Le Neve, *Fasti Ecclesiae Anglicanae 1066–1300*, ed. Diana Greenway (London, 1968—); *Lincoln* (1977), 126; *St. Paul's* (1968), 47. For Godfrey's earliest date as archdeacon of Richmond, Clay, *Honour of Richmond*, pt. 1, 4: xxv, 117; also John Nichols, *The History and antiquities of the county of Leicestershire*, 4 vols. (London, 1795–1815), 2:82, no. 14(5), Croxton Cartulary. For Derby, Adrian Morey and C. N. L. Brooke, eds., *The Letters and Charters of Gilbert Foliot* (Cambridge, 1967), 322, no. 251.

152. C. R. Cheney and Bridgett E. A. Jones, eds., *Canterbury 1162–1190*, vol. 3 of *English Episcopal Acta* (London, 1986), 33, nos. 52, 53; Searle, *Chronicle of Battle Abbey*, 268–70, 320–24.

to assist him in this lawsuit. Godfrey also gained—sometime before his elevation to the episcopate—the church at Bampton, Oxfordshire.[153]

Whether or not Godfrey de Lucy ever enrolled in a faculty of law, his studies and his experience in the Church gave him some knowledge of Roman and canon law principles. If he had actually resided for any time at Exeter, he could have learned some canon law from Bishop Bartholomew, who was a noted canonist.[154] Even though Godfrey was often absent in the king's service from his benefices, they required him to conduct some ecclesiastical business, giving him familiarity with church courts. A papal letter sent to him after he had become bishop of Winchester addressed him as "you who are wise and experienced in the law [*jus*]."[155]

Clearly, Godfrey had the academic background required for the authorship of *Glanvill*. His lengthy litigation with the monks of Battle Abbey over the church of Wye, 1173–76, gave him some practical experience in the church courts' operations, for Battle's advocate was Master Gerard Pucelle, a learned canonist.[156] Godfrey had, in addition, the necessary knowledge of the laws and customs of the curia regis, which he had gained from almost a decade on the bench beside Ranulf de Glanvill.

Godfrey had first-hand experience with feudal rules of inheritance because of the complicated succession to his father's holdings, which gave rise to lawsuits lasting from Richard I's reign down to the 1230s. The difficulties arose from the fact that many of Richard de Lucy's lands were not inherited, but were acquisitions; he could thus divide them in various ways among his heirs. The *caput* of the Lucy estates, the Honor of Ongar, was not a barony held in-chief of the crown, but consisted of thirty knights' fees carved out of other honors. Richard's elder son, Geoffrey, who died *circa* 1170/73, was heir to this honor, but he had predeceased his father, leaving as his heirs minor sons; after they died without heirs (*ante* 1194), the honor passed to their two sisters for partition.[157] Godfrey was custodian of Ongar for his nephews and nieces, *circa* 1181–94, and he obtained part of its estates as his

---

153. C. W. Foster and Kathleen Major, eds., *Registrum antiquissimum* of the cathedral church of Lincoln (Lincoln Record Society, 29, 1931), 3:265, no. 923.

154. *Fasti, Lincoln*, 126; Adrian Morey, *Bartholomew of Exeter, Bishop and Canonist* (Cambridge, 1937), 38, 103.

155. Cheney, *Becket to Langton*, 29.

156. Searle, *Chronicle of Battle Abbey*, 320–24.

157. J. H. Round, "The Heirs of Richard de Lucy," *The Genealogist*, n. s., 15 (1906): 129–33; idem, "The Honour of Ongar," *Transactions of Essex Archaeological Society*, n. s., 7 (1900): 142–52. See also Emilie M. Amt, "Richard de Lucy, Richard II's Justiciar," *Medieval Prosopography* 9 (1988): 61–87.

own inheritance. Some Lucy lands, however, went to descendants of Richard de Lucy's daughters.[158]

This complicated succession raised the same questions of feudal custody and inheritance that were treated in Book Seven of *Glanvill*, among them questions concerning the partition of estates among heiresses that led Holt to look to Glanvill or Geoffrey fitz Peter for its authorship. In addition, Godfrey's position as younger brother of a deceased elder brother made him potential heir to the Lucy honor, raising the question of the precedence of a younger brother over his nephews. This foreshadowed the *casus regis,* or the rival claims of John and Arthur of Brittany to the English crown.

It is possible that Godfrey came directly to the bench from the schools. He first appears at the curia regis in 1169, when he joined other royal servants in witnessing a grant,[159] but his active career in the king's service only began with his appointment to the judiciary in 1179. Once his judicial career began, he had few other responsibilities, and he seems to have concentrated his attention on the courts.[160] He was not a multi-purpose royal servant, holding simultaneously office in the shires, in the king's household, and at Westminster. He performed few tasks other than judicial except for his custody of the abbey of St. Mary, York, from 1184 to 1186, and his two journeys abroad as Henry II's ambassador.[161]

Godfrey de Lucy, then, fits well the description of the author of *Glanvill*: an experienced judge working alongside the justiciar, loyal to Henry II, grounded in scholastic reasoning, acquainted with Roman and canon law, experienced in the ecclesiastical courts, and acquainted with great pioneers such as Richard de Lucy who had worked with Henry II in initiating his legal reforms, making Godfrey master of English law and custom. Furthermore, he had a strong personal interest in mastering the feudal law of inheritance because of his father's

---

158. *Victoria County History, Essex* 4:160; *Rotuli de dominabus* (Pipe Roll Society 35, 1885), 40; *Pipe Roll 2 Richard I* (Pipe Roll Society, n. s., 1, 1925), 104; *Pipe Roll 6 Richard I* (Pipe Roll Society, n. s., 5, 1928), xxi, 24, 28; *Curia Regis Rolls* (Public Record Office, 1923—), 8:25–26. For claims by descendants of Richard de Lucy's daughters, see this case and F. W. Maitland, ed., *Bracton's Note Book* (Cambridge, 1887), 3: no. 1764.

159. Stenton, *Pleas* 3: lv.

160. Turner, *English Judiciary,* 51. Godfrey's only colleague among the justices without multiple responsibilities was Robert of Wheatfield, a layman.

161. *Pipe Roll 31 Henry II* (Pipe Roll Society 34, 1913), 77; *Pipe Roll 32 Henry II* (Pipe Roll Society 36, 1914), 84; *Pipe Roll 33 Henry II* (Pipe Roll Society 37, 1915), 97. William Stubbs, ed., *Gesta Henrici secundi Benedicti Abbatis,* 2 vols. (Rolls Series 49, 1867), 1:334, to Normandy in 1184 to treat with the French king and the Flemish count; *Pipe Roll 32 Henry II,* 179, for an unknown overseas distination.

complex legacy. Finally, unlike the other candidates, Godfrey was not so deluged with administrative responsibilities that he had no time free for reflection and writing.

Even though the evidence points toward Godfrey de Lucy as *Glanvill*'s author, there is a possibility that most of these candidates were contributors to the treatise. Certainly, it is a result of discussion among judges. Some early manuscripts of *Glanvill* cite conflicting opinions and name seven judges, mainly in marginal or interlinear notations. All were men who sat on the bench with Godfrey de Lucy, with the exception of one, his father Richard de Lucy. William Basset had served as a royal justice since 1168, while two others—Hubert Walter and Hugh Bardolf—joined the judiciary in the year of his death, 1185. Two of the justices had participated in the great 1176 eyre following the Council of Northampton: Glanvill and William Basset, plus a third not cited for his opinions, Michael Belet.[162] An analogy with S. E. Thorne's view of the composition of the great thirteenth-century legal treatise attributed to Henry of Bracton may teach us something: Thorne has shown that *Bracton* grew out of a series of small tractates on particular topics. Thorne credits William of Raleigh with inspiring the work of writing the individual pieces and then weaving them together to make a single work.[163]

Could the twelfth-century treatise have been composed in a similar way? Hall concluded that the alpha text of *Glanvill* was written without division into books and chapters; it was instead divided into an uncertain number of *tractatus*. The internal cross-references are to these *tractatus*; for example, "in the *tractatus* concerning pleas of land," and "in the treatise on warranty," or "in this present treatise."[164] Woodbine dated the alpha text later, seeing it as a polishing of an earlier beta text by a clerk who introduced Romanist terminology. Perhaps Woodbine was half-right. Possibly the author of the alpha text was putting together and polishing several tractates that he and some of his colleagues on the bench had composed, shaping them into a single work.

Such a method of composition would explain scholars' inability to agree upon a single model for the work, for some parts of it seem to be based upon writs, while others do not conform so closely to this pattern. Those books in the present version that veer farthest from the

---

162. The others among the seven cited are Robert of Wheatfield and Osbert fitz Hervey, Hall, *Glanvill,* xliv-xlv. Two judges, both relatives of Glanvill, were named Osbert fitz Hervey, one served 1191–1206, while another served occasionally in the 1180s. Richard Mortimer, "The Family of Ranulf de Glanville," *Bulletin of the Institute of Historical Research* 54 (1981): 5–10.

163. Thorne, *Bracton,* preface and xiv, xxxv.

164. R. W. Southern, "A Note on the text of 'Glanville'," *English Historical Review* 65 (1950): 83–84; Hall, *Glanvill,* xli, 4.3, 4.6, 5.3, 10.15, 12.8, 13.11, 13.15.

writs are seven, ten, and fourteen. Book Seven, one of the longest ones, abandons commentary on writs for long stretches to consider substantive laws of feudal inheritance. It best illustrates Milsom's version of the common law's growth: customary feudal relationships hardening into rules as a result of the royal justices' regulation. Book Ten, treating debt, a category of cases for which the curia regis provided few remedies, shows the strongest attempt to apply Roman law to England. Book Fourteen, which purports to cover criminal law, betrays its author's lack of interest in the topic.

Perhaps several members of the justiciar's staff at Westminster contributed to a work that Godfrey de Lucy shaped into its final form. Perhaps Ranulf de Glanvill was the guiding genius behind this treatise in a fashion similar to William of Raleigh's sponsorship of *Bracton*. At the least, Howden's "obscure words" suggest that Glanvill advised and encouraged the author. By 1185, the justiciar had recruited several of his *familiares* as judges, among them his nephew Hubert Walter.[165] The justices and clerks who spent so much time traveling together and working together on eyres formed a tightly bound little band of colleagues and friends.[166] It is not difficult to imagine them collaborating on a handbook of the law that they were pioneering. Neither is it difficult to visualize Godfrey de Lucy as the one among them most capable of knitting their efforts together into a single, coherent work.

Maitland closed his discussion of *Glanvill*'s authorship by stating, "The question is interesting rather than important."[167] The problem surely interests any student of English legal history, but it has broader importance, for it illustrates links between the schools and learning, the law, and society. The author is a representative of those graduates of the schools who were streaming into secular government in the late twelfth century, placing their learning at the service of the king and his subjects.

Note

Sir James Holt spells out a bit more his support for Geoffrey fitz Peter as author of *Glanvill* in his Sewanee Mediaeval Colloquium Lecture, "The *casus regis*: the Law and Politics of Succession in the Plantagenet Dominions 1185–1247," *Law in Mediaeval Life and Thought*, ed. Edward B. King and Susan J. Ridyard, *Sewanee Mediaeval Studies*, 5 (The Press of the University of the South, 1990).

165. Turner, *English Judiciary*, 77–78.
166. Donald Sutherland, "The Brotherhood and the Rivalry of English Lawyers in the General Eyre," *American Journal of Legal History* 31 (1987): 3. Sutherland calls attention to the fraternal spirit among justices and their associates on the last general eyres, which must have had its beginnings with Glanvill and colleagues.
167. Pollock and Maitland, *History of English Law* 1:165.

6

The Reputation of Royal Judges under the Angevin Kings

In twelfth and thirteenth-century England complaints that justice was being sold were common, culminating with King John's tacit admission in *Magna Carta*. Coupled with these complaints were charges of corruption against royal judges, or against royal *aulici, curiales,* or *familiares,* since until the middle of Richard I's reign no professional judiciary existed. Even in King John's time, *familiares regis* still served as judges. Yet a core of royal servants specializing in justice, "professionals" in a certain sense, had been created. Historians since Maitland have generally held a high opinion of these judges. According to Maitland, under Henry II and Richard I, "English law was administered by the ablest, the best educated men in the realm . . . ." F.M. Powicke wrote that the judiciary of Henry III was "probably the most stable and helpful, as it was the most intelligent, element in the State at this time."[1] How are we to reconcile historians' high opinion of the royal justices with their contemporaries' low opinion? Were the chroniclers simply drawing stock figures in their depictions of corrupt judges, or was their picture drawn from life?

Royal officials, including judges, proved popular targets for the pens of twelfth-century moralists and satirists, some of whom wrote out of personal bitterness, having failed in the contest for royal patronage and high office.[2] Capable of condemning *curiales* in classical Latin style was John of Salisbury. He knew many of Henry II's courtiers, and he came to despise them, especially those in clerical orders. Indeed, the theme of his *Policraticus* can be said to be "the incompatibility of the type of character required for the royal administration with the religious and ecclesiastical duties of a church-

---

[1]Frederick Pollock and F.W. Maitland, *The History of English Law,* 2 vols. (2nd ed.; Cambridge, 1898), 1:132; cf. pp. 160-61, 169-70; F.M. Powicke, *King Henry III and the Lord Edward* (Oxford, 1947), p. 143. Cf. C.T. Flower, *Introduction to the Curia Regis Rolls,* Selden Society, 62 (London, 1944), p. 498; Doris M. Stenton, *English Justice between the Norman Conquest and the Great Charter 1066-1215,* Memoirs of the American Philosophical Society, 60 (Philadelphia, 1964), pp. 82-86.

[2]Examples that immediately come to mind are Peter of Blois and Gerald of Wales. See Egbert Türk, *Nugae Curialium: Le règne d'Henri II Plantagenet (1145 [sic]-1189) et l'èthique politique,* Centre de Recherches d'histoire et de philologie, Hautes Études médiévales et modernes, 28 (Geneva, 1977), p. 188.

man."[3] Throughout his book, John of Salisbury complained of the venality, avarice, and sycophancy of royal officials. He made harsh remarks about royal justices, writing that they seemed "rather extortioners than judges."[4] He blamed Henry II for his selection of judges, finding him either ignorant of the law or contemptuous of it by choosing such greedy men. John had especially sharp comment about itinerant justices:

> What I have said concerning governors and other judges should apply also to proconsuls, whom our countrymen commonly call itinerant or "wandering" justices. The name is erroneous, but still it fits, because, following their own desire in pursuit of avarice, they "wander" from the path of equity and plunder the people.[5]

John condemned the venality of all Henry II's officers. He pointed out that "money is the sole driving force" for expediting any business at the royal court.[6] He added that not only must money be paid for action but for inaction as well: "Not merely is there no act, no word to be had without payment, but they will not even keep silent unless paid a price; silence itself is a thing for sale."[7] John recognized, however, that royal servants depended at least partly on payments from petitioners. He wrote, "I am willing to concede that court officials may accept gifts so long as they do not shamelessly extort them."[8]

A correspondent of John of Salisbury, Ralph Niger, denounced Henry II bitterly in one of his chronicles. He complained that the king had brought to England to install as officials "shameful slaves, common foot soldiers of the household."[9] He accused Henry of quibbling overmuch in contending causes so that he might sell justice. Ralph Niger was not alone in his accusation that the king was a delayer and seller of justice. Later Gerald of Wales made the same charges against Henry II.[10]

---

[3] Hans Liebeschutz, *Medieval Humanism in the Life and Writings of John of Salisbury,* Studies of the Warburg Institute, 17 (London, 1950), p. 17. Cf. Ralph V. Turner, "Clerical Judges in English Secular Courts: the Ideal versus the Reality," *Medievalia et Humanistica,* n. s. 3 (1972): 83-84.

[4] *Policraticus,* v, 10, 11, 15; vi, 1; *The Statesman's Book of John of Salisbury,* John Dickinson, trans. (New York, 1927), pp. 114-45, 174-79. John accused royal judges of being ignorant of law and lacking in goodwill, "as is proved by their love of gifts and rewards, exercising the power which they have in the service of avarice or advancing the fortunes of their own flesh and blood," v, 11, p. 125.

[5] *Policraticus,* v, 15, p. 145. The Latin allows a play on the word *errantes.*

[6] Ibid., v, 10, p. 114.

[7] Ibid., p. 116.

[8] Ibid., p. 117.

[9] Robert Anstruther, ed., *The Chronicles of Ralph Niger,* Caxton Society, 13 (London, 1851), Chronicle II, pp. 167-69.

[10] *Giraldi Cambrensis Opera,* ed. J.S. Brewer et al., Rolls Series (London, 1861-91), 5:304; 8:160; also 8:183-86, where he recorded the dream of a Lincolnshire knight, directed by St. Peter to warn Henry II of his misdeeds. One of the knight's admonitions was "concerning the rendering of justice freely and without cost."

Walter Map, one of Henry II's clerks and occasionally an itinerant justice, composed *De nugis curialium,* a collection of court gossip.[11] A typical courtier, Map flattered the king for his legal ability, but he also commented satirically on the quality of royal justice. He complained of such delays in settling cases that many died or spent all their money before their suits were settled, and he pointed out that money was the source of all pardons.[12] He blamed corruption on the base birth of the judges, whom he claimed to be often the sons of serfs, seeking through clerical careers to rise above their station. He cited the Roman poet Claudian, "Nothing is harder than the lowly whenever he riseth to high degree."[13]

A disappointed courtier, Peter of Blois, also denounced the lives of lawyers and *curiales* in his letters.[14] He gave perhaps the most detailed criticism of Henry II's royal justices in a letter addressed to the king sometime after early 1182.[15] Peter sought to warn Henry II of the abuses of his itinerant justices, foresters, sheriffs, and other officials in a letter which would at the same time demonstrate his own learning, studding it with strings of quotations from Scripture, the classics, and Roman law. He complained that the people had to bear the burden of multitudes of royal ministers, who were like locusts in that as soon as some left others arrived. He gave a detailed picture of the faults of Henry's judges, writing that the justices on eyre "frequently err themselves, while they search out the errors of others." He quoted the Sermon on the Mount (Matt. 5:6), "How blest are those who hunger and thirst to see right prevail . . . ." Then he went on to say, "Those who judge your poor hunger and thirst only for money, ignoring justice and prudence." Like Walter Map, he complained of the low origin of many of the justices, pointing out that royal officials chose unsuitable men for selfish reasons, and that noble men resented those judges of inferior station who had no claim to their offices other than their

---

[11] *De Nugis Curialium,* ed. M.R. James, revised by C. N. L. Brooke and R. A. B. Mynors (Oxford, 1983). For a description of the work, see Antonia Gransden, *Historical Writing in England c.550 to c.1307* (Ithaca, N.Y., 1974), pp. 243-44.

[12] *De Nugis Cur.*, v, 6, p. 241; v, 7, pp. 252-53.

[13] Map also tells of an abbot who became an itinerant justice, and "spurred on the spoiling of the poor, hoping perchance to win a bishopric through the favour gained from his spoils," in *Master Walter Map's Book,* Frederick Tupper and Marbury Bladen Ogle, trans. (London, 1924), p. 8.

[14] Jacques Paul Migne, ed., *Patrologia Latina, cursus completus* (Paris, 1844-64), 207, no. 14, col. 43. Peter complained of courtier's vain hopes for worldly gain, writing that the courtier's life is "death to the soul," and quoting *Ecclesiasticus* (7:1-7), "Seek not of the Lord pre-eminence, neither of the king the seat of honor . . . . Seek not to be judge . . . ." For Peter's denunciation of lawyers, see no. 26, cols. 91-92.

[15] *Pat. Lat.*, 207, no. 95, cols. 298-302. It can be dated by the fact that Peter identified himself as "archdeacon of Bath."

connection with the king's *familiares*.

Peter's chief complaint was that justice was so costly to the poor. He called the king's attention to justices who sought gifts, who would not grant writs (*litterae*) unless promised money. He warned, "Whoever sells writs in this way puts on sale the justice of God . . . which he is bound to exhibit freely." He concluded his letter by warning Henry II of his responsibility for his servants' sins and urged him to "judge most strictly the judges of your kingdom."

Complaints about curialists continued in the thirteenth century. Two scholar-bishops, Robert Grosseteste and St. Edmund of Abingdon, denounced clerics in the royal service who neglected their care of souls to pursue the king's interests. The bishop of Lincoln was scandalized by the appointment of the abbot of Ramsey as an itinerant justice, and he complained to St. Edmund.[16] The scholarly archbishop of Canterbury denounced courtiers in a sermon. Applying an allegorical interpretation to the Old Testament account of King Ahab's death (III Kings, 22), he equated the false prophets who had caused his disaster with royal counselors:

> . . . . false counsellors, grasping persons, flatterers, the hard of heart, and oppressors of the poor. With such people the court of every prince and great man is filled. Whoever, therefore, wishes to lead a good life, let him depart from court.[17]

Near the end of the thirteenth century, the corruption of royal justices and their punishment by Edward I inspired the *Narratio de Passione justiciariorum*. The king, following his return from Gascony in 1289, removed from office a number of his officials; among them were ten judges, including the chief justices of King's Bench and Common Pleas. The *Passion* describes the justices' fall, satirizing their sufferings in "a ribald travesty of biblical texts."[18] Its author writes of their misdeeds before their dismissal, noting that "they sat with the rich in secret places to murder the innocent and their right hand was full of bribes."[19]

Moral and satirical writers, then, made three chief criticisms of courtiers: excessive ambition, sycophancy, and greed. In their view, royal judges were

---

[16]H.R. Luard, ed., *Letters of Robert Grosseteste,* Rolls Series (London, 1861-63), 1:105-8, *epistola* xxvii. Later he sought removal of the abbot of Croyland from the itinerant judicature (p. 262, no. lxxxii).

[17]Clifford H. Lawrence, *St. Edmund of Abingdon* (London, 1960), p. 131, citing BL. Harleian MS. 325, f. 163v.

[18]F.M. Powicke, *The Thirteenth Century 1216-1307* (Oxford, 1953), pp. 361-66.

[19]T.F. Tout and Hilda Johnstone, eds., *State Trials of the Reign of Edward I,* Royal Historical Society, Camden 3rd Series, 8 (London, 1906), pp. 93-99. Harry Rothwell, ed., *English Historical Documents,* vol. 3: *1189-1327* (London, 1975), pp. 922-24, gives a translation of the *Passio*. For another poem, slightly later, on the venality of judges, see Thomas Wright, ed., *Political Songs of England,* Camden Society, 6 (1839):224-30.

guilty of these three faults, and especially of the third one, greed. They made surprisingly little criticism on the grounds of incompetence or ignorance of the law.

Chroniclers regarded the judicial eyres as more concerned with increasing royal revenues than with rendering justice; and indeed, a large part of the itinerant justices' work was administrative and financial, not limited to hearing pleas. Roger Howden complained of the cost of the 1198 eyre under Richard I. He wrote, "By these and other vexations, whether just or unjust, the whole of England from sea to sea was reduced to poverty."[20] The Dunstable annalist recorded cryptically that when the itinerant justices came to Cornwall in 1233 everone fled to the woods in fear of them.[21] An extremely biased source, Matthew Paris, viewed the itinerant justices as rapacious royal financial agents. He wrote of the justices of the 1240-41 eyre, "Under the pretence of justice, they collected a huge sum for the use of a King who squandered everything."[22]

Comments on individual judges are rarely encountered, but when they are, they are so cryptic that they offer little real evidence for their careers.[23] An exception is the dramatic condemnation of the life of a royal justice found in the "Vision of Thurkill." It is a description of the punishments in hell awaiting sinners from all levels of society, written in 1206 by Ralph of Coggeshall. Among the sinners is a royal justice, who can be identified as Osbert fitz Hervey, a judge with long experience on the bench under Richard I and John.[24] Ralph described him as "one most expert in worldly law," and "famous throughout England among high and low for his over-

---

[20]*Chronica Magistri Rogeri de Houdene,* ed. William Stubbs, Rolls Series (London, 1868-71), 4:62. Howden also described the visit of the itinerant justices to Boston fair in 1202, where merchants paid heavy fines for the privilege of ignoring the assize of cloth. His comment is, "The said justices gained much money for the King's use, to the injury of many" (4:172).

[21]*Annales Monastici,* ed. H.R. Luard, Rolls Series (London, 1864-69), 3:135. This story has become "a stock example of the eyre's unpopularity," but the situation was unusual because no eyre had been held in Cornwall for over thirty years. C.A.F. Meekings, "The Eyre *ad omnia placita*" (paper read at the Anglo-American Conference of Historians, July 1954, kindly lent to the author by Mrs. Meekings).

[22]*Mattaei Parisiensis, Monachi Sancti Albani, Chronica Majora,* ed. H.R. Luard, Rolls Series (London, 1872-83), 4:51 (Hereafter cited as *Chron. Maj.*). Similarly, Paris referred to money raised by Henry in 1254 as "Whatever he could extract from the rapines of the itinerant justices" (5:458).

[23]Gerald of Wales labelled William of Ste.-Mère-Èglise, one of Henry II's aides and Richard I's judges, *curia sequela est et domini regis familiaris* (*Opera,* 1:260).

[24]H.L.D. Ward, ed., *Journal of the British Archaeological Association,* 31 (1875): 420-59. Ralph did not mention the justice's name, but the identification seems clear. The date of death mentioned in the "Vision"—1206—corresponds with the death of Osbert. Also Ralph, monk at an Essex house, would have known of Osbert, of East Anglian origin and with landholdings there.

flowing eloquence and experience in the law."[25] Most of what was written about the judge is less complimentary, however. He was accused of greedily gaining wealth by taking gifts from litigants on both sides of lawsuits; and worse still, he died without making a will in which he could dispose of his ill-gotten gain with pious gifts. As punishment, the demons in hell invented new tortures, forcing him to gulp down burning coins, then running an iron wheel up and down his back, forcing him to vomit up the coins.[26]

Occasionally chroniclers made brief comments on judges, such as Matthew Paris' remarks on William de Ralegh's consecration as bishop of Norwich in 1239. William was a longtime royal judge, chief justice of the court *coram rege,* and the authority most cited by *Bracton.* The chronicler quoted Luke (15:10), "There is joy among the angels of God over one sinner who repents;" and he expressed the hope that Ralegh, like Matthew, who had fled from taxation to the apostolate, would fly from curial occupations to a summit of great sanctity.[27] Matthew Paris had a practice of penning scathing obituaries for those royal justices he believed had injured his house of St. Albans. He wished to point out that punishment caught up with them. He claimed that Henry of Bath had enriched himself with rents, manors, gold and silver second to none of the justices, and that on a single eyre he had accumulated over 200 librates of land.[28] A number of other judges of Henry III are remembered in Matthew Paris' obituaries.[29]

The chroniclers, even when denouncing royal justices for their misdeeds, usually admitted their knowledge of the law. Matthew Paris' obituary of Thomas of Moulton, sheriff and justice for John and Henry III, described him as "learned in the law, but coveting too much to enlarge his possessions."[30] Paris acknowledged that Henry of Bath was a *miles literatus, legum terrae peritissimus.* He described another of Henry III's justices, John of Lexington, as *vir magnae auctoritate et scientiae.*[31] Another chronicler gave a more detailed description of John's legal training, calling him "learned in both laws, namely canon and civil law."[32] An anonymous

---

[25]Ibid., p. 452.
[26]Ibid., pp. 452-53.
[27]*Chron. Maj.,* 3:617-18.
[28]Ibid., 5:213.
[29]Adam fitz William is described as "a man of the shrewdest sort in worldly affairs and the riches which come from them," in *Gesta Abbatum Monasterii Sancti Albani,* ed. H.T. Riley, Rolls Series (London, 1867-69). Roger of Whitchester is described as a judge who "strove wholly to please the royal will" (*Chron. Maj.,* 5:716).
[30]Ibid., 4:49.
[31]Ibid., 5:213, 384.
[32]*Annales Monastici,* ed. H.R. Luard, Rolls Series (London, 1864-69), 1:345, annals of Burton.

St. Albans chronicler wrote that Roger of Thirkleby and Gilbert of Preston, itinerant justices in Berkshire in 1258-59, were chosen by the community of the land because "they were expert in the law and the most just in exercising judgments."[33]

Yet cases of incompetence or carelessness on the part of justices on eyre can be found easily enough on the plea rolls. One of King John's itinerant justices, Hugh Bardolf, once allowed his chaplain and constable to hear a case in his absence. Because they had wrongly allowed the assize to proceed, even though the tenants had vouched a warrantor and presented charters, the justices at Westminster had the task of correcting their careless act and restoring the victims to their property.[34] The king's council in 1219 found that a group of itinerant justices had wrongly and unjustly hanged two suspects.[35] The head of the party of itinerant justices, Jocelin of Wells, had not been present when sentence was given. Evidently, he had not wanted to share responsibility for a judgment that he regarded as a miscarriage of justice.[36] Later one of the justices of gaol delivery in the summer of 1234 came to the justices at Westminster to tell of his disagreement with the judgment of his colleagues concerning nine prisoners held for homicide.[37] About the same time itinerant justices were amerced for hearing an assize of darrein presentment after a lapse of six months and in spite of an essoin made by the tenant. They pleaded ignorance, and their amercement was remitted, "because they had acted through ignorance rather than through malice."[38] Examples of errors by the justices at Westminster are far less frequent. The first correction by the justices *coram rege* of an error made by the justices of the bench came in 1236. The judges were summoned before King Henry III, where they acknowledged that they had proceeded wrongly, "but that they did not know how better to proceed in the matter."[39]

Medieval English monarchs rarely commissioned "official" histories to combat the anti-government bias of monastic chroniclers.[40] Yet Henry II

---

[33]*Flores Historiarum per Matthaeum Westmonasteriensem collecti,* ed. H.R. Luard, Rolls Series (London, 1890), 2:247.

[34]*Curia Regis Rolls,* ed. C.T. Flower et al. (London, 1922—), 3:87, 97.

[35]Ibid., 8:80-81.

[36]As an ecclesiastic, Jocelin had a legitimate excuse for absenting himself from a "judgment of blood."

[37]Ibid., 15:248, no. 1089, John de Braitoft.

[38]Ibid., 15: 368, no. 1429. A fourteenth-century itinerant justice also confessed his ignorance of the law. Answering a complaint against him, he stated that he was a man of arms and did not know the laws and that his colleague, a man of law, had made all judgments, G.O. Sayles, ed., *Select Cases in the Court of King's Bench under Edward I,* 2, Selden Society, 58 (London, 1938), p. cxxvi.

[39]F.W. Maitland, ed., *Bracton's Note Book* (London, 1887), 3:179-80, no. 1166.

[40]Antonia Gransden, "Propaganda in English Medieval Historiography," *Journal of Medieval History,* 1 (1975): 363-81.

had learned courtiers who were capable of writings which challenged the usual charges against his judges. Some of the writers were royal justices themselves. Not surprisingly, the treatise on English law known as *Glanvill* praises Henry's *curia regis:*

> No judge there is so audacious as to presume to turn aside at all from the path of justice or to digress in any respect from the way of truth. For there, indeed, a poor man is not oppressed by the power of his adversary, nor does favour or partiality drive any man away from the threshold of judgment . . . . *[*The King*]* is ever guided by those of his subjects most learned in the laws and customs of the realm whom he knows to excell all others in sobriety, wisdom and eloquence, and whom he has found to be most prompt and clear-sighted in deciding cases on the basis of justice and in settling disputes, acting now with severity and now with leniency as seems most expedient to them.[41]

Richard fitz Neal, author of the *Dialogus de Scaccario,* served Henry II and his successors not only at the Exchequer but also as judge of common pleas and on eyre in the counties. In his book, he took care to assure his readers that the Exchequer did not function arbitrarily, but followed established rules. He wrote in the Dedication:

> To be sure, the Exchequer has evolved its own rules, not by hazard, but by the deliberation and decisions of great men; and if those rules be observed in every particular, the right of individuals will be maintained, and the reverence due to the Treasury will come to *[*the King*]* in full . . . .[42]

Walter Map shared Richard fitz Neal's favorable view of the Exchequer, finding it "one place in which money can do no miracles, for the glance of the king seems ever fresh there."[43] Fitz Neal's view of the itinerant justices, however, veered far from that of Map. His account of their work was: "They, giving audience in each county, and doing full justice to those who considered themselves wronged, saved the poor both money and labour."[44]

Peter of Blois, who condemned courtiers, had praise for them elsewhere. In 1180, he wrote a letter to the clerk of the royal household, expressing the view that civil servants ought not to be condemned but rather praised:

> Even if they cannot have leisure for prayer and contemplation, *[*they*]* are nevertheless occupied in the public good and often perform works of salvation . . . . I think it is not only laudable but glorious to assist the king, to hold office in the State, not to think of oneself, but to be all for all.[45]

---

[41] G.D.G. Hall, ed. and trans., *Tractatus de Legibus et Consuetudinibus Regni Anglie qui Glanvilla vocatur,* Medieval Texts (London, 1965), Prologue, p. 2.
[42] Charles Johnson, ed. and trans., *Dialogus de Scaccario,* Medieval Texts (London, 1950), p. 3; cf. pp. 7, 13. This translation is from *English Historical Documents,* vol. 2, 1042-1189, ed. David Douglas and George W. Greenway (London, 1968), p. 492.
[43] He concluded, "I heard a judgment there given in favour of a poor man against a rich one," *De Nugis Cur.,* v, 7, p. 253 of James ed.
[44] *Dialogus,* Johnson ed., p. 77.
[45] *Pat. Lat.,* 207, no. 150, col. 440, partial trans. in R.W. Southern, *The Making of the Middle Ages* (London, 1953), pp. 212-13.

In his work as secretary to two archbishops of Canterbury, Peter wrote letters in defense of clerics employed as royal justices. He drafted a letter to the pope for Richard of Dover, defending three bishops whom Henry II had named royal justices in 1179. The letter pointed out that it was useful for bishops to serve on the bench, where they could protect the Church's liberties, monastic property, and the needs of widows, orphans, and the poor.[46] Later, Peter wrote a letter for Hubert Walter, seeking exemption from the rules of residence for a cathedral canon who was a royal justice. His argument was that since the cleric was occupied in "the public business of the king," he was devoting himself to the welfare of all.[47]

The chronicler Master Ralph de Diceto knew many prominent persons at the court of Henry II. He had great respect for the king, and in his history, he wrote favorably of his legal reforms.[48] Ralph praised Henry II for turning to the episcopate, "the sanctuary of God," in 1179 to seek judges who would not oppress the poor or favor the rich. Ralph excused their involvement in worldly matters in violation of canon law, offering as an excuse, "the importunity of the king, his good intentions, and his actions pleasing to God and meet for the praise of men."[49] Yet the three bishops—Geoffrey Ridel, John of Oxford, and Richard of Ilchester—were longtime *familiares regis*, notorious as Henry II's counsellors in his conflict with Becket.

Gervase of Chichester had been their opponent, one of Becket's counsellors, but in his old age he mellowed, admitting that clerics' service in secular government was unavoidable. In his Homilies on Malachias he wrote:

> We do not forbid clerks to do honest service to princes; we only detest the fact that they do it by reason of obsequiousness and greed and that they enjoy it so much.... It will not detract from churchmen's worth and merit if they decide to attach themselves to princely courts and follow laymen's camps, provided that their motive is love and desire to correct the princes or to forward the business of chruches, and providing that they do not harbor ambitions secretly.[50]

The critics of the judges seem to outnumber their supporters. How then are we to evaluate these comments by contemporary writers? Were they justified in their condemnation of royal justices for their ambition, sycophancy, and greed? The judges of the Angevin kings—except for the authors of *Glanvill,* the *Dialogus de Scaccario,* and Bracton's treatise—wrote little that might cast some light on their view of themselves. The earliest surviving letters of royal justices date from the early years of

---

[46]*Pat. Lat.,* 200, no. 96, cols. 1459-61.
[47]Master Thomas of Hurstbourne, *Pat. Lat.,* 207, no. 135, cols. 403-4.
[48]*The Historical Works of Master Ralph of Diceto, Dean of London,* ed. William Stubbs, Rolls Series (London, 1876), 1:434.
[49]*Ralph de Diceto,* 1: 435; trans. in *English Historical Documents,* 2:481-82.
[50]BL. MS. Royal, 3.B.x, f.88[r-v], quoted by Beryl Smalley, *The Becket Conflict and the Schools* (Oxford, 1972), p. 227.

Henry III. The plea rolls do not record principles of judicial conduct, for most cases concluded with a jury's verdict, supposedly a statement of fact.

Yet it is possible to arrive at a reasonable evaluation of the royal judges' performance, responding to their critics. The criticisms of the justices' ambition reflect uneasiness at the growing social mobility, as newcomers rising through the civil service came to threaten the static, hierarchical social structure which conservative writers found comfortable. The men who first formed a professional judiciary in England clearly were ambitious. They were often the first of their family to enter the king's service, and they sought to make of their posts a step on the path to higher social standing.[51] Michael Belet, a judge for both Henry II and Richard I, was able to launch his son Master Michael Belet on a successful career in the civil service by 1199. Master Michael, who succeeded his father as *pincerna* and held other posts, gained three rectories and other proprties as a result of his service to John and Henry III.[52] Simon of Pattishall, perhaps the ablest of King John's justices, founded a family which would remain prosperous into the fourteenth century. Two sons followed him in the royal service, one of whom became bishop of Coventry and Lichfield.[53] Most judges in clerical orders who obtained bishoprics, however, had assisted the king in other capacities.[54] Judges with the most spectacular rise were *familiares regis,* who served the king in a wide range of responsibilities. Typical of these is William Briwerre, who began his career under Henry II as a minor forest officer and ended it under Henry III as a powerful baron.

Sycophancy is a difficult quality to assess, but from what can be discovered of the judges' outlook, they were at the least eager to please their

---

[51] Of fifteen professionals under King John, five were the first of their family to leave their names on the public records: William Briwerre, Walter of Creeping, Simon of Pattishall, James of Potterne, and Master Ralph of Stokes. Seven were from middling knightly families who had some property recorded in final concords, etc.: John of Guestling, Richard of Herriard, Osbert fitz Hervey, Roger Huscarl, Godfrey de Insula, Master Henry (Blund) of London, and Henry of Whiston. Only three had any relatives in the royal service. See the author's "The Judges of King John: Their Background and Training," *Speculum,* 51 (1976): 450-51. Of ten professionals under Richard I, five were of undistinguished origin: Richard Barre, archdeacon of Ely; Geoffrey fitz Peter, the future justiciar; Osbert fitz Hervey; Master Thomas of Hurstbourne; and William de Ste.-Mère-Eglise.

[52] Alfred B. Emden, *A Biographical Register of the University of Oxford to A.D. 1500,* 3 vols. (Oxford, 1957-59), 1:159-60.

[53] See Ralph V. Turner, "Simon of Pattishall", below, p. 212.

[54] Justices serving Richard and John who became bishops include Richard fitz Neal, William de Ste.-Mère-Église, Master Eustace of Fauconberg, and Master Henry of London, all of whom had other important posts. William Ralegh and William of York are two of Henry III's justices who became bishops, and who served him mainly on the bench.

royal master. They were primarily the king's servants, holding other posts along with their places on the bench. They had no sense of being set apart from other branches of the civil service; they were men "who approached their task from the point of view of the organizer, the higher civil servant."[55] The views expressed in *Glanvill,* the Dialogus de *Scaccario,* and *Bracton* on their duties reflect the feelings of other professional royal servants acting as judges. No doubt, the royal justices, viewing themselves first of all as the king's servants, shared the outlook of Richard fitz Neal. He had an exalted view of kingship, defending the doctrine that kings were accountable only to God.[56] In the *Dialogus,* he took pains to assure his pupil that the laws of the Exchequer were not arbitrary, though he admitted that the king sometimes acted arbitrarily. He acknowledged that Henry II denied justice: "For to some he shows the fullness of justice freely out of regard for a service rendered solely out of charity; but to others, by the law of human circumstance, he will not yield for love or money . . . ."[57]

Richard fitz Neal probably represents the feeling of most royal justices that their chief responsibility was to safeguard the king's interest. His pupil made the point, "I observe that with all your moderation you never lose sight of the king's interests."[58] Richard made a similar point, explaining that great men sat at the Exchequer "not merely for the King's profit, but to honour his excellence and royal state."[59] *Bracton* recognized the judges' responsibility for the king's interest in his account of the itinerant justices' oath. According to him, they swore to do right to rich and poor alike, to carry out the articles of the eyre, and to do what is right and just in hearing please of the crown. But he added after the oath, "Let each of them be instructed to promote, to the best of his ability, the advantage of the lord king."[60]

Royal judges often gained experience in financial posts before their appointment to the bench, and they continued to have financial responsibilities. They recognized a duty to increase royal revenues, as can be seen in a letter by one of Henry III's justices. William of York wrote several letters to

---

[55] T.F.T. Plucknett, "The Relations between Roman Law and English Common Law down to the Sixteenth Century," *University of Toronto Law Journal,* 3 (1939-40):32.
[56] *Dialogus,* ed. Johnson, pp. 1-3.
[57] Ibid., p. 120, translation from *English Historical Documents,* 2:564. Fitz Neal also admitted the arbitrary nature of the forest law (*Dialogus,* pp. 59-60).
[58] Ibid. p. 109. Cf. p. 13, "Yet the purpose of all the offices *[at the Exchequer]* is the same, namely to watch over the King's interests, due regard being paid, however, to equity, according to the established rules of the Exchequer."
[59] Ibid., p. 28.
[60] Samuel E. Thorne, trans., *Bracton on the Laws and Customs of England,* 4 vols. (Cambridge, Mass., 1969-77), 2:309, f.109.

his patron, the royal chancellor, in the years 1226-1228. His letters, written with frankness, are rare evidence for the thoughts of a royal justice at the beginning of his career.[61] He took pride in his part in raising royal revenues, boasting that his eyre in 1227 was producing forty marks a day for the king.[62]

Royal justices could visualize their monarch in three capacities: as the source of all justice in England; as the greatest feudatory in the kingdom, lord of many lands; and as a living individual of vast power, whose *ira* and *malevolentia* were to be feared. Possible conflicts among these three roles made the judges' task a difficult one. They recognized that most cases should proceed *secundum legem et consuetudinem Angliae*,[63] but at the same time they recognized the reality of the royal *voluntas*. Old notions of the "tutorial" character of the ruler meant that justice could be seen as a royal grace, not a right but a privilege granted to the people. Judges must have been uncertain where law and custom left off and the king's will began.[64]

Because the monarch was the source of all justice, he had a necessary role in the work of the courts. The justices recognized his role, and they sometimes marked cases *loquendum cum rege*.[65] For example, many suits touched the king in his capacity as feudal lord, and the justices were careful to consult him on questions about royal grants or charters.[66] Twelfth- and thirteenth-century justices knew that the king was a man who could do wrong. From time to time, they witnessed the king's anger: he closed his courts to certain suitors because of his ill-will toward them, or they heard allegations of disseizin *per voluntatem regis*. Yet the courts offered little help to victims of the king's arbitrary acts before the second decade of Henry III's reign.[67] The impact of the royal will on the courts can be exag-

---

[61] C.A.F. Meekings, "Six Letters concerning the Eyres of 1226-28," *English Historical Review*, 65 (1950): 494-95.

[62] Ibid., p. 499, no. iv.

[63] *Curia Regis Rolls*, 8:198, 237; 10:52, 148; 13:96, no. 414; 14:191, no. 936; 375, no. 1751; 15:425, no. 1662.

[64] J.C. Holt, *Magna Carta* (Cambridge, 1965), p. 90; Walter Ullmann, *Principles of Government and Politics in the Middle Ages* (London, 1961), p. 156, and *Law and Politics in the Middle Ages* (Ithaca, N.Y., 1975), p. 58.

[65] See Ralph V. Turner, *The King and his Courts: The Role of John and Henry III in the Administration of Justice 1199-1240* (Ithaca, N.Y., 1968), pp. 127-35, 157, 242.

[66] Henry III's justices stated, "The testimony of the lord king by charter or by word of mouth exceeds all other proof," *Bracton's Note Book*, 2:182-83, no. 239. They also declared that the king was not bound by the regular forms of action in his pleadings, H.G. Richardson and G.O. Sayles, eds., *Select Cases of Procedure without Writ under Henry III*, Selden Society, 90 (London, 1941), p. 36, no. 34.

[67] Ralph V. Turner, "The Royal Courts Treat Disseizin by the King: John and Henry III, 1199-1240," below, pp. 251-68.

gerated, however. Most "common pleas" came to a conclusion without the king's intervention. The judges seem generally to have taken seriously their oath to render justice impartially to all. The plea rolls indicate that in those cases where royal justices had occasion to express opinions—questions of procedure or problems with the law's uncertainty—they sought a reasonable resolution of the problem with concern for the best interests of the contending parties. For example, only two of about 240 cases brought by widows seeking their dower suggest any irregularity, and they were both dismissed without reaching a conclusion due to King John's intervention, not due to the justices' action.[68]

While we can only speculate on the feelings of earlier judges about their responsibilities, a group of itinerant justices in the minority of Henry III pronounced their views clearly in a letter. They protested the action of the council in reversing one of their judgments for political expediency.[69] They stated their concept of their duty in dignified language:

> Since you chose us—we did not choose ourselves—and since you appointed us in this eyre for the peace of the lord king and his kingdom, bound to do justice to one and all, rich and poor without respect of persons, it would seem becoming and honorable . . . that you should not so readily at the suggestion of /certain persons/ believe evil of us . . . . We call Him as witness of our consciences and the searcher of hearts and the knower of secrets that, sitting as a tribunal, we have done nothing of our certain knowledge according to our understanding and intelligence which ought to displease God or men of good will.[70]

They went on to ask that the judgment they had given "in accordance with the due custom of the kingdom" be allowed to stand. These justices were not professional royal servants, but were important in their own right: the bishop of Lincoln; a nephew of the regent, William Marshall; and a baron, a former leader in the rebellion against King John. In this period just after *Magna Carta,* they took seriously their responsibility for rendering justice impartially to all men regardless of the king's wishes. Their complaint was effective in this case, causing the council to reconsider. Possibly itinerant justices, who were often prominent local men, not professional civil servants, were more likely to express independent views.

More easily measurable than ambition or sycophancy is the influence of greed upon the judges, whether their own greed, or that of the king which they hoped to satisfy. The profits of justice were an important source of

---

[68] Sharon T. Ady (M.A. Thesis, Florida State University, 1974).
[69] A suit between the count of Aumale and Gilbert de Gant, *Rolls of the Justices in Eyre for Lincolnshire (1218-19) and Worcestershire (1221),* ed. Doris M. Stenton, Selden Society, 53 (London, 1934), p. 61, no. 151.
[70] *Royal and other Historical Letters Illustrative of the Reign of Henry III,* ed. W.W. Shirley, Rolls Series, (London, 1862-68), I:21; Lady Stenton, trans., *Rolls for Lincolnshire and Worcestershire,* p. lii.

revenue for the Angevin kings, and their judges were very much aware of this, as William of York's letter indicates. Demands of fees for writs, fines to expedite proceedings, and amercements were simply parts of the system. Large sums, or falcons and warhorses, were accepted by the justices on the king's behalf in return for special favors. Such offerings were eagerly sought during John's reign, especially after 1207.[71] Few of these payments can be labelled outright bribery, for they sought to speed the course of a case or to secure some special procedure, not to influence actual judgment.[72]

Amercement was a possibility for anyone involved in an action in the royal courts, not only plaintiffs and tenants but also attorneys, jurors, pledges, and others. As Maitland said, "Any litigant who hoped to get to the end of his suit without an amercement must have been a sanguine man . . . ."[73] Judges had an interest in amercements, for the expenses of justices on eyre were often paid out of the funds that they collected.[74] Yet the justices did sometimes take pity on poor litigants. Notes of pardons of amercements "on account of poverty" appear often on the plea rolls.[75]

Were additional profits from justice, beyond what went into the royal treasury, available to the judges? They sometimes benefitted handsomely from their offices, or from the connections they offered. Favors were accepted freely from litigants in spite of *Bracton*'s warning borrowed from *Ecclesiasticus* (20:31) that "Presents and gifts blind the eyes of judges."[76] Royal justices thought nothing of accepting pensions or grants of land from important people or monastic houses in return for their legal advice. By the end of the thirteenth century and throughout the fourteenth century, justices were regularly accepting annual retaining fees from great men. Public criticism of this practice grew during the course of the fourteenth century, prompting Parliament to make periodic attempts at reform.[77] Neither did justices find it unfitting to accept the hospitality of prominent

---

[71] Flower, *Intro. to Curia Regis Rolls*, pp. 480-495.
[72] Flower, p. 496. Cf. Turner, *King and his Courts*, pp. 274-75.
[73] Pollock and Maitland, 2:519.
[74] Geoffrey Templeman, *The Sheriffs of Warwickshire in the Thirteenth Century*, Dugdale Society, Occasional Papers, no. 7 (Oxford, 1948), p. 22.
[75] Turner, *King and his Courts*, pp. 155-56.
[76] Bracton, 2: 302-3, f. 106b. See Richard de Anesty's account of his payment of 17½ marks to Henry II's justices (*English Historical Documents*, 2:457).
[77] J.R. Maddicott, "Law and Lordship: Royal Justices as Retainers in Thirteenth-and Fourteenth-Century England," *Past and Present*, Supplement 4 (Oxford, 1978). See also G.O. Sayles, ed., *Select cases in the Court of King's Bench*, 1, Selden Society, 55 (London, 1936), pp. lxxvi-viii; and ibid., 7 (74 for 1971), p. xxv. In the early thirteenth century, Simon of Pattishall held land of four monastic houses possibly granted to him in return for legal advice, Turner, "Simon of Pattishall," below, 209, 211.

county families when they made their eyres, even though their hosts might have suits pending.[78]

All this must be put into context, however. A thin line did separate acceptable gifts from unacceptable "bribes." Even John of Salisbury conceded that courtiers could accept gifts, but that they must not "shamelessly extort" them. Before the mid-thirteenth century the king did not pay his justices regular salaries; they depended upon his periodic gifts, uncertain grants of expense money, and custodies of lands.[79] After salaries became customary, they remained inadequate, and royal officials were expected to exploit their posts by taking gifts from petitioners. Judges continued to receive gifts for "expediting" pleas down into the seventeenth century.[80]

The rapid rise of some royal justices seems to validate the charge of greed leveled against them. Men of little substance were able to secure leases, custodies, and permanent grants that raised them into the ranks of substantial landholders. An early example is Osbert fitz Hervey, condemned in the "Vision of Thurkill." He began his career as an obscure East Anglian knight, but at his death he had an income of over £240.[81] This was more than the £202 average annual income of a baron at the beginning of the thirteenth century.[82] Judges in clerical orders perhaps found it easier to accumulate wealth, since the king could reward them with benefices. Martin of Pattishall, prominent on the bench in Henry III's early years, had ecclesiastical preferments valued at 1600 marks; and William of York had preferments worth £800 when he became senior justice *coram rege*.[83] Again the judges' activity must be put into context. They were only one group of royal servants seeking to climb a step or two higher on the social ladder. Other *curiales* succeeded in climbing much higher and more quickly.

---

[78]C.A.F. Meekings, ed., *Crown Pleas of the Wiltshire Eyre, 1249,* Wilts. Archaeol. and Nat. Hist. Soc. Records Branch, 16 (1961), pp. 13-14, for the hospitality of the bishop of Winchester. The Dunstable chronicle in *Annales Monastici,* 3:174, notes two itinerant justices at Dunstable for two days *ad custum prioris.*

[79]Sayles, *Select Cases in King's Bench,* 1: lxxi; Meekings, *Crown Pleas of Wiltshire,* pp. 12-13.

[80]As the impeachment of Sir Francis Bacon shows. What Trevor-Roper wrote about payment of public officials in the Renaissance must have been true centuries earlier. H.R. Trevor-Roper, "The General Crisis of the Seventeenth Century," in *Crisis in Europe 1560-1660,* ed. Trevor Aston (New York, 1967), p. 79. For judges' conduct in Renaissance England, see J.H. Baker, ed., *The Reports of John Spelman,* Selden Society, 94 (London, 1978), 2: 141-42.

[81]*Pipe Roll 8 John,* Pipe Roll Society, new series (London, 1942), pp. 33, 35; *Pipe Roll 9 John* (1946), p. 113.

[82]Sidney Painter, *Studies in the History of the English Feudal Barony,* Johns Hopkins Univ. Studies in Hist. and Pol. Sci., series 61, no. 3 (Baltimore, 1943), p. 170.

[83]C.A.F. Meekings, "Robert of Nottingham, Justice of the Bench, 1244-6," *Bulletin of the Institute of Historical Research,* 41 (1968): 236. Another justice of Henry III who piled up possessions was Robert of Lexington, C.S. Holdsworth, ed., *Rufford Charters,* Thoroton Soc. Rec. Ser., 29 (Nottingham, 1972), 1: xcii-v.

In spite of all the complaints about sale of justice, ordinary freemen flocked to the royal courts. The end of the twelfth and beginning of the thirteenth century saw a surge of suits in the royal courts which continued throughout the thirteenth century: civil pleas rolls of Henry III's reign contain on the average 400 to 500 cases.[84] No doubt, many royal justices were ambitious, sycophantic, and greedy, and complaints about these failings were frequent. Far less frequent, even among writings of their severest critics, were complaints of the judges' incompetence or ignorance of the law, even though such was sometimes the case, at least among the itinerant justices. Apparently most Englishmen found royal justices' standards of conduct acceptable. Certainly the standard they found in the courts of the Angevin kings was no lower than that of the ecclesiastical courts, including the papal *curia* at Rome.[85] Chroniclers and moralists wrote for their own purposes, a high moral one in the case of John of Salisbury, one of petty vindictiveness in the case of Matthew Paris. Whatever their purpose in condemning the judges, they were advocating an ideal in conflict with the realities of medieval life, given the inadequate provision for payment of royal officers and the propensity of petitioners for offering them gifts.

[84] M.T. Clancy, ed., *Civil Pleas of the Wiltshire Eyre, 1249,* Wiltshire Records Society, 25 (Devizes, 1971), p. 9.

[85] For writings critical of the Church courts, see J.A. Yunck, *The Lineage of Lady Meed* (Notre Dame, 1963).

7

The *Miles Literatus* in Twelfth- and Thirteenth-Century England: How Rare a Phenomenon?

Must we assume that medieval administrators were always accompanied by clergymen to read to them, write their letters, and figure their accounts? A misconception about the Middle Ages that dies hard is that laymen were by definition illiterate and that the Church alone could provide kings and princes with professional administrators. The growth of a literate laity is usually associated with the rise of towns and tradesmen, not with the nobles and knights of the countryside.[1] T. F. Tout, for example, assumed that the *miles literatus* was a "rare phenomenon" in England even as late as the mid-thirteenth century. Like too many others, he presupposed the static character of medieval life, unaware that the lives of the nobility changed sharply after about 1100. And the myth of lay illiteracy has survived despite the challenge of studies published as long ago as the 1930s.[2] True, the works of both James

---

I wish to thank Michael Clanchy of Glasgow University and Edward J. Kealey of Holy Cross College for their helpful comments. I also wish to thank Eleanor Rathbone for allowing me to consult her unpublished dissertation, "The Influence of Bishops and Members of Cathedral Bodies in the Intellectual Life of England, 1066-1216" (University of London, 1935).

[1] The statements found in textbooks on the history of Western civilization are less surprising than those found in medieval texts: "But reading, which fills so many hours for the modern man of leisure, was literally a closed book to most of the medieval nobility"; Wallace K. Ferguson and Geoffrey Bruun, *A Survey of European Civilization*, 1 (4th ed., Boston, 1969): 221. "Since the elder son of nobility, who was to inherit the lands, was ordinarily occupied with the long, arduous training in the use of weapons required for knighthood, he usually had no formal education to speak of"; William Langer *et al.*, *Western Civilization*, 1 (2d ed., New York, 1975): 314. "The education of the noble youth consisted of little else than training for the profession of arms"; Robert S. Hoyt, *Europe in the Middle Ages* (2d ed., New York, 1966), 303. "Neither nobles nor peasants found it useful to educate their children academically," but "the sons of medieval merchants were taught to read and write Latin"; Jeffrey Burton Russell, *Medieval Civilization* (New York, 1968), 494. "Schooling was peculiarly an urban phenomenon. . . . Unlike the nobles, a high proportion of tradesmen could read"; Charles T. Wood, *The Quest for Eternity: Medieval Manners and Morals* (Garden City, N.Y., 1971), 113-14. And histories of education repeat the same clichés: "The nobility had little concern with academic learning in any form. . . . The warrior knight became the aristocratic ideal and his training in military accomplishments had little concern with literacy"; James Bowen, *A History of Western Education* (London, 1975), 21, 25-26. Carlo M. Cipolla has recognized that around 1100 educational opportunities increased, but he has also linked this change to the *bourgeoisie*: "Two cultures developed side by side: an urban culture that was essentially literate, and a rural culture essentially illiterate"; Cipolla, *Literacy and Development in the West* (Harmondsworth, Middlesex, 1969), 55, and also see *ibid.*, 41-44, 55-56.

[2] Marc Bloch, *La société féodale*, 2 vols. (Paris, 1939-40), translated by L. A. Manyon as *Feudal Society*, 2 vols. (London, 1961), 1: 79-80; V. H. Galbraith, "The Literacy of the Medieval English Kings," *Proceedings of the British Academy*, 21 (1935): 201-37; James Westfall Thompson, *The Literacy of the Laity in the Middle Ages* (Berkeley and Los Angeles, 1939); and Lynn Thorndike, "Elementary and Secondary Education in the

Westfall Thompson and V. H. Galbraith chiefly considered the education of princes and great nobles, not simple knights; and Galbraith concluded that a significant level of lay literacy arose only when the vernacular pushed Latin aside. Yet Thompson was able to suggest that "the English nobility of the high Middle Ages were more familiar with Latin than is commonly assumed."[3]

Recent research in Anglo-Norman and Angevin royal administration reveals that Thompson's speculation was close to the mark. The Angevin kings were not as dependent upon the Church for their civil servants as has been thought. Those who did the day-to-day work that made Angevin government so effective were largely laymen, and they came chiefly from the knightly class, not the *bourgeoisie*. Henry II and his sons made increasing use of written records in their governments; and a process of "bureaucratization" was clearly underway. This reliance upon the written record can be seen in the writs, pipe rolls, plea rolls, feet of fines, and chancery enrollments. The value of written records was soon appreciated by those outside the government. By the mid-thirteenth century, if not earlier, manorial bailiffs maintained written accounts, and even villeins kept charters to record their sales and purchases of small parcels of land.[4]

Although sheriffs, barons of the exchequer, justices of the bench, and other officials may have employed scribes to do their writing for them, that is not necessarily a sign of their illiteracy. Reading and writing were not yet linked together, as they are today. Writing was a specialized craft not easily mastered—a point illustrated in an earlier age by Einhard's account of Charlemagne's futile efforts to learn to write long after he had learned to read. And in the twelfth century even monastic houses hired scribes for routine secretarial work.[5] Nevertheless, the royal officials needed to be able to read the writs and rolls for themselves. Those two puncturers of myths in English medieval history, H. G. Richardson and G. O. Sayles, have been busy here, seeking to establish "that laymen engaged in public administration involving the use of written documents were sufficiently literate for the task."[6] Their essay points up the need for a closer look at the problem of the *miles literatus* in twelfth- and thirteenth-century England.

Since it is unlikely that all of the laymen in the royal government can have

---

Middle Ages," *Speculum*, 15 (1940): 400-08. For Tout's assumptions, see his *Chapters in the Administrative History of Medieval England*, 6 vols. (Manchester, 1920-37), 1: 205, 288 n. 2, 3: 202. On the changing character of medieval society around 1100, see Bloch, *Feudal Society*, 2: 422.

[3] Galbraith, "Literacy of Medieval English Kings," 225; and Thompson, *The Literacy of the Laity in the Middle Ages*, 180. But K. B. McFarlane, unlike Galbraith, found evidence for a continued sound grounding in Latin among the aristocracy for the late Middle Ages; McFarlane, *The Nobility of Later Medieval England* (Oxford, 1973), chap. 6: "The Education of the Nobility in Later Medieval England."

[4] M. M. Postan and C. N. L. Brooke, eds., *Carte Nativorum*, Northampton Record Society (Northampton, 1960), xxxviii, xliii; and Dorothea Oschinsky, *Walter of Henley and Other Treatises on Estate Management and Accounting* (Oxford, 1971), 64.

[5] Eginhard, *Vie de Charlemagne*, ed. and trans. Louis Halphen (Paris, 1923), 29-30; and David Knowles, *The Monastic Order in England, 943-1216* (Cambridge, 1953), 520.

[6] Richardson and Sayles, *The Governance of Mediaeval England from the Conquest to Magna Carta* (Edinburgh, 1963), 277. And more generally, see *ibid.*, chap. 15: "Statecraft and Learning."

been unlettered in Latin, answers to three questions must be sought: Did laymen hold government posts that required literacy? What is the evidence for laymen literate in Latin? And where did such laymen learn their letters? It may not be possible to answer these questions in a fully satisfying fashion, for little direct evidence for education of the laity survives from before the fourteenth century. But, even though answers must be tentative and based in part on speculation, it is long past time to raise the questions.

THE MADDENINGLY IMPRECISE USE of the term *clericus* in Latin ("clerk" in English) presents a semantic obstacle in trying to answer these questions. When authors—medieval or modern—use the term, do they mean it in the religious sense of "cleric," one who is in holy orders or at least tonsured? Or do they mean it in the bookish sense of an accountant, secretary, scribe, or scholar? According to Charles du Cange, in the twelfth century the terms *clerici* and *scholares* were not yet synonomous. Leona Gabel has further shown that in the time of Henry I the term *clericus* meant "a clerk in holy orders"— that is, presumably in major orders—and that by the reign of Henry III the term was also applied to those who had first tonsure; by the fourteenth and fifteenth centuries, it applied to all who could demonstrate their literacy.[7] It is paradoxical that, in those centuries when more and more laymen were gaining an ability to read, literacy should have come to stand as the legal test for clerical status. To extend the jurisdiction of its courts, the Church encouraged a broad definition of clerical status and readily tonsured those who sought it.[8] The possibility of gaining benefit of clergy in late medieval England by reading a verse of Scripture has doubtless contributed to the modern myth of the illiteracy of the laity throughout the Middle Ages.

When one became a *clericus* in the religious sense is significant for defining the status of students in the Middle Ages. Scholars have long assumed that students in the schools were *clerici*—tonsured, in clerical garb, and subject to the ecclesiastical courts, whether or not they were in one of the seven major orders of the Church. M.-M. Davy has demonstrated that before 1200 students, at least in Paris, were not necessarily considered members of the clergy, and only in that year did they fall fully under canon law and the Church courts.[9] Students' clerical status, assumed only because of their student status, did not commit them to ecclesiastical careers upon completion of their studies. According to canon law, tonsuring was not an irreversible process, and it alone did not admit one to minor orders, although a candidate was usually tonsured at the time of his admission to the first of the minor orders.

---

[7] Du Cange, *Glossarium mediae et infimae latinitatis*, 10 vols. in 11 (Paris, 1883–87), 3: 367–70; and Gabel, *Benefit of Clergy in England in the Later Middle Ages* (Northampton, Mass., 1928–29), 62–65.

[8] M.-M. Davy, "La situation juridique des étudiants de l'Université de Paris au XIIIe siècle," *Revue d'histoire de l'Église de France*, 17 (1939): 300–04.

[9] *Ibid.*, 300. But see Hastings Rashdall, *The Universities of Europe in the Middle Ages*, ed. F. M. Powicke and Alfred B. Emden, 1 (2d ed., Oxford, 1936): 393–95; and Margaret Deanesly, "Medieval Schools to ca. 1300," in J. B. Bury *et al.*, eds., *Cambridge Medieval History*, 5 (Cambridge, 1929): 767–68.

Nothing prevented those who actually took minor orders from later choosing a secular occupation and living a secular life, even marrying. They could then be "clerks" in the bookish sense—though no longer in the religious sense— and serve as notaries or "clerical odd-job men" to draw up legal documents.[10] Many of the *milites literati* may fall into such a category: men who had once taken minor orders but who subsequently devoted themselves entirely to worldly work. Only those who were in major orders—subdeacons or higher— were likely to find permanent careers in the Church, holding benefices with care of souls.

Another word that wants a definition in keeping with medieval usage is *literatus*. What could be more confused than Matthew Paris's description of Paulin Piper, one of Henry III's royal officers, as "quidam miles literatus sive clericus militaris"?[11] Du Cange has noted that *literatus* was a synonym for *clericus* and was also used in monastic writings to distinguish choir monks from lay brothers or *conversi*.[12] Clearly, medieval writers often meant more by the term than merely the ability to read. A more accurate translation in many cases might be "learned"—that is, soundly grounded in classical literature.[13] Critics of ecclesiastical officers often called them *illiterati*, which certainly did not mean the inability to read a text.[14] For example, an opponent of Ralph Neville, a thirteenth-century bishop of Chichester and royal chancellor, called him a "curialem . . . et illiteratum."[15] Royal administrators may have been then *illiterati* in the Latin of their contemporaries because of their ignorance of rules of classical rhetoric, but not "illiterate" in today's English usage. A *miles literatus*, a "learned knight," was rare enough to arouse comment by a chronicler, but not a knight who was merely literate in today's sense. There were, then, three levels of literacy in the twelfth and thirteenth centuries: (1) the professional man of letters; (2) the cultivated amateur; and (3) the pragmatic reader. The adjective *literatus* applies to the first two but not the third.[16] Most knights were at least pragmatic readers, functional literates in today's terms, capable of handling simple Latin as a tool in their many tasks of government.

---

[10] R. R. Bolgar, *The Classical Heritage and Its Beneficiaries from the Carolingian Age to the End of the Renaissance* (Cambridge, 1954), 416 n. 195; "Tonsure," *New Catholic Encyclopedia*, 14 (1967): 199; Rashdall, *Universities of Europe in the Middle Ages*, 394–95; and H. G. Richardson, "The Oxford Law School under John," *Law Quarterly Review*, 57 (1949): 335. Gervase of Tilbury was one cleric, a canonist, who sought a secular career and eventually married; H. G. Richardson, "Gervase of Tilbury," *History*, 46 (1961): 114. Gervase of Chichester, one of Becket's *eruditi*, complained of those who abandoned clerical orders in order to take secular posts; Beryl Smalley, *The Becket Conflict and the Schools* (Oxford, 1976), 226.

[11] Matthew Paris, *Chronica majora*, ed. H. R. Luard, Rolls Series, no. 57, 7 vols. (London, 1872–84), 5: 242.

[12] Du Cange, *Glossarium mediae et infimae latinitatis*, 5: 127.

[13] On use of the terms in fourteenth-century England, see McFarlane, *The Nobility of Later Medieval England*, 235.

[14] For the problem of defining literacy and illiteracy, see Cipolla, *Literacy and Development in the West*, chap. 1.

[15] For this epithet of Simon Langton, see Matthew Paris, *Chronica majora*, 3: 207. In the eleventh century, the prior of Bec was also described as an *illiteratus*; John A. Giles, ed., *Vita Lanfranci*, 1 (Oxford, 1844): 281–83.

[16] For the development of this classification, see M. B. Parkes, "Literacy of the Laity," in D. Daicher and A. Thorlby, eds., *The Medieval World* (London, 1972), 555–77.

By the time of Henry II, royal government was growing rapidly, expanding its scope of activity, and requiring more officers. The king continued to depend upon the clergy for many of his servants. The office of treasurer traditionally went to a cleric until 1340, when it was first given to a knight. A cleric also always held the office of chancellor until 1340. Since the chancellor was often a bishop, his secretaries were clerics, in many instances members of his episcopal household. Indeed, clerics continued to play prominent roles in English government until the fall of Thomas, Cardinal Wolsey in the sixteenth century. Medieval monarchs may have felt that clerics made more pliable servants—ones less likely to put family interests first, less likely to build up landed inheritances. But clerical civil servants were almost as susceptible to these temptations as laymen. Thus, medieval kings relied mainly upon clergymen to staff their secretariats neither because they were celibate nor because they were the only available literates but because they could hold ecclesiastical benefices, which made it possible to provide their livings—their pay—at the Church's expense.

The lay element in royal administration, however, increased after the mid-twelfth century, and perhaps earlier. The sheriff was generally a layman, first from among the baronage and later from among the knights.[17] He had lay assistants, undersheriffs, who had about the same social rank as the estate stewards of great barons. The novelty of Henry I's policy of raising new men "from the dust" to help him govern may be questioned, but there can be no dispute that he depended heavily upon laymen in governing England. William T. Reedy has identified eleven itinerant justices under Henry I, all of whom appear to have been laymen; and C. Warren Hollister has more recently described Henry I's *curiales*, many of whom were laymen.[18] Later, one of Henry II's judicial experiments was to assign five members of his household—two clerics and three laymen—to hear pleas.[19] The first of the "chief justiciars," Roger of Salisbury, was an ecclesiastic, but under Henry II and his sons the post frequently fell to a layman. Seven of the thirteen justiciars who held office from the time of Henry I until the extinction of the position under Henry III were laymen, and four of the clerics served under Richard I. The chamberlains of Henry I and of Henry II and his sons were always laymen of knightly rank, and the chamber staff included more laymen than clerics. The stewards of the royal household were also laymen, even though they had to be able to keep accounts; and one of them—Henry III's steward, John of Lexington—was praised by the chroniclers for his learning.[20]

---

[17] Occasionally a bishop held a shrievalty. For examples, see Public Record Office, *Lists and Indexes*, vol. 9: *List of Sheriffs for England and Wales from the Earliest Times to A.D. 1831* (London, 1898).
[18] Reedy, "The Origins of the General Eyre in the Reign of Henry I," *Speculum*, 41 (1966): 698–704; and Hollister and John W. Baldwin, "The Rise of Administrative Kingship: Henry I and Philip Augustus," *AHR*, 83 (1978): 867–90 (above). Also see—for Geoffrey of Clinton, Henry I's chamberlain—R. W. Southern, *Medieval Humanism and Other Studies* (New York, 1970), 214.
[19] William Stubbs, ed., *Gesta Regis Henrici Secundi*, 1, Rolls Series, no. 50 (London, 1867): 207–08.
[20] According to Matthew Paris, John of Lexington was a man of great authority and knowledge (*scientia*), and, according to the Chronicle of Burton, he was a layman skilled in civil and canon law; Matthew Paris, *Chronica majora*, 5: 384; and H. R. Luard, ed., *Annales Monastici*, 1, Rolls Series, no. 36 (London, 1864): 345. Even the stewards of private households kept accounts of daily expenses. The earliest surviving one dates

More significant than those who held some formal title in Angevin government were the *familiares regis* or *curiales*, men of diverse social standing who had the king's confidence and who were ready to serve him in any capacity: as sheriffs, custodians of castles, barons of the Exchequer, itinerant justices, ambassadors abroad, even generals. Their work was so wide-ranging that it is impossible to list them under any one branch of government.[21] Although their names appear frequently in the records, not much is known about them. No one has made a detailed study of the *familiares* of Henry II, but many—perhaps most—of them were laymen.[22] Sidney Painter has identified five trusted agents who were among King John's *familiares*, men below the great officers of state but almost their equals in administrative responsibility: William Marshal, William de Braose, Peter des Roches, Hugh Bardolf, and William Briwerre.[23] Of these five key figures, only one—Peter des Roches—was in clerical orders.

Some of the "men of all work" can be identified through the feet of fines, records of agreements made at the exchequer, on eyres, or later before the bench at Westminster. Many of the Angevin kings' *familiares* spent part of their time as judges; their names thus survive as witnesses to the final concords. A significant number of names on these records are those of laymen. In the years before 1179, when a group of justices was appointed to hear pleas, Henry II periodically sent out groups of itinerant justices, many of whom were also barons of the exchequer. Of over forty men, some can only be identified by their names on the feet of fines, but, of those about whom more is known, at least twenty-six were laymen and only five were clerics. Between 1179 and 1189, forty-eight different justices witnessed fines made at Westminster, and twenty of these were laymen. Raoul C. van Caenegem has calculated that of all of Henry II's judges only about a dozen, "not even ten percent of the total force of justices," had the title *magister*, which is indicative of formal study at a cathedral school.[24] During the reign of Richard I, some sixty men served on the bench. Certain names recur often enough that those men can be considered professional royal servants specializing in the work of justice, even though it is not yet appropriate to speak of a professional judiciary. Five of the ten professionals who served Richard were laymen. Of the roughly ninety

---

from 1265, that of the countess of Leicester; see Margaret Labarge, *A Baronial Household of the Thirteenth Century* (New York, 1965), 13, 60.

[21] W. L. Warren, *Henry II* (Berkeley and Los Angeles, 1973), 310; and Doris M. Stenton, "England: Henry II," in Bury et al., *Cambridge Medieval History*, 579–80. For one very precise definition of Henry I's *curiales*, see Hollister and Baldwin, "The Rise of Administrative Kingship: Henry I and Philip Augustus," 887, table 3 (above).

[22] For the names of some of them, see Warren, *Henry II*, 308–14; and Stenton, "England: Henry II," 579–81.

[23] Painter, *The Reign of King John* (Baltimore, 1949), 70–71.

[24] Van Caenegem, *The Birth of the English Common Law* (Cambridge, 1973), 23. For the justices of this period, see Doris M. Stenton, ed., *Pleas before the King or His Justices, 1198–1202*, Selden Society, 4 vols. (London, 1952–66), 3: app. 1: "The Development of the Judiciary, 1100–1215," xlvii–ccxciv. Of the forty-eight justices of the years 1179–89, another twenty were ecclesiastics, including eight bishops, while the status of eight is unknown. For biographical details, unfortunately not always reliable, see Edward Foss, *The Judges of England* (London, 1848), vols. 1–2.

men who assisted King John as judges, many were great men of the kingdom sitting briefly with the king or local notables with temporary appointments as itinerant justices, but fifteen regularly served as royal judges at Westminster. Eleven of these fifteen were laymen. During the minority of Henry III, four of the seven justices sitting with regularity at Westminster were laymen.[25] Frederic William Maitland stressed the ecclesiastical character of the English judiciary in the age of Glanvill, and T. F. T. Plucknett agreed that the English judiciary was largely clerical in composition until 1300.[26] But a look at the lists of judges under Henry II, his two sons, and his grandson shows a large lay contingent a century earlier. England, moreover, was not alone in having numbers of laymen learned in the law. The Latin Kingdom of Jerusalem produced a remarkable group of jurists who were laymen of noble rank and acquainted with a broad range of legal literature.[27]

WERE THESE LAYMEN who carried out so many tasks of government in twelfth-century England all illiterates? The constantly increasing number of written documents with which they had to cope implies at least their pragmatic literacy. Yet the traditional view is that they were unable to read and that they relied upon clerks to maintain the necessary records.[28] V. H. Galbraith, an expert on medieval public records, maintained that the clergy monopolized record keeping as long as the government's language remained Latin and that only a return to the vernacular broke that monopoly.[29] But as Thompson, Richardson and Sayles, and others have pointed out, laymen learned in Latin were not unknown in the years following 1100. References to literate laymen can occasionally be found in chronicles; other evidence is less direct. Galbraith's own work on the literacy of the English monarchs supplies such indirect evidence, for the education of the magnates' children must have paralleled that of the royal heirs. Galbraith pointed out that the kings before 1100 were largely illiterate; in the twelfth and thirteenth centuries princes were taught to read Latin; and by the late Middle Ages they learned French and English, as first French and then English replaced Latin as the language of government.

Henry I *Beauclerc* has an exaggerated reputation for learning that did not arise until long after his death. Charles W. David has made a detailed study of the sources of the king's reputation and concluded, "It cannot be doubted

---

[25] Those who served at least ten terms on the bench are counted as professionals. Possibly, the relatively large number of lay justices who served under John is in part due to John's quarrel with Pope Innocent III, for clerics could not serve an excommunicate king. For Henry III's justices, I consulted an unpublished list compiled by the late C. A. F. Meekings, who kindly allowed me to use it.

[26] Frederick Pollock and F. W. Maitland, *History of English Law before the Time of Edward I*, 1 (2d ed., Cambridge, 1898): 133–35, 205; and Plucknett, "The Place of the Legal Profession in the History of English Law," *Law Quarterly Review*, 48 (1932): 328–40.

[27] Jonathan Riley-Smith, *The Feudal Nobility and the Kingdom of Jerusalem, 1174–1277* (London, 1973), chap. 6: "A School of Feudal Jurists," 121–44.

[28] Tout, for example, stated, "As in the exchequer, knights [of the chamber] could only keep account by tallies, and could not write letters at all. . . . There was, therefore, an imperative need in the camera for a staff of experts in writing and finance"; *Chapters in the Administrative History of Medieval England*, 1: 116.

[29] Galbraith, "Literacy of the Medieval English Kings," 225, 229–30.

that Henry had his opportunity to learn Latin, and that he did acquire a considerable, though by no means complete, mastery of the language. But it is equally certain that his great fame as a learned king is the product of a later age, not of the age in which he lived."[30] Henry's first wife, Matilda, was a woman with a strong interest in letters, which she had learned under an aunt who was a nun. And their court was clearly a cultural center, where youths such as Henry's natural son, Robert of Gloucester, and his nephew, Stephen of Blois, as well as the sons of other aristocrats came to learn Latin letters.[31]

Henry II provides evidence for the greater emphasis given to studies by the mid-twelfth century, for he had an excellent education. He attracted to his court a brilliant group of writers, who commented favorably upon his learning in their works. And he made certain that all of his sons mastered the elements of Latin. Each boy had a *magister* or *preceptor*, one of the *familiares regis*, charged with general supervision of his upbringing. The *preceptor* of the young Henry was Thomas Becket, who may not have taken his responsibility too seriously; he left the boy's formal schooling to tutors.[32] Peter of Blois wrote a letter in which he expressed the fear that the knightly side of the young Henry's education was being emphasized at the expense of the liberal arts. Certainly, the young king's career indicates that the fear was justified, for the code of chivalry weighed more heavily in motivating him than did the classics. Yet Gervase of Tilbury, who belonged to his household for several years, wrote a book of jests for him and started a second work on the assumption that he would be able to read them.[33] Richard I is usually linked in modern minds with French chivalric literature, but he was equally at ease with Latin. He knew the language well enough to correct the grammar of Hubert Walter, archbishop of Canterbury.[34] The youngest of Henry's sons, John, was first sent to the monks and nuns of Fontevrault; later, he was handed over to Ranulf de Glanvill, the justiciar, who served as his *magister*. King John certainly had some interest in literature, for he owned a collection of the classics and devotional works that he left for safekeeping at Reading Abbey.[35]

---

[30] David, "The Claim of King Henry I to be Called Learned," in Charles H. Taylor and John L. LaMonte, eds., *Anniversary Essays in Medieval History by Students of Charles Homer Haskins* (Boston, 1929), 56. Galbraith agreed with David; "Literacy of Medieval English Kings," 211–12. But Thompson wrote, "It seems probable that Henry I was a better scholar, and more entitled to his title of Beauclerc, than Professor David would permit us to believe"; *The Literacy of the Laity in the Middle Ages*, 170.

[31] M. Dominica Legge, "L'influence littéraire de la cour d'Henri Beauclerc," in Fred Dethier, ed., *Mélanges offerts à Rita Lejeune*, 1 (Gembloux, 1969): 679–87; R. H. C. Davis, *King Stephen* (Berkeley and Los Angeles, 1967), 4; and Leslie Stephen and Sidney Lee, eds., *The Dictionary of National Biography* [hereafter *DNB*], 22 vols. (London, 1885–1901), *sub nom.* "Matilda" and "Robert of Gloucester."

[32] For contemporary comments on Henry II's learning, see, for example, Walter Map, *De nugis curialium*, ed. M. R. James, C. N. L. Brooke, R. A. B. Mynors (Oxford, 1983), 237–42; Gerald of Wales, *Opera*, ed. J. S. Brewer, J. F. Dimock, and G. F. Warner, 8 vols., Rolls Series, no. 21 (London, 1861–91), 5: 302–06, 6: 213–15, as cited in Warren, *Henry II*, 208. For the king's education, see Warren, *Henry II*, 38–39; for that of his sons, see Thompson, *The Literacy of the Laity in the Middle Ages*, 178.

[33] Letter of Peter of Blois, written in the name of the archbishop of Rouen, in Jacques-Paul Migne, ed., *Patrologiae cursus completus . . . series Latina*, 207 (Paris, 1862): cols. 210–12; and Richardson, "Gervase of Tilbury," 105. Also see Thompson, *The Literacy of the Laity in the Middle Ages*, 178.

[34] Gerald of Wales, *Opera*, 3: 30.

[35] W. L. Warren, *King John* (Harmondsworth, Middlesex, 1966), 41; Austin Lane Poole, *From Domesday Book to Magna Carta, 1087–1216*, vol. 3 of *The Oxford History of England* (2d ed., Oxford, 1955), 243; and Thompson, *The Literacy of the Laity in the Middle Ages*, 179.

When the death of John left the nine-year-old Henry III as king, responsibility for the boy's formal schooling lay with Peter des Roches, while his training for knighthood was in the charge of Philip of Aubenay.[36] Galbraith and Thompson, stressing the rise of French as a literary language by the thirteenth century, have tended to doubt Henry III's ability to read Latin.[37] But everything known of his character and interests points toward the assumption that he had mastered Latin at least as well as his fathers and uncles had.

The care that Henry I took in the education of Robert of Gloucester, his illegitimate son, shows that not just royal heirs were thought to need schooling in the early twelfth century. Robert's early education was entrusted to the bishop of Lincoln, Robert Bloet, who had a reputation as a patron of letters. His pupil grew up to become the patron of several writers, most notably William of Malmesbury.[38] The ideas of the earls and barons about the education of their children cannot have been different from those of their lord, the king. A son of Hugh Otwell, earl of Chester, must have gained some skill in letters, for he was a *tutor et paedagogus* at the court of Henry I. Whether he was in clerical orders is unknown.[39] Two great nobles who had remarkable reputations for learning were Waleran of Meulan, earl of Worcester, and his twin brother Robert, earl of Leicester. In 1118, when the twins were fourteen, they were sent to the court of Henry I for advanced schooling. The next year, when the pope and the king met in Normandy, the two boys astonished the cardinals with their dialectical skill. And the testimony of Geoffrey of Monmouth for Waleran and of Richard fitz Neal for Robert, for example, points to the learning of these two young nobles.[40] Another great noble who demonstrated his learning in Latin and likewise received his education at the court of Henry I was Brian fitz Count, lord of Wallingford, an ardent advocate of the empress Matilda. He wrote a pamphlet—which, unfortunately, no longer survives—in support of Matilda's claims against Stephen and a letter—which does survive—denouncing those who had broken their oaths and abandoned her. His letter, "though not unimpeachable in the point of Latinity, bears out his reputation as a man of some learning and acute intelligence."[41]

---

[36] F. M. Powicke, *King Henry III and the Lord Edward: The Community of the Realm in the Thirteenth Century*, 1 (Oxford, 1947): 9.

[37] Galbraith, "Literacy of the Medieval English Kings," 215; and Thompson, *The Literacy of the Laity in the Middle Ages*, 180.

[38] For Bloet, see Henry of Huntingdon, *Historia Anglorum*, ed. Thomas Arnold, Rolls Series, no. 74 (London, 1879), 298–300, as cited in Martin Brett, *The English Church under Henry I* (Oxford, 1975), 174–75. Brett notes that possibly another royal bastard was entrusted to Alexander, Robert Bloet's successor; *English Church under Henry I*, 175. For William of Malmesbury, see G. E. Cockayne, *The Complete Peerage of England, Scotland, Ireland, Great Britain, and the United Kingdom*, ed. V. Gibbs et al., 13 vols. (London, 1910–59), 5: 686 n. a.

[39] Richardson and Sayles, *The Governance of Mediaeval England*, 272–73.

[40] William of Malmesbury, *Gesta Regum Anglorum*, ed. William Stubbs, 2, Rolls Series, no. 90 (London, 1889): 482; Geoffrey of Monmouth, *Historia regum Brittaniae*, ed. Jacob Hammer (Cambridge, Mass., 1951), prefatory letter; and Charles Johnson, ed., *Dialogus de Scaccario* (London, 1950), 57.

[41] H. W. C. Davis, "Henry of Blois and Brian fitz Count," *English Historical Review* [hereafter *EHR*], 25 (1910): 298–99.

ALTHOUGH ELUSIVE, ISOLATED EVIDENCE of educated laymen of lesser rank survives from the first half of the twelfth century. Among the letters of Herbert, bishop of Norwich, is one written at the beginning of the century that praises the style of a lay correspondent, a certain John, who may have been a former student at the Norwich priory school.[42] Orderic Vitalis, the Anglo-Norman chronicler, described some Norman knights who entered the house of Saint Evroul as "well versed in learning," and he explained that some of them were able to take charge of the administration of the abbey's business affairs. He described the knights who protected the abbey of Maule as coming often to the cloister to discuss with the monks "practical as well as speculative matters."[43] In the late 1130s a Yorkshire baron, Walter Espec, possessed a copy of Geoffrey of Monmouth's *Historiae regum Brittaniae*, which he lent to another northern landholder, Ralph fitz Gilbert. Ralph's wife, Constance, a Hampshire heiress, then lent the book to Geoffrey Gaimar, who used it in the composition of *L'estoire des Engleis*.[44] According to Gaimar, Constance was a woman of some education, for she had paid a silver mark for a *Life of Henry I* written by the historian David, and "en sa chambre sovent le lit."[45]

Sanson de Nantuil made a French translation of the Proverbs of Solomon in the middle of the century as an aid to the study of the Latin text for Roger de Condet, a boy of about twelve. The lad was the son of Robert de Condet, a Lincolnshire knight, and of Alice, who was probably a daughter of Earl Ranulf of Chester.[46] Philip, son of Earl Patrick of Salisbury, went off to Italy to study in the law schools of Bologna in the 1160s while retaining his lay status. In the late twelfth century Gilbert fitz Baderon, lord of Monmouth, had a collection of books in his castle, both French and Latin, according to the poet—Hue de Rutland—whose patron he was. A master was engaged for the grandsons of the earl of Oxford sometime around 1187.[47]

By the late twelfth century, evidence that literacy had spread beyond the clergy, the monarch, and the great barons becomes easier to find. In the courtly romances it is not uncommon to see indications of literacy among noblemen—or even among ladies—where in the earlier *chansons de geste* literate laymen were regarded as something upon which to remark.[48] Gerald of Wales

---

[42] Herbert de Losinga, *Epistolae Herberti de Losinga, Osberti de Clara et Elmeri Prioris Cantuariensis*, ed. Robert Anstruther, Caxton Society (London, 1846), nos. 45, 58, as cited in Richardson and Sayles, *The Governance of Mediaeval England*, 272. James W. Alexander has suggested that the layman was a former student at the priory school.

[43] Orderic Vitalis, *The Ecclesiastical History of Orderic Vitalis*, ed. and trans. Marjorie Chibnall, 4 vols. (vols. 2-5) (Oxford, 1969-75), 3: 118-19, 206-07.

[44] M. Dominica Legge, *Anglo-Norman Literature and Its Background* (Oxford, 1963), 28, 277.

[45] Legge, "L'influence littéraire de la cour d'Henri Beauclerc," 683. David's life of Henry I seems to have been in verse, set to music, and most likely in Anglo-Norman, not Latin; Antonia Gransden, *Historical Writing in England, c. 550-c. 1307* (Ithaca, N.Y., 1974), 211.

[46] Legge, *Anglo-Norman Literature and Its Background*, 38-42. Roger was born ca. 1138/39 and died before 1201.

[47] Richardson, "Gervase of Tilbury," 105-06; Legge, *Anglo-Norman Literature and Its Background*, 85-86, 95; and Richardson and Sayles, *The Governance of Mediaeval England*, 273.

[48] For references, see Eric Auerbach, *Literary Language and Its Public in Late Latin Antiquity and in the Middle Ages* (New York, 1965), 291-93. For example, one romance, *Floir and Blancheflor*, describes its hero as able to read Latin, to write on parchment, and to read books of the pagans.

mentioned a *miles literatus* who amused himself by composing Latin verses. Gerald also apologized for the simple style of one of his books, adding that he wished to make it accessible to "laymen and princes not too well grounded in letters"—a sure indication that he thought they could at least read simple Latin.[49] In King John's time, the sons of one baron, Richard de Umfraville, who were sent as hostages to the royal court, were accompanied by their tutor.[50] Simon de Montfort seems to have had a thorough education, as shown by his scholarly and spiritual interests throughout his life. He was so concerned about the education of his two eldest sons that he followed the early practice of sending them off to the household of a bishop, Robert Grosseteste, for instruction. Simon's eldest son learned his letters at least well enough to write out his father's will in his own hand, though in French, not in Latin.[51]

The medieval Church, fearful that clerics would be tainted by sharing in the shedding of blood, legislated continually against their participation in secular government.[52] By the beginning of the thirteenth century, some canonists and theologians were aware that there were adequate numbers of literate laymen for service in the secular courts. Certainly that was the case in Italy, homeland of so many canon lawyers. Peter the Chanter and Robert of Courson, two theologians at Paris with "a passionate interest in practical morality," advised secular princes to assign literate laymen to draft documents ordering sentences of death.[53] Moralists and satirists like Walter Map and Nigel Wireker also complained against the employment of clerics in royal government.[54] Apparently, they were confident that the king could find sufficient numbers of educated laymen to replace the clergymen. A series of diocesan and provincial councils of the English Church passed legislation aimed at giving practical meaning to the principle of clerical withdrawal from worldly affairs, particularly after the Fourth Lateran Council barred the clergy from participation in blood judgments.[55]

The most abundant evidence of lay literacy comes from the careers of royal servants, who clearly had to be able to read Latin to carry out their tasks. As Richardson and Sayles have stated, "We may presume, then, that a layman who exercised an office demanding the use of written instruments was literate. . . ."[56] To support this conclusion, a look at the seven laymen who held the office of justiciar is useful. Unquestionably, an ability to read the rolls, writs,

---

[49] Gerald of Wales, *Opera*, 8: 310, and *Expugnatio Hibernica*, in *Opera*, 5: 207–08.
[50] Warren, *King John*, 201.
[51] Margaret Labarge, *Simon de Montfort* (London, 1962), 22–23, 76; and Charles Bémont, *Simon de Montfort*, trans. E. F. Jacob (Oxford, 1930), app. A: 778.
[52] On this question, see Ralph V. Turner, "Clerical Judges in English Secular Courts: The Ideal versus the Reality," below, 159-79.
[53] John W. Baldwin, *Masters, Princes, and Merchants: The Views of Peter the Chanter and His Circle*, 1 (Princeton, 1970): 17, 185.
[54] Turner, "Clerical Judges in English Secular Courts," below, 169-70.
[55] *Ibid.*, 262-63.
[56] Richardson and Sayles, *The Governance of Mediaeval England*, 274. Or, as McFarlane has written of late medieval royal officials, "We are entitled to believe those who appeared to function did so until the contrary is proved"; *The Nobility of Later Medieval England*, 229-30.

charters, and chirographs was a requirement for any occupant of that office.[57] The earl of Leicester's reputation for learning was noted in the *Dialogus de Scaccario*.[58] His colleague and successor, Richard de Luci, came from a lower level of the landed classes, yet he clearly was "an able administrator and a skilled judge"; his role in drafting the Constitutions of Clarendon provides ample evidence of his learning.[59] Ranulf de Glanvill, his successor, came from a similar social level, but he had such a reputation for learning that the *Treatise on the Laws and Customs of England* has been attributed to him from the thirteenth century forward. Recently, he has been proposed as the author of two other works: a crusading chronicle of the conquest of Lisbon and an account of an East Anglican shire-moot.[60] Earl William de Mandeville, a close friend and counsellor to Henry II, died before he could assume office. He had some interest in vernacular letters, for he was a patron of Anglo-Norman poets; possibly he was the Count William to whom Marie de France dedicated her *Fables*.[61] Geoffrey fitz Peter, "one of the most learned of justiciars," came from a family of professional royal servants. He possibly began his career as clerk in the circle of Ranulf de Glanvill, then moved on to hold a number of posts, becoming the chief assistant of Hubert Walter before his own appointment as justiciar. Doris M. Stenton has speculated that he was the author of the treatise traditionally attributed to Glanvill.[62] Like his predecessors, Hubert de Burgh came from the class that was later called "country squires." He had been chamberlain to John when the future king was count of Mortain; when John was crowned, Hubert became a royal chamberlain. Thus, he was an experienced administrator before he was named justiciar. Following his fall from Henry III's favor, when he fled to sanctuary, the king commanded that no letters should reach him and even commanded that his psalter be taken from him—surely an indication of his literacy.[63] Another experienced administrator, Stephen de Segrave, succeeded to the justiciarship. According to Matthew Paris, Segrave deserted the clergy for knighthood out of arrogance and sought to resume wearing the tonsure on losing royal favor.[64] No other evidence supports this story, but, if Segrave had attended school in his youth, he may once have been tonsured.

---

[57] Richardson and Sayles, *The Governance of Mediaeval England*, 274; and Francis West, *The Justiciarship in England, 1066-1232* (Cambridge, 1966), 45-47.

[58] Johnson, *Dialogus de Scaccario*, 57; and see page 936, above.

[59] Stenton, "England: Henry II," 578; and West, *The Justiciarship in England*, 39.

[60] On his learning, see Roger of Howden, *Chronica*, ed. William Stubbs, 2, Rolls Series, no. 51 (London, 1869): 215; and Gerald of Wales, *Opera*, 8: 258. On his authorship of the two works, see J. C. Russell, "Ranulf de Glanvill," *Speculum*, 45 (1970): 69-70.

[61] Sidney Painter, "To Whom Were Dedicated the *Fables* of Marie de France?" *Modern Language Notes*, 47 (1933): 367-69, reprinted in Fred A. Cazel, ed., *Feudalism and Liberty* (Baltimore, 1961), 105-10.

[62] F. M. Powicke, *Stephen Langton* (Oxford, 1928), 115; *DNB*, sub nom. "Geoffrey fitz Peter"; West, *The Justiciarship in England*, 99, 109-10; and Stenton, *Pleas before the King or His Justices, 1198-1202*, 1: 9-10. In earlier work, Lady Stenton had considered Glanvill's authorship to be "most probable"; "England: Henry II," 578.

[63] Michael Weiss, "The Castellan: The Early Career of Hubert de Burgh," *Viator*, 5 (1974): 235-36; and *Close Rolls of Henry III, 1231-1234* (London, 1905), 161.

[64] Matthew Paris, *Chronica majora*, 3: 293.

There is evidence that lesser office holders in Angevin government were also literate. Certainly if the justiciar was literate, then the laymen who sat at the exchequer with him as barons or on the bench as justices must also have been literate. Sheriffs had to be capable of reading the royal writs sent to them, and their responses often required them to make a written record, returning information to Westminster *per breve suum* or *litteris suis sigillatis*.[65] One sheriff in 1159 gave a moneylender his promise to repay, purportedly written in his own hand.[66] An illiterate sheriff or custodian would have been at a great disadvantage when he presented his accounts for auditing at the exchequer. The tallies and checkered cloth used by the barons of the exchequer do not imply illiteracy on the part of those presenting accounts there.[67] Those laymen who were *familiares* of King John could not have performed their varied functions without an ability to read—Reginald of Cornhill, for example, was sheriff of Kent, chamberlain of London, custodian of mints and exchanges, collector of the fifteenth, and justice of the bench. Another valued agent was William Briwerre—sheriff, royal justice, custodian of escheats, and warden of the stanneries. He played an important part in drafting borough charters and was apparently one of the king's chief negotiators with the boroughs.[68]

Several thousand knights in the counties who held no permanent administrative posts were enlisted in the work of royal government as jurors, coroners, and commissioners of various sorts. In these capacities they were brought more and more into contact with written records. Search for social status and for local political influence made them seek office in their shires, and literacy was an obvious advantage in fulfilling the functions of office. Furthermore, the business of managing their own affairs—leases, lawsuits, estate accounts, business correspondence—meant that literacy was becoming increasingly necessary for them. Richardson and Sayles have collected documents "couched in uncouth Latin" that they believe were written by twelfth-century laymen unaided by clerks.[69]

By the thirteenth century, practical treatises, written for the instruction of laymen, appeared for four professions: common lawyers, estate stewards or bailiffs, conveyancing clerks, and accountants. Of course, these four fields were closely related, and an individual might concern himself with more than one of them. [70] Legal treatises and registers of writs were being compiled for

---

[65] William A. Morris, *The Medieval English Sheriff to 1300* (Manchester, 1927), 115, 212-22, 146-47.

[66] Hilary Jenkinson, "A Moneylender's Bonds of the Twelfth Century," in H. W. C. Davis, ed., *Essays in History Presented to Reginald Lane Poole* (Oxford, 1927), 190, 206.

[67] Richardson and Sayles, *The Governance of Mediaeval England*, 279-82. Tallies had the name of the person paying and the reason for payment written on them; these notched sticks continued to be cut until 1783 (and the burning of old ones may have caused the destruction of the Houses of Parliament in 1834); R. L. Poole, *The Exchequer in the Twelfth Century* (London, 1912), 86-91.

[68] Painter, *Reign of King John*, 81, 137, 147; and W. R. Powell, "English Administrative Families in the Twelfth- and Thirteenth-Centuries with Special Reference to the Cornhill Family" (B. Litt. Thesis, Oxford, 1952), 116. Briwerre witnessed forty-four of the ninety-eight borough charters issued in John's reign; Powell, "English Administrative Families," 109.

[69] Richardson and Sayles, *The Governance of Medieval England*, 275-77. In general, see Nicholas Orme, *English Schools in the Middle Ages* (New York, 1973); but Orme has been doubtful that literacy was widespread until the triumph of the vernacular in the reign of Richard II; *ibid.*, 33-34.

[70] Oschinsky, *Walter of Henley and Other Treatises on Estate Management*, 62.

members of the legal profession. As early as the time of King John, the plea rolls describe a professional attorney coming before the court *cum suo libro*, some sort of record he kept of the suits in which he was involved.[71] By the mid-thirteenth century knights of the counties had so many public responsibilities that they needed legal expertise. Little handbooks, compilations of law tracts, legal texts, and other documents appeared in order to supply that need.[72] The stewards of great estates in the thirteenth century were usually men of knightly rank who kept their accounts in Latin.[73] Evidence for their literacy comes from rentals, customals, and treatises on estate management composed for their guidance. The earliest treatises on estate management date from the middle of the thirteenth century, although they were much more common in the early fourteenth century. Among the earliest is that of Walter of Henley, written about 1285. Henley did not write his book until he became a Dominican friar, but it was based on his earlier experience: he was a knight who had received a good education, including some study of Latin, and who had served as a manorial bailiff.[74] The earliest surviving estate accounts, kept in Latin, date from the early part of the century, while the earliest treatises on accounting appeared a little later, around 1225.[75]

WHERE DID THESE LAYMEN LEARN THEIR LETTERS? The usual view of knightly education is that it stressed skill in arms and courtesy learned in the household of some great noble and that the nobility looked at bookish learning with indifference, if not contempt. By the mid-twelfth century, however, warfare and chivalry were no longer adequate for the education of knights, and a third discipline—letters—was becoming essential. John of Salisbury wrote that he had supported himself at Paris by taking the children of nobles as pupils.[76] Some nobles sent their sons off to cathedrals to be schooled in bishops' households. Others sent theirs to that of the king. The courts of Henry I and Henry II included schoolmasters who gave instruction not only to the kings' children but also to other noble youths sent to court for their upbringing.[77] Numbered among such youths was an Italian, a relative or protégé of Rolando Bandinelli, the future Pope Alexander III, commended to Henry II's court by Arnulf, bishop of Lisieux. Other aristocratic households included, in

---

[71] C. T. Flower et al., eds., *Curia Regis Rolls*, 6 (London, 1933): 228.

[72] For discussions of the compilation of Robert Carpenter, for example, made about 1260–61, see Noël Denholm-Young, "Robert Carpenter and the Provisions of Westminster," *EHR*, 50 (1935): 22–35; and C. A. F. Meekings, "More about Robert Carpenter of Hareslade," *EHR*, 72 (1957): 260–69. Meekings has stated that the "resulting book seems to be unique now" but that in "Robert's day . . . there must have been many such compilations"; "Robert Carpenter of Hareslade," 269.

[73] Labarge, *A Baronial Household of the Thirteenth Century*, 63; and Oschinsky, *Walter of Henley and Other Treatises on Estate Management*, 64.

[74] Oschinsky, *Walter of Henley and Other Treatises on Estate Management*, 56, 145–46.

[75] *Ibid.*, 64, 226, pipe roll of Winchester, 1208/9.

[76] John of Salisbury, *The Metalogicon of John of Salisbury*, ed. and trans. Daniel D. McGarry (Berkeley and Los Angeles, 1955), 98, lib. II, cap. x.

[77] William Stubbs, *Seventeen Lectures on the Study of Medieval and Modern History* (Oxford, 1900), 163. Orderic Vitalis told of two Norman knights—Robert II of Grandmesnill and Ralph the "Ill-tonsured"—who as early as the mid-eleventh century had gone to school; *Ecclesiastical History*, 2: 40, 76.

imitation of the royal court, a tutor or at least a chaplain who could give lessons in Latin. Hubert Walter, for example, testified that he had received his early education in the household of his uncle, Ranulf de Glanvill.[78]

What opportunities were there for sons of humbler knights—those young men who did not go off to a noble household to serve as pages—to secure an education? An early twelfth-century master exaggerated when he wrote that "throughout Normandy and England, not only in the cities and castles but also in small villages, there are as many practised school-masters as there are tax-collectors and other royal officials."[79] But opportunities for elementary and secondary education were more widely available in England than is generally recognized. The universities could not have arisen unless pupils had been prepared by a network of primary schools. There were many schools in England where boys might have studied Latin grammar and a few where they might have gained some business training, including a smattering of law. But schools were not the sole source of literacy; boys could learn to read in less formal settings. No doubt, most boys in the twelfth and thirteenth centuries learned their Latin from parish priests, the priests' assistants, parish clerks, or their own mothers.[80]

In pre-Conquest England monastery schools had been open to boys who were not destined for the religious life, even though the schools' main duty was to train children dedicated to the cloister. Most likely, they accepted the sons of some of the leading families of the shire to study alongside the novices. Norman monasticism had no such tradition, except possibly at Bec, but some of the English abbeys continued to accept sons of important neighbors after the Conquest.[81] Monasteries in the twelfth century still provided instruction for some boys who were not destined for the monastic life; Richard fitz Neal, for example, received his early education at the monastery of Ely, Thomas Becket at the priory of Merton, and Robert of Beaumont at the abbey of Abingdon. As late as the mid-thirteenth century, boys from neighboring gentry families were boarded at monasteries to learn their letters in the abbot's household; and some houses instructed poor youths—almonry boys— for charity's sake and for their service as acolytes at the daily masses.[82]

---

[78] Frank Barlow, ed., *The Letters of Arnulf of Lisieux*, Camden Society, 3d ser., no. 61 (London, 1939), 20–21, no. 15; and Charles R. Young, *Hubert Walter, Lord of Canterbury and Lord of England* (Durham, N.C., 1968), 4. In the Crusader Kingdom in the mid-thirteenth century Philip of Novarra, a learned jurist, urged nobles to hire capable tutors for their sons; Riley-Smith, *Feudal Nobility and the Kingdom of Jerusalem*, 130. This was already the practice of the kings of Jerusalem; William of Tyre, for example, served as tutor to the young Baldwin IV; *ibid.*, 101.

[79] Letter to Theobald of Etampes, as cited in R. W. Southern, "Master Vacarius and the Beginning of an English Academic Tradition," in J. J. G. Alexander and M. T. Gibson, eds., *Medieval Learning and Literature: Essays Presented to Richard William Hunt* (Oxford, 1976), 268, 268 n.

[80] Thorndike, "Elementary and Secondary Education in the Middle Ages," 401–03; and Orme, *English Schools in the Middle Ages*, 66–67. For a description of a parish priest in the late eleventh century hurrying to administer the last rites *cum suis veniens scolaribus*, see Thomas Arnold, ed., *Memorials of St. Edmund's Abbey*, 1, Rolls Series, no. 90 (London, 1890): 81. Mary Martin McLaughlin has suggested that noblewomen were capable of instructing their children in simple Latin; McLaughlin, "Survivors and Surrogates," in Lloyd de Mause, ed., *History of Childhood* (New York, 1974), 125.

[81] Knowles, *The Monastic Order in England, 943–1216*, 488–91; and Orme, *English Schools in the Middle Ages*, 226.

[82] Johnson, *Dialogus de Scaccario*, xiv, 57; Warren, *Henry II*, 55–56; J. Stevenson, ed., *Chronicon Monasterii de Abingdon*, 2, Rolls Series, no. 2 (London, 1858): 229; and Orme, *English Schools in the Middle Ages*, 64–65.

Following the Conquest other types of schools gave organized classes in Latin grammar and more advanced subjects.[83] These schools can be grouped in four categories: (1) the "song schools" that instructed young choristers and outside pupils in elementary Latin at the nine secular cathedrals and at some collegiate churches; (2) grammar schools in London and a number of other important towns and at practically every English cathedral; (3) schools of *ars notaria* or what might be called "business schools" that taught the drafting of letters and legal documents, accounting, and some common law; and (4) "higher schools" at some cathedrals, at Northampton, and at Oxford that gave advanced instruction in the liberal arts, philosophy, and theology and sometimes in Roman and canon law comparable to that given later in the universities.[84] By the mid-twelfth century, these cathedral schools were accepting pupils who had no intention of progressing beyond minor orders into the priesthood.[85]

If laymen in the king's service earned any education beyond the elementary level, it was likely to have been at the "business schools." Before the opening of these schools, any advanced training was purely practical, based on the students' observations of experienced judges and other officials at work. Later, the Inns of Court attracted sons of noble families who sought to study the common law.[86] By the early thirteenth century a need for specialists with some academic training in the law had already appeared. As early as the reign of King John, Oxford seems to have become a center of business studies—*ars dictaminis*, accounting, and some elementary law—a curriculum that prepared youths for careers as common lawyers, estate stewards, conveyance clerks, or accountants. In the early thirteenth century several Englishmen composed treatises on the *ars dictaminis*, which are extant.[87] Another collection that has survived includes treatises on letter-writing, sample letters, and other materials, probably collected at Oxford as early as the first third of the thirteenth century.[88] These subjects were never part of the university curriculum but were studied in separate schools at Oxford into the fifteenth century.

Another question concerns the study of Roman law and its possible influence on the political thought of the men in the king's service, for Roman law did arouse much interest in twelfth- and thirteenth-century England. Roman legal studies had their beginning in England during the reign of King Stephen

---

[83] For a list—albeit incomplete—of schools at nineteen different places in the years 1066–1149, see Orme, *English Schools in the Middle Ages*, 294.

[84] H. G. Richardson, "The Schools of Northampton in the Twelfth Century," *EHR*, 56 (1941): 595–605, and "The Oxford School of Law under John," 319–38; and Orme, *English Schools in the Middle Ages*, 64–65, 75–76, 80, 293–325.

[85] Bolgar, *The Classical Heritage and Its Beneficiaries*, 194.

[86] "Knights, barons and also other magnates and nobles of the realm place their sons in those inns, although they do not intend them to be imbued by a professional knowledge of the laws nor to live by its practice, but upon their patrimonies alone"; John Fortescue, *De Laudibus Legum Angliae*, ed. S. B. Chrimes (Cambridge, 1942), 118.

[87] Geoffrey de Vinsauf, John of Garland, Gervase of Melkley, and, somewhat earlier, Peter of Blois all composed treatises on the *ars dictaminis*. See Noël Denholm-Young, "The Cursus in England," in F. M. Powicke, ed., *Oxford Essays in Medieval History Presented to Herbert Edward Salter* (Oxford, 1934), 75–80; and C. H. Haskins, "The Early *Artes Dictandi* in Italy," in his *Studies in Medieval Culture* (Oxford, 1929), 191.

[88] H. G. Richardson, "An Oxford Teacher of the Fifteenth Century," *Bulletin of the John Rylands Library*, 23 (1939): 447–49.

with the arrival of the Italian Master Vacarius. Although he established no school, there is some evidence for the study of Roman law at a number of centers by the mid-twelfth century.[89] Legal studies at these schools, however, cannot have attained a level comparable to that of the school that appeared at Oxford by the end of the twelfth century.[90] Generally, legal studies were on a lower level, using various compendia and condensations, not the *Digest* or the *Institutes* of Justinian. They grew out of a study of rhetoric, part of the *trivium*, for rhetorical studies had long included some legal teachings. The texts used in the medieval English schools must have resembled those of the early Italian law schools: the *ordo judiciarius* and the formulary for the *ars notaria*.

The first, the *ordines judiciarii*, were primarily manuals of procedure, attempting to remedy the deficiencies of contemporary canon and secular law by reference to Roman law. Sometimes they took on the characteristics of the formularies and vice versa.[91] Several *ordines* written in either England or Normandy survive, the best known of which is by William Longchamp, Richard I's justiciar.[92] Portions of another *ordo judiciarius* survive as part of an Oxford compilation dating from the reign of King John. It may be derived from an earlier *ordo* studied in the twelfth-century schools at Northampton.[93]

Another instrument for transmission of some Roman legal principles studied in the "business schools" was the notarial formulary. A course of study, the *ars notaria*, arose in medieval Italian municipal schools out of the *ars dictaminis*. It concentrated on the drafting of legal documents, and the formulary presented models for notaries public to follow. Portions of the Oxford compilation seem to represent an attempt by a master in early thirteenth-century Oxford to compile a formulary similar to those of Italy for use by English students preparing for careers in episcopal or noble secretariats. By the end of the thirteenth century, compilations of texts for study in the "business schools" included not only formularies for legal documents and manuals of procedure but also treatises on accounting and estate management.[94]

The *ordines judiciarii*, notarial formularies, and other texts indicate that it was possible for students who did not attend a university to gain some technical training for a business career. H. G. Richardson has described such students as young men "who were seeking employment in the households of the larger landowners, where they would write their lord's letters, and keep

---

[89] For studies at Exeter, Hereford, Lincoln, Northampton, and St. Albans Abbey and possibly at London and York, see Stephan Kuttner and Eleanor Rathbone, "Anglo-Norman Canonists of the Twelfth Century," *Traditio*, 7 (1949-51): 321-23; and Kathleen Edwards, *The English Secular Cathedrals in the Middle Ages* (Manchester, 1949), 188-90.

[90] Kuttner and Rathbone, "Anglo-Norman Canonists of the Twelfth Century," 323. Also see Southern, "Master Vacarius and the Beginning of an English Academic Tradition," 257-86.

[91] Richardson, "The Oxford School of Law under John," 336.

[92] For the text of Longchamp's *Practica legum et decretorum*, see E. Caillemar, "Le droit civil dans les provinces anglo-normandes," *Mémoires de l'Académie de Caen* (Paris, 1883).

[93] Richardson, "An Oxford Teacher of the Fifteenth Century," 327, and "The Oxford School of Law under John," 319-38.

[94] Richardson, "The Oxford School of Law under John," 325, 328; and Dorothea Oschinsky, "Medieval Treatises on Estate Accounting," *Economic History Review*, 17 (1947): 57, and *Walter of Henley and Other Treatises on Estate Management*, 62, 234.

his courts and his accounts, and draw up for him conveyances and leases and other instruments as occasion arose."[95] They might find a post with an abbot or bishop, with a sheriff or some other royal official, or perhaps with the king himself. Younger sons of knights who had to seek their fortunes or ambitious sons of humbler freemen very likely sought the training that would qualify them for such positions.

Once young men had completed their "business" course of six months to a year, they were ready to begin their careers, and any further training that they received came through everyday experience. Richard fitz Neal claimed that his treatise on the operations of the exchequer was more valuable than books of the philosophers, providing information that was *non subtilia sed utilia*.[96] A practical apprenticeship in some minor clerical post was preferred to a university degree as the proper preparation for a life of government service. Yet, obviously, an apprentice-clerk already had to have some knowledge of Latin letters, some primary education, before he could read Richard's treatise.

To ANSWER IN REVERSE ORDER THE THREE QUESTIONS raised earlier, it is clear that opportunities offered themselves for laymen to learn Latin grammar and to receive some specialized training in the twelfth and thirteenth centuries. As Lady Stenton wrote, "If men of position were illiterate, it was because they made no effort to learn rather than that provision for their teaching was not available."[97] It is also clear, although the evidence is perhaps less illuminating, that more and more laymen were taking advantage of the available means of learning. Changes in government, requiring written records of all kinds, were making pragmatic literacy a necessity for the knightly class in the high Middle Ages. Finally, significant numbers of laymen in Angevin England did hold government posts that required literacy. That an adequate supply of literate knights existed to fill the new offices growing up in royal government is proven by the king's ability to find laymen to fill them, laymen who performed tasks that certainly required that they know Latin.

[95] Richardson, "The Oxford School of Law under John," 334.
[96] Johnson, *Dialogus de Scaccario*, 5.
[97] Doris M. Stenton, *English Society in the Early Middle Ages* (4th ed., Harmondsworth, Middlesex, 1971), 251.

8

Religious Patronage of Angevin Royal Administrators, *c.* 1170–1239

Ecclesiastical benefactions by English barons have provided topics for a number of scholars, but the professional civil servants, proto-bureaucrats, who first appeared in the twelfth century, are another group whose gifts to the Church deserve more study. In England, such men appear as early as Henry I's time, but they become more numerous in the reign of his grandson, Henry II. At first, such royal servants were men of all work, doing whatever the king assigned to them at the *curia regis,* in the counties, and abroad. By the last years of Henry II and in the reigns of his sons, however, some specialization was taking place, and this becomes easier to see in Henry III's early years.

It is next to impossible to probe these royal administrators' minds. They left few letters, no personal recollections, and they earned only a few anecdotes—mainly hostile—in the chronicles. For a number of years, I have been studying a group of fifty-two of these men, whose careers span the last third of the twelfth and the first third of the thirteenth centuries, chosen first chiefly because of their connection with the work of royal justice. They form a representative sample, ranging in rank from the justiciar to knights of the counties, from archbishops to men in minor orders, including roughly equal numbers of clergy and laity. They range from close associates of the king to largely local officials (see Appendix I).

These royal officials are sometimes depicted as either ruthless plunderers of Church property or as superstitious purchasers of salvation. They were often both at the same time, yet they were not incapable of genuine religious feeling or charitable concern. A diligent search can produce some information about their devotional practices. The twelve who became bishops present special problems, for some of them retired from active royal service, and gifts made after they left court may reflect a changed outlook. Some evidence for the donations of two-thirds of the fifty-two survives. In addition, there is some evidence about their wills and their choice of burial-places (Appendix IV). I must confess failure, however, with 25% (15 of 52) for whom I have no evidence whatsoever.

The most solid evidence of religious feeling is the gifts that these administrators made to religious houses, especially establishing new houses. Twelve (23%) founded a total of twenty-six new religious houses (Appendix II). These twelve fit quite easily into the mold of the *curiales,* new men from knightly families of the counties, rising through their own efforts and through royal favor. For them, a new monastic foundation signified not only their piety; it also showed their associates that they had "arrived." These twelve men were high-ranking royal officials who stood close to the center of power. Indeed, six of them held the office of justiciar. Another, William Briwerre, came close to exercising the power of a justiciar without the title. He was labelled one of John's *consiliarii iniquissimi* by the chroniclers, yet he was lavish in his religious foundations, using his new-found wealth to endow four new religious houses, among them Torre Abbey, the richest Premonstratensian house in England.[1] If William Briwerre was the champion founder of monasteries among the laymen, Peter des Roches held the championship among the clerics. A longtime associate of King John, who rose to be bishop of Winchester and justiciar, he figured prominently in Henry III's struggle to establish his personal power. Peter founded five religious houses and planned two more, which were built following his death. The least prominent founder was Master Ralph of Norwich, who founded an Austin priory at Chetwode, Bucks, in 1245. With its modest endowment, it never had more than three or four canons.[2] Master Ralph did not rise as high as some of his colleagues, but he did serve Henry III as chancellor of Ireland and came close to becoming archbishop of Dublin.[3]

New men seeking to purchase prestige may have been more generous than members of the old nobility. Only one of the twelve founders, William de Warenne, baron of Wormegay, came from the old baronage. Although he was a longtime official under King John, he did not quite fit into the inner corps of royal counselors. Royal administrators' gifts might be compared to those of Ranulf III, earl of Chester, a powerful representative of the old aristocracy among the barons of John and young Henry III. His biographer has termed him "a pinchpenny patron," noting that he founded only one monastery, a Cistercian house costing little to found, a translation of a pre-existing house. The earl's donations to houses of other orders were even less generous.[4]

In the final decades of the twelfth century, the rate for founding new religious houses was slowing compared to earlier in the century. Nonetheless, the years between Becket's murder and the coming of the friars saw continued growth for the regular canons, with about a hundred houses established. It comes as no surprise, then, that most of the twenty-six new foundations by this group of twelve Angevin royal servants housed regular canons: seven Augustinians and

---

[1]Howard M. Colvin, *The White Canons in England* (Oxford, 1951), p. 159.
[2]David Knowles and R. Neville Hadcock, *Medieval Religious Houses, England and Wales* (London, 1971), p. 153.
[3]*Dictionary of National Biography*, s.v. "Norwich, Ralph de"; for added details see C.A.F. Meekings, ed., *The 1235 Surrey eyre*, Surrey Record Society 31 (1979), 1:224.
[4]James W. Alexander, *Ranulf of Chester, a Relic of the Conquest* (Athens, Ga., 1983), pp. 37-42.

five Premonstratensians. Three belonged to other orders, while the remaining eleven were hospitals. Scholars have long observed that self-made men such as royal *curiales* preferred the regular canons to older orders of Benedictines or Cistercians. The smaller size of canons' houses reduced their costs at a time when less land was available for endowments. Founders may also have felt that canons followed the apostolic life more devotedly than did the Black or White monks.[5] According to Gerald of Wales' account of a conversation with Ranulf de Glanvill, the justiciar rejected the Benedictines because of their gluttony. He similarly rejected the Cistercians because they were too greedy, often falsifying charters for their advantage. Glanvill concluded that only regular canons were innocent of these sins, and he founded a house of White canons and one of Black canons.[6] Glanvill included in his charter of foundation for Leiston Abbey a clause aimed at preventing the canons from hoarding money in order to buy additional lands.[7] He wanted to ensure that they would spend their income on charity and hospitality, not on expansion of their properties.

The Cistercians had supposedly barred further foundations of their order in 1152, but one *curialis*, William Briwerre, founded Dunkeswell Abbey, Devon, in 1201.[8] Three more Cistercian houses were planned, but their patrons died before they could complete them. Hubert Walter, King John's chancellor and archbishop of Canterbury, was planning a Cistercian house at Wolverhampton two years before his death; and he had acquired considerable property for it, but the project was abandoned at his death in 1205.[9] Peter des Roches was preparing to found two Cistercian abbeys at the time of his death in 1238, one in England and one in his native France. Foundation of the English house, Netley Abbey, Hampshire, went forward under his executors' direction. Peter also bequeathed money for the French house, La Clarté Dieu, founded in Touraine in 1240.[10]

The friars arrived in England in the early 1220s, and they first lived entirely off charity, not accepting endowments. Soon, however, they won popularity and patronage. Hubert de Burgh, Henry III's justiciar, had a great interest in the

[5]Colvin, pp. 36-38; C.R. Cheney, *Hubert Walter* (London, 1967), p. 28; John C. Dickinson, *The Origins of the Austin Canons and their Introduction into England* (London, 1950), pp. 125-30; Richard Mortimer, "Religious and secular motives for some English monastic foundations," in Derek Baker, ed., *Religious Motivation: Biographical and Sociological Problems for the Church Historian, Studies in Church History* 15 (Oxford, 1978): 83-84.
[6]*Geraldi Cambrensis Opera*, ed. J.S. Brewer, Rolls Series (1861-91), 4:144-45.
[7]Richard Mortimer, ed., *Leiston Abbey Cartulary and Butley Priory Charters,* Suffolk Record Society, *Suffolk Charters* (1979), 1:76-77.
[8]William Dugdale, *Monasticon Anglicanum,* 6 vols. in 9 (new ed.; London, 1846), 5:678; George Oliver, *Monasticon diocesis Exoniensis* (Exeter, 1846), pp. 393, 396-97.
[9]Colvin, p. 135; Charles R. Young, *Hubert Walter* (Durham, N.C., 1968), p. 159.
[10]Knowles and Hadcock, p. 122; C.A.F. Meekings, "The Early Years of Netley Abbey," *Journal of Ecclesiastical History* 30 (1979): 1-2, reprinted in *Studies in 13th Century Justice and Administration* (London, 1981).

Dominicans and became one of the earliest benefactors of their London house.[11] Peter des Roches also played an important role in introducing the Dominican order to England. The earliest group of Dominicans to reach England were Italians who came with him from the Continent in 1221.[12] The new arrivals won Peter's goodwill, and he wished to settle them in his diocese of Winchester; as early as 1225 he tried to establish a Dominican house at Portsmouth, but the project failed. By 1235, however, he had established a house for forty or fifty friars at Winchester.[13]

A native English order, the Gilbertines, had grown rapidly in the second half of the twelfth century. Many of their monasteries were double houses of both nuns and canons. Geoffrey fitz Peter, longtime administrator for Henry II and his sons, founded a Gilbertine mixed house in 1193—before he became justiciar—at Shouldham, Norfolk.[14] This was the only house for women among those founded by this group of royal servants, and it was the last of the Gilbertine mixed houses to be established.

The largest number of religious foundations—nine or possibly eleven—fall into the category of hospitals.[15] The term hospital lacked any precise meaning in the Middle Ages. Hospitals were not simply houses for the sick; many were almshouses or shelters for the aged, serving the purpose of modern nursing homes; and at the same time, they functioned as hostels for pilgrims and other wayfarers. Sometimes the distinction between a hospital and a smallish house of canons, monks, or nuns is quite blurred, for both dispensed hospitality to needy travelers. In the first half of the twelfth century, an average of two hospitals had opened each year in England. An increase in incidence of leprosy created a need for new hospitals; and by the second half of the century growing numbers of pilgrims were seeking shelter, creating an additional need.[16] This form of charity indicates also a new sense of social responsibility, a desire to achieve practical as well as spiritual ends, that was widespread in the twelfth century.[17] The hospitals founded by eight royal administrators in the late twelfth-early thirteenth centuries were more concerned with poverty than with public health.

---

[11] W.A. Hinnebusch, *The Early English Friars Preachers* (Rome, 1951), pp. 20-21.
[12] Knowles and Hadcock, p. 218; Hinnebusch, pp. 3, 443.
[13] Hinnebusch, p. 107; Knowles and Hadcock, p. 219.
[14] *Monasticon*, 6(2): 974-75.
[15] See Appendix II. Confusion about the number results because Peter des Roches refounded St. Thomas Hospital, Southwark, at a new location (Knowles and Hadcock, p. 393). Is this a new foundation? Geoffrey fitz Peter granted land to William of Wrotham for the purpose of founding the hospital at Sutton at Hone, Kent (ibid., p. 396). Is Geoffrey founder? Rotha Mary Clay, *The Medieval Hospitals of England* (London, 1909), p. 229, lists him as co-founder.
[16] See Clay, *passim;* and Edward J. Kealey, *Medieval Medicus, A Social History of Anglo-Norman Medicine* (Baltimore, 1981).
[17] For hospital building in 12th-century Italy, see Marvin Becker, *Medieval Italy, Constraints and Creativity* (Bloomington, Ind., 1982), p. 101.

Their foundations were mainly for maintenance of the poor; only two had care of lepers as their chief duty (Appendix II). Some of the most ambitious and grasping royal servants were among the eight who founded hospitals. They included four justiciars and three curialist bishops.

Compassion for the poor was becoming a familiar sentiment throughout Europe in the twelfth century, not only to professional royal servants. The Church had long taught that possession of property carried with it an obligation to provide alms for the poor. Writers on kingship so stressed the monarch's obligation to protect the poor that it was becoming almost a cliché. Even King John, rarely considered a model of piety, took the message to heart and granted generous sums for charity.[18] Apparently royal officials were also taking the message to heart, for writers commented favorably on their concern for the poor and oppressed.[19] Not only were the king's administrators endowing hospitals; his justices were frequently pardoning amercements "on account of poverty," especially during the minority of Henry III.[20]

Besides founding hospitals, these new men expressed concern for the poor through gifts to existing almshouses. Noticeable among them are several bishops who gave gifts for the maintenance of paupers. Richard of Ilchester as bishop of Winchester took charge in 1185 of a hospital for the poor, founded by his predecessor. It had fed a hundred men daily at Winchester, but Richard doubled the number.[21] Hubert Walter had a fondness for over-lavish living, yet he too showed compassion for the poor. Around 1190, when the monks of Reading founded a hospital for thirteen paupers, Hubert—then bishop of Salisbury—added funds to support thirteen additional poor men daily. Later as archbishop, he gave revenues to a hospital at Eastbridge, Canterbury, which provided shelter for pilgrims and other poor travelers.[22] Still later Henry of London, once he had become archbishop of Dublin, made gifts to St. Thomas' Abbey, an Augustinian house at Dublin, to aid the canons in their care for paupers.[23]

[18]Charles R. Young, "King John of England: An Illustration of the Medieval Practice of Charity," *Church History* 29 (1960): 270-72. See also Paul R. Hyams, *Kings, Lords and Peasants in Medieval England: The Common Law of Villeinage in the Twelfth and Thirteenth Centuries* (Oxford, 1980), p. 261.

[19]E.g. *Radulphi de Diceto opera historica*, ed. William Stubbs, Rolls Series (1876), 1:415, describing Richard of Ilchester's work as viceroy in Normandy; or the abbot of Reading's description of Hubert Walter as a young judge, Giles Constable, "An Unpublished Letter by Abbot Hugh II of Reading," *Essays in Medieval History Presented to Bertie Wilkinson*, ed. T. A. Sandquist and M.R. Powicke (Toronto, 1969), pp. 29-31.

[20]Ralph V. Turner, *The King and His Courts: The Role of John and Henry III in the Administration of Justice, 1199-1240* (Ithaca, N.Y., 1968), pp. 155-56.

[21]Knowles and Hadcock, p. 404.

[22]Young, *Hubert Walter*, p. 163. William Briwerre gave a manor to Mottisfont Priory to provide food and shelter for four paupers, *Monasticon*, 6(1): 481.

[23]*Register of the Abbey of St. Thomas, Dublin*, ed. John T. Gilbert, Rolls Series (1889), pp. 294-95, no. 341.

Rarely do we know any more about motives for making gifts to religious foundations than the pious formulas repeated in charters. Obviously, the traditional belief of laymen that they could vicariously share in the merit that the good deeds their monks earned weighed heavily. Or their confessors may have advised them to atone for some grievous sin with a generous gift. In the case of Geoffrey fitz Peter, however, a concrete explanation for his foundation of a pilgrim hostel at East Tilbury, Essex, does survive. Pope Innocent III in 1205 gave Geoffrey leave to postpone carrying out his crusading vow for three years, on grounds that the war between the English and French kings created conditions too dangerous to allow him to leave England. In return, the justiciar promised among other things to found a hospital (*xenodochium*) for poor travelers.[24] Geoffrey had first taken the cross at the time of Richard Lionheart's crusade, and he never fulfilled his vow.

By the end of the twelfth century, the great period for founding new monasteries and convents had ended, and religious benefactions were likely to take the form of gifts to existing houses. Presents to already established houses could range in value from a manor to a silk cloth. Such gifts are not as easy to trace as are new foundations. Nevertheless, I have enough evidence about the gifts of my group of royal officials to offer some generalizations.

Patrons of religious houses presented gifts of altar plate, service books, or vestments on various occasions. For example, the hospitality that monks extended to visiting dignitaries usually brought gifts from their guests in return.[25] More significant, however, are additions to monastic endowments (Appendix III). About a third of the group of royal servants made grants of land, rents, or churches to religious houses, several giving to more than one house. Sixteen (30%) chose the Austin canons as recipients of their gifts. The second most popular order was Citeaux with seven of them giving to nine different Cistercian houses. Closely following in popularity were the Premonstratensian canons. Old Benedictine monasteries received gifts from only four royal servants. It has been stated that *curiales* frequently made benefactions to Westminster Abbey, since it stood in their sight when they were at work at the Bench or Exchequer.[26] This group showed no particular enthusiasm for the Westminster monks, however; only two—Geoffrey fitz Peter and Richard of Ilchester—made them gifts.[27]

---

[24]C.R. and Mary G. Cheney, ed., *The Letters of Innocent III* (Oxford, 1967), p. 205, no. 633.
[25]E.g. Hubert Walter's gift of a chasuble to the celebrant at mass on his visit to the Carthusians of Witham, E. Margaret Thompson, *The Carthusian Order in England* (London, 1930), pp. 74-76. Also William Briwerre gave the abbey of Prémontré two silver chalices (Colvin, pp. 152-53). Adam fitz William gave St. Albans a silk cloth (*Matthaei Parisiensis Chronica Majora*, ed. H.R. Luard, Rolls Series [1872-84], 6: 390).
[26]Emma Mason, "Timeo barones et donas ferentes," in Derek Baker, ed., *Religious motivation*, p. 68.

There were nine donations to nunneries of various orders: four to Benedictine sisters, two to Cistercians, and one each to Gilbertines, Augustinian canonesses, and Premonstratensians. Noticeably lacking are gifts to military orders—Hospitallers and Templars—which had such a strong appeal to the feudal baronage. The only gift to one of the military orders dates from early in the period, probably in 1157, when Richard de Lucy granted a manorial rent to the Hospitallers.[28]

The main type of grant to monasteries was land, ranging in quantity from an entire manor to a few acres. Monks and nuns must have particularly valued urban property for the cash rents it produced, and several royal officers granted land and buildings in towns.[29] Advowsons proved to be popular gifts as laymen's practical advantages in being patrons of churches tended to decline. Also a growing uneasiness among lay patrons about their role in the appointment of parish priests may have hastened the movement to give them away to religious houses.[30] Although gifts of churches to the religious orders grew enormously in the twelfth century, less than a quarter of the fifty-two handed over churches in their gift.

A number of considerations guided these men in their choice of houses for their benefactions. Hardly any of them came from old families which had founded houses in the years before Henry II's accession, although they did occasionally become patrons of long established houses through marriage, custody of an heir, or other chance. Patronage did not necessarily ensure a flow of favors from the lay protector, however. Later generations often took little interest in houses their families had founded, although they continued to insist on their prerogatives as patrons.[31] Indeed, patrons expected material benefits, and sometimes bitter quarrels resulted between monks and their patrons. Geoffrey fitz Peter found himself patron of Walden Abbey through his marriage in 1190 to the

---

[27]Geoffrey fitz Peter made a gift in return for their commemoration of his mother's *obit*, Westminster Abbey Muniment Book 11, f. 492b; the bishop of Winchester gave two churches to the infirmary, ff. 570b-571.

[28]Michael Gervers, ed., *Cartulary of the Knights of St. John of Jerusalem in England*, British Academy, Records of social and economic history, new series 6 (Oxford, 1982), p. 135, no. 216.

[29]E.g. Thomas of Moulton gave all his land and buildings in Boston to the nuns of Bullington (F.M. Stenton, *Transcripts of charters Relating to Gilbertine Houses*, Lincoln Record Soc., 18 [1922]: 95, no. 10; 99, no. 22). Simon of Pattishhall gave a house and land at Stamford, Lincs, to Pipewell Abbey (*Calendar of Charter Rolls*, Public Record Office [1903—], 1: 205). Geoffrey fitz Peter gave Shouldham Priory twelve London shops (*Victoria County History, Norfolk*, 2: 412).

[30]Brian R. Kemp, "Monastic Possession of Parish Churches in England in the Twelfth Century," *Journal of Ecclesiastical History* 31 (1980): 134-35.

[31]This was true of the Clares, J.C. Wood, "Fashions in monastic endowment: the foundations of the Clare family, 1066-1314," *Journal of Ecclesiastical History* 32 (1981): 446. William Briwerre showed little interest in his father's convent of Polsloe.

heiress to the Mandeville barony, but he and the monks soon quarrelled, and a series of lawsuits resulted. The monks left a vivid account of the conflict, in which they complained that Geoffrey "took several properties away from us and gave them to his own men to hold, and we do not know of any good work to ascribe to him."[32]

The chief consideration in choosing houses to benefit was proximity to the donor's estates. It was a point of pride for newly prominent lords to patronize a religious house near the *caput* of their collection of lands. Closely connected with this is concern for family, for donors were likely to favor convents and monasteries near the estate from which the family had sprung, with which their family had already some ties. Indeed, family feeling may have had as much importance as religious devotion. Eleven royal servants made gifts to houses with which they had some family connection. Frequently, their gifts went to foundations that sheltered the remains of family members. Geoffrey fitz Peter showed particular concern for the resting places of his kin. He had his first wife's body moved from its original burial-place to his new nunnery of Shouldham; and he gave land to the monks of Winchester Cathedral, which housed his father's tomb.[33] Sometimes the signs of love and respect are still touching. Michael Belet provided funds for the Austin canons of East Rhuddam to keep a lamp perpetually burning over his mother's tomb, a light that we know has long since been extinguished.[34]

Another factor that encouraged donations to a particular house was the presence of a relative among its inmates. Royal administrators of this period, however, were more likely to have brothers or sons among the secular clergy, for whom they were seeking benefices, than they were among the cloistered; and surprisingly few seem to have had sisters, daughters, or nieces who were nuns. Only once can a gift by one of the fifty-two administrators be connected with family members residing among the religious. William de Warenne had a sister who was a nun of St. Mary at Carrow, Norfolk; and this doubtless explains his gift of land to the convent.[35]

---

[32]*Monasticon*, 4: 140; see Susan Wood's account of the conflict, *English Monasteries and their Patrons in the Thirteenth Century* (Oxford, 1955), pp. 167-70.

[33]*Monasticon*, 6(2): 974; BL Add. MS. 29,436, ff. 31v-32. Others' gifts: Hubert de Burgh to Walsingham Priory, his mother's resting place; William de Warenne to Lewes Priory, where his father died a monk; Roger fitz Reinfrid to St. Mary Clerkenwell, burial site for his wife and mother; Robert of Lexington to Rufford, his father's burial-place; and Thomas of Moulton to Spalding, site of his grandfather's grave.

[34]Coxford Cartulary, Norfolk and Norwich Record Office, SUN/8, nos. 41-52, 467. His mother was buried in the church of Thorpe Market, Norf., which he had given to the canons.

[35]C.T. Clay, ed., *Early Yorkshire Charters*, 8, *Honour of Warenne*, Yorks Archaeological Society, Record Series, extra Series (1949), p. 32; *Victoria County History, Norfolk*, 2: 128. William Briwerre did provide funds in order that two sisters-in-law could become nuns at Polsloe (P.R.O. DL 36/2/127).

Medieval men regarded their lives as a preparation for death, and they sometimes selected their own burial places years before dying. The first clauses of wills often expressed the dying person's wishes concerning disposal of his body. The burial places of twenty-one of our group are known with certainty, and those of six can be conjectured (Appendix IV). Gifts often went to the religious house they had chosen for their final resting place. William de Warenne chose St. Mary Overy, Southwark for his tomb, although he had founded Wormegay Priory. He gave the Southwark priory sixty acres.[36] Robert of Lexington, a royal justice through the first half of Henry III's reign, changed his mind about his burial place twice. He first chose Rufford, a Cistercian abbey to which his father had made gifts. Then he decided upon Newstead Priory, an Augustinian house, and gave land to it. Finally, he turned back to his first choice of Rufford, possibly influenced by his brother, who was prominent in the Cistercian order.[37] Both the monasteries that Robert had considered were Nottinghamshire houses, located near the Lexington family seat (Laxton). It was not uncommon in the Middle Ages for the heart or viscera to be deposited apart from the rest of the body in another church. Peter des Roches' heart was placed at the Cistercian Abbey of Waverley, while his body rested in his cathedral church at Winchester. Geoffrey fitz Peter was buried in the Gilbertine priory he had founded at Shouldham, but part of his body—heart? viscera?— was at the Austin priory of Holy Trinity, Aldgate.[38]

In only a few instances can we see connections to feudal lords or patrons influencing these royal officers' monastic benefactions. Hugh Bardolf's grant of a carucate and pasturage for 500 sheep to Barlings Abbey may have been due to the fact that he was a tenant of the abbey's founder.[39] Roger fitz Reinfrid felt indebted enough to his patron, Richard de Lucy, to confer a church in his gift on Lesnes Abbey, Richard's foundation.[40] Stephen of Segrave's family had long been tenants of St. Mary de Pré, Leicester, an Augustinian abbey to which he made gifts. Obviously, he had close ties with the abbey, for he sought sanctuary there on his fall from power in 1234, and he returned there to die in 1241. The abbot of St. Marry de Pré called for celebration of a mass on the anniversary of Segrave's death, "as if for their own advocate."[41] The ultimate lord and patron of

---

[36] *Monasticon,* 6(1): 169, 171.
[37] C.H. Holdsworth, *Rufford Charters,* Thoroton Society, Record Series, 29 (Nottingham, 1972), 1: xciii-xcv.
[38] For Peter des Roches' burial, *Matthew Paris,* 3:489; for Geoffrey fitz Peter, *Monasticon,* 4: 140; *Descriptive Catalogue of Ancient Deeds,* Public Record Office (London, 1890-1915), 2: 91, 93.
[39] *Monasticon,* 6(2): 916. The lord of the land he gave at Riseholm, Lincs, was Ralph de Haia (Knowles and Hadcock, p. 185).
[40] *Monasticon,* 6(1): 457.
[41] *Complete Peerage,* 2: 596-601. For his death, see *Matthew Paris,* 4:169. For the abbot's charter, see John Nichols, *The History and Antiquities of the County of Leicester* (London, 1795-1815), 2(1): 115.

all royal servants, the king, seems to have had little influence on their giving. They showed no noticeable preference for monasteries that enjoyed royal favor. Henry II favored houses of extremely ascetic orders, such as Carthusians, for royal foundations.[42] King John's one monastic foundation, Beaulieu Abbey, secured donations from none of his chief counselors, only from the relatively obscure Henry de Pont-Audemer.

Religious donations did show devotion to the monarch, however, with foundation charters commonly soliciting prayers for the king as well as for the founder and his family. The foundation charters of William Briwerre's houses, for example, indicate his devotion to the Angevin Monarchy. At a chapel that Briwerre maintained at Northampton, a special mass was said for the souls of the four kings he had served.[43] He gave a gold chalice to Worcester Cathedral on its restoration following a fire in 1217, and he attended its rededication, along with Henry III and a host of dignitaries.[44] Worcester, far from his estates, must have held a special place in his thoughts because it sheltered King John's remains.

A special time for bestowing gifts on religious houses was at the approach of death, when one made his last will. Most men dying in the twelfth and thirteenth centuries chose to leave part of their property to the Church, perhaps to make restitution for misdeeds. Many also sought to provide for commemoration of their anniversaries with special prayers or food-offerings to the poor.[45] Medieval Christianity attached great importance to "making a good death," confessing one's sins, receiving the last rites, and disposing of one's property.

Chronicles abound with uplifting accounts of good deaths and also with equally edifying descriptions of not such good deaths. Chroniclers were careful to condemn those who died intestate. Three royal servants in my group earned writers' scorn for dying without making wills: Geoffrey Ridel, bishop of Ely; and two laymen, Osbert fitz Hervey and Adam fitz William.[46] Matthew Paris reveled in recording the sudden death of Adam fitz William, whom he resented for having wronged St. Albans Abbey. He accused one of Adam's friends, a fellow royal justice, of falsely swearing that Adam had made a testament so that his goods could be distributed among his kin. The chronicler delighted in re-

---

[42] Elizabeth M. Hallam, "Henry II, Richard I and the Order of Grandmont," *Journal of Medieval History* 1 (1975): 165-86; and "Henry II as a founder of monasteries," *Journal of Ecclesiastical History* 28 (1977): 113-32.

[43] M.T. Martin, *Percy Chartulary*, Surtees Society, 117 (1909): 381-82.

[44] *Annales Monastici*, ed. H.R. Luard, Rolls Series (1864-69), 4: 409, 418).

[45] E.g. William Briwerre gave specific lands and rents to Mottisfont Priory for his and his wife's anniversaries (*Monasticon*, 6(1): 481). See also Michael M. Sheehan, *The Will in Medieval England* (Toronto, 1963), pp. 231-32, 259-62.

[46] For Osbert fitz Hervey, see the "Vision of Thurkill," H.L.D. Ward, ed., *Journal of the British Archaeological Association* 31 (1875): 452-53. For Geoffrey Ridel, see *Radulphi de Diceto opera*, 2: 68.

cording the death of Adam's widow in childbirth before she could enjoy her legacy.[47]

Few English wills survive before the mid-thirteenth century, and I have found none from any of the fifty-two royal administrators. A few details about several are available, however, revealing names of executors and some bequests. Four appointed clerics as their executors. Master Thomas of Hurstbourne, longtime clerk of Henry II and Richard I, named as his executors the prior of Merton and the abbot of a Cistercian house at Stratford Langthorne, Essex; but we know nothing about the terms of his will.[48] Hubert Walter appointed two members of his household, James Savage and Master Elias of Dereham.[49] Peter des Roches also included Elias of Dereham among his executors; he had four, headed by Ralph de Neville, bishop of Chicester and royal chancellor.[50] Peter left funds for completing two Cistercian monasteries he had been planning. Hubert de Burgh is the only layman about whose will anything is known. It shows his interest in the Dominicans, for he named Brother Walter of the Order of Preachers one of his executors, and he left them considerable sums of money.[51] Often wills included bequests for socially useful purposes, such as feeding the poor. An example is the will made by Richard fitz Neal, bishop of London, which left a modest sum of money to the chapter of St. Paul's for alms.[52]

Ralph of Coggeshall's description of Hubert Walter's last hours is typical of accounts of "good deaths" that chroniclers liked to give. The archbishop lay ill for four days before he died on 13 July 1205, and he remained conscious long enough to prepare for a Christian death. He made his confession, he ordered a will which he had drawn up years earlier to be read for his approval, and he sent for his old friend the bishop of Rochester to perform the last rites.[53] The arch-

[47]*Gesta Abbatum monasterii S. Albani,* ed. H.T. Riley, Rolls Series (1867-69), 1: 329-30.
[48]*Ninth Report of the Royal Commission on Historical MSS.* (London, 1883-84), 1: 26, 49a, D & C St. Paul's.
[49]Young, *Hubert Walter,* p. 166.
[50]Others were P. archdeacon of Winchester and Luke des Roches, archdeacon of Surrey, Meekings, "Netley Abbey," p. 1. King John addressed letters to Geoffrey fitz Peter's executors, but the close rolls do not record their names, *Rotuli litterarum clausarum,* Record Commission (1833-34), 1: 154b, 162b.
[51]*Calendar of Liberate Rolls,* Public Record Office (1917—), 2: 242. *Calendar of Documents Relating to Ireland,* ed. H.S. Sweetman and G.F. Handcock (London, 1875-86), 1: 45. The executor of Hugh Bardolf's will was another royal official (Reginald of Cornhill, *Pipe Roll 6 John,* p. 212).
[52]Maria Hackett, ed., *Registrum eleemosynariae D. Pauli Londoniensis* (London, 1827), p. xlviii. Fitz Neal also left a cope, two reliquaries, and two pastoral staffs to St. Paul's (C.N.L. Brooke and Gillian Kier, *London 800-1216: The Shaping of the City* [Berkeley, Calif., 1975], p. 272). Eustace de Fauconberg, bishop of London, also left a will, although its terms are not known (*Close Rolls Henry III, 1227-31,* Public Record Office [1902], pp. 56-59).
[53]*Radulphi de Coggeshall Chronicon Anglicanum,* ed. J. Stevenson, Rolls Series (1875), pp. 156-59; Young, *Hubert Walter,* pp. 162-63.

bishop left the monks of Christchurch, Canterbury, splendid sets of vestments, jewelry, altarplate, all the paraphernalia of his "principal chapel," on condition that they spend 300 marks for the good of his soul. When King John saw the worth of these goods, he seized them and eventually gave them to his new bishop of Winchester, Peter des Roches.[54]

Laymen too could meet death in edifying ways which earned them chroniclers' praise. Matthew Paris, usually so critical of *curiales,* found Stephen of Segrave deserving of a favorable obituary because of the way in which he met death. Stephen prepared for death with pious gifts, then returned to his old refuge at St. Mary de Pré, Leicester, to die in the habit of an Austin canon.[55] Two other laymen among the royal servants retired to monasteries to await their end. Richard de Lucy entered the abbey of Lesnes shortly after he had founded it, to die there as a canon; and William Briwerre retired to his foundation, Dunkeswell Abbey, in order to die in the Cistercian habit.[56] Ecclesiastics too sometimes withdrew to monasteries to prepare for death. William de Sainte-Mère-Eglise gave up his responsibilities as bishop of London in 1221 and retired to St. Osyth's Priory, where he died as an Austin canon in 1224.[57]

No doubt, few of the Angevin kings' servants, whether laymen or clerks, had much real spirituality. They certainly did not let their Christianity stand in the way of their service to the monarch or their own greed, if they even understood that their activities were incompatible with their religion. Yet men considered the king's "evil counselors" and blamed for their master's arbitrary acts could be exceedingly generous in endowing churches, monasteries, and hospitals. The dean and chapter of Exeter Cathedral remembered William Briwerre not as one of King John's greediest agents, but as *nobilis vir laudabilis memoriae . . . beneficus noster.*[58] Worldly royal clerks, promoted by the king to bishoprics, could devote energy and expenses to cathedral building on a grand scale.[59] Doubtless, such men saw God as a force of power more than of love, as a letter

---

[54]*Gervase of Canterbury: Historical Works,* ed. William Stubbs, Rolls Series (1879-80), 2: 98, 413-14.

[55]*Chronica Majora,* 4: 169.

[56]For Richard de Lucy, J.C. Dickinson, "The English Regular Canons and the Continent in the Twelfth Century," *Transactions of the Royal Historical Society,* fifth series, 1 (1951): 85; and Oliver, *Monasticon dioc. Exon.,* p. 393.

[57]*Dictionary of National Biography,* s.v. "William of Sainte-Mère-Eglise."

[58]Oliver, *Monasticon Exon.,* p. 53.

[59]Godfrey de Lucy rebuilt the eastern end of Winchester Cathedral, adding the Lady Chapel, *Monasticon,* 1: 196. John of Oxford completed construction of Norwich Cathedral and built an infirmary for the monks, *Bartholomaei de Cotton Historia Anglicana,* ed. H.R. Luard, Rolls Series (1859), p. 393. Richard fitz Neal watched over construction at St. Paul's, *Ralph of Coggeshall,* p. 89. Henry of London built the nave of Christ Church Cathedral, Dublin, and in his last years began raising funds to rebuild St. Patrick's Church as a cathedral, Aubrey Gwynn and R. Neville Hadcock, *Medieval Religious Houses, Ireland* (London, 1970), pp. 72, 171.

of Hubert de Burgh written during a military expedition indicates. He writes that no one can triumph over his enemies unless led by the Lord of Hosts.[60] Yet Hubert could find consolation in the Christian religion when he had fallen into disgrace and fled into sanctuary.[61]

This group of royal servants' religious benefactions indicates that they took seriously the Church's teachings as they understood them, that they recognized some obligation to share their often ill-gotten gain with God and with the poor, and that they prepared for death in accordance with the Christian practices of their day. We cannot hope to understand the minds of men like William Briwerre or Peter des Roches, who amassed enormous wealth through dubious means and then used it to found religious houses. We can only compare them to more familiar "new men," nineteenth-century American "robber barons" who similarly amassed great fortunes and then spent them building libraries, museums, and universities. Twelfth- and thirteenth-century administrators' pious gifts perhaps showed greater concern for the poor, but they had much the same purpose as the charitable contributions of modern self-made men: the purchase of self-respect and of the respect of others.

[60]Fred A. Cazel, "Religious Motivation in the Biography of Hubert de Burgh," in *Religious Motivation*, ed. Derek Baker, pp. 115-16, citing P.R.O., Anc. Correspondence SC 1/6 101.
[61]*Close Rolls Henry III, 1231-34*, Public Record Office (1905), p. 161. Henry III ordered Hubert's psalter taken away from him.

Note

On William Briwerre as a patron of the Cistercians, see now Christopher Holdsworth, "The Cistercians in Devon," in *Studies in Medieval History Presented to R. Allen Brown*, ed. Christopher Harper-Bill, Christopher Holdsworth, Janet L. Nelson (Boydell Press, 1989).

Appendix I
Selected Royal Administrators, c. 1170-1239

Hugh Bardolf: Knight, rose to baronial rank.
(d. 1203) Sheriff, *dapifer,* baron of Exchequer, royal justice.

Richard Barre: cleric, archdeacon of Lisieux, c. 1173-1190; archdeacon of Ely,
(d. 1202/13) 1190—
Royal clerk and diplomat, justice.

William Basset: Knight.
(d. 1185) Sheriff, baron of Exchequer, royal justice.

Michael Belet, Sr. Knight.
(d. 1201) *Pincerna,* sheriff, justice.

William Briwerre: Knight, rose to baronial rank.
(d. 1226) Sheriff, baron of Exchequer, royal justice.

Hubert de Burgh: Knight, became earl of Kent, 1227.
(d. 1243) Justiciar, 1215-1232.

Walter of Creeping: Knight.
(d. 1217/23) Royal justice.

Master Eustace of Cleric, of baronial family.
Fauconberg: Bishop of London, 1221-28.
(d. 1228) Treasurer, 1217-28.

Osbert fitz Hervey: Knight.
(d. 1206) Undersheriff, royal justice.

Richard fitz Neal: cleric, archdeacon of Ely,
(d. 1198) bishop of London, 1189-98.
Treasurer, 1159-96.

Geoffrey fitz Peter: Knight, became earl of Essex, 1199.
(d. 1213) Chief forester, justiciar, 1198-1213.

Roger fitz Reinfrid: Knight.
(d. c. 1198) Sheriff, royal justice.

Adam fitz William: Knight.
(d. 1238) Royal justice, escheator.

Ralf Foliot: Cleric, archdeacon of Hereford, 1192-93/99.
(d. 1198/99) Chancery clerk and royal justice.

Adam de Furnellis: Knight.
(d. c. 1189) Sheriff and keeper of the Stannaries.

Ranulf de Glanvill: Knight, rose to baronial rank.
(d. 1190) Sheriff, justiciar, 1180-89.

John of Guestling: Knight.
(d. c. 1220) Royal justice.

Ralf Hareng: | Knight.
(d. 1230) | Sheriff and royal justice.

Richard of Herriard: | Knight.
(d. 1208) | Royal justice.

Thomas of Heydon: | Cleric.
(d. 1235) | Royal clerk and justice.

Hubert Walter: | Cleric, dean of York, bishop of Salisbury, 1189-93; archbishop
(d. 1205) | of Canterbury, 1193-1205
Justiciar, 1193-98; chancellor, 1199-1205.

Master Thomas of | Cleric.
Hurstbourne: | Exchequer clerk, justice.
(d. 1200/1201)

Roger Huscarl: | Knight.
(d. c. 1230) | Royal justice in England and Ireland

Richard of Ilchester: | Cleric, archdeacon of Poitiers, 1162/63-1173; bishop of
(d. 1188) | Winchester, 1173-88.
Royal clerk, baron of Exchequer, justice.

Master Godfrey de Insula: | Cleric.
(d. after 1215) | Justiciar's clerk and justice.

William de Insula: | Knight.
(d. 1239) | Sheriff and royal justice, marshal of Exchequer.

Jocelin: | Cleric, archdeacon of Lewes (Chichester).
(d. 1202/1203) | Royal clerk and justice.

Robert of Lexington: | Cleric.
(d. 1250) | Sheriff, custodian of lands, royal justice.

Henry of London: | Cleric, archdeacon of Stafford, archbishop of Dublin, 1213-28.
(d. 1228) | Justiciar of Ireland, 1213-15, 1221-24.

Godfrey de Lucy: | Cleric, archdeacon of Richmond and of Derby, 1182/84-89;
(d. 1204) | bishop of Winchester, 1189-1204.
Royal Justice.

Richard de Lucy: | Knight, rose to baronial rank.
(d. 1179) | Justiciar, 1168-78/79.

Richard de Mucegros: | Knight.
(d. 1237) | Sheriff and royal justice.

Thomas of Moulton: | Knight, rose to baronial rank.
(d. 1240) | Sheriff and royal justice.

Master Ralph of Norwich: | Cleric.
(d. 1258/59) | Exchequer clerk, royal justice, chancellor of Ireland, 1249-56.

John of Oxford: | Cleric, dean of Salisbury, 1165-75;
(d. 1200) | Bishop of Norwich, 1175-1200.
Royal clerk and justice.

Martin of Pattishall: Cleric, archdeacon of Norfolk, 1225-28;
(d. 1229) dean of St. Paul's, 1228-29.
 Judicial clerk and justice.

Simon of Pattishall: Knight.
(d. 1216/17) Sheriff and royal justice.

Henry de Pont-Audemer: Knight.
(d. 1223?) Royal justice.

James of Potterne: Knight.
(d. c. 1220) Sheriff and royal justice.

William of Raleigh: Cleric, bishop of Norwich, 1239-43;
(d. 1250) bishop of Winchester, 1243-50.
 Royal justice.

Geoffrey Ridel: Cleric, archdeacon of Canterbury, 1163-73;
(d. 1189) bishop of Ely, 1173-89.
 Royal clerk, acting chancellor, 1162-73, justice.

Peter des Roches: Cleric, bishop of Winchester, 1205-38.
(d. 1238) Justiciar, 1214, royal counselor.

William Ruffus: Knight.
(d. after 1194) Chamber officer, *dapifer,* royal justice.

William de Ste.-Mère-Eglise: Cleric, dean of Mortain, bishop of London, 1198-21.
(d. 1224) Chamber clerk, Keeper of Jews, justice.

Geoffrey le Sauvage: Knight.
(d. 1230) Royal justice.

Stephen of Segrave: Knight, rose to baronial rank.
(d. 1241) Sheriff, justice, justiciar in 1234.

Master Robert Shardlow: Cleric.
(d. 1253) Diplomat, justice, senior justice in Ireland, 1243—

Master Ralf of Stokes: Cleric.
(d. 1219/24) Justiciar's clerk, justice.

William de Warenne: Baron of Wormegay.
(d. 1209) Royal justice and justice of Jews.

Robert of Wheatfield: Knight.
(d. 1193/94) Sheriff and royal justice.

Henry of Whiston: Cleric in minor orders.
(d. after 1209) Baron of Exchequer and justice.

William of York: Cleric, provost of Beverley, 1239-46,
(d. 1256) bishop of Salisbury, 1246-56.
 Chancery clerk and royal justice.

Appendix II
New Foundations*

Austin canons:
Butley Priory, Suff.—Ranulf de Glanvill
Chetwode Priory, Bucks—Ralph of Norwich
Hartland Abbey, Devon—Richard of Ilchester
Lesnes (Westwood), Kent—Richard de Lucy
Mottisfont Priory, Hants—William Briwerre
Selbourne Priory, Hants—Peter des Roches
Wormegay Priory, Norf.—William de Warenne

Premonstratensians:
Halesowen Abbey, Worcs.—Peter des Roches
Leiston Abbey, Suff.—Ranulf de Glanvill
Titchfield Abbey, Hants—Peter des Roches
Torre Abbey, Devon—William Briwerre
West Dereham, Norf.—Hubert Walter

Cistercians:
Dunkeswell Abbey, Devon—William Briwerre
Projected:
    La Clarté Dieu, France—Peter des Roches
    Netley Abbey, Hants—Peter des Roches
    Wolverhampton, Staffs—Hubert Walter

Dominicans:
Winchester Friary, Hants—Peter des Roches

Gilbertine nuns:
Shouldham Priory, Norf.—Geoffrey fitz Peter

Hospitals:
  Pauper/pilgrim:
Bridgewater, Somerset, St. John—William Briwerre
Dover, Kent, Maison Dieu or St. Mary—Hubert de Burgh
Dublin, St. James at the Steyne—Henry of London
East Tilbury, Essex St. Mary—Geoffrey fitz Peter
Portsmouth, God's House—Peter des Roches
Skirbeck near Boston, Lincs, St. John Baptist—Thomas of Moulton
Southwark, Surrey, St. Thomas (refounded)—Peter des Roches
Sutton Home, Kent, Holy Trinity or St. Mary—Geoffrey fitz Peter
West Somerton, Norf., St. Leonard—Ranulf de Glanvill

  Lepers:
Berkhamstead, Herts, St. John Baptist—Geoffrey fitz Peter
Winchester, Hants, Mary Magdalen—Richard of Ilchester

*Appendix II relies chiefly on Rotha Mary Clay, *The Medieval Hospitals of England* (London, 1909); William Dugdale, *Monasticon Anglicanum* (London, 1846); Aubrey Gwynn and R. Neville Hadcock, *Medieval Religious Houses, Ireland* (London, 1970); and David Knowles and R. Neville Hadcock, *Medieval Religious Houses, England and Wales* (London, 1971).

Appendix III
Gifts to Established Religious Houses

Benedictines:
    Luffield Priory, Bucks/Northants—Ralph Hareng[1]
    Spalding Priory, Lincs—Thomas of Moulton[2]
    Westminster Abbey—Geoffrey fitz Peter[3], Richard of Ilchester[4]
    Wetheral Priory, Cumberland—Thomas of Moulton[5]
    Winchester Cathedral Priory—Geoffrey fitz Peter[6]

Cluniacs:
    Prittlewell Priory, Essex—William de Ste-Mère Eglise[7]

Cistercians:
    Beaulieu Abbey, Hants—Henry de Pont-Audemer [8]
    Calder Abbey, Cumberland—Thomas of Moulton[9]
    Cleeve Abbey, Somerset—Hubert de Burgh[10]
    Combe Abbey, Warws.—Stephen of Segrave[11]
    Dore Abbey, Herefs—Hubert de Burgh[12]
    Holm Cultram, Cumberland—Thomas of Moulton[13]
    Pipewell Abbey, Northants—Simon of Pattishall[14]
    Rufford Abbey, Notts—Robert of Lexington[15]
    Stoneleigh, Warws.—Stephen of Segrave[16]

Austin canons:
    Aldbury, Surrey—Godfrey de Lucy[17]
    Aldgate, London, Priory—Ralph Hareng[18]
    Bourne Abbey, Lincs—Thomas of Moulton[19]
    Coxford Priory, Norf.—Martin of Pattishall(?)[20]
    Dunmow, Essex—Roger fitz Reinfrid[21]

[1]*Luffield Priory Charters*, ed. G. R. Elvey, jt. pubns. of Northants Record Soc. and Bucks Record Soc., 18 (1975), 2: nos. 396, 397.
[2]B.L. MS. Harl. 742, ff. 95d-96d.
[3]Westminster Abbey Muniments Book 11, f. 492b.
[4]Ibid., ff. 570-571.
[5]*Complete Peerage*, 9: 401, note 'c'.
[6]Dugdale, *Monasticon*, 6(2): 974.
[7]Cheney and Cheney, *Letters of Innocent III*, no. 862.
[8]*The Beaulieu Cartulary*, ed. S.F. Hockey, Southampton Records Ser., 17 (1974): no. 146.
[9]*Monasticon*, 5: 340-41.
[10]*Monasticon*, 5: 732-33.
[11]William Dugdale, *The Baronage of England* (London, 1675-76), p. 672.
[12]*Monasticon*, 5:556.
[13]*Complete Peerage*, 9: 401, note 'c'.
[14]*Cal. Charter Rolls*, 1: 205.
[15]*Rufford Charters*, 1: xciii-xcv.
[16]*Cal. Charter Rolls*, 2: 52.
[17]*Cal. Charter Rolls*, 3: 430.
[18]*Cartulary of Holy Trinity, Aldgate*, ed. G.A.J. Hodgett, London Record Soc. Pubns., 7 (1971): no. 1004.
[19]*Cal. Charter Rolls*, 4: 29.
[20]Coxford Cartulary, no. 167.
[21]B.L. MS. Harl. 662, f. 62.

	East Ruddham (later Coxford)—Michael Belet[22]
	Ipswich, Suff.—John of Oxford, bp. of Norwich[28]
	Laude Priory, Leics—William Basset[24]
	Lesnes, Kent—Godfrey de Lucy[25], Roger fitz Reinfrid[26]
	St. Gregory, Canterbury—Hubert Walter[27]
	St. Mary de Pré, Leicester—Stephen of Segrave[28]
	Newstead Priory, Notts—Robert of Lexington[29]
	St. Denys Priory, Hants—William Briwerre[30]
	St. Mary Overy, Southwark—William de Warenne[31]
	St. Thomas' Abbey, Dublin—Henry of London[32]
	Walsingham Priory, Norf.—Hubert de Burgh[33]
Premonstratensian canons:	Barlings Abbey, Lincs—Hugh Bardolf[34]
	Dale Abbey, Derby—Robert of Lexington[35]
	St. Radegund's, Bradsole, Kent—Hubert de Burgh[36]
	Welbeck Abbey, Notts—William Briwerre[37], Geoffrey fitz Peter[38]
Dominicans:	London, Holborn—Hubert de Burgh[39]
Knights Hospitallers:	Essex—Richard de Lucy[40]
	Houses of Women
Benedictines:	Cambridge, St. Radegund Priory—Godfrey de Insula[41]
	Godstow Abbey, Oxon.—Ralph Hareng[42]

[22]Coxford Cartulary, nos. 41-52, 467.
[23]Knowles and Hadcock, p. 161.
[24]William Farrer, *Honors and Knights' Fees*, (London, 1923-25), 2: 310.
[25]*Fourteenth Report of the Royal Comm. on Hist. MSS.*, app. 8, p. 194.
[26]*Monasticon*, 6: 457.
[27]*kentish Cartulary of the Order of St. John of Jerusalem*, ed. Charles Cotton, Kent Archaeol. Soc., Kent Records (1930), p. 77.
[28]*Cal. Charter Rolls*, 2: 52.
[29]*Rufford Charters*, 1: xcv.
[30]*Ancient Charters*, ed. J.H. Round, Pipe Roll Soc., 10 (1888): no. 66.
[31]*Monasticon*, 6: 169, 171.
[32]*Register of St. Thomas, Dublin*, Rolls Series, no. 341.
[33]*Monasticon*, 6: 74.
[34]*Cal. Charter Rolls*, 2: 390.
[35]*Cartulary of Dale Abbey*, ed. Avrom Saltman, Derbys Archaeol. Soc. and Historical MSS. Comm. (1966), pp. 359-60.
[36]*Monasticon*, 6(2): 942.
[37]*Cal. Charter Rolls*, 4: 71.
[38]Colvin, *White canons*, pp. 68-69.
[39]Matt. Paris, *Chronica Majora*, 4: 243-44.
[40]Gervers, ed., *Cart. of Knights of St. John in England*, no. 216.
[41]*Curia Regis Rolls*, Public Record Office (1923–), 9: 26-27.
[42]*English Register of the Godstow nunnery*, ed. Andrew Clark, E.E.T.S. orig. ser., 142 (1911): nos. 86, 249-51.

	Kingston St. Michael Priory, Wilts—Richard of Herriard[43]
	Norwich, St. Mary Carrow—William de Warenne[44]
Cistercians:	Wintney Priory, Hants—Godfrey de Lucy[45], Richard of Herriard[46]
Gilbertines:	Bullington Priory, Lincs—Thomas of Moulton[47]
Augustinians:	London, St. Mary Clerkenwell Priory—Roger fitz Reinfrid[48]
Premonstratensian canonesses:	Dublin, Grace Dieu, St. Mary Priory—Henry of London[49]

[43] *Monasticon*, 4: 399.
[44] *Early Yorks Charters*, 8: 32.
[45] *Cal. Charter Rolls*, 4: 394.
[46] *Cal. Charter Rolls*, 4: 393, 397; B.L. MS. Cott. Claud., D iii, f. 146^v.
[47] Stenton, ed., *Charters Relating to Gilbertine Houses*, nos. 10, 22.
[48] *Cartulary of St. Mary Clerkenwell*, ed. W.O. Hassell, Royal Hist. Soc. Camden Ser., 3rd Ser., 71 (1949): nos. 101, 105.
[49] Gwyn and Hadcock, p. 317.

Appendix IV
Places of Burial

Bishops buried in their cathedrals:
    Eustace de Fauconberg at St. Paul's, London
    Richard fitz Neal at St. Paul's, London
    Richard of Ilchester at Winchester
    Henry of London at Christ Church, Dublin
    Hubert Walter at Canterbury
    Godfrey de Lucy at Winchester
    John of Oxford at Norwich
    Geoffrey Ridel at Ely
    Peter des Roches at Winchester (His heart buried at the Cistercian Abbey of Waverley)
    William of York at Salisbury

Bishops buried elsewhere:
    William de Ste-Mère-Eglise, resigned bishopric of London, buried at St. Osyth's Priory, Essex, in Austin canon's habit
    William of Raleigh at Tours Cathedral, France, *en route* to Rome

Others:
    Michael Belet at parish church of Thorpe Market, Norf., or at East Ruddham Priory (?)
    William Briwerre at Dunkeswell Abbey in habit of a Cistercian monk
    Hubert de Burgh in Dominican chapel, Holborn, London
    Geoffrey fitz Peter at Shouldham Priory; part of his body at Holy Trinity, Aldgate
    Roger fitz Reinfrid at St. Mary Clerkenwell, London (?)
    Ranulf de Glanvill died in the Holy Land, Third Crusade
    Robert of Lexington at Rufford Abbey
    Richard de Lucy at Lesnes in an Austin canon's habit
    Richard de Mucegros at St. Peter's Abbey, Gloucester (?)
    Thomas of Moulton at Spalding Priory (?)
    Simon of Pattishall at Pipewell Abbey
    Henry de Pont-Audemer at Beaulieu Abbey (?)
    Stephen of Segrave at Leicester Abbey as an Austin canon
    William de Warenne at St. Mary Overy, Southwark
    Robert of Wheatfield at Thame Abbey (?)

(?) Uncertain, my own conjecture, based on the fact that they had relatives buried in the places given.

9

Clerical Judges in English Secular Courts:
The Ideal versus the Reality

St. Paul advised Christians that "no man that warreth for God entangleth himself in the things of this world,"[1] and councils of the Church constantly legislated against involvement of the clergy in worldly affairs, concerned that time would be taken from a cleric's chief concern, the care of souls. Yet throughout the Middle Ages, lay rulers relied upon members of the clergy to serve them as judges, secretaries, and other administrative agents. Bishops were also barons, dual personages in the eyes of twelfth- and thirteenth-century canonists and theologians. The result was an intermingling of the two orders – laity and clergy – that confronted ecclesiastical leaders with a conflict between their ideal and the reality of medieval society. There was the ideal of St. Paul's advice, and there was the reality that the Church was deeply entangled in secular affairs, with its clergy holding powerful posts at the courts of princes.

The revolution in government of the twelfth and thirteenth centuries with growth of bureaucracies made the mingling of clerics in secular matters more common than ever. Henry II and his sons in England needed civil servants who could only come from the clergy. Bishops, abbots, and lesser clergy served the Angevin kings as clerks, itinerant justices, and more rarely, sheriffs.[2] The royal administration was largely staffed with clerics, not only because they were literate, but also because the king could be certain that their ecclesiastical benefices would provide them an income. This situation posed a number of problems.

Under the circumstances, pluralism and absenteeism were obvious consequences.[3] Rectors of some rural churches and archdeacons of some

---

[1] II Timothy 2:4.

[2] According to C.R. Cheney, *From Becket to Langton, English Church Government, 1170–1216* (Manchester, 1956), pp. 24–25, seventeen bishops, or a third of the episcopate, served as royal justices, while at least two served as sheriffs. Marion Gibbs and Jane Lang, *English Bishops and Reform, 1215–1272* (Oxford, 1934), p. 167, list seven bishops and eleven abbots who served Henry III as itinerant justices.

[3] On the question of pluralism, see A. Hamilton Thompson, "Pluralism in the Medieval Church; with notes on Pluralists in the diocese of Lincoln, 1366," *Associated Architectural and Archeological Societies, Reports and Papers (1915)*, xxxiii, 35–73.

dioceses were constantly absent in the king's service. Other royal clerks were not priests or deacons, but though only in minor orders were eligible for lucrative benefices, and appointed poorly paid deputies to perform their ecclesiastical duties. The most convenient benefices for royal servants were cathedral prebends, since they provided a good income yet according to canon law were without care of souls. This meant that the holder, if in higher orders, could lawfully hold another benefice with care of souls.[4] C. N. L. Brooke has estimated that about a quarter of cathedral prebendaries were regularly absent in the king's service in the twelfth century, although in some cases the number could rise higher.[5] Although popes, councils, and bishops inveighed against pluralism throughout the Middle Ages, the pluralists' consciences seem to have been little troubled.

Another problem was possible conflicts of interest for clerics obliged to serve both Church and king. Which would receive their first loyalty in case of conflict? Perhaps medieval men did not see conflict as necessary, since both Church and monarchy served the same end, the security of the *Respublica Christiana*. Yet the problem could arise for bishops who held high office in the royal government. The chancellor was traditionally a member of the clergy who could look forward to appointment to a bishopric, and who might then resign his office, as did Thomas Becket, or who might continue to hold it.[6] Possibly some sought papal dispensation before accepting appointment to secular posts. William of Malmesbury wrote in his *De Gestis Regum Anglorum* that Roger of Salisbury, Henry I's justiciar, had shunned the king's courts until three different Archbishops of Canterbury and the pope had allowed him to share in the work of secular justice. William then noted that Roger's secular responsibilities did not cause him to neglect his ecclesiastical duties.[7] Nigel Wireker, a satirical writer of the late twelfth century, hinted that bishops sometimes sought papal "indulgences" before serving as secular judges.[8] But no more direct evidence of such papal dispensations survives.[9] Lesser royal clerks who shifted back and forth from ecclesiastical to royal duties must have had a

---

[4] Thompson, p. 62; Kathleen Edwards, *The English Secular Cathedrals in the Middle Ages, a Constitutional Study with Special Reference to the Fourteenth Century* (Manchester, 1949), pp. 37–38.

[5] C.N.L. Brooke, "The Composition of the Chapter of St. Paul's 1068–1163," *Cambridge Historical Journal*, x (1951), 120.

[6] Cheney, p. 22: Geoffrey Ridel, named Bishop of Ely, and Geoffrey Plantagenet, named Archbishop of York. Gibbs and Lang, *English Bishops and Reform*, p. 165: the bishops of Durham, Chichester, Bath and Wells, and Worcester were also chancellors; the bishops of Coventry and Lichfield, Carlisle, Ely, London, and York resigned the office of chancellor on being raised to their bishoprics.

[7] William of Malmesbury, *De Gestis Regum*, ed. William Stubbs (Rolls Series [London, 1887–89]), ii, 484.

[8] *Anglo-Latin Satirical Poets of the Twelfth Century*, ed. Thomas Wright (Rolls series [London, 1872]), i, 219.

[9] Cheney, p. 24.

blurred sense of distinction between the two spheres, as had their episcopal masters. As Sir Frank Stenton wrote of one of them, "We may doubt whether Jocelin, archdeacon of Chichester, deliberately assumed a new habit of mind when he passed from a session of the king's court to sit in that of his own archdeaconry." [10]

The Church could condone the employment of these clerics in the civil service in the hope that they were helping to improve standards of government, softening with Christian teaching the harshness of barbarian and feudal custom. But at the same time, the Church was trying to draw a sharper distinction between clergy and laity. Clergy in the twelfth century were being encouraged to dress in a distinctive way, to remain celibate, to refrain from hunting and hawking; in short, to stress their status as a superior order apart from the world at large.[11] St. Bernard enveighed against those clerics who insisted on imitating the lives of the laity, writing in *De consideratione*, "Indeed, in dress they are soldiers, in profession clergy, in conduct neither. For they neither fight like soldiers nor preach like clerics. To which do they belong? In wishing to belong to both, they desert both, confuse both."[12]

The ideal of the Church that clergy should stand apart from worldly concerns placed clerics in the royal service in an awkward position. If they were to continue to serve the king, they could not avoid violating certain ecclesiastical canons. Councils from the time of the early Church had constantly legislated against involvement of members of the clergy in worldly affairs, particularly as advocates in the law courts. The Apostolic Canons, a collection made sometime before the mid-fourth century, included the decree, "Let not a bishop, priest, or deacon undertake worldly business; otherwise let him be deposed," while the canons of other early councils included similar measures.[13] Gratian summarized the canons in his great twelfth-century collection of canon law, adding a warning to bishops that they ought not to involve themselves in secular causes in the courts.[14]

Gratian, aware that some service by the clergy in government offices was unavoidable, sought to define the types that would be acceptable. He wrote

[10] "Acta Episcoporum," *Cambridge Historical Journal*, iii (1929), 9.

[11] Cheney, pp. 104–6.

[12] Jacques Paul Migne, *Patrologia Latina, cursus completus* (Paris, 1844–64), clxxxii, cols, 771–72, *De consideratione*, lib. iii, cap. v.

[13] Giovanni D. Mansi, *Sacrorum concilorum nova et amplissima collectio* (Florence and Venice, 1758–98), i, col. 30, canon vi, trans. Philip Schaff and Henry Wace, eds., *A Select Library of Nicene and Post-Nicene Fathers of the Christian Church* (second series), *The Seven Ecumenical Councils* (New York, 1900), xiv, 594. The Council of Chalcedon, 451, decreed that no cleric should be involved in worldly business except the guardianship of minors, care of widows, orphans, and the defenseless (Mansi, vii, col. 359, canon iii); *Nicene and Post-Nicene Fathers*, xiv, 269.

[14] *Decretum*, P. i, dist. lxxxviii, c. 3, 4, in E.A. Friedburg, ed., *Corpus iuris canonici* (Graz, 1959), i, col. 307.

that priests could act as judges, provided that they had gained a dispensation for the swearing of oaths; but he warned that should they be involved in the shedding of blood, they would be degraded.[15] In a further discussion of clerics involved in sentences of death or mutilation, Gratian repeated a canon of the Council of Toledo in 675 which declared that those who handle the sacraments of the Lord were not to be permitted to participate in blood-judgments, and those priests who ignored this precept were to be degraded and punished with perpetual imprisonment.[16] Although Gratian recognized the Church's opposition to the shedding of blood, he also recognized the need for capital punishment; elsewhere in the *Decretum*, he gave examples from the law of the Old Testament as evidence of divine sanction for the death penalty. Following St. Augustine's teaching, he added that those who executed the wicked by authority of the law and not by their own authority could not be considered in violation of the Church's commandments.[17]

All these canons plus those of ecclesiastical councils held since the appearance of Gratian's *Decretum* were summarized in 1234 in Pope Gregory IX's *Decretales* under the title "That neither clerics nor monks ought to involve themselves in secular affairs."[18] The chief canons to be added were those of the Third and Fourth Lateran Councils, 1179 and 1215. Pope Alexander III at the Third Lateran Council demanded that clerks hand over their offices held of secular princes, including the office of judge *(justiciarius)*;[19] and Pope Innocent III prohibited clerks from pronouncing or carrying out sentences of blood, from writing or dictating letters directing capital punishment, from participating in trials by ordeal or combat.[20]

Throughout the twelfth and thirteenth centuries, provincial and diocesan synods legislated against clerical involvement in secular affairs. In 1138, an ecclesiastical council at London prohibited clerics from acting as tax collectors *(exactores)* or stewards *(praepositi)* for laymen;[21] and in 1172 a council at Avranches, Normandy, barred clergy and Jews from exercising secular jurisdiction, threatening clerics who did so with loss of their benefices.[22] The Council of Westminster in 1175 once more pointed out the

---

[15] *Decretum*, P. ii, causa xxiii, quest. viii, c. 29, cols. 963–64. For views of other canonists, see Robert L. Benson, *The Bishop-Elect, a Study in Medieval Ecclesiastical Office* (Princeton, 1968), pp. 321–23.

[16] *Decretum*, c. 30, col. 964; Mansi, xi, col. 141, canon vi.

[17] *Decretum*, P. ii, causa xxiii, quest. v, c. 7, col. 932. For Augustine's teaching see *Pat. Lat.*, xxxiii, *epistola* xlvii, cols. 184–87; *epistola* cliii, cols. 653–65; *De Civitate Dei*, xix, 6.

[18] *Decret. Greg. IX*, lib. iii, tit. 1, in *Corpus iuris canonici*, ii, cols. 657–60.

[19] Ibid., cap. iv, col. 658.

[20] Ibid., cap. ix, cols. 659–60. For the full text, see Mansi, xxii, cols. 1006–7, canon xviii.

[21] David Wilkins, *Concilia Magnae Britanniae et Hiberniae* (London, 1737), i, 418; cited in Cheney, p. 21.

[22] Roger Howden, *Gesta Regis Henrici Secundi*, ed. William Stubbs (Rolls Series [London, 1867]), i, 34.

prohibitions against the clergy's participation in judgments of blood and against their holding the secular offices of sheriff or steward.[23] The same prohibition against priests in secular offices was among the canons of a council held by Walter of Coutances, Archbishop of Rouen, in 1189.[24] Yet Walter's whole career was a violation of this canon. He was an Englishman from Cornwall, prominent for years in the chamber and chancery, Keeper of the Seal, and King Richard's justiciar, 1191–93. As justiciar, he went on judicial eyres and presided over the exchequer and the bench at Westminster. His ecclesiastical career rose with his administrative career: he was Archdeacon of Oxford, then Bishop of Lincoln, translated to Rouen in 1184.[25]

In 1213 and 1214, Archbishop Stephen Langton held a council which enacted statutes to regulate the conduct of the clergy in the diocese of Canterbury. They included prohibitions against priests participating in secular administration, acting as advocates in judgments of blood, or in any secular cases unless their own or those of poor people.[26] These prohibitions appear among the articles adopted by a number of English diocesan synods in the thirteenth century: statutes of Bishop Richard Poor for the diocese of Salisbury, 1217–19, reissued for Durham, 1228–36; statutes of Bishop William of Blois for Worcester, 1229; *Constitutiones cuiusdam episcopi*, 1225–30(?); statutes of Richard de Wich for Chichester, 1245–52; and statutes of William of Bitton for Bath and Wells, 1258(?).[27]

The Fourth Lateran Council's action in denouncing clerical involvement in blood judgments is reflected in the canons of some English councils. A council of the province of Canterbury in 1222 adopted an article prohibiting any beneficed clerk or anyone in holy orders from writing or dictating letters inflicting a penalty of blood, or from being present where a judgment of blood was being handed down or carried out.[28] Similar articles were included in the legislation of Bishop Walter de Cantilupe for Worcester, of William Raleigh for Norwich and, after his translation, for Winchester, and later of John Gervais for Winchester.[29] Bishop Robert Grosseteste was strong in his opposition to clerics who served in secular offices. He was more specific in statutes that he issued for his diocese of Lincoln in 1239, stating that clerics should not serve as sheriffs or secular justices or hold offices

[23] *Gesta Henrici Secundi*, i, 85; also Mansi, xxii, col. 148, canon iii.
[24] Mansi, xxii, col. 583, canon x.
[25] Francis West, *The Justiciarship in England, 1066–1232* (Cambridge, 1966), pp. 74–78.
[26] F.M. Powicke and C.R. Cheney, *Councils and Synods with Other Documents Relating to the English Church* (Oxford, 1964), pp. 25–27, articles 1, 10.
[27] Ibid., pp. 60, 63–64, articles 1, 11, Salisbury; p. 180, article 61, Worcester ii; pp. 186–87, articles 32, 40, *Constitutiones cuiusdam episcopi*; p. 456, article 25, Chichester; p. 607, article 34, Bath and Wells.
[28] Ibid., p. 110, article 13.
[29] Ibid., pp. 310, 314, articles 57, 75, Worcester, 1240; p. 348, article 16, Norwich, 1240–43; p. 406, article 19, Winchester ii, 1247; p. 712, article 51; Winchester iii.

(*ballivas*) that obliged them to be accountable to laymen.[30] This measure was borrowed by Bishop William Raleigh for his statutes of Norwich and Winchester.[31] His issuing such statutes shows that they were not taken too seriously in thirteenth-century England, for he had a long career on the bench, rising to the rank of senior justice of the court *coram rege* in 1234, before becoming a bishop in 1239. All the time that he was a justice of the king's court he was also rector of a village church, treasurer of Exeter, and a canon of St. Paul's.[32] As C. R. Cheney, an authority on the legislation of the medieval English Church, admits, the synodal statutes largely "represented unattained ideals."[33]

Attempts by the episcopate to enforce the canons in England could take more positive forms than legislation by diocesan synods. Serving as sheriff was a more outrageous violation of the canons than occasional service on the bench, and few clerics served in the office under Henry II and his sons. Among those who did was Hugh de Nonant, Bishop of Lichfield and Coventry and Sheriff of Warwick, Leicestershire, and Staffordshire about the end of the twelfth century.[34] Baldwin, Archbishop of Canterbury and a former Cistercian abbot, threatened action against Hugh in 1190, pointing out that such work was "against the dignity of the episcopal office." But Hugh was "crafty, bold, and shameless," a cleric who had served for years at the court of Henry II. Although he promised to resign the shrievalties, he did not, and Baldwin had to make preparations for his trial.[35]

One of those who most strongly opposed the participation of clerics in secular government was the saint and former Carthusian monk, Hugh of Avalon, Bishop of Lincoln at the end of the twelfth century. His monastic biographer noted that when he became bishop, many of the canons of Lincoln were also "members of the king's council and household, and were distinguished politicians and scholars."[36] Hugh soon set to work to change

[30] Ibid., p. 271, article 16; repeated in a list of rules for priests, no. 16, p. 276. Another rule forbade priests to study civil law, p. 277, no. 37.

[31] Ibid., p. 348, article 17, Norwich; p. 406, article 20, Winchester ii.

[32] For Raleigh's career, see C.A.F. Meekings, "Martin Pateshull and William Raleigh," *Bulletin of the Institute for Historical Research*, xxvi (1953), 157–79.

[33] Cheney, "Statute-Making in the English Church in the Thirteenth Century," *Proceedings of the Second International Congress of Medieval Canon Law (Monumenta iuris canonici*, series C, i [Vatican City, 1965]), p. 414.

[34] Charles L. Kingsford, "Hugh de Nonant," *Dict. Nat. Bio.*, ed. Sidney Lee (London, 1900), xiv, 545–48; Cheney, *Becket to Langton, p.* 25. Others were Hilary, Bishop of Chichester and sheriff of Sussex, 1154–55 and 1160–62, Henry Mayr-Harting, "Hilary, Bishop of Chichester (1147–1169) and Henry II," *Eng. Hist. Rev.*, lxxviii (1963), 213, 216; and Geoffrey Plantagenet, illegitimate son of the king, Archbishop of York, also sheriff of York, 1194, Cheney, p. 25.

[35] Ralph de Diceto, *Opera Historica*, ed. William Stubbs (Rolls Series [London, 1876]), ii, 77; *Dict. Nat. Bio.*, xiv, 547.

[36] *Magna Vita Sancti Hugonis*, ed. and trans. Decima L. Douie and Dom Hugh Farmer (London, 1961–62), i, 92.

this situation, for in his view royal clerks holding cathedral prebends "devastate and plunder all the churches like rapacious birds of prey."[37] His biography records his policy: "It was exceptional for him to make either royal clerks or the clergy of any other cathedral canons of his church, because he expected those on whom he conferred the revenues of the canonries of his church to reside at Lincoln."[38] His policy soon caused a crisis, for Henry II expected to continue his practice of maintaining his clerks with ecclesiastical appointments. When the king demanded that the bishop grant a prebend to a royal clerk, Hugh refused, stating his reasons strongly:

> Ecclesiastical benefices should not be conferred on royal officials, but on ecclesiastics, since their holders should not serve at court, at the treasury or the exchequer, but as the Scripture enjoins, at the altar. The lord king has the wherewithal to pay his own servants, he has the possessions with which to reward those who transact secular business for him. It is only right for him to let those who are serving the King of Heaven enjoy the provision made for their needs, and not allow them to be deprived of the salary due to them.[39]

Fortunately, Hugh could speak freely to the king, since they were friends. This one firm refusal freed the bishop from any future requests from Henry II for prebends for his clerks, but he had to fight the battle again with Richard I in 1197. Richard tried to force twelve of the Lincoln canons to serve him abroad at their own expense, but St. Hugh refused to permit it, telling the king, "I have never constrained my clerks to serve the king, nor will I do so."[40]

King Richard's agent in this affair was Hubert Walter, a prime illustration of the clerical preoccupation with secular affairs that St. Hugh so strongly opposed. Hubert Walter seems to have had little awareness of any distinction between his two roles as an officer of the Church and a servant of the king; he once said that he "had both swords committed to his custody."[41] Hugh tried to be certain whether his instructions from the archbishop came in his capacity as head of the English Church or as the king's representative. As his biographer wrote, "Wherever he [Hubert Walter] ordered or advised anything which pertained rather to the material than to the spiritual sword, the man of God [Hugh] had no scruples about saying to him as we read in

---

[37] Ibid., p. 119.
[38] Ibid., pp. 119–20.
[39] Ibid., p. 115. A similar view is expressed on p. 120: "He said emphatically that, as they who served at the altar were rightly partakers with the altar, it was unjust that the endowments of the altar should go to those who never served there. This seemed to him a species of robbery...."
[40] Ibid., ii, 111–13; see also Introduction, i, xix.
[41] Ibid., ii, 28.

Acts that the apostles did to the high priests, 'It behooves us to obey God rather than men.'"[42]

Hubert Walter had no scruples about using the clerks of his and other bishops' households to assist him in his duties as justiciar and chancellor, so that a number of them also served at the exchequer and on the bench at Westminster.[43] A letter written for him by Peter of Blois about 1195 reflects his feeling that he could call freely upon the cathedral clergy to staff the civil service, and that their service to the king exempted them from the usual rules of residence. The letter requested that the chapter of Salisbury Cathedral permit the absence of one of their canons because he was needed for the king's service:

> Since reverence is everywhere due to the great ones of the earth and especially and above all to the king, the exchequer account and the necessities of the state exempt from the general rule those who do the business of the king or kingdom; for in all walks of life he sufficiently fulfills his duties, although absent, who devotes himself to the welfare of all. Therefore, because the faithfulness and industry of Master Thomas of Hurstbourne in the public business of the king is abundantly proved, we do not wish you to compel him to reside as long as he is so occupied.[44]

The attitude toward secular service by clerics of a later Archbishop of Canterbury, Master Richard Grant, contrasts with Hubert Walter's complacency. Richard Grant's appointment to the archbishopric in 1227 came from the pope, not the king; and unlike Hubert Walter, he had no background in royal administration.[45] When Richard visited Rome in 1231, he protested to the pope against the involvement of English clergy in secular government. He complained that bishops "were sitting at the king's exchequer, bringing forward secular causes, and giving judgments of blood to the neglect of their pastoral cares." He added that they were encouraging beneficed clergy and priests to follow their example, "mixing themselves in secular cares and judgments of laymen."[46] Although the pope promised his aid in ending these abuses, Richard died soon; and apparently nothing came of his complaint.

Perhaps the strongest opponent of the employment of clerics as royal judges was Robert Grosseteste, mid-thirteenth century scholar-bishop of Lincoln. In 1236, he challenged Henry III's appointment of the abbot of Ramsey as an itinerant justice, complaining to Edmund Rich, Archbishop

---

[42] Ibid., 29; Acts 5:29.

[43] C.R. Cheney, *English Bishops' Chanceries, 1100–1250* (Manchester, 1950), pp. 17–19; Charles R. Young, *Hubert Walter, Lord of Canterbury and Lord of England* (Durham, N.C., 1968), pp. 58–59.

[44] *Pat. Lat.*, ccvii, cols. 403–4, *epistola* 135; C.R. Cheney, trans., *Hubert Walter* (London, 1967), p. 158.

[45] William Hunt, "Richard Grant," *Dict. Nat. Bio.*, viii, 401–2.

[46] Roger Wendover, *Flores Historiarum*, ed. H. G. Hewlett (Rolls Series [London, 1886–89]), iii, 14.

of Canterbury.[47] He pointed out in his letter that the canons and constitutions of councils forbade any cleric, much less a Benedictine abbot, to sit in judgments of blood, and he asked the archbishop to counsel the king to withdraw his appointment.[48] In a second letter, Grosseteste stated his dissatisfaction with the archbishop's response to his first request. The archbishop had twice replied that it would be better to await a council's discussion, but Grosseteste cited Scripture, canon law, and a letter of Gregory the Great to prove that clerical participation in secular justice was already clearly labelled a sin. Bishops who have clerics in their care themselves sin, therefore, by allowing them to sin in this way.[49]

Later the Bishop of Lincoln wrote a long letter to the archbishop, actually a treatise considering six areas of conflict between the crown and the Church.[50] He cited the royal writs appointing abbots as itinerant justices, and then he made his first point that "it can be shown infallibly that abbots assuming by their command the burden of judicial office sin gravely."[51] He continued, saying that they sin not only because they will be drawn into judgments of blood but also because they will be drawn away from spiritual things toward lower ones, citing the usual passages from St. Paul in support.[52] Also, he stressed the separation of the tasks of the two powers with judgment in secular matters clearly belonging to the temporal sphere.[53] Grosseteste anticipated that some clerics who were also barons owing feudal services might cite Christ's words, "Render unto Caesar ..." But he answered that they need not perform personally their judicial responsibilities any more than they performed personally their military service.[54]

Grosseteste, like St. Hugh of Lincoln, was preoccupied with the clergy's responsibility for the care of souls, and he feared that secular duties would divert them from their first duty. He fought against presentation of clerics holding posts in the royal government to benefices having care of souls, causing him to oppose some of the ablest men in the kingdom.[55] But his fellow-bishops did not share his concern. They were like Hubert Walter, finding no harm in having substitutes to fulfill the functions of cathedral

[47] *Letters of Robert Grosseteste*, ed. H. R. Luard (Rolls Series [London, 1861–63]), i, 105–8, *epistola* xxvii. Later, in 1239, he sought removal of the abbot of Croyland from the list of itinerant justices, p. 262, no. lxxxii.

[48] For a discussion of the letter, see J.H. Srawley, "Grosseteste's Administration of the Diocese of Lincoln," in D.A. Callus, ed., *Robert Grosseteste, Scholar and Bishop* (Oxford, 1955), p. 165; Francis S. Stevenson, *Robert Grosseteste, Bishop of Lincoln* (London, 1899), pp. 171–72.

[49] *Letters*, p. 111, no. xxviii; Callus, p. 166; Stevenson, p. 172.

[50] *Letters*, pp. 205–34, no. lxxii. For a list of the six points, see Stevenson, pp. 173–74.

[51] *Letters*, p. 205.

[52] Ibid., p. 206. I Cor. 6:4; II Tim. 2:4.

[53] Ibid., pp. 208–10.

[54] Ibid., p. 213.

[55] A protégé of William Raleigh, ibid., p. 63, no. xvii; Hugh Pateshull, p. 97, no. xxv; Robert Passelewe, pp. 349–50, no. cxxiv; Ralph Neville, pp. 188–90, no. lxii.

canons who were absent in the royal service. Grosseteste held to a stricter view, however, maintaining that prebends had care of souls and that appointment of absentee royal clerks endangered those souls.[56] The tradition of royal service was so strong that he had little success in winning the support of the archbishop or the other English bishops. Grosseteste did gain, however, the support of Pope Gregory IX, who authorized him to proceed against the clergy of his diocese who were sheriffs and justices.[57]

The bishop refused to admit Robert Passelewe, a longtime royal clerk, to a church to which the king had presented him because he had been a justice of the forest. In a letter to Henry III, Grosseteste again attempted to define the distinction between the temporal and spiritual spheres, so that each might attend to its proper sphere. He advised that "spiritual things be dealt with by ecclesiastical and spiritual men, secular things by secular men; namely military things by military men, and corrections and reforms of excesses and defects in those things that touch the commonwealth of the kingdom to be dealt with by secular persons...."[58] His position involved him in another quarrel with the Archbishop of Canterbury, for Passelewe appealed to Boniface of Savoy and gained admission to the church. Grosseteste wrote still another letter to the archbishop, complaining of his action and repeating his arguments against the mingling of secular and spiritual responsibilities.[59] Grosseteste, then, saw clearly the conflict between the Church's teaching on the clergy's withdrawal from secular government and their actual involvement. He so feared the consequences for the care of souls that he was willing to contend against Henry III himself, but his struggle did little to change conditions in thirteenth-century England.

Several moralists and satirists in twelfth- and thirteenth-century England complained of the employment of clerics as royal judges. The most learned of all these was John of Salisbury in the time of Henry II. John's close association with two archbishops of Canterbury, Theobald and Thomas Becket, acquainted him well with Henry's clerical courtiers. Certainly he knew many of them as his associates in the archbishop's household.[60] He came to despise royal courtiers, as he made clear throughout his *Policraticus*, complaining of their venality, avarice, and sycophancy. He wrote to a petitioner who was seeking a position for a friend in the royal household, warning that he would be torn between loyalty to the Church and obedience to the king: "If you act rightly and defend the liberty of the Church, the authority of the king bars the way; whereas if you act ill, the authority of the

---

[56] W.A. Pantin, "Grosseteste's Relations with the Papacy and the Crown," in Callus, pp. 179–83.

[57] *Entries in the Papal Registers relating to Great Britain*, ed. W.H. Bliss (Public Record Office [London, 1894]), i, 155, July 1236. In 1247, Innocent iv sent Grosseteste a similar letter, ibid., p. 230.

[58] Grosseteste, *Letters*, p. 349, no. cxxiv; Pantin, in Callus, p. 199.

[59] *Letters*, pp. 353–56, no. cxxvi.

[60] For biographical information, see W.J. Millor and H.E. Butler, *Selected Letters of John of Salisbury* (London, 1955), i, introduction, xii–xvi.

law of God cries out against you on every side." And he asked, "What could be more filthy, more shameless and unscrupulous than an old priest turned informer? Will he do such outrage to his conscience and his reputation merely to please the satellites of the court?"[61]

Typical of the curialist clerks whom John of Salisbury condemned was Walter Map, a clerk of Henry II's household, who often served as an itinerant justice and who collected ecclesiastical benefices as a reward for his royal service. He held prebends at St. Paul's and Lincoln, was named Chancellor of Lincoln, and finally Archdeacon of Oxford.[62] He was known as a wit, the author of *De nugis curialium*, a sharp satire on conditions in the Church and at court. Even though he served as a royal judge, he opposed the employment of clerics, but for reasons far different from John of Salisbury's. His opposition was based on snobbism. He noted that clerical judges were often harsher than lay ones, which he explained by their base birth, citing the Roman poet Claudian, "Nothing is harder than the lowly whenever he riseth to high degree."[63] Then he told a story to illustrate his point:

> It came to pass recently, moreover, that a certain abbot took upon himself to become one of the justices, and he more cruelly than any layman, spurred on the spoiling of the poor, hoping perchance to win a bishopric through the favour gained from his spoils; upon him, however, after a few days, vengeance came, and made him turn his teeth upon himself, and to die gnawing off his hands.[64]

Another satirist who commented unfavorably on the secular activities of clerics was Nigel Wireker, a monk of Canterbury toward the end of the twelfth century, who wrote the popular poem *Speculum stultorum*. He was a kinsman or countryman of William Longchamp, Bishop of Ely, chancellor, papal legate, and briefly justiciar under Richard I.[65] He wrote his only prose work, *Contra curiales et officiales clericos*, in 1193–94 to convince Longchamp of the incompatibility of the offices of chancellor and bishop. His fifth point concerned the bishop's activities at the exchequer. He asked, "Whatever does sitting at the king's exchequer and hearing these accounts and conversations from dawn to dusk have to do with divine matters?" And he answered that there, "The concern is for securing coins, not for salvation of souls, for collecting coppers, not for rescuing souls of sinners from the devil." [66]

---

[61] Ibid., pp. 144–45, no. 94, undated, to an unknown petitioner.
[62] Charles L. Kingsford, "Walter Map," *Dict. Nat. Bio.*, xii, 994–97.
[63] Walter Map, *De nugis curialium*, ed. Thomas Wright (Camden Society, 1 [London, 1850]), p. 9.
[64] Ibid, trans. Frederick Tupper and Marbury Bladen Ogle (London, 1924), p. 8.
[65] John A. Herbert, "Nigel Wireker," *Dict. Nat. Bio.*, xiv, 507–8.
[66] *Anglo-Latin Satirical Poets*, i, 202.

A writer who shared Nigel Wireker's views about the impropriety of bishops serving at the exchequer was Gerald of Wales, a harsh critic of Hubert Walter. His pique at the archbishop's opposition to his promotion to the bishopric of St. David's may have colored his opinion.[67] He made outrageous accusations to the pope, charging that Hubert Walter had ordered a *Te Deum* sung to celebrate the killing of 3000 Welshmen in battle against the English in 1198. He added, "So on that occasion he made an evil use of both the swords committed to him, and to speak the truth, it was an evil thing that he should at that time have had both swords at once in his grasp."[68] Again Gerald complained to the papal court of the archbishop's background of secular offices and his continuing concern for them. He asked, from where was Hubert called to be archbishop? And he answered:

> From the Exchequer; and what is the Exchequer? It is the seat of the public Treasury in England, a sort of square table at London, where royal dues are collected and accounted for. This was the academy, this the school, in which he has already grown old, from which he was summoned to all the grades of his dignities, like nearly all the English bishops... A year ago he was Justiciar, and when that office was taken from him by the Court at Rome, he managed at once to get himself appointed the king's Chancellor. And when of late he lost that honor he spared no effort till he recovered it... For as a fish cannot live out of water, so he cannot live without his Court and worldly cases, since he is either wholly ignorant of the words of the Apostle or conceals the fact that he has ever read them, to wit "no man that warreth for God entangleth himself in the things of this world."[69]

Was Hubert Walter required to resign the justiciarship by the pope, as Gerald maintained? Certainly as the chief of the king's justices he could not avoid violating the prohibitions against clerical participation in judgments of blood.[70] But the only confirmation of Gerald's statement comes from the chronicler Roger Howden, who states that Innocent wrote Richard I in 1198, asking him to release the archbishop from his secular duties and warning him not to appoint any other prelates or priests to secular offices.[71] The lack of any confirmation of Innocent's letters from other English sources or from papal records makes the accuracy of Howden's account doubtful.[72] It seems, then, that the reasons given in Richard's letter

---

[67] F.M. Powicke, *The Christian Life in the Middle Ages* (Oxford, 1935), "Gerald of Wales," pp. 126–29.

[68] Giraldus Cambrensis, *Opera*, ed. J.S. Brewer *et al.* (Rolls Series [London, 1861–91]), *De Invectionibus* iii, 25; cited in Young, pp. 120–21.

[69] Giraldus Cambrensis, iii, 28, *De Invectionibus*; trans. H.E. Butler, *The Autobiography of Giraldus Cambrensis* (London, 1937), p. 215.

[70] See Cheney, *Hubert Walter*, pp. 93–94, and Young, pp. 128–29, for a flagrant violation, the case of William fitz Osbert.

[71] Roger Howden, *Chronica*, ed. William Stubbs (Rolls Series [London, 1868–71]), iv, 47–48.

[72] C.R. and Mary G. Cheney, *The Letters of Innocent III concerning England and Wales (a Calendar)* (Oxford, 1967), p. 10, nos. 47–48, include the letters, although their only source is Howden. Cheney,

accepting the archbishop's resignation – the burdens of work and poor health – are the real reasons for his leaving the justiciarship.[73] Additional doubt is cast upon Innocent's role in Hubert Walter's removal from the justiciarship by the lack of any papal complaint in 1199, when he became King John's chancellor.

Although writers in England were concerned about clerics serving secular rulers in judicial and financial posts, they rarely treated the question in theoretical terms. It was theologians and canonists on the Continent who wrote the formal treatises. A significant group of theologians at Paris around the end of the twelfth century was the circle of Peter the Chanter. He and his pupils manifested in their writings "a passionate interest in practical morality,"[74] which caused them to consider the role of the clergy in secular government. Several members of the Chanter's circle were Englishmen. The best known is Stephen Langton, from Lincolnshire, a master of theology at Paris before he became Archbishop of Canterbury.[75] But there was also Master Robert de Courson, author of a *Summa* that demonstrates knowledge of Roman and canon law as well as theology, and later a legate for Pope Innocent III.[76] Master Thomas of Chobham, who returned from Paris to serve the Bishop of Salisbury in various posts, wrote a popular penitential, the *Summa confessorum*.[77]

Peter the Chanter and his pupils tended to follow Gratian and the canonists in treating the problem of the clergy's participation in secular judgments.[78] They tended to lose sight of the basic objection that time spent on worldly matters was time that could be better spent on spiritual concerns, splitting hairs over what a cleric who served the king could or could not do to avoid the taint of shedding blood. Their discussion of clerical participation in judgments of blood can be separated into two topics: first, the problem of bishops as secular lords exercising jurisdiction over their tenants; second, the problem of "curialist" clerks, serving as secretaries at princely courts.

Gratian, in his *Decretum,* had recognized that there were bishops "who – not content with tithes and first-fruits – possess lands, towns, castles, and cities," and that these bishops owed certain secular services to the prince of

---

Becket to Langton, pp. 25–26, accepts Howden with some reservations. West, *Justiciarship,* p. 96, and Young, pp. 129–30, reject his account.

[73] *Foedera, conventiones, litterae,* ed. Thomas Rymer (Record Commission [London, 1816]), i, pt. 1, 71; cited in Young, p. 130.

[74] John W. Baldwin, *Masters, Princes, and Merchants: The Social Views of Peter the Chanter and his Circle* (Princeton, 1970), i, 17.

[75] Ibid., pp. 25–26.

[76] Ibid., p. 19.

[77] *Summa confessorum,* ed. F. Broomfield (Analecta mediaevalia Namurcensia, 25 [Paris and Louvain, 1968]), xxviii–xxxviii.

[78] Baldwin, i, 178.

whom they held such properties.[79] Peter the Chanter, like Gratian, recognized that bishops had a dual character.[80] Their secular character obviously required them to hold courts where opponents fought duels, suspects underwent ordeals, and convicted criminals were hanged. Yet Peter advised against prelates' participation in passing sentences of death.[81] Stephen Langton, Thomas of Chobham, and Robert of Courson also recognized that bishops sometimes had police powers through their positions as agents of the secular prince, and they felt that the bishops had such powers rightfully. But all three agreed that their power to punish criminals should be exercised only through lay officers.[82] Clearly, they were following the twelfth-century canonists who had considered the problem of bishops with *regalia*. They had recognized that bishops sometimes had jurisdiction over cases involving death or mutilation, but had recommended that they appoint lay representatives to pass judgment and execute sentence in such cases.[83] Robert of Courson compared the bishop's situation to that of a lay ruler lacking a hand who orders his servant to do what he himself cannot do; that is, he has the right to judge and to execute, but not the force.[84]

Peter the Chanter also discussed the problem of lesser clerics assigned various tasks by the secular ruler whom they served. One duty which was arousing debate in the late twelfth century was the blessing of the instruments of proof used in ordeals. Peter forbade clerics to participate in ordeals, for those convicted by such proof were subsequently executed or mutilated, possibly involving them in the shedding of innocent blood.[85] He did admit that a clergyman could give advice to judges outside of court, if he gave it in such general terms that he could not be identified with any individual decision.[86] His solution, allowing clergymen to give general but not specific advice, was adopted by Thomas of Chobham, Robert of Courson, and Stephen Langton.[87]

---

[79] *Decretum*, P.I, causa xxiii, quest. viii, c. 20, 25, cited in Robert L. Benson, "The Obligations of Bishops with 'Regalia': Canonistic Views from Gratian to the early Thirteenth Century," *Proceedings of the Second International Congress of Medieval Canon Law*, pp. 125–26. See also his book *The Bishop-Elect* on the whole question of the dual character of bishops.

[80] Peter the Chanter, *Verbum abbreviatum*, MS. cited by Baldwin, i, 186.

[81] *Pat. Lat.*, ccv, col. 220; cited by Baldwin, i, 188–89.

[82] Baldwin, i, 187–88. Chobham, *Summa confessorum*, p. 424. The prelate's seneschal could hang malefactors by the authority of the law or of the prince.

[83] Benson, "Obligations of Bishops," pp. 129–30.

[84] Courson, *Summa*, MS. cited in Baldwin, i, 188.

[85] *Pat. Lat.*, ccv, cols. 226–27; John W. Baldwin, "The Intellectual Preparation for the Canon of 1215 against Ordeals," *Speculum*, xxxvi (1961), 631–32.

[86] Peter the Chanter, *Summa de sacramentis et animae consiliis*, ed. Jean-Albert Dugauquier (Analecta mediaevalia Namurcensis, 4, 7, 16, 21), par. 324: iii (2a) 386, cited by Baldwin, i, 185, 189.

[87] Baldwin, i, 189; citing Chobham, *Summa*, p. 305, Courson, *Summa*, MS., and Langton, *Questiones*, MS.

The Chanter discussed "curialist" clerics, who might be involved in judgments of blood through service as secretaries to princes. Gratian in his *Decretum* had considered the case of one who drafted a legal document ordering a sentence of death, and he had concluded that the drafter working at the command of a secular official was free from guilt.[88] Another canonist, Huguccio, concluded that if the secretary was a cleric, he sinned by involving himself in a judgment of blood, and that such sinful clerics were to be barred from advancement in holy orders.[89] His view was incorporated into canon law with the Fourth Lateran Council's decrees. Peter the Chanter and his pupil Robert of Courson followed Huguccio, advising secular rulers to assign the drafting of such documents to literate laymen.[90] The Chanter returned to his distinction between general and specific advice, however, allowing clerics to draw up general decrees concerning punishment of criminals but forbidding them to draft individual death sentences.[91] Robert did feel it necessary to point out that the pope often granted dispensations to royal clerks barred from advancement by canon law.[92] Yet he must have known that employment of clerics in posts that technically barred them from advancement was so common that they rarely bothered to seek dispensations.

Discussions such as those centering on what documents clerics could and could not draft illustrate the approach of the canonists and theologians. Such an approach could have little influence on the practice of clerics at princely courts, and it overlooked the basic question of their presence at court at all. Yet the canons of councils from earliest times had urged the clergy to avoid the courts of princes.[93] It is difficult to detect any results from the speculations of the Chanter and his circle, other than influence on the decrees of the Fourth Lateran and of some diocesan synods.

The only member of Peter the Chanter's school to deal directly with the question of ecclesiastics as royal justices was Thomas of Chobham, who wrote his *Summa confessorum* about 1216 in England with English priests in mind. He recognized that it is meritorious for secular judges to condemn the wicked, but he warned that clerics must not participate in any way in sentencing men to death or mutilation.[94] He wrote, "So great is the dread of human blood that even a judge who justly slays the wicked, if he enters

---

[88] *Decretum*, P. ii, causa xxiii, quest. iv, c. 46, col. 924.

[89] Huguccio, *Summa*, MS., cited by Baldwin, i, 185.

[90] Chanter, *Summa de sacramentis*, par. 162: iii (2a), 36; Courson, *Summa*, MS.: cited by Baldwin, i, 185.

[91] Chanter, *Summa de sacramentis*, par. 332: iii (2a), 401; Baldwin, i, 185. Clerics could draft sentences imposing only fines.

[92] Courson, *Summa*, MS.; Baldwin, i, 178.

[93] Council of Sardica, canon vii, *Nicene and Post-Nicene Fathers*, xiv, 422; repeated by Gratian, *Decretum*, P. II, causa xxiii, quest. viii, c. 28, col. 963.

[94] *Summa confessorum*, pp. 304–5, 422–25.

the religious life or wishes to be made a cleric, cannot be promoted to holy orders."[95] Chobham did concede, however, that clerics could participate in judgments of blood if the prince assured them of the security of the accused's life and limb.[96]

Since the opposition to the king's use of clerics in courts and chanceries was so ineffective, there was little need for theoretical defenses of the practice. Some supporters and servants of Henry II, however, did comment favorably on his employment of ecclesiastics in government. Richard fitz Neal, author of the *Dialogus de scaccario*, illustrates the increasingly important role that clergy played in royal administration as a result of the bureacratic revolution of the twelfth century. He served Henry II as a clerk of the exchequer, treasurer, judge of common pleas, and itinerant justice. At the same time that he was rising in the royal administration, he was rising in the ecclesiastical hierarchy; he was archdeacon of Ely and Colchester, a canon of St. Paul's, and finally Bishop of London, succeeding Gilbert Foliot.[97] The statements that he made on the royal power could have come from the period before the Investiture Contest; the Church's efforts at a sharper separation between the two spheres made no impression on him. In the *Dialogus*, he wrote:

> For there is no power but of God. There is clearly, therefore, nothing incongruous, or inconsistent with the clerical character in keeping God's laws by serving kings as supreme and other powers, especially in those affairs which involve neither falsehood nor dishonour. And we ought to serve them by upholding not only those excellences in which the glory of kingship displays itself but also the worldly wealth which accrues to kings by virtue of their position.[98]

Peter of Blois expressed views also reminiscent of theocratic concepts. He is typical of the new academically trained men who sought careers as civil servants in the twelfth century. His work as secretary to two archbishops of Canterbury brought him into contact with Henry II's courtiers, and he possibly hoped to join them in the king's service, gaining ecclesiastical preferment as a reward.[99] In one of his letters, Peter defended the clerks of the household of the Archbishop of Canterbury from the criticism of a grammarian that their lives as courtiers should be most harshly condemned.[100] He recognized that many members of the archbishop's household also served the king, but he saw nothing wrong in this, for their

---

[95] Ibid., p. 423.
[96] Ibid., p. 425.
[97] *Dialogus de Scaccario*, ed. Charles Johnson (London, 1950), introduction, pp. xiv–xvi.
[98] Ibid., p. 1.
[99] For his career, see J. Armitage Robinson, *Somerset Historical Essays* (London, 1921), pp. 100–40; R.W. Southern, *Medieval Humanism* (New York, 1970), pp. 105–30.
[100] *Pat. Lat.*, ccvii, *epistola* vi, cols. 16–18; response to Master Ralph of Beauvais.

higher standard of right and justice meant that they could help solve all the knotty problems of the kingdom. Surely such work was more valuable than grammatical exercises!

In another letter, addressed to the clerks of the royal household in 1180, Peter of Blois stated more clearly his view that service to the king need not conflict with Christian duties.[101] First, he apologized for his criticisms of courtiers in an earlier letter,[102] explaining that he had been in bodily distress and danger of death when he wrote it. He wrote that while it could be dangerous to linger at court, he did not condemn civil servants, "who even if they cannot have leisure for prayer and contemplation, are nevertheless occupied in the public good and often perform works of salvation." He recognized that "those who are admitted into the sanctum of royal familiarity can do and say much by which the need of the poor is lessened, religion is fostered, justice is done, and the Church is expanded."[103]

These views seem to have been shared by Peter's master, Archbishop Richard of Canterbury. In 1179, the same year that the Third Lateran Council legislated against clerics serving as secular judges, Henry II named three bishops as royal justices.[104] Peter, as the archbishop's secretary, drafted a letter to the pope for his master, making the point he would later make in his own letter: it was useful to have bishops in important positions in the king's council, where they could protect ecclesiastical liberties, monastic property, and the interests of widows, orphans, and the poor.[105] He made no attempt to deny directly the charge that the bishops were guilty of sharing in judgments of blood. Probably the archbishop would not have gone as far as Peter would in his letter to the royal clerks. He made a statement about the sanctity of kingship much like those that had been made in the midst of the Investiture struggle. He wrote, "I admit that it is a holy thing to aid the king, for he is holy and the Anointed of the Lord: neither did he receive in vain the sacrament of royal unction, the power of which, if anyone is ignorant or doubtful, is made fully evident by the disappearance of inguinal plague and the cure of scrofula."[106]

Sometimes Peter had less favorable feelings toward ecclesiastics in the king's service. His feelings were partly due to genuine doubts about their secular preoccupations, but possibly also due to bitterness at his own failure to gain any post higher than archdeacon. Once he wrote to his friends in the king's service, reminding them that the life of a courtier is "death to the soul," and quoting with approval *Ecclesiasticus*, "Seek not of the Lord

---

[101] Ibid., *epistola* cl, cols. 439–42; R.W. Southern, *The Making of the Middle Ages* (London, 1953), pp. 212–13, partial trans.

[102] *Pat. Lat.*, ccvii, *epistola* xiv.

[103] Ibid., *epistola* cl, col. 440.

[104] Cheney, *Becket to Langton*, pp. 22–23: the bishops of Ely, Norwich, and Winchester.

[105] *Pat Lat.*, cc, *epistola* xcvi, cols. 1459–61.

[106] Ibid., ccvii, *epistola* cl, col. 440.

pre-eminence, neither of the king the seat of honour... Seek not to be judge...[107] Peter recognized the temptation to put professional advancement ahead of spiritual growth that the king's service presented to clerics. He urged one of Henry II's clerks to turn away from study of law, the key to advancement in the civil service, and take up theology and devotional literature. He wrote, "There are two things which drive men strongly to the study of law, ambition for honors and vain appetite for glory." [108]

Master Ralph de Diceto, dean of St. Paul's, began writing his histories about the time that Peter of Blois was writing his letters. A secular cleric like Peter, he had studied at Paris and knew many leading figures of the royal court, and was in a position to produce capable historical work.[109] He had great respect for Henry II, and he wrote favorably of his judicial reforms. He also commented on the king's selection of three bishops as royal judges in 1179. As might be expected from an intimate of Bishop Gilbert Foliot of London, Ralph praised his prince for turning to the "sanctuary of God" to find judges who would not oppress the poor or favor the rich, and he excused the prelates for violating canon law by accepting the posts.[110] He wrote, "If then these prelates should occupy themselves in secular business, contrary to the ordinances of Canon Law, and should be called to account for this, let them instantly oppose to the rigour of the canons the importunity of the king, his good intentions, and his actions pleasing to God and meet for the praise of men."[111] Ralph did recommend that the bishops follow the example of Roger of Salisbury, who would not serve as Henry I's justiciar until he had a dispensation from the pope and the Archbishop of Canterbury.[112] As noted above, there is no evidence that the bishop of Salisbury had troubled himself to secure such dispensations.

As Ralph de Diceto indicated, Henry II frequently called on bishops and abbots to serve him as itinerant justices.[113] Then in 1178, when he took a step toward creating a permanent professional court, he specified that two justices should be clerics and three, laymen.[114] By the early 1240's, the professional judicature had grown large enough to staff entirely the eyres, but many of these professionals continued to be clerics.[115] Three of the

[107] Ibid., *epistola* xiv, col. 43; for similar views, see *epistola* xlii, cols. 122–25. Ecclesiasticus 7:1–7.
[108] *Pat. Lat.*, ccvii, *epistola* cxl, col. 416.
[109] R.L. Poole, "Ralph de Diceto," *Dict. Nat. Bio.*, v, 217–19.
[110] Diceto, *Opera*, i, 435; trans. David Douglas, ed., *English Historical Documents*, ii, *1042–1189* (Oxford, 1953), pp. 481–82.
[111] Trans. *English Historical Documents*, ii, 482.
[112] Diceto, i, 435.
[113] E.g. eyre of 1179, Doris M. Stenton's list of justices, *Pleas before the King or his Justices, 1198–1212*, iii (Selden Society, 83 [London, 1966]), pp. lxi–lxii. For King John's appointments, see her table, pp. lxxix–ccxciv.
[114] Howden, *Gesta Regis Henrici Secundi*, i, 207–8; trans. *English Historical Documents*, ii, p. 482.
[115] C.A.F. Meekings, *Crown Pleas of the Wiltshire Eyre, 1249* (Wilts Archaeological and Natural History Society, xvi [Devizes, 1961]), p. 11. Also my *English Judiciary in the Age of Glanvill and Bracton*, p.206.

greatest judges of the thirteenth century – Martin Pateshull, William Raleigh, and Henry de Bracton – were clerics holding benefices with care of souls.[116]

No particular effort seems to have been made to prevent these judges from hearing judgments of blood. Henry II's Constitutions of Clarendon in 1164 did release bishops present at the king's court as royal vassals from participation in judgments of blood. Article 11 noted that they should sit in judgment with the king's barons "until a case shall arise of judgment concerning mutilation or death."[117] Yet they must have continued to participate in such judgments, for the Archbishop of Canterbury's consistory in 1179 declared that bishops might "with tranquil spirit" decide cases involving a penalty of blood, if they were acting in their capacity as barons.[118]

Although little is known of how the royal justices did their work, nothing indicates that those who were clerics took care to absent themselves when judgments of blood came before the panel. Doris M. Stenton suggests that the itinerant justices may have held concurrent courts,[119] which might have allowed the clerics to concern themselves with civil pleas, while the laymen heard criminal cases. The rolls themselves rarely offer any clues concerning which judges heard which pleas, for they record judgments only as *"judicium est ... ," "consideratum est...."* But sometimes a justice's name creeps into the account of a case; for example, two appeals of felony in 1232 were postponed for hearing before William Raleigh.[120] Certainly ecclesiastics as late as the middle years of Henry III did not hesitate to accept appointments as justices of gaol delivery trying accused criminals, which would have required them to impose the death penalty.[121]

An examination of the published *curia regis* rolls and numerous assize rolls has revealed only one case in which it is recorded that an ecclesiastic

---

[116] Meekings, "Martin Pateshull and William Raleigh," *Bulletin of the Institute for Historical Research,* xxvi (1953), 157–79; H. G. Richardson, *Bracton, the Problem of His Text* (Selden Society, Supplementary Series [London, 1965]), pp. 1–3. For another example, see Meekings, "Robert of Nottingham, Justice of the Bench, 1244–6," *Bulletin of the Institute for Historical Research,* xli (1968), 132–38. Robert was only a subdeacon, but he held benefices worth 150 pounds. See also Meekings, "Roger of Whitchester (d. 1258) ," *Archaeologia Aeliana,* 4th series, xxxv (1957), 100–28. He was rector of two churches.

[117] William Stubbs, ed., *Select Charters and other Illustrations of English Constitutional History* (rev. ed.: Oxford, 1913), p. 16; trans. *English Historical Documents,* ii, 721.

[118] Diceto, i, *Ymagines,* p. 436.

[119] *Pleas before the King,* iii, xxxi.

[120] *Curia Regis Rolls* (Public Record Office [London, 1923–]), xiv, 456, no. 2133; 507, no. 2351. Also evidence that Raleigh did not hesitate to hear criminal cases is an abjuration of the realm, p. 92, no. 464.

[121] Appointment of Martin Pateshull, 1225, *Rotuli Litterarum Clausarum* (Record Commission [London, 1844]), ii, 76b; William Raleigh to give counsel to laymen appointed, 1232, *Patent Roll, 1225–32* (Public Record Office [London, 1903]), p. 516; William of York, 1235, *Close Roll, 1234–37* (Public Record Office [London, 1908]), p. 159; and *Calendar of Patent Rolls, 1232–7* (Public Record Office [London, 1906]), p. 442: appointment to hear pleas of the crown, 1244.

absented himself from a judgment of blood. In this case in 1219, the judge – Jocelin, bishop of Bath and Wells – may have wanted his absence recorded because he disagreed with his colleagues' treatment of the case.[122] It is not certain that his clerical status had any connection with his absence. In 1230, the bishop of Bath did not hesitate to witness a command that prisoners be brought before justices of gaol delivery, even though he must have known that hanging would be the fate of many of them.[123]

The first legislation that indicates any real attempt to guard against clerical participation in judgments of blood came only in 1299. The Statute of Fines stated that the justices sent to the counties to take the assizes should also be justices of gaol delivery. If one of the justices should be a cleric, the statute provided that the other justices should select some knight of the shire to replace him for the hearing of criminal cases.[124] By the end of the thirteenth century, however, far fewer clerics were acting as royal judges. The peak period for clerical justices had been the late twelfth century, when Henry II had called upon his abbots and bishops to make judicial circuits. T. F. T. Plucknett considers 1300 to have marked a turning point in the recruitment of royal justices. According to him, royal clerks and administrative agents supplied most of the judges before that date; but by then, a group of laymen – professional attorneys – had grown up to supply them.[125] It was the growth of a group of laymen learned in the law, then, that ended the appointment of clergymen as secular judges, not the canons of the Church.

It is clear that the Church's opposition to clerical participation in judgments of blood had little effect on secular rulers' appointments of judges. A great gap separated the ideal expressed in decrees of councils, complaints of moralists, and commentaries of canonists and theologians from the practice of the Angevin kings. About the only men who tried seriously to bring the reality into conformity with the ideal were bishops of a monastic or scholarly background, a minority of the English episcopate, such as St. Hugh of Lincoln or Robert Grosseteste. Not even the canonists and theologians questioned the rulers' right to the service of the clergy; they were aware of the intermingling of the two orders, and they only tried to limit through technicalities anything that would leave blood on the hands of clerics.

---

[122] *Curia Regis Rolls*, viii, 80–81. For a discussion of the case, see Ralph V. Turner, *The King and His Courts* (Ithaca, N.Y., 1968), pp. 193–95.

[123] *Close Roll, 1227–31*, p. 388.

[124] *Statutes of the Realm* (Record Commission [London, 1810–28]), i, 129–30.

[125] Plucknett, 'The Place of the Legal Profession in the History Of English Law," *Law Quarterly Review*, xlviii (1932), 328–40. The change did not come suddenly, however; seven of the fifteen justices of King's Bench under Edward I were clerics; *Select Cases in the Court of King's Bench under Edward I*, ed. G.O. Sayles (Selden Society, lv [London, 1936]), i, lxiii.

Certainly, the entanglement of ecclesiastics in secular affairs had the effect of reducing their pastoral care to secondary importance, and it encouraged men of little or no spirituality to seek clerical careers. Yet something can be said for the benefits to both Church and monarchy that came from cooperation. Clerical judges who had some training in Roman and canon law, who had at least some concept of Christian charity, did much to aid the growth of English common law. F. W. Maitland wrote of Henry II, "His most lasting triumph in the legal field was this, that he made the prelates of the church his justices." [126] Peter of Blois and Ralph de Diceto recognized that if the Church wished to lead society toward Christian goals, then the clergy had to take positions of leadership in secular government.

---

[126] F. Pollock and F.W. Maitland, *A History of English Law* (2nd ed.: Cambridge, 1898), i, 132.

Genealogy of the Belet Family

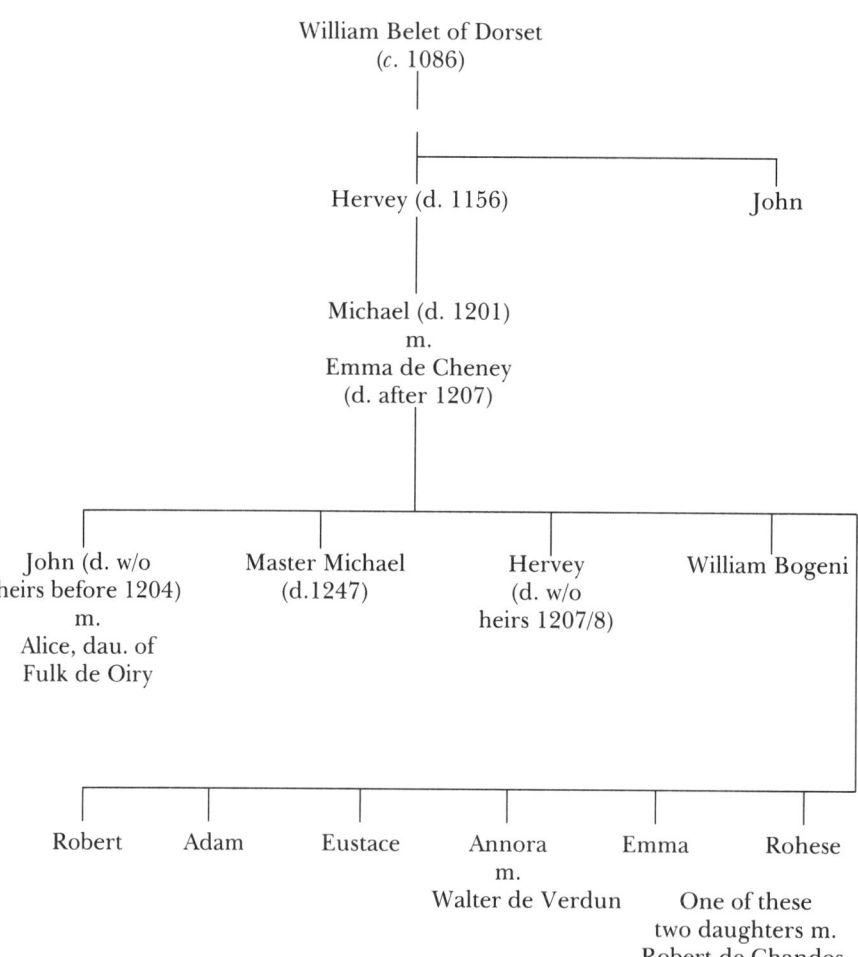

Richard Barre and Michael Belet: Two Angevin Civil Servants

The late twelfth and early thirteenth centuries witnessed a revolution in English government as significant as G.R. Elton's "Tudor Revolution". The earlier revolution introduced government by means of written documents, in other words, the beginning of bureaucracy with professional civil servants, specialized offices, and reduction of governmental activity to routine.[1] Numerous studies exist of this process of professionalization and specialization of the courts of the Angevin kings. Most are impersonal, however, describing the growth of departments of state as institutions, neglecting the element of human personality. This is partly the simple result of the difficulty of knowing the civil servants participating in the changes, for many left little more than their names behind them, if that. Yet we can reconstruct the lives and even the thoughts of some of them, in spite of difficulties. There were some who thought deeply about their work and wrote manuals such as the *Dialogus de Scaccario* or the legal treatises attributed to Glanvill and to Bracton, attempting "to invest the routine of government with an intellectual generality".[2]

Three groups of men administered the government of Henry II and his sons, if one counts the knights of the shires who served in part-time posts as coroners, jurors, and on other temporary commissions. Surrounding the king was a circle of a dozen or so men, "loosely formed and constantly shifting", consisting of bishops, barons, and lesser ranking clerics and knights, some holding definite office and others without any title.[3] This group, on whom the king relied for advice, formed the *privata familia regis*. A useful, though imperfect, way of identifying this group is by counting the number of royal charters that they witnessed.[4]

---

[1] See John W. Baldwin and C. Warren Hollister, "The Rise of Administrative Kingship: Henry I and Philip Augustus", *American Historical Review*, 83 (1978): 867–905; Michael T. Clanchy, *From Memory to Written Record, England 1066–1307*, second edition (Oxford, 1993); and H.G. Richardson and G.O. Sayles, *The Governance of Mediaeval England* (Edinburgh, 1963).

[2] R.W. Southern, *Medieval Humanism and Other Studies* (Oxford, 1970), p. 176.

[3] W.L. Warren, *Henry II* (Berkeley and Los Angeles, 1970), p. 304; J.E.A. Jolliffe, *Angevin Kingship* (London, 1955), pp. 142–49.

[4] A count of charter witnesses for Henry II's last decade reveals 160 names, but only 10 witnessed 15 or more charters: Ranulf de Glanvill, 33; Walter of Coutances and William de Humez, constable, 16 each; 15 each for Hugh de Cressy, Richard, bishop of Winchester, Geoffrey, bishop of Ely, William fitz Ralph, Norman seneschal, Ralph fitz Stephen, Michael Belet, and Hugh, Bishop of Durham.

Below the level of royal intimates lay a larger group of over a hundred, sometimes stationed in the royal household but as likely to be at Westminster or in the counties, who carried out policies determined by the first group. These men remain largely unknown, lumped together by chroniclers as *curiales* or *familiares regis*, although they were not in fact always close to the king. Such terms actually may apply more accurately to the first group of men accompanying him on his travels. The names of those in the second and third groups seldom appear in the chronicles except to be berated as a body for their crimes of ambition, greed, and sycophancy. Royal charters do not always reveal their presence at court, for not all these *curiales* acted as charter witnesses. It is possible to know such second-rank royal servants, however, by the later years of Henry II, when other records begin to survive in larger numbers; more ecclesiastical and private charters become available, and there are the pipe rolls, superbly indexed in the Pipe Roll Society's editions. Particularly important are the feet of fines, first officially recorded during Hubert Walter's justiciarship, which enable historians to reconstruct the judicial bench from 1194 onwards.[5]

Two such second-rank royal servants whom I hope to rescue from obscurity are Michael Belet, a knight, and Richard Barre, a cleric. Neither man figures prominently in the chronicles, yet each had a significant share in royal government for almost half a century. Both royal servants began their careers in the service of Henry II, around 1160–65, and they continued to serve him and his sons until about 1200. In the time of Richard I, their sphere of activity shifted away from the royal presence, and they became attached to the justiciar's staff at Westminster. A reconstruction of their lives sheds light on the process of professionalization and specialization in late twelfth-century English government.

Although a group of professional royal servants appears clearly enough in the time of Henry II, specialization – or identification of an individual with a particular office – is less easy to observe. Some *curiales* shifted so often from one sphere of responsibility to another that it is impossible to connect them with any single branch of government. Nonetheless, such royal officials tend to fall into three chief groups. First were those constantly in the king's company, members of his household who followed him to and from the Continent. Second were members of the justiciar's staff, working in the house of the exchequer at Westminster. Third were those active mainly in the counties as sheriffs, itinerant justices, or constables of castles; some of these were primarily local notables who rarely strayed far from their native shires. These groups were not mutually exclusive, for movement from one of the three to another was frequent and easy. A sheriff, for

---

[5] See lists of justices reconstructed by Doris M. Stenton, using feet of fines: "The Development of the Judiciary, 1100–1216", in *Pleas before the King or his Justices, 1198–1212*, 3, Selden Society vol. 83 (London, 1966).

example, came to Westminster twice a year for the audit of his accounts; and he might remain there for some time, joining the bench to hear pleas. Men moved in the opposite direction as well – from the center outward – as they moved from the royal household to the shires into posts as sheriffs, or from Westminster as itinerant justices or as tax collectors throughout the kingdom. Sometimes reassignments were permanent, as with Barre and Belet.

Specialization in government can be seen in the lives of Richard Barre and Michael Belet. The former, a cleric, had a career chiefly on the Continent as a royal clerk and diplomatic envoy until Henry II's death. The latter, a layman, was royal butler (*pincerna*) and a sheriff, active in England. Their careers under Henry II indicate that the royal household had different members, depending upon whether the king was in England or France. Both men eventually gave up their old tasks to concentrate on judicial activity in the reign of Richard Lionheart.

It is not certain whether Richard Barre grew up in England or in Normandy. His surname probably comes from the Norman village of La Barre, east of Lisieux (Dépt. Eure). A kinsman, Hugh Barre, was archdeacon of Leicester in the early and mid 1150s, and perhaps it was he who encouraged young Richard to go off to the schools. They had other kinsmen, the Sifrewasts, Berkshire knights who continued to hold fees on the other side of the Channel at Chiffrevast, their ancestral center in Normandy.[6] More can be told of Belet's background. He was of knightly birth, descended from a Domesday tenant of lands in Dorset and heir to the manor of Sicheston, Lincolnshire, and four knight's fees in Northants and Oxfordshire, part of the barony of Chipping Warden.[7] Both men share, then, the sort of middling rank from which many of Henry Plantagenet's servants came.

We know more about the education of Richard Barre than we do about that of many twelfth-century figures. Historians assume that a number of Henry II's servants received training in Roman law on the Continent, but rarely can they point to a specific individual who studied at one of the continental legal centers.[8] We do know that Richard Barre studied at

---

[6] Lewis Loyd, *The Origin of Some Anglo-Norman Families*, Harleian Society, 103 (1951), p. 98; *The Cartulary of Missenden Abbey*, ed. John G. Jenkins, 2 vols., Buckinghamshire Archaeological Society, Records Branch (1939, 1962), 1: 220, no. 247; 2, nos. 275–76. For Hugh Barre, see *Fasti Ecclesiae Anglicanae, 1066–1300, Lincoln*, ed. Diana E. Greenway (London, 1977), p. 33.

[7] On Michael's ancestry and inheritance, see *Dictionary of National Biography*, s.n. "Belet, Michael"; *Victoria History of the Counties of England, Oxfordshire*, ed. Arthur Doubleday, William Page, Louis Salzman, and Ralph Pugh (London and Westminster, 1900–), 9: 175–76; C.T. Flower, *Introduction to the Curia Regis Rolls*, Selden Society, 62 (London, 1943), p. 123. *Red Book of the Exchequer*, ed. Hubert Hall, 3 vols., Rolls Series (London, 1897), 1: 331; William Farrer, *Honors and Knights' Fees*, 3 vols. (London and Manchester, 1923–25), 2: 417. Also I consulted unpublished notes of the late C.A.F. Meekings.

[8] See my, "Roman Law in England before the Time of Bracton", above Chapter 4.

Bologna sometime before 1150, where he was a fellow student of Stephen of Tournai, an eminent canonist who lived at Orleans and Paris before he became bishop of Tournai in 1192. He proved an important link between the Bolognese decretists and the Anglo-Norman school of canon law that was growing up in the 1160s.[9] Stephen wrote to Richard years after their studies together to congratulate him on his appointment as archdeacon of Ely, recalling their student days in Bologna.[10]

If it is difficult to learn anything about a cleric's education in the twelfth century, it is impossible to know about a layman's studies. The usual assumption is that youths of the knightly class did not study letters at all, but that is incorrect. Most sons of knights learned some rudimentary Latin, and even those who did not know Latin could read Anglo-Norman. This form of French was the spoken language of the Anglo-Norman aristocracy, and a literature in that tongue was flourishing at noble households in twelfth-century England.[11]

A tradition of legal expertise, entirely oral, was strong among twelfth-century knights. Attendance at the courts was both a feudal and a public obligation, both a duty and a diversion. Knights sharpened their skills in pleading through years of attending the courts of feudal honors, shire, and hundred, first as youthful observers and later as participants. Eventually, they had to preside over their own manorial courts or the courts of lords whom they served as stewards. Also increasing litigiousness meant that they had to be acquainted with the land law and feudal custom in order to defend their own holdings. Some of them won such reputations for eloquence and learning in the law that they became semi-professional pleaders, speaking for others in the courts. By the second decade of Henry II's reign, plaintiffs occasionally appointed pleaders to make their "counts" in court, although the evidence is limited before the first decade of the thirteenth century.[12] Since there were no schools and hardly any textbooks for study of English law before the treatise *Glanvill* about 1187, we must assume that Michael Belet's knowledge of English law came from practical experience.

Anyone seeking a position in the middle ages needed a patron if he did not have a powerful family to assist him. Second-rank royal officials often

---

[9] *New Catholic Encyclopedia*, ed. David I. Eggenberger, 18 vols. (New York, 1967), s.v. "Stephen of Tournai"; Stephan Kuttner and Eleanor Rathbone, "Anglo-Norman Canonists of the Twelfth Century", *Traditio*, 7 (1949–51): 293, 296.

[10] *Lettres d'Etienne de Tournai*, ed. J. de Silve (Paris, 1893), pp. 246–47, no. 275; see translation, Appendix II below.

[11] On lay Literacy, see my, "The *Miles Literatus* in Twelfth- and Thirteenth-century England: How Rare a Phenomenon?", above, Chapter 7; also Clanchy, *From Memory to Written Record*, second edition, pp. 224–52, 328–34.

[12] Robert C. Palmer, "The Origins of the Legal Profession in England", *Irish Jurist*, new series 11 (1976): 126–35; for a more conservative estimate of twelfth-century pleaders, see Paul Brand, *The Origins of the English Legal Profession* (Oxford, 1992), pp. 46–49.

served in the households of some influential *familiaris regis* before joining the king's service. A number of them came to the *curia regis* by way of the justiciar's or chancellor's staffs. This cannot be demonstrated for our two men, however. Richard Barre's first post seems to have been with Robert de Chesney, bishop of Lincoln, or Nicholas, archdeacon of Huntingdon, whose charters he witnessed *c.* 1160/64.[13] How he got from English ecclesiastical circles to the royal court in Normandy by 1165 cannot be known.

Michael Belet secured his post as *pincerna* or royal butler through inheritance; the Belet family had gained the office in the time of Henry I.[14] The *pincerna* had responsibility for supplying wine, firewood, and other supplies to royal castles, the court, and the army. We do not find the title applied to Michael before 1171, but he was charged with transporting wine to Woodstock for the king as early as 1166.[15] Although the English kings generally frowned upon hereditary offices, they did not mind some household posts being filled through inheritance due to the king's ability to keep a close watch on them.[16] Michael Belet seems to have carried out his duties as *pincerna* only in England, however, not with the king across the Channel.[17]

Besides being royal *pincerna*, Belet served as sheriff of Worcestershire, 1175–85, and then as sheriff of Warwickshire and Leicestershire, 1186–89.[18] Sheriffs in the days after Henry II's 1170 Inquest of Sheriffs were no longer magnates, but were either local notables or professional royal servants. Many were non-residents with other royal responsibilities, spending much of their time with the king or at Westminster and depending upon deputies to administer their shires.[19] In those days, sheriffs often served as itinerant justices although not usually in their own shires; and, beginning in 1176, Belet went on judicial eyres nearly every year, visiting

---

[13] *English Episcopal Acta, Lincoln 1067–1185*, ed. David M. Smith (London, 1980), pp. 73–74, no. 112; p. 77, no. 119; p. 132, no. 212. See also Westminster Abbey Muniment Book 11, f. 227.

[14] *The Book of Fees*, Public Record Office, 3 vols. (London, 1921–31), 1: 70.

[15] *Pipe Roll 12 Henry II*, Pipe Roll Society, 9 (London, 1888), p. 116. Michael may have become a royal servant earlier, for he was pardoned of scutage as early as 1158–59, *Red Book of the Exchequer*, 1: 17, and again in 1160–62 (p. 699); see also *Pipe Roll 7 Henry II*, Pipe Roll Society, 4 (London, 1884), p. 96. For later examples of his work as *pincerna*, see *Pipe Roll 18 Henry II*, Pipe Roll Society, 18 (London, 1894), p. 37; *21 Henry II*, Pipe Roll Society, 22 (London, 1897), pp. 15, 187, 203; and *31 Henry II*, Pipe Roll Society, 34 (London, 1913), p. 120.

[16] For another example of working hereditary officials, see Emma Mason, "The Mauduits and their Chamberlainship of the Exchequer", *Bulletin of the Institute of Historical Research*, 49 (1976): 1–23.

[17] The only evidence for Michael Belet's being with the court on the Continent is a charter he witnessed at Rouen sometime in the early 1180s, *Recueil des actes de Henri II*, ed Léopold Delisle and Elie Berger, 4 vols. (Paris, 1909–27), 2: 248.

[18] *Public Record Office, Lists and Indexes*, 9, *List of Sheriffs* (London, 1898), pp. 144, 157.

[19] David A. Carpenter, "The Decline of the Curial Sheriff in England, 1194–1258", *English Historical Review*, 91 (1976): 1–3.

at one time or another almost every corner of England.[20] It is likely that he had been accompanying the justices in September 1176 before he joined them as a judge, for senior men who were not yet considered "of judicial mettle" seem to have traveled with the itinerant justices, assisting them or replacing them as needed.[21] Most likely, when Michael Belet was not with the royal household, he divided his time between his shrievalty and Westminster. He was present at a number of exchequer sessions in the 1180s, witnessing final concords as one of the royal justices.

Charter witness lists are about the only concrete proof that persons were present with the king frequently enough to be considered *curiales* or *familiares regis*. Michael Belet joined Henry II's court on the king's visits to England, for he witnessed some twenty charters between 1175 and 1189, a significant number.[22] Absence from charter witness lists is not necessarily proof that a person was absent from court, however. Richard Barre rarely witnessed royal charters for Henry II, yet he clearly counted on occasion as a member of the *privata familia regis*. In 1169, when the king appointed Richard as his agent to the papal court, he described Richard and his associates as *clerici et familiares nostri*.[23]

Thomas Becket and his supporters viewed Richard Barre as one of the king's "evil counselors", and they denounced him bitterly. From 1169 to 1171, Richard Barre's activities centred around Henry II's diplomatic campaign against the archbishop of Canterbury. Richard went on a diplomatic mission to the papal *curia* in January and February 1170. Then, early in 1171, following Becket's murder, he went on a second mission to the pope, accompanied by four bishops and charged with the delicate task of assuaging the papal anger against the king. Richard's companions informed Henry II that he was solicitous of his honor and working usefully on his behalf. While the delegation was not fully successful, they did succeed in forestalling an interdict on England and excommunication of the king.[24]

It was not long after this that Richard Barre became archdeacon of Lisieux, most likely as a result of Henry II's influence with Bishop Arnulf

---

[20] See Stenton "Development of the Judiciary 1100–1216". At the Michaelmas Exchequer 1180, p. lxiii; April 1182, p. lxvi; Michaelmas 1182, p. lxvii; Oct. 1184, p. lxviii; Nov. 1185, p. lxx; Easter 1186, p. lxxi; Nov. 1188, p. lxxv; and Jan. and April 1189, p. lxxvii. For eyres, see pp. lvii-clxxv.

[21] Stenton "Development of the Judiciary, 1100–1216", pp. lvii-lviii.

[22] Robert W. Eyton, *Court, Household and Itinerary of Henry II* (London, 1878), pp. 196, 241, 246, 272–74, 277, 290; Delisle and Berger, *Recueil des actes de Henri II*, 2: 122, 210, 248, 307. Henry was in England for about 7 of the 14 years, 1175–89.

[23] *Materials for the History of Thomas Becket*, ed. J.C. Robertson, Rolls Series, 7 vols. (London, 1875–85), 7: 85, no. 564. Becket called the envoys *principes prophetiae falsae* and "Goliaths in the camp of Achitophel", *Materials*, 7: 15, no. 536; 20, no. 537; 59–60, no. 554; 271, no. 654.

[24] Eyton, *Court, Household and Itinerary of Henry II*, pp. 134, 152; *Gesta Regis Henrici secundi Benedicti Abbas*, ed. William Stubbs, Rolls Series, 2 vols. (London, 1867), 1: 19; *Rogeri Hovedene Chronica*, ed. William Stubbs, Rolls Series, 4 vols. (London, 1868–71), 2: 25–28; *Materials for History of Becket*, 7: 227, 440–43, 443–45, 471–75, 475–87.

and as a reward for his services as envoy to the papal *curia* in 1171. Among his colleagues in the chapter at Lisieux were other clerics who would be active in Angevin government. Gilbert de Glanvill (archdeacon 1151 x 1185), bishop of Rochester (1185–1214), served alongside Richard as a royal justice in the 1190s; John of Alençon (1182 x 1195) served Richard Lionheart as vice-chancellor, 1189–90.[25] Like other cathedral canons in the king's service, Richard Barre probably resided at Lisieux only during those periods when Henry II's court was nearby in Normandy. A few surviving documents locate him at Lisieux or Rouen, involved in ecclesiastical matters, in the 1170s and 1180s.[26] There is little to indicate, however, that he visited England during the years that he was Henry's clerk.[27]

In 1188, after Henry II had taken the cross as part of his penance, he chose Richard Barre for another diplomatic mission, sending him off to the German emperor, the king of Hungary, and the Eastern emperor to seek safe passage across their lands for his crusade.[28] In the interval between his journeys to Rome and to the East, Richard Barre had served briefly (1172–73) as chancellor at the court of Henry the Younger, one of a group of household officials chosen for the boy by his father. Considerable resentment arose between members of the young king's household of his own choosing, impetuous knights who gave their young lord first loyalty, and officials selected by Henry II, who remained dedicated to the old king's interests. When Young Henry and a number of his companions defected to the French king's court in March 1173, Richard and several colleagues refused to follow them and returned to Henry II's household to serve him during the great rebellion that followed. Barre brought with him the seal of Young Henry, who had to have a new seal cut at Paris.[29]

---

[25] Carolyn Poling Schreiber, *The Dilemma of Arnulf of Lisieux* (Bloomington, Indiana, 1990), p. 58.

[26] 17 June 1179, Richard Barre was among witnesses to the display of St. Romanus's body at Rouen, Archives Départementales de la Seine-Maritime, G.3666; 1180, Richard Barre, along with other Lisieux clergy, was fined by the Norman Exchequer, *Magni Rotuli Scacarii normanniae*, ed Thomas Stapleton, Society of Antiquaries of London, 2 vols. (London, 1840–4), 1: cxxxi-cxxxii, 103; 17 July 1183, letter of Pope Lucius III to the bishop of Lisieux, abbot of Gestain, and R[ichard] archdeacon of Lisieux, Johannes Ramacker, *Papsturkunden in Frankreich*, 2, *Normandie* (Berlin, 1932), no. 228; undated and damaged charter of Rotrou, archbishop of Rouen, concerning Richard, *Archives Départementales du Calvados*, H.7771; undated confirmation of Bishop Arnulf of Lisieux, which Richard Barre, archdeacon, witnessed, Léonce de Glanville, *Histoire du prieuré de St. Lo de Rouen*, 2 vols. (Rouen, 1890–91), 2: 342, no. xxxc. I owe these references to Professor David S. Spear.

[27] His only recorded appearance is at Oxford, Sept, 1172, Stenton, *Pleas before the King or his Justices*, 3: lvi. He may have been in England *c.* 1175–77, when he was involved in litigation concerning the church at Burbage, Wilts., *Charters and Documents Illustrating the History of the Cathedral, City and Diocese of Salisbury*, ed. W. Rich Jones and W. Dunn Macray, Rolls Series (London, 1891), pp. 40–41, 60.

[28] *Radulphi de Diceto Opera Historica*, ed. William Stubbs, Rolls Series, 2 vols. (London, 1876), 2: 51–54.

[29] *Rogeri Hovedene Chronica*, 2: 46; *Gesta Regis Henrici secundi*, 1: 43.

The careers of both Michael Belet and Richard Barre underwent significant change following Henry II's death and Richard I's accession. The new king removed most of his father's sheriffs, including Michael Belet. As Richard Lionheart frantically sought to raise funds for his crusade, he sold offices right and left, and Belet had to offer £100 for confirmation as *pincerna regis*.[30] Richard I was rarely in England, but on his first visit in the summer and autumn of 1189, Belet joined him for a time. He witnessed six of the new king's charters, hardly enough to class him as a royal intimate.[31]

Richard Barre came to England with William Longchamps, who had been chancellor for the new king in Poitou. Longchamps accompanied Richard I to England in 1189, becoming chancellor and briefly justiciar; he was also named papal legate and bishop of Ely. Barre's new patron was a man of considerable learning, author of a little treatise on civil and canon law procedures, *c.* 1181–89.[32] Longchamps sought to bolster his position as England's viceroy by naming his own dependents to government posts; for example, sheriffs of five shires were members of his *familia*.[33] He became a victim of Count John's enmity and nascent anti-alien feeling among the English baronage, however, and they forced him out of the justiciarship early in the king's absence. It was due to Longchamps' patronage that Richard Barre left Lisieux to begin a new career as archdeacon of Ely by 1190.[34] Shortly after their arrival in England that summer, Barre joined a party of itinerant justices in the eastern counties near Ely.[35]

In the reign of Richard I, Michael Belet and Richard Barre moved away from the royal household and into the orbit of the justiciar; both came to work mainly as royal justices. They brought two different types of experience to the courts: Belet's was that of the practical administrator, acquainted with the customs of shire and hundred, while Barre's learning was in written law taught in the schools. Belet was already experienced in judicial

---

[30] *Pipe Roll 2 Richard I*, Pipe Roll Society, new series, 1 (London, 1925), p. 102. The fine had two purposes: for the *pincernaria* and for justice in a lawsuit.

[31] Lionel Landon, *The Itinerary of Richard I*, Pipe Roll Society, new series 13 (London, 1935); pp. 11, 12, 20, 22. Approximately 200 charters were issued, Aug.–Dec. 1189, and the ten leading attestors witnessed at least 75 charters, Richard Heiser, "The Royal *Familiares* of King Richard I", *Medieval Prosopography*, 10 (1989): 39, Appendix.

[32] E. Caillemar, "Le Droit civil dans les provinces anglo-normands", *Memoires de l'Académie de Caen* (Paris, 1883), p. 49.

[33] Richard R. Heiser, "The Sheriffs of Richard the Lionheart: A Prosopographical Survey of Appointments, Politics, and Patronage, 1189–1199" unpublished Ph.D. dissertation, Florida State University (Tallahassee, 1993), p. 174.

[34] *Fasti Ecclesiae Anglicanae 1066–1300, Monastic Cathedrals*, ed. Diana E. Greenway (London, 1971), p. 50. Stephen of Tournai's letter makes clear that Longchamps was Barre's patron. Also in April 1191, Richard witnessed the settlement of a dispute at Canterbury, decided before Longchamps, *Documents Preserved in France, Illustrative of the History of Great Britain and Ireland*, 1, *918–1206*, ed. J.H. Round, Public Record Office (London, 1899) p. 17, no. 63.

[35] Stenton, *Pleas before the King or his Justices*, 3: lxxiv; see also Francis West, *The Justiciarship in England, 1066–1232* (Cambridge, 1966), p.71.

work, having first been a justice in 1176. In those days, sheriffs often served as itinerant justices, although not usually in their own shires. Belet had also served as a justice at Westminster in the 1180s, so that he was an experienced judge by the time of Richard Lionheart's coronation. That – coupled with his knowledge of local conditions – explains why Longchamps chose him to accompany him on the eyre to Norfolk and Suffolk in 1191. Belet was active on the Bench at Westminster, 1190–92; then his activity almost ceased, 1193–97; but it returned to a high level until his death, which seems to have occurred while he was on eyre in the summer of 1201.[36]

Longchamps' fall from power in October 1191 interrupted Richard Barre's judicial career until Richard Lionheart's return from captivity. He was not called to the royal courts until 1194, when he went on eyre in the autumn and then, on its completion, joined the Bench at Westminster.[37] The archdeacon of Ely was one of five "professionals" who began their judicial careers in 1194; and he would be the fourth most frequent witness to final concords, 1195–99.[38] Before then, it is difficult to differentiate between barons of the exchequer and justices of the Bench.[39] Richard Barre's appointment to the judiciary is evidence for more specialization in the work at Westminster, for he had no financial experience and in no way could be considered a baron of the exchequer. When the new justiciar Hubert Walter chose Richard, he was looking for a legal expert. Doubtless, he was impressed by the archdeacon's knowledge of Roman law and his experience in the church courts.

The separation of judicial from financial work was not yet complete, however, not even after 1194. Indeed, one of the main purposes of the 1194 eyre was to raise money for Richard I's ransom. Itinerant justices' work was almost as much administrative as judicial, and they frequently assessed aids and tallages in the counties they visited. Occasionally, justices were recruited for specifically financial purposes. In 1197 Richard Barre went to Norfolk and Suffolk to amerce merchants who had sold grain to the king's enemies in Flanders, in violation of a royal embargo.[40]

---

[36] His name disappears from the list of judges on 16 June, but the others continued their work until early July, Stenton, *Pleas before the King or his Justices*, 3: clxxv. Other evidence for Belet's death in 1201 is his son's fine for the marriage of his sister, *Rotuli de Oblatis et Finibus*, ed. T. Duffus Hardy, Record Commission (London, 1835), p. 180. Had Michael the elder been alive, he would have controlled his daughter's marriage.

[37] Stenton, *Pleas before the King or his Justices*, 3: xcvi, and eyre to the Southeast, p.c.

[38] The other new justices in 1194 were Ralph Foliot, William de Sainte-Mère-Eglise, Richard of Herriard, and William de Warenne of Wormegay. The three who surpassed Barre in witnessing final concords were Osbert fitz Hervey, Simon of Pattishall, and Richard of Herriard.

[39] For a survey of scholarly opinion on the question of a judicial bench at Westminster separate from the barons of the Exchequer, see my, "The Origins of Common Pleas and King's Bench", above, Chapter 2.

[40] *Pipe Roll 10 Richard I*, Pipe Roll Society, new series 9 (London, 1932), pp. xix–xx, 92.

After 1194 the archdeacon of Ely was almost continuously in the law courts until January 1200. When he went on eyres, they were usually to the East Anglian counties, convenient to Ely. After the accession of King John, Richard Barre had less work as a judge. John had a long memory, and he would have mistrusted Barre because of his friendship with William Longchamps, with whom he had tangled during his struggle for power following Richard Lionheart's departure for the Third Crusade.

Both Michael Belet and Richard Barre, then, were concentrating much of their energies on the courts in Richard I's reign. For both, this represented a shift from earlier activity. Both continued to serve until early in John's reign. Belet's final illness seems to have fallen upon him during an eyre to the southwestern counties in the early summer of 1201, and apparently he died shortly afterwards. King John's enmity explains Barre's departure from the bench. He went on eyre in early autumn 1199 to Midland shires, then returned to Ely where he busied himself with ecclesiastical affairs. Bishop Eustace was an expert in canon law, active as an ecclesiastical judge, and he would have valued his archdeacon's legal expertise.[41] In the spring of 1198, before Barre retired from Westminster, Bishop Eustace appointed him his attorney for all pleas, especially those against the abbot of Bury St. Edmunds.[42] Sometime between 1198 and 1213, the archdeacon joined his bishop and the prior of Barnwell as papal-appointed mediators of a dispute between a monastic house and a parish priest.[43] The date of Richard Barre's death is uncertain, possibly as late as 1213, but no earlier than 9 August 1202, the last date on which he was definitely alive.[44]

Royal office could bring rich reward and higher social rank. What success did our two royal servants have in improving their positions? Obviously, those closest in the king's confidence, giving him advice on matters of great moment, reaped richer rewards than those occupied with routine administration. Three of Henry II's intimates in the Becket conflict – Richard of Ilchester, Geoffrey Ridel, and John of Oxford – were rewarded with bishoprics, while Richard Barre had to be content with an archdeaconry. Laymen who won admission to the king's innermost councils could

---

[41] Barre witnessed 6 episcopal charters and other acts for Bishop Eustace, Cambridge University Library: MS. Add. 3020, ff. 169–169^v; Ely Cartulary, Liber M, ff. 150–158b; British Library: Ms. Harl. 391, f. 101^v. He also witnessed a grant to the Austin canons at Ipswich, *c.* 1192 x 1210, *Catalogue of Ancient Deeds*, Public Record Office, 6 vols. (London, 1890–1915), 2: 182, no. A3347; a grant to York Minster sometime after 1197, C.T. Clay, *York Minster Fasti*, Yorkshire Archaeological Society, Record Series, 2 (1958–59): 123, no. 81; and a grant to the nuns of St. Radegund, Cambridge, *c* 1198 x 1213, *The Priory of St. Radegund, Cambridge*, ed. Arthur Gray, Cambridge Antiquarian Society (1898), p. 109, no. 180.

[42] *Curia Regis Rolls*, Public Record Office, 17 vols. (London, 1923–), 1: 33.

[43] *Lancashire Pipe Roll*, ed. William Farrer (Liverpool, 1902), pp. 330–31.

[44] *Fasti Ecclesiae Anglicanae, 1066–1300, Monastic Cathedrals*, p. 50. In 1202 he was active as an ecclesiastical judge, *Letters of Pope Innocent III Concerning England and Wales*, ed. C.R. and Mary G. Cheney (Oxford, 1967), p. 62, no. 379; p. 10, no. 431.

experience sudden advance in their status. Geoffrey fitz Peter, for example, first joined the royal service during Henry II's last decade; by early in Richard I's reign, his lands had expanded from lesser knightly holdings to a great barony, the Mandeville honor; and one of King John's first official acts was to belt him as an earl.[45] Men such as Barre and Michael Belet, who never achieved such intimacy with their monarch, had to settle for lower levels of reward than the dozen or so men at the heart of government.

What reward did they win? No provision for regular payment of salaries to royal servants emerges before the time of Henry III. The old feudal method of providing for household officials was through granting of serjeanty tenures. Michael Belet, as hereditary butler, held manors at Sheen (today Richmond) and Bagshot, Surrey, part of the royal forest of Windsor.[46] The king provided for his other officers through a variety of *ad hoc* arrangements. One method of maintenance for civil servants throughout the middle ages was a system by which they charged the public fees for performance of duties, illustrated by the charges that chancery clerks imposed for drafting documents.[47] Officials of all sorts, even judges, expected to exploit their posts by accepting payments from petitioners that, to modern eyes, appear remarkably like bribes. Some royal officers became retainers of abbots, bishops, and barons, using their inside knowledge of the workings of government agencies to guard their paymasters' interests. Doubtless, such a practice prevailed from the earliest days of such offices, although little documentation survives before the early fourteenth century.[48] Sheriffs "farmed" their offices, paying the king a fixed portion of the revenues they raised from the shire and keeping the rest for profit. That the profits were great is proven by the sums offered for appointment. There is no evidence, however, that Michael Belet purchased his two shrievalties. Royal officials also received grants of money or goods, such as robes or game and timber from the royal forests. No record of such gifts to Richard Barre or Michael Belet survives, since records of such gifts were recorded mainly on the liberate rolls, the earliest of which date from King John's second year.[49]

Positions in the royal service brought other, indirect benefits, with the special protection that the king extended to certain favored servants and their families, giving them demesne status, *sicut proprio dominica mea*.[50]

---

[45] Ralph V. Turner, *Men Raised from the Dust: Administrative Office and Upward Mobility in Angevin England* (Philadelphia, 1988), chap. 3, "Geoffrey fitz Peter, Earl of Essex".

[46] *Victoria County History, Surrey*, 4: 411; *Red Book of the Exchequer*, pp. 456, 561. According to the inquest of 1210–12, Bagshot was held by service of *veltraria*, i.e. leading hounds on hunts.

[47] For an account of chancery fees under Richard I and John, see Sidney Painter, *The Reign of King John* (Baltimore, 1949), pp. 94–95.

[48] See my, "The Reputation of Royal Judges under the Angevin Kings", above, pp.103–18.

[49] *Rotuli de Liberati ac de misis praestitis*, ed. T. Duffus Hardy, Record Commission (London, 1844).

[50] Jolliffe, *Angevin Kingship*, pp. 90–94.

King John extended such protection to Michael Belet's widow. In 1203, when she was vouched to warranty in a suit at Westminster, the plea was adjourned *sine die* "because Emma by command of the lord king has peace concerning all pleas".[51] Some royal officials, such as barons of the exchequer, enjoyed exemptions from payment of scutage and other levies. Michael Belet was pardoned of scutage as early as 1161. The king's officials also received excuses from court appearances while occupied on his business. When they brought their own lawsuits, they escaped the fees that ordinary litigants had to pay for writs or chirographs.[52]

The king could readily reward his clerks with ecclesiastical benefices in his gift. He could also press others into presenting royal clerks to churches in their gift, or perhaps they willingly presented them in the hope of securing friends at court. Richard Barre had his archdeaconry of Lisieux until 1190, and then one at Ely. Archdeacons had so many opportunities for rewards, both lawful and unlawful, that some twelfth-century moralists feared that every road to salvation was barred to them.[53] Barre had other ecclesiastical sources of income: prebends at two cathedrals – Hereford and Salisbury – and a church presented him by the monks of Waltham Abbey. The Hereford prebend provided him with income from two churches, Moreton and Whadon, Gloucestershire. His Salisbury prebend also consisted of income from two churches on the royal manors of Hurstbourne Tarant and Burbage, producing annually 42 marks. In addition, Richard held a lay tenure, a portion of the Sifrewast family lands.[54]

It is useful to compare Richard Barre's reward to that of other clerics in the king's service. His benefices seem comparable to those of other royal servants not within the inner circle of king's friends. We can compare his benefices with those of Ralph Foliot, a royal clerk who became a justice about the same time. Foliot could rely upon his influential uncle, Bishop Gilbert Foliot, to aid his career. The bishop was "a man with a powerful

---

[51] *Curia Regis Rolls*, 2: 266.

[52] Pardons of scutage, *Red Book of the Exchequer*, pp. 17, 50, 699; *Pipe Roll 7 Henry II*, p. 96; *12 Henry II*, p. 116. For privileges of Barons of the Exchequer, see *Dialogus de Scaccario*, ed. and trans. Charles Johnson, Medieval Texts (London, 1950), pp. 46–48. Belet's son, Master Michael, summoned for a lawsuit in 1206, neither appeared nor essoined, but sent a servant with the king's letters of general protection, *Curia Regis Rolls*, 4: 188. On securing documents free of charge, see Clanchy, *From Memory to Written Record*, second edition, p. 46.

[53] John of Salisbury, reminding Nicholas de Sigillo of his earlier statement, *The Letters of John of Salisbury*, ed. W.J. Millor, H.E. Butler, C.N.L. Brooke, Oxford Medieval Texts, 2 vols. (Oxford, 1955–79), 2: 25, no. 140.

[54] *Fasti Ecclesiae Anglianae, 1066–1300, Salisbury*, ed. Diana E. Greenway (London, 1991), pp. 78–79. Barre had his Salisbury prebend at least since late 1175, *Charters and Documents of Salisbury*, Rolls Series, pp. 11, 40–41. By 1180–85 he had his Hereford prebend, Z.N. Brooke and C.N.L. Brooke, "Hereford Cathedral Dignitaries" [corrections], *Cambridge Historical Journal*, 8 (1946): 180. The monks of Waltham presented him with the church of Bradburgham (?), British Library, MS. Harl. 391, ff. 101^v, 110; Cott. Tiber. C.IX, ff. 152–152^v. For his lay fee, see *Cartulary of Missenden Abbey*, 2: 20, no. 267.

sense of family", and at Hereford and later at London, he provided generously for relatives.[55] Ralph Foliot was archdeacon of Hereford by 1182, and he later became a canon of St. Paul's Cathedral and parson of three churches.[56] Master Thomas of Hurstbourne, another of Richard's justices who had begun his career under Henry II, acquired similar benefices. He was parson of three churches, two at the presentation of an early patron, the abbot of Glastonbury, and one from the king's gift. He also held prebends at two cathedrals, Salisbury and St. Paul's.[57]

No monarch could afford to give many of his servants permanent grants alienated from the royal demesne, but the Angevins often gave them temporary custody of land or wardship of minors as a source of income.[58] Richard Barre held custody of some £20 worth of escheated land in Buckinghamshire in 1197–98.[59] A king was unlikely to make a permanent grant of land to a layman, since it would not return to him in the way that ecclesiastical livings would. Yet most royal servants increased their landholdings with or without direct royal grants. Another royal justice, Simon of Pattishall, expanded his holdings from approximately one knight's fee to six during a quarter-century of service on the bench.[60] Michael Belet did not increase his holdings quite so dramatically, but he doubled the four knight's fees he had inherited.

Most knights hoped for marriage to an heiress who would bring them more land. Some striking changes in status came from marriage to a rich heiress, as illustrated by William Marshal's acquisition of the earldom of Pembroke through marriage to its heiress. Michael Belet made a good marriage; whether on his own initiative or through royal favor is unclear. Michael married Emma de Cheney, a member of a family whose pedigree stretched back to the Norman Conquest. Her uncle, William de Cheney, had been sheriff of Norfolk in the mid twelfth century. She was coheir to

[55] Adrian Morey and C.N.L. Brooke, *Gilbert Foliot and His Letters* (Cambridge, 1965), pp. 44–45.

[56] Z.N. Brooke and C.N.L. Brooke, "Hereford Cathedral Dignitaries", *Cambridge Historical Journal*, 8 (1944): 16; *Fasti Ecclesiae Anglicanae, St. Paul's London*, ed. Diana E. Greenway (London, 1968), p. 65. Foliot was parson of Chaddersley Corbet, Worcs., *Pleas before the King or His Justices*, 1: 312–13, no. 3180; of Cradley, Herefs., *Charters and Records of Hereford Cathedral*, ed. W.W. Capes, Cantilupe Society (Hereford, 1908), pp. 34–35; and Potton, Beds., British Library, MS. Cott. Vesp. E. xvii, f. 20.

[57] Ashbury, Berks., and Christian-Malford, Wilts., *Adami de Domerham historia de rebus gestis Glastoniensibus*, ed. Thomas Hearne, 2 vols. (Oxford, 1727), 2; 487; Hurstbourne, Hants., *Vetus Registrum Sarisberiense*, ed. W.H.R. James, Rolls Series, 2 vols. (London, 1883–84), 1: 242; *Fasti Ecclesiae Anglicanae, St. Paul's*, p. 81. For Salisbury, see a letter of Hubert Walter in *Patrologia Latina cursus completus*, ed. J.-P. Migne (Paris, 1844–64), 208: cols. 403–04.

[58] J.E. Lally, "Secular Patronage at the Court of Henry II", *Bulletin of the Institute of Historical Research*, 49 (1976): 174–84.

[59] *Pipe Roll 9 Richard I*, Pipe Roll Society, new series 8 (London, 1931), p. 206; *10 Richard I*, p. 15, land of William of Clinton.

[60] See my, "Simon of Pattishall, Early Common Law Judge from Northamptonshire", below, pp. 199–213.

wide lands in Norfolk, bringing to her husband the manor of Rudham, a fee of two knights with a weekly market.[61]

Concern for family was characteristic of royal servants, like all medieval men, and they sought good marriages and other opportunities for their offspring. Michael Belet and his wife had a large family of three daughters and seven sons. Their eldest son, John Belet, married a daughter of Fulk de Oiry, tenant of significant estates in the Lincolnshire fenland.[62] Clearly, he had taken a wife of comparable social standing, though hardly superior. John's life was spent fighting for the Angevins against the French king's forces in Normandy, and he died there sometime before 1204, leaving a landholding at Vire. Following his death, the Norman exchequer rolls record a fine of £140 for custody of his land and heir. In 1207 his widow settled a dispute with her father-in-law for her dower lands in Oxfordshire, Northamptonshire, and Lincolnshire.[63]

The second son of Michael and Emma, Michael, junior (d. 1247), chose to enter the clergy; he earned a master's degree, probably at Oxford. He followed his father into the king's service, becoming a royal clerk as early as 1199; and he had a successful career as a royal servant, rewarded with three ecclesiastical livings. Like a number of clerics, he incurred King John's illwill during the Canterbury succession crisis, but he offered a 500-mark fine to regain the king's favor and remained in the royal service under Henry III.[64] By 1206 he had succeeded his father as *pincerna regis* and was in possession of the serjeanty manors that went with the post.[65] A third son was Hervey Belet, who held his mother's manor of Rudham, Norfolk. Later

---

[61] For William de Cheney, see J.H. Round, "Early Sheriffs of Norfolk", *English Historical Review*, 35 (1920): 480. In 1203, Emma de Cheney gave a carucate of the manor at Syderstone and Barmer to her son Michael Belet, *Curia Regis Rolls*, 2: 208, 266; later the entire manor was in her son Hervey's hands, Coxford Cartulary, ed. H.W. Saunders, *Original Papers of the Norfolk and Norwich Archaeological Society*, 17 (1909–10), p. 467; also a 1285 confirmation of Hervey Belet's gift of the manor to the Coxford canons, *Calendar of Charter Rolls*, Public Record Office, 6 vols. (London, 1903–27), 2: 302, For the market, see Henry II's charter, British Library MS. Add. 47784, f. 8; also *Original Papers of the Norfolk and Norwich Archaeological Society*, 17: 333.

[62] *Rotuli Litterarum clausarum*, ed. T. Duffus Hardy, Record Commission, 2 vols. (London, 1833–44), 1: 12b. On Fulk, see J.C. Holt, *The Northerners* (Oxford, 1961), p. 55; Painter, *Reign of King John*, p. 133.

[63] *Rotuli Saccarii Normanniae*, 2: ccxlvi. In 1195, an offering of £260 for his chattels and debts was recorded, 1: lvii. Ralph Ridel (Tyrell?) owed a mark and 2 palfreys for having John's widow as wife, *Pipe Roll 6 John*, Pipe Roll Society, new series, 18 (London, 1940), p. 139. Her father offered 100 marks a year later for her marriage and for her dower, *Pipe Roll 7 John*, Pipe Roll Society, new series 19 (London, 1941), p. 211.

[64] *Biographical Register of the University of Oxford*, ed. Alfred B. Emden, 3 vols. (Oxford, 1957–59), 2: 159. Fine, *Pipe Roll 13 John*, Pipe Roll Society, new series 28 (London, 1953), p. 12.

[65] *Pipe Roll 1 John*, Pipe Roll Society, new series 10 (London, 1933), pp. 145, 185, 196, 228, 240; *Rotuli Chartarum*, ed. T. Duffus Hardy, Record Commission (London, 1837), 100b. Master Michael Belet offered £100 fine for the *pincernaria*, *Pipe Roll 6 John*, p. 123.

Hervey gave it to the Austin canons of Coxford to endow a hospital.[66] Hervey died without issue sometime before 1216, but Master Michael Belet was acting as head of the family even before his brother's death. Little is known of their brothers and sisters beyond their names, recorded on the foundation charter of Wroxton Priory, Oxfordshire, a house of Austin canons that Master Michael founded in 1217 or shortly afterwards for the souls of his family.[67]

It is next to impossible to peer into the minds of royal servants such as Michael Belet or Richard Barre. We can assume that they, like other royal officials, held an exalted view of the royal power and felt a responsibility to protect the king's interest and to increase his revenues.[68] They doubtlessly shared the conventional view of society that their colleague Richard fitz Neal set forth in his *Dialogus de Scaccario*. Fitz Neal expressed the usual prejudices of the knightly class against merchants, whose greed, combined with fear of openly displaying their wealth, he found shameful.[69] We can assume from Michael Belet's ecclesiastical benefactions that he was conventionally pious. He made several gifts to the Austin canons at East Rudham, Norfolk (later Coxford), a house that had been founded by his wife's family. Austin canons ranked high among the religious orders favored by the Angevin kings' servants. Piety and filial devotion combined in Belet's provision of funds for a lamp to burn perpetually over his mother's tomb in the church of Thorpe Market, Norfolk.[70]

Tantalizing material survives for speculation about Richard Barre's outlook, more than we have for most twelfth-century civil servants. His friendships hint at intellectual interests and a measure of Christian spirituality. Richard's services to King Henry II during the Becket struggle indicate his royalist sympathies. He shared the rather old-fashioned ideas on relations between the royal and ecclesiastical powers held by Arnulf, bishop of Lisieux, whom he served as archdeacon after 1171. The views of his bishop conformed to early twelfth-century compromises that had ended the conflicts of the Gregorian reform movement, an ideal of co-operation between the two powers with bishops continuing to act as secular

---

[66] William Dugdale, *Monasticon Anglicanum*, new edition by John Caley, Henry Ellis, Bulkeley Bandinel, 6 vols. in 8 (London, 1817–30), 6: 369; *Calendar of Charter Rolls*, 2: 302.

[67] *Monasticon*, 6: 485.

[68] E.g. the justice William of York's views, C.A.F. Meekings, "Six Letters concerning the Eyres of 1226–8", *English Historical Review*, 72 (1957): 260–69; reprinted in Meekings, *Studies in 13th-Century Justice and Administration* (London, 1981).

[69] *Dialogus de Scaccario*, pp. 108–11.

[70] *Victoria County History, Norfolk*, 2: 378. Emma de Cheney gave the canons 40 A. and confirmed her father's gift of the 2 churches of Rudham, Farrer, *Honors and Knight's Fees*, 3: 320; Coxford Cartulary, *Original Papers of the Norfolk and Norwich Archaeological Society*, 17: 286, 297, 356; nos. 129, 130, 400.

advisers as well as spiritual counselors to monarchs.[71] An awareness of some principled motivation helps us to see Richard as more than a careerist clerk, concerned only with his own advancement.

The canonist Stephen of Tournai valued Richard's friendship, which dated from their student days at Bologna.[72] The archdeacon doubtlessly shared views on the two powers that Stephen put forward in his *Summa Decretorum*, written in the 1160s. Stephen restated the Gelasian tradition of two separate authorities – priesthood and kingship – within a single Christian commonwealth. His treatment of the problem of clerical immunity from criminal prosecution in the secular courts closely resembled Henry II's views set forth in the Constitutions of Clarendon. Anglo-Norman canonical treatises written before 1190 borrowed from Stephen of Tournai, but one of them, *Summa de multiplici iuris divisione*, adds a new category of clerical cases for the king's court: *res ad ius principis pertinentes*. The source for this statement supporting royal jurisdiction over some cases involving clerics seems to have been the English concept of the King's Peace.[73] Richard Barre certainly knew Stephen of Tournai's views, and he would have felt that they justified his service with Henry II in the conflict with Becket. Perhaps it is not too far-fetched to nominate Richard as a candidate for authorship of the anonymous *Summa de multiplici iuris divisione*.

Richard's friendship with William Longchamps also reveals some intellectual pretensions. This Norman cleric had an interest in learning, having written a legal treatise before coming to England to take up his triple posts as chancellor, bishop, and papal legate. He was also interested in biblical studies. Herbert of Bosham wrote for him a commentary on the *Hebraica*, St. Jerome's translation of the Psalter; and Richard Barre dedicated to him a work on the Scriptures, *Compendium de veteri et novo testamento*, which he completed while at Ely. The archdeacon compiled important passages of each book of the Bible, arranged them topically, and labelled them with marginal subject-headings "as do the experts in Roman law".[74] Certainly his authorship of a biblical compendium sets him apart from other curialists, perhaps indicating some depth of Christian devotion.

I hope that this study indicates that the civil servants of the Angevin kings outside the circle of magnates, bishops, and great officers of state need not remain nameless and faceless. They were individuals whose names, friends,

---

[71] Carolyn Poling Schreiber, *The Dilemma of Arnulf of Lisieux*.

[72] *Lettres d'Etienne de Tournai*, p. 347.

[73] Richard M. Fraher, "The Becket Dispute and Two Decretist Traditions: The Bolognese Masters Revisited and Some New Anglo-Norman Texts", *Journal of Medieval History*, 4 (1978): 347–68.

[74] On Herbert of Bosham, see Beryl Smalley, *The Becket Conflict and the Schools* (Totowa, N.J., 1973), pp. 72–73. Richard Barre's *Compendium* is British Library MS. Harl. 3255 and Lambeth Palace MS. 105.

families, and interests can be known. We need not accept blindly the accusations that twelfth- and thirteenth-century chroniclers, moralists, and satirists routinely hurled at these *curiales*.[75] They were definitely ambitious, sometimes greedy, and the system of patronage that prevailed made them sycophantic, as their critics charged. Yet they took seriously their responsibilities as royal servants, and the Angevins' administrative machine could not have functioned so smoothly without such men to keep its wheels turning. Richard Barre and Michael Belet illustrate the combination of qualities found among the civil servants of Henry II and his sons. In the two were combined "book learning and oral learning", "an academic approach and a practical one", both ideas and action.[76]

Appendix

Translation of the Latin letter of Stephen of Tournai, congratulating Richard Barre on his promotion to archdeacon of Ely, from J. de Silve, editor, *Lettres d'Etienne de Tournai* (Paris, 1893), pp. 346–47, no. 275.

To Richard, archdeacon of Ely.
On your translation from Lisieux to the city of Ely it is uncertain to me whether I ought to rejoice or to grieve. If you should turn your attention to the principles of oratory, you are translated from the planet of the Cyprian [i.e. Venus] to the sun, from whirring orbits to the stability of splendor: this change should be pleasing, if your move did not mutually separate us. I entreat you, that you beware in this transfer, that you do not, as you once said to me jokingly about certain neighbors of those parts, begin to err in reckoning and not wish to celebrate Pentecost around Easter. I believe that if you should fall anytime into that error, you have become the companion of those about whom the Apostle says: "But you have been purified, but you have been sanctified, but you have been justified." [I. Cor. vi, 11] What else indeed should be assumed of an archdeacon, unless that he should be solicitous first of his own salvation, second of those subject to him.

I wish you so to be moderate between the concerns of the court and merry conversations with colleagues after work, that neither should the former press you down with burdens nor should the latter dissipate you with easy

---

[75] Ralph V. Turner, *The English Judiciary in the Age of Glanvill and Bracton* (Cambridge, 1985), pp. 290–98.

[76] The phrases are from Michael T. Clanchy, *England and its Rulers, 1066-1272* (Glasgow, 1983), pp. 160–61.

leisure. You who were beloved by your fellow scholars now will be admired by your fellow curialists. Let me say that *curiales* is not from *cruor* [blood], but from *curia*, where sometimes the foolish is held serious, the serious is held foolish, where it is rare for anyone to wish to have an equal, never a superior. Remember a couplet of that poem, which rather in a poetic than prophetic, but nevertheless in a true spirit, was spoken to you by a certain man in your Bolognese hideaway:

> You will handle the causes of bishops and the business of kings, who prepare you for riches and pleasures.

Greet for me your lord bishop, legate, chancellor [William Longchamps], and frequently admonish him that, in this triple position, he acknowledge himself to be the servant of the Trinity, and if he should recognize that he is above men, let him confess that he is below his Creater. I love him because he loves you, although the joyousness of his reputation and the sublimity of his life commend him as deserving of love in his own right.

11

Simon of Pattishall, Early Common Law Judge from Northamptonshire

The village of Pattishall lies a few miles south-west of Northampton and to the north of Towcester, just off Watling Street. It was the home of Simon of Pattishall, an early professional in government, specializing in judicial activity. His name surfaces in the records in 1190, and it disappears after 1216.[1] His time of activity coincides with an important period for English common law: the years between "Glanvill" and *Magna Carta*.

Simon was one of that group of royal judges who mark the beginning of bureaucratic government in England, as professionals began to perform specialized tasks by the last years of the twelfth century. By the time of King John, about ninety men acted at various times as royal judges, either at the Bench at Westminster, with the court following the king, or as itinerant justices in the counties. Many of these had temporary appointments, making circuits in the counties; but a core of fifteen concentrated on the work of the courts, so that they can be regarded as early members of a professional judiciary.[2] Simon of Pattishall's is perhaps the most respected name among the fifteen. He had the longest career, earning such a reputation as a judge that his plea rolls were preserved.[3] He founded a judicial dynasty, for his clerk, Martin of Pattishall, became a judge, as did his clerk, William Raleigh, probable author of the great treatise on English law that bears the name of his clerk, the justice Henry de Bracton, editor and reviser of the work.

The background from which Simon of Pattishall came seems little different from that of his colleagues on the bench. Most of John's judges came from the class that would later be called "country squires"; few came

---

[1] G.E. Cockayne, ed., *The Complete Peerage*, new edition (London, 1910–59), x, 312, "h"; Sidney Lee, ed., *Dictionary of National Biography* (London, 1900–), xv, 474.

[2] They served at least ten terms at Westminster or with the court *coram rege*, plus making eyres.

[3] Doris M. Stenton, ed., *The Earliest Lincolnshire Assize Rolls*, A.D. 1202–1209 (Lincoln Record Society, xxii, 1926), pp. xxii-xxiii; *English Justice between the Norman Conquest and the Great Charter, 1066–1216* (American Philosophical Society, Philadelphia, 1964), p. 98, n. 4. In 1219 – after Simon's death – a dispute before the Bench could be settled by consulting his roll, *Curia Regis Rolls* (Public Record Office, London, 1923–), viii, 99.

from families that approached baronial rank.⁴ Very little can be known of Simon's family, except that they were Northamptonshire freeholders. The family name of Pattishall or "Pateshull" comes from a village in Towcester Hundred, Northamptonshire. The 1166 Inquest of Knights' Fees lists two men of the village bearing the surname Pattishall, each with a fifth part of a knight's fee belonging to the honor of Wahull.⁵ It has been suggested that a family of hereditary rural deans resided at Pattishall, and that Simon may have been a member of that family, but the evidence to support this view is inadequate.⁶ Evidence that he did come from the village of Pattishall is provided by a final concord by which he promised to make payment there each year of a mark to a certain widow.⁷ Also the pipe roll for 1192 lists him as holder of a knights' fee of the honor of Wahull, which must have been the same land that Pattishalls – presumably his ancestors – had held in 1166.⁸

Simon first appeared in the administrative records as a royal agent in 1190, soon after the accession of Richard I; but he must have begun his administrative career earlier, in the reign of Henry II. What preparation did Pattishall have for the posts he would hold? An important part of the professionalization in government under Henry II and his sons was an increasing use of written records. Although the education of laymen in the twelfth and thirteenth centuries is a murky area, the *miles literatus* can be sighted more often than is usually recognized. As Richardson and Sayles stated, "We may presume…that a layman who exercised an office demanding the use of written instruments was literate."⁹ Younger sons of knights or ambitious sons of humbler freemen sought training that would qualify them for positions as clerks or stewards with a baron or bishop, a sheriff or some other royal officer. Since Simon was such a layman, with duties that demanded literacy, he must have learned his Latin letters somewhere.

Opportunities for elementary and secondary schooling were more widely available in the middle ages than is generally realized. By the early thirteenth century, there were many schools where boys could study Latin grammar. Simon, like other boys in the twelfth century, probably learned his first Latin from his parish priest, from the parish clerk, or perhaps at his

---

⁴ Only two of the fifteen: Eustace of Fauconberg and Richard de Mucegros.

⁵ *Complete Peerage*, x, 311.

⁶ William Farrer, *Honors and Knights Fees* (London and Manchester, 1923–25), I. 92, citing a crown debt owed by Roger dean of Pateshull in 1201; but *Complete Peerage*, x, 311–12, n."f", points out that Roger merely held a benefice at Pattishall, while he was dean of Brackley.

⁷ Public Record Office, Feet of Fines, Northants. 171/11/177.

⁸ *Pipe Roll 3 and 4 Richard I* (Pipe Roll Society, new series, 1926), p. 201; Farrer, *Honors and Knights Fees*, i. 92.

⁹ H.G. Richardson and G.O. Sayles, *The Governance of Mediaeval England from the Conquest to Magna Carta* (Edinburgh, 1963), p. 274. See my "The *Miles Literatus* in Twelfth- and Thirteenth-Century England: How Rare a Phenomenon?" above Chapter 7.

mother's knee.[10] He may have boarded at a monastery to learn his letters in the abbot's household, as was customary among knightly families until the mid-thirteenth century. Or if his family was poor, he might have served at the monastery as an almonry boy.[11] But once he had received an elementary education that enabled him to conduct correspondence or keep accounts, further training came through practical experience.

It is most unlikely that Simon ever studied at a university or even at one of the business schools or schools of *ars notaria* that existed in England in the early thirteenth century, and possibly earlier.[12] He was not unusual in not having taken a university degree. Only three of the sixty or so men who served Richard I as judges had the title *magister*, and only eight out of about ninety judges under King John.[13] Of the small number of judges who might be termed professionals in the reigns of Henry II's two sons, only three seem to have studied Roman law.[14] Simon's preparation for his judicial career had to be chiefly practical, *non subtilia sed utilia* in the words of the *Dialogus de Scaccario*.[15] Pattishall probably served an apprenticeship in the household of some baron or royal official, moving into Henry II's service through the support of his patron.[16]

Any ambitious young man seeking a career as a civil servant needed a patron, someone already at court to sponsor him. Personal servants of royal officials often carried out public responsibilities even though they were not technically in the king's employ. Judges' personal clerks kept "official" records. These clerks sometimes became royal justices themselves, so that we can almost speak of "judicial dynasties". There is no evidence, however, that Simon served as a judge's clerk. A more likely possibility for patronage was through service to some baron or bishop, and once he gained high office, his clients could win an introduction to court. For example, Hubert Walter brought many members of his household from Canterbury into royal government when he was justiciar and later chancellor. Three of Simon's colleagues in the judiciary seem to have come to their posts through their service with Geoffrey fitz Peter, King John's justiciar,[17] and

[10] Nicholas Orme, *English Schools in the Middle Ages* (New York and London, 1973), pp. 66–67. Mary Martin McLaughlin, "Survivors and Surrogates", *History of Childhood*, ed. Lloyd de Mause (New York, 1974), p. 125, suggests that noblewomen were capable of instructing their children in simple Latin.
[11] Orme, pp. 243–45, 248.
[12] H.G. Richardson, "The Schools of Northampton in the Twelfth Century", *Eng. Hist. Rev.*, lvi (1941), 595–605; "The Oxford Law School under John", *Law Qtrly. Rev.*, lvii (1941), 319–338.
[13] See my, "Roman Law in England before the Time of Bracton", above Chapter 4.
[14] Ibid., p. 24.
[15] Charles Johnson, ed., *Dialogus de Scaccario* (London, 1950), p. 5.
[16] Noel Denholm-Young, *Seignorial Administration in England* (Oxford, 1937), p. 70; Doris M. Stenton, ed., *Rolls of the Justices in Eyre for Lincolnshire (1218–19) and Worcestershire (1221)* (Selden Society, liii, 1934), p. xvi.
[17] Richard of Herriard, James of Potterne, and Master Ralph of Stokes.

it is likely that Simon also entered the royal service through Geoffrey. Others could have had the king as their initial patron. Throughout the early middle ages, stories were told of humble chaplains or huntsmen who attracted the king's attention, won his favor, and rose to high rank, great wealth and power.

Often justices had gained practical experience in other aspects of royal administration, particularly in finances, before their appointment. Most of the early thirteenth-century judges seem to have been associated with the Exchequer, even though technically they were not *clerici de scaccario*.[18] In 1190 – the year in which Simon also first sat at the Bench – he was custodian of escheats in Northamptonshire, and the next he was given custody of Northampton Castle.[19] These posts point toward some tie with Geoffrey fitz Peter, who was sheriff of Northamptonshire, 1190–94; and in 1194, he replaced Geoffrey as sheriff. In 1193 and 1194 Simon was sheriff of Essex and Hertfordshire, again replacing Geoffrey fitz Peter.[20] When Richard I returned to England in the spring of 1194, he shifted a number of sheriffs, sending Simon to his native county of Northampton, where he remained sheriff after John became king, until the spring of 1203.[21] In February 1198, King Richard named Simon one of the four "keepers of the Jews", a central office created in 1194 to collect debts owed to Jewish moneylenders.[22] He still had some involvement in Jewish matters in 1204, accounting to the Exchequer for a fine offered by a Jew charged with counterfeiting.[23] King John continued to show his confidence in Simon even when he had grown mistrustful of many of his subjects. In 1212, the king entrusted him with custody of Fotheringay Castle in Northamptonshire, which had been taken away from the earl of Huntingdon.[24] One of John's ways of strengthening his security was by taking hostages from those he suspected. In October 1214, he committed one of his hostages to Simon.[25]

---

[18] Frank Pegues, "The *Clericus* in English Royal Administration", *Eng. Hist. Rev.*, lxx (1956), 541.

[19] *Pipe Roll 2 Richard I* (Pipe Roll Society, new series, 1925), pp. 6, 26; *Chronica Rogeri de Hovedene*, ed. William Stubbs (Rolls Series, London 1868–71), iii, 136, indicates that he became custodian of Northampton Castle on 28 July 1191.

[20] *Public Record Office Lists and Indexes*, ix, *List of Sheriffs for England and Wales from the Earliest Times to A.D. 1831* (London, 1898), p. 43; *Pipe Roll 7 Richard I* (Pipe Roll Society, new series, 1929), p. 217, shows that he was sheriff in 1194.

[21] Brian E. Harris, *The English Sheriffs in the Reign of King John* unpublished M.A. Thesis (Nottingham, 1961), Appendix I, "A list of Sheriffs ...," p. 200.

[22] *Pipe Roll 10 Richard I* (Pipe Roll Society, new series, 1932), pp. 125, 165, 210. According to H.G. Richardson, *English Jewry under the Angevin Kings* (London, 1960), p. 136, Simon was replaced in 1200.

[23] *Pipe Roll 6 John* (Pipe Roll Society, new series, 1940), p. 191.

[24] Simon was custodian along with another Northants man, Walter of Preston, *Rotuli Litterarum Clausarum* (Record Commission, London, 1833), i, 122b; *Rotuli Litterarum Patentium* (Record Commission, London, 1835), p. 94b.

[25] *Rot. Lit. Pat.*, p. 104b.

The justices' financial work calls to mind the close ties between the Bench and the Exchequer. It is possible to admit the judges' involvement in finances without admitting the claims of some scholars that the "justices of the Bench" and the "barons of the Exchequer" were identical groups.[26] Whatever may have been true earlier, by the middle years of Richard's reign the two branches of government were growing apart.[27] Yet long after two distinct groups of financial officers and judges came into sight, the justices continued to concern themselves with finances. Sometimes Simon accepted fines when men seeking some favor from the king found it more convenient to offer it to a judge visiting their county than to send it to the Exchequer.[28] Letters close concerning crown debts occasionally reveal Simon carrying out financial tasks connected with his native county of Northampton.[29]

Justices on eyre were a vital link in the chain connecting the shires, hundreds, and boroughs with royal government. It was convenient for the justices to act as tax assessors when they went to the counties. Taking tallage of the towns of the royal demesne was normally included among the itinerant justices' duties, and many pipe roll entries tell of Simon's work of tallaging.[30] Collection of the carucage was also the responsibility of the itinerant justices, and Simon of Pattishall helped to collect that short-lived tax in 1198 and 1200.[31] Another task assigned to Simon and other judges was the investigation in 1213 following John's reconciliation with the pope into damages done to churches during "the time of discord between the king and the clergy of England."[32]

In spite of his work in finances, Simon of Pattishall's career illustrates a tendency toward specialization in royal government. Under Henry II and his sons, much administrative activity was conducted by men whose work was so wide-ranging that they cannot be linked with one branch of government only. The chroniclers simply describe them as *curiales* or

---

[26] As H.G. Richardson maintained, *Memoranda Roll 1 John*, (Pipe Roll Society, new series, 1943), introduction, pp. xii–xv; Richardson and Sayles, *Governance*, p. 210.

[27] Francis J. West, "The *Curia Regis* in the Late Twelfth and Early Thirteenth Centuries", *Historical Studies (Australia and New Zealand)*, vi (1954), 173–85; Brian Kemp, "Exchequer and Bench in the later twelfth century: separate or identical tribunals?" *Eng. Hist. Rev.*, lxxxviii (1973), 559–73; my "The Origins of Common Pleas and King's Bench" above Chapter 2.

[28] E.g. oblations *per Simon de Pattishall* in *Rotuli de Oblatis et Finibus* (Record Commission, London, 1835), pp. 127, 131, 132, 349.

[29] *Rot. Lit. Claus.*, i, *34*, May 1205, Simon to show the sheriff a debt; p. 126, Oct. 1212, Simon returned to the chamber 15 marks for the widow of Walter of Wahull.

[30] E.g. *Pipe Roll 1 John* (Pipe Roll Society, new series, 1933), pp. 84, 218, 227; *Pipe Roll 5 John* (1938), pp. 63, 104, 252; *Pipe Roll 7 John* (1941), p. 104; *Rotuli de Liberate ac de Misis et Praestitis* (Record Commission, London, 1844), pp. 89, 100.

[31] *Pipe Roll 1 John*, pp. 29, 36, 78, 84, 217, 227, 267; Doris M. Stenton, ed., *Pleas before the King or his Justices, 1198–1202*, Selden Society, lxvii, lxviii, lxxxiii, lxxxiv, (1948–67), i, 137.

[32] *Rot. Lit. Claus.*, i, 164b, Simon assigned to the archbishopric of Canterbury.

familiares regis, and in King John's time such royal *familiares* as William Briwerre or Hugh Bardolf were frequently judges. Although Simon did occasionally perform other tasks, he can best be described as a professional royal servant specializing in the work of justice.

Simon's judicial career began in 1190, when he was one of the justices itinerant in Kent, Surrey, and Middlesex. That summer and autumn he sat at the Bench at Westminster for the first time, and he remained there until the summer of 1207. During those years, he joined other justices on eyre when the court at Westminster was adjourned. He did not always go on circuit to his native region as was normal for justices, but visited several different parts of England. Whenever King John visited the kingdom, Simon joined his court, sitting as a justice *coram rege* in 1200, 1201, in 1204–1205, and in 1207. After Trinity term 1207, he no longer returned to Westminster, but remained with the court following the king through Easter term 1214.[33]

King John clearly respected Simon of Pattishall's judicial ability, for the monarch kept him a member of his court *coram rege* almost continuously from its creation until its collapse at the time of the rebellion. Simon was present at the great council at Northampton on 7 July 1199 shortly after John's coronation.[34] He was also with the king on his next visit to England after the coronation, February–April 1200.[35] At that early point in his reign, John seems to have selected Simon as one of the judges for his newly created court *coram rege*.[36] By 1209 John had closed the court at Westminster, and the king – moved by his suspicious nature and by the hostility growing out of his quarrel with the pope – concentrated justice in the hands of a few trusted judges travelling with him. It was a small band, composed largely of laymen because clerics feared to serve an excommunicate master. Simon was constantly one of them, along with three other professionals.[37] He was the senior member of the band, the only one whose experience extended to the days of Glanvill and Hubert Walter.

Business of the court *coram rege* had to be suspended in the summer of 1210 during King John's campaign in Ireland, and he sent for Simon of Pattishall to help him reform the Irish legal system.[38] John was determined to bring Ireland more closely under his control, and he turned to his most experienced judge to help establish English laws and customs there. John's

---

[33] Stenton, *Pleas before King or Justices*, iii, "Development of the Judiciary, 1100–1216", pp. lxxix–ccxciv.

[34] Stenton, *Pleas before King or Justices*, i, 49–50.

[35] *Cartae Antiquae Rolls 1–10* (Pipe Roll Society, new series, 1939), pp. 61, 124–25, no. 104, 248.

[36] Stenton, *Pleas before King or Justices*, i, 78.

[37] James of Potterne, Henry de Pont-Audemer, and Roger Huscarl.

[38] *Rot. de Lib. ac de Mis.*, p. 188, 10 marks payment to the men who arranged Simon's crossing to Ireland.

departure for his expedition to recover his continental territories brought another closing of the court *coram rege* and a brief revival of the Bench before the baronial rebellion forced the suspension of all normal government work. In 1214 and 1215, right up to the outbreak of fighting, Simon of Pattishall was back at Westminster hearing pleas. In 1216, in the midst of civil war when the regular machinery of government had broken down, King John still relied upon Simon as a judge.[39] Clearly, Simon had moved into that suspicious monarch's inner circle of counselors.

C.A.F. Meekings wrote, "We are...very much in the dark about the mechanical side of business in the Bench."[40] Nevertheless, the surviving plea rolls do cast some light on Simon of Pattishall's part in the work of the courts, and they reveal him as bearing special responsibilities. When he went on eyre, he was always leader of the band of justices with whom he rode.[41] If the justices apportioned their work by allowing their non-professional colleagues the simpler task of taking the assizes, then Simon sometimes had to revise their work, making marginal notes on their scrolls.[42]

Darkness still surrounds the making and keeping of plea rolls. By 1232 the chancellor had a clerk resident at the Bench to take charge of the rolls and writs.[43] But in the time of King John, each justice had his own clerk, and each one seems to have kept a roll.[44] Since a major concern of the monarch was with the profits of justice, one of the rolls was marked with the amercements and turned over to the treasurer. Certainly that was true of the assize rolls,[45] and when Simon was an itinerant justice, his roll was the authoritative one. The mere fact of the preservation of his rolls would point towards this.[46] But further evidence is the notation on one of the eyre rolls that it was to be handed over to "Martin the clerk of Lord Simon of Pattishall", so that he could turn it over to the sheriff.[47] Late in John's reign, Simon had the responsibility for sending the roll of amercements from the court *coram rege* to the treasury.[48]

It does seem that in whatever court Simon sat he and his clerk had special record-keeping responsibilities. From the first years of John's reign, entries

[39] *Rot. Lit. Claus.*, i, 270, 30 Mar. 1216 Simon commanded to take an assize of darrein presentment at Northampton.

[40] "Martin of Pateshull and William Raleigh", *Bull. Inst. Hist. Research*, xxvi (1953), 164.

[41] Pipe Roll lists of amercements refer to eyres of "Simon of Pattishall and his companions".

[42] Stenton, *Pleas before King or Justices*, i, 129–30.

[43] Pegues, "The *Clericus* in English Administration", p. 546.

[44] Cyril Flower, *An Introduction to the Curia Regis Rolls* (Selden Society, lxii, 1943), p. 10, points out that duplicate and even triplicate rolls of sessions have survived.

[45] *Dial. de Scacc.*, p. 77.

[46] Of twelve eyre rolls surviving from John's reign, eleven are from eyres in which Simon was leader, Stenton, *Eng. Justice*, p. 98, n. 4.

[47] Stenton, *Pleas before King or Justices*, ii, 148, no. 537, assizes at Launceston, 18 June 1201.

[48] *Pipe Roll 14 John* (Pipe Roll Society, new series, 1955), and *Pipe Roll 16 John* (1962), *passim*.

on the fine rolls reveal Simon's work of accepting and recording oblations offered for writs, adjournments, and other favors.[49] Both the Bench and *coram rege* rolls refer to writs which were in the keeping of Simon of Pattishall.[50] He witnessed many of the judicial writs which commanded sheriffs to carry out the court's judgments or, in some cases, to hold inquests to obtain further information.[51] After 1205 Simon's clerk, Martin of Pattishall, kept notes on the agreements between litigants which would be needed in drawing up the chirographs recording their final concords. Several entries on the plea rolls concerning final concords state that Martin had the necessary note.[52] Records of payments to messengers sent with letters for Simon of Pattishall suggest that he was the link between the justices following the king and the Exchequer staff sitting at Westminster.[53]

Little can be said about the significance of the judgments which Simon gave because the documents tell so little. The plea rolls rarely record general statements of legal principles, and when they do, it is difficult to connect the decision with any one judge, since panels of three, four, or more justices heard pleas.[54] The plea rolls record judgments in impersonal language: *judicium est ...*, or *consideratum est ...* Another difficulty is the English dependence upon the jury, which meant little separation of substantive law from procedure. The aim of proceedings was to frame some question – either in the original writ or through pleadings by the opposing parties – that the jury might answer. Its answer could bring the case to a conclusion without ever deciding the issue of substantive law.[55] This pattern left less scope for authoritative pronouncements by judges than in countries of Roman law.

Still another difficulty is that the time had not yet come when justices would turn to the judgments of their predecessors as binding authorities. Occasionally the early legal treatises would note the work of an individual judge, but only as "an illustration of the custom of the court."[56] A London legal collection from the time of King John records contention between

[49] *Rot. de Obl. et Fin.*, pp. 15, 19, 255, 318.
[50] Stenton, *Pleas before King or Justices*, ii, 291, no. 986; *Curia Regis Rolls*, iii, 48, 230.
[51] E.g. *Rot. Lit. Claus.*, i, 5b, 22b, 23, 51b, 102, 125.
[52] *Curia Regis Rolls*, ii, 279; iii, 347; iv, 46, 48, 177.
[53] *Documents illustrative of English History in the 13th and 14th Centuries from the Records of the Queen's Remembrancer in the Exchequer* (Record Commission, London, 1844), p. 243, from *rotuli misae* 14 John (1212). For a letter addressed to Pattishall concerning a court case, see Herbert E. Salter, ed., *Cartulary of Osney Abbey* (Oxford Historical Society, 1929–36), v, 57, no. 575A. The bishop of Coventry informed Simon that a church in litigation was not vacant.
[54] Simon once postponed a suit when he found all his colleagues on the bench absent, *Curia Regis Rolls*, v, 151.
[55] John P. Dawson, *A History of Lay Judges* (Cambridge, Mass., 1960), pp. 126–27; T.F.T. Plucknett, *Early English Legal Literature* (Cambridge, 1958), p. 103.
[56] Frederick Pollock and F. W. Maitland, *The History of English Law before the Time of Edward I* (Cambridge, 2nd edition, 1898), i, 138. E.g. some mss. of 'Glanvill' indicate opinions of individual judges in the margins, G. D. G. Hall, ed. (London, 1965), introduction, pp. xliii–xlvii.

Simon of Pattishall and another justice over a point of procedure. A London goldsmith had killed his wife, sought sanctuary in a church, then abjured the realm. When pleas of the crown were heard, however, a question arose about amercement of his pledges, since they did not have him present before the king's justices. Simon of Pattishall argued that the pledges should be quit, for the goldsmith had abjured the realm with the king's permission; since royal justice had been kept safe, the evildoer punished, and the king's will done, the pledges should go free. Although Simon's colleague disagreed, his view prevailed, and the pledges escaped amercement.[57]

Bracton's treatise cites nearly 500 decisions, chiefly those of Martin of Pattishall and William Raleigh, whose rolls were copied into *Bracton's Note Book*. It does cite, however, two cases supposedly from rolls of Simon Pattishall. In one, the question is the validity of a gift of land when both donor and donee remain in seizin throughout the donor's life; and the answer is that the gift is invalid.[58] In the other, the question concerns adjournment of suits involving minors until they come of age. Actually, the date of the case on which *Bracton* based the discussion is 1237, a plea seeking from Henry III custody of Salisbury Castle and the hereditary shrievalty of Wiltshire.[59] In the course of the proceeding, the claimaint points out an earlier plea heard before Simon of Pattishall in the time of King John. *Bracton* concluded from Pattishall's having allowed the earlier plea to go forward that the exception of minority is no excuse for dismissal if the suit touches the king.[60]

One case survives from the eyre rolls where judgment – or rather refusal to give judgment – can be linked to Simon of Pattishall. A mort d'ancestor came before Simon and his companions taking the assizes in 1201, which must have brought to their minds the *casus regis*, John's doubtful succession to the crown on Richard's death instead of his nephew, Arthur of Brittany. The tenant asked the court's judgment whether a younger brother or a nephew, son of a deceased elder brother, was the nearer heir. Obviously, the similarity to the circumstances surrounding John's succession placed Simon and his companions in an awkward position. They were unwilling to give judgment, adjourning the assize indefinitely "because judgment is pending by the will of the lord king."[61]

[57] Martin Weinbaum, *London unter Eduard I. und II.* (Stuttgart, 1933), ii, 65, from British Library, Add. MS. 14252, f. 114v-117r, no. 21; summarized by Mary Bateson, "A London Municipal Collection of the Reign of John", *Eng. Hist. Rev.*, xvii (1902), 709.

[58] *On the Laws and Customs of England*, ed. and trans. Samuel E. Thorne (Cambridge, Mass., 1968–77), ii, 152, f. 50b.

[59] *Bracton's Note Book*, ed. F.W. Maitland (Cambridge, 1887), iii, 248–49, no. 1235, brought by William Longsword.

[60] Bracton, iv, 313, f. 422b.

[61] *Pleas before King or Justices*, ii, 144, no. 528.

What can be said of Simon's attitude toward his work? No notions of seventeenth-century common law judges or twentieth century high court justices must be read back into the thirteenth century. Simon was the king's servant first and the law's servant only second. He must have been aware of the importance of the profits of justice to the king, and he probably took pride – like one of Henry III's itinerant justices later – in the royal revenues that he raised.[62]

The king's will was a powerful factor in judgments, to be taken into account along with custom and law. Pattishall and his fellow justices consistently sought to protect King John's interests, consulting him about royal charters and grants, about difficult cases, or about suits involving prominent persons.[63] The king had little cause for concern about protection of his rights when Simon of Pattishall was sitting on the bench. Furthermore, Simon was aware that John kept his eye constantly trained on the courts. Indeed, the king once amerced him and a fellow justice 100 marks because they granted two barons license to agree in an appeal of felony without royal permission.[64]

What provision did the king make for payment of Simon? It was easy to support royal servants who were in clerical orders by giving them ecclesiastical benefices, but Pattishall was a layman. Other means of support were temporary custodies of lands in the king's hand, grants of escheats, wardships, or income-producing offices. Only by the early thirteenth century do records reveal regular payments to justices. Earliest records of salaries for justices at Westminster date from 1218, when they received twice-yearly payments of 100 shillings. The chief justice of King's Bench under Edward I received an annual salary of 60 to 100 marks.[65] Some of his colleagues, however, received no definite salary, but only irregular grants 'for their expenses' or 'of our [the king's] special grace'.[66] By the 1240s justices on eyre were paid allowances amounting from 20 marks to £40 to cover the added expenses of riding on circuit.[67] From time to time, Henry III made gestures of gratitude toward his justices by giving them robes,

---

[62] W.W. Shirley, ed., *Royal Letters, Henry III* (Rolls Series, London, 1862–66), i, 421–22, no. 350: William of York to the chancellor, enthusiastically stating that his sessions had averaged 40 marks a day for the king.

[63] Ralph V. Turner, *The King and His Courts: The Role of King John and Henry III in the Administration of Justice, 1199–1240* (Ithaca, N.Y., 1968), *passim*.

[64] *Pipe Roll 9 John* (Pipe Roll Society, new series, 1946), p. 207; *Rot. de Obl. et Fin.*, pp. 412, 417. The plea roll account does not indicate that the justices gave the two parties leave to agree, *Curia Regis Rolls* v, 58–59. Later the two justices were pardoned, *Rot. Lit. Claus.*, i, 113, 114, 20 April 1208.

[65] G.O. Sayles, *Select Cases in the Court of King's Bench under Edward I*, (Selden Society, lv, 1936), i, lxxxi. See also my *English Judiciary in the Age of Glanvill and Bracton* (Cambridge, 1985), p. 245.

[66] Sayles, pp. lxxi–lxxii.

[67] C.A.F. Meekings, *Crown Pleas of the Wiltshire Eyre, 1249* (Wilts. Archaeo. and Natural Hist. Soc., Records Branch, xvi, 1961), p. 12.

game, or timber from the royal forests.⁶⁸ The only record of King John making such a gesture to Simon of Pattishall is a gift of two casks of good Angevin wine.⁶⁹ The king did, however, sometimes pardon him of debts due at the Exchequer.⁷⁰

In spite of the expenses the justices encountered on their eyres, their office could produce income. A normal method of maintenance for civil servants throughout the middle ages was a system of fees. This applied to the courts, with the justices and their clerks collecting part of the fees paid by litigants, such as charges for sealing judicial writs.⁷¹ But judges profited from their posts in other ways, some of which would appear remarkably like bribery to modern eyes. Benefits might range from hospitality offered by local nobles to justices on eyre to permanent pensions paid by magnates or monastic houses to justices of the Bench.⁷² No doubt, these patrons expected some consideration when their cases came into court, at least a speedier hearing than less affluent litigants might expect. Possibly some of the grants of land to Simon represented efforts by important landholders to put him on retainer. William de Béthune, advocate of St. Vaast, Flanders, who secured Simon the grant of a manor in 1207, had been involved in lengthy litigation for possession of his English barony.⁷³ Could this have been a reward for Simon's legal services? Or could grants of land by four monastic houses have represented attempts to ensure favorable treatment of their court cases? It must be borne in mind that medieval men accepted as normal a certain amount of venality in all courts, up to the papal *curia* at Rome.

Most royal judges were able to add to their landholdings, and to push their sons up a rung higher on the social ladder. This is true of Simon, even though he received no remarkable rewards from his royal master. Since he was not a cleric, he could not be rewarded with a bishopric; neither was he married to a rich heiress, an easy way of rewarding a faithful knight. Simon did marry, but if his wife brought any land to her husband, it is not recorded.⁷⁴ Neither did Simon ever attain a great office of state as did two

---

⁶⁸ Ibid.

⁶⁹ *Rotuli Chartarum* (Record Commission, London, 1837), p. 70, cited in Edward Foss, *The Judges of England* (London, 1848), ii, 101.

⁷⁰ E.g. the remainder of his farm of the county in 1209, an amercement in 1207, and scutage in 1212, *Pipe Roll 13 John* (Pipe Roll Society, new series, 1953), pp. 91, 267.

⁷¹ Meekings, *Crown Pleas of Wilts. Eyre*, p. 13; Margaret Hastings, *The Court of Common Pleas in the Fifteenth Century* (Ithaca, N.Y., 1947), p. 83.

⁷² Meekings, p. 13; Sayles, *Select Cases in Court of King's Bench*, i, lxxvi-lxxviii.

⁷³ *Rot. Chart.*, p. 184b.

⁷⁴ *Complete Peerage*, x, 312, note 'g', tentatively identifies her as Amice, daughter of William le Chivaler, lord of the manor of Tolleshunt, Essex, based on a 1316 plea, *Year Books of 10 Edward II (1316–1317)* (Selden Society [Year Books Series, xx], lii, 1934), pp. 113–21. But the Simon mentioned (d. 1274) must have been the grandson of Simon I.

of his colleagues on the bench.[75] Nevertheless, he was able to build up his landholdings, adding to the one knights' fee he had in 1190. Apparently, he wished his home at Pattishall to form the heart of his holdings, for they were concentrated around his native village in Northamptonshire with some holdings in adjoining counties – Bedfordshire, Buckinghamshire, and Oxford to the south, and Lincolnshire, Nottinghamshire, and Rutland to the north – although he did have some holdings farther away in Suffolk, Surrey, and Yorkshire. Simon not only acquired estates in the country, but also some urban property in Northampton and at Stamford, Lincolnshire.

From time to time, King John granted property to Simon, particularly temporary possession of escheats. John often made such grants to men who had his favor, but he rarely gave them great hereditary holdings. The grants he gave could easily be withdrawn in case royal wrath was aroused.[76] In 1199 Simon held at farm the land of John de Mallium at Willaveston, Rutland.[77] The next year, the king granted him by charter two houses in Northampton for 16 pence yearly, part of the escheat of Benedict the Jew of York.[78] In 1201 Simon held the escheated land of Josce of Wallingford in Northamptonshire; he held it by charter and by the service of eighteen geese.[79] For a period between the death of the count of Perche in 1202 and the grant of his lands to one of the king's natural sons in 1204, Simon of Pattishall had custody of the count's lands.[80] In 1205 and 1206 Simon had custody of the lands of Matilda de Cauz, a widow in the king's wardship, at Milton Malsor west of Pattishall and south of Northampton, part of the honor of Laxton.[81] Simon already held other lands of the honor of Laxton nearby. By 1212 Simon held at the king's will the escheated manor of Waddesdon, Buckinghamshire, a manor that pertained to the honor of Wallingford.[82]

Pattishall was able to accumulate holdings in addition to those granted him by the king. He held some land lying in royal forests, though not held of the king: 60 acres in King John's wood called Le Hay and 120 acres at his heath of Estley.[83] In 1190 Simon assumed a debt of £30 owed the king by Robert fitz Hugh, a member of a prominent Northamptonshire family,

---

[75] Eustace de Fauconberg became treasurer in 1217, and Henry of London became justiciar of Ireland in 1221. Both were clerics, and also became bishops.

[76] J.C. Holt, *The Northerners* (Oxford, 1961), p. 226.

[77] *Pipe Roll 1 John*, p. 20. He accounted for 20 shillings.

[78] *Rot Chart.*, p. 52, 26 April 1200.

[79] *Pipe Roll 3 John* (Pipe Roll Society, new series, 1936), p. 178.

[80] *Rot. Lit. Claus.*, i, 1, 3b.

[81] *Pipe Roll 7 John*, p. 226; *Pipe Roll 8 John*, p. 176, he owed 40 shillings.

[82] Hubert Hall, ed., *Red Book of the Exchequer* (Rolls Series, London, 1897), ii, 600. In May 1215, the estate was given to another, *Rot. Lit. Claus.*, i, 200; *Memoranda Roll 10 John* (Pipe Roll Society, new series, 1957), pp. 138–39, no. 10.

[83] *Rot. Chart.*, p. 131b, 11 May 1204; p. 152, 1 June 1205, land held by Simon of William fitz Hamo and of the monks of Bradwell.

and in return Robert granted him his land at Heyford. Simon was to hold the land for an annual rent of a pound of pepper to Robert and ten shillings to its chief lords.[84] In 1200 Simon held half a knights' fee in Whatefield, Suffolk, of the abbey of Bury St. Edmunds;[85] he also held of Bushmead Priory, Bedfordshire, land which was part of the barony of Eaton Socon.[86] In April 1201 Simon completed a final concord with William de Lefremund by which William granted his grandfather's one and a half knights' fees in Milton Malsor and Collingtree, Northamptonshire, part of the honor of Laxton, to Simon.[87] Earlier, William had acknowledged Simon's right to advowson of the medieties of the churches of Milton Malsor and Collingtree.[88] During the years 1201–12, Simon was paying scutage on a quarter of a knight's fee in Surrey.[89] In 1202, nine bovates in Great Panton, Lincolnshire, were quitclaimed to Simon in return for his payment of one silver mark.[90] Sometime before 1207 Simon de Beauchamp, constable of Bedford Castle, gave Pattishall a mill at Linslade, Buckinghamshire.[91] In 1207 Simon had his part in nine virgates at Hillesdon, also in Buckinghamshire, confirmed by Ralph Tricket, a member of an old Bedfordshire family.[92] Also Simon accepted a grant of a croft in Pattishall plus the manor of Cold Higham and Grimscot, very near Pattishall, from the prior of Dunstable; and he accepted four virgates in Eascote, also near Pattishall, from the abbot of Cirencester.[93] In 1209 at William de Béthune's request, King John granted Simon and his heirs the manor of Rothersthorpe, not far from his other Northamptonshire holdings. Simon was to hold the manor, part of the honor of Chocques, by the service of one knight and payment of £10 annually.[94] When scutages were assessed in 1211, Simon paid on one and a half knights' fees at Knaresborough, Yorkshire.[95] In the pipe roll for 1214, Simon owed three shillings for two bovates at Swillington, Yorkshire, which

---

[84] *Pipe Roll 2 Richard I*, p. 6; *Pipe Roll 3 and 4 Richard I*, pp. 157–58.

[85] *The Chronicle of Jocelin of Brakelond*, ed. H.E. Butler (Edinburgh, 1949), p. 89.

[86] Farrer, *Honors and Knights Fees*, iii, 251; *The Book of Fees* (Public Record Office, London, 1921–31), ii, 888.

[87] F.M. Stenton, *Facsimiles of early Charters from Northamptonshire* (Northamptonshire Record Society, iv, 1930), pp. 156–57. Confirmation by King John, *Rot. Chart.*, p. 95b, 1 May 1201.

[88] *Curia Regis Rolls*, i, 120.

[89] *Red Book of the Exchequer*, i, 148.

[90] *Feet of Fines for the County of Lincoln, John* (Pipe Roll Society, new series, 1954), pp. 74–75, no. 159, assize of mort d'ancestor brought by Geoffrey fitz Guy.

[91] Joyce Godber, ed., *Cartulary of Newnham Priory* (Bedfordshire Hist. Record Soc., xlii, 1963), p. 17, no. 15.

[92] Farrer, *Honors and Knights Fees*, i, 93.

[93] Ibid.; C.D. Ross, ed., *The Cartulary of Cirencester Abbey, Gloucestershire* (London, 1964), ii, 559–60, no. 665, a rent of one mark. G.H. Fowler, ed., *A Digest of the Charters preserved in the Cartulary of the Priory of Dunstable* (Bedfordshire Hist. Record Soc., x, 1926), p. 109, no. 312. Rent of 4/13/- plus a pound of incense, and hospitality two to three times yearly, also 100 shillings of gersum paid.

[94] *Rot. Chart.*, p. 184b, 5 Mar. 1209.

[95] *Pipe Roll 13 John*, p. 91.

he had held for three years.[96] Also in 1214, Simon quitclaimed one virgate at Winton, Lincolnshire, in exchange for property in the town of Stamford. He gained a loft in the parish of St. John's Church with two shops below and an oven on the north side of the church, which he was to hold for seven pence yearly rent.[97]

Simon of Pattishall never came close to holding the thirty knights' fees that can be considered "the minimum for a fair sized barony."[98] The length of time some of his grants lasted cannot be known; some were permanent, others only temporary. If he could have kept them all until the end of his life, however, he would have held five and three-quarters knights' fees plus other lands of varied sizes and some burgage tenures. Certainly he was a considerable landholder, comfortably within the knightly, if not baronial class. His sons continued to prosper in the king's service. One of them, Walter (d. 1232), served Henry III as sheriff and itinerant justice; and he made a good marriage, which brought him property in Bedfordshire.[99] Another son, Hugh (d. 1241), served Henry III as Exchequer clerk, treasurer, and royal justice until he became bishop of Coventry and Lichfield in 1240.[100] Pattishall had founded a family which would remain prosperous into the fourteenth century.[101]

Yet Simon may have remained unsatisifed with his rewards, for the only important post that he held was senior justice *coram rege*. He had held the office of sheriff, often a source of profit, only until 1203, he was justice of the Jews only briefly, and he held no great number of profitable custodies or wardships. He did not rise to wealth and power either as rapidly or as high as did other royal officers who formed a clique of *familiares regis*. Did Simon's disappointment at his lack of reward lead him to lean toward the rebels against John? The king's distrustful nature caused him to turn against Simon for a time, with or without reason. A sign of John's reduced confidence in Simon is his return to the Bench at Westminster for Easter term 1215 after years as senior justice *coram rege*. Later that spring, on 12 May, a royal writ commanded the seizure of his lands and the sale of his chattels.[102] Possibly, as Christopher Cheney suggested, Simon had to join the rebellion to protect his property once the rebels occupied Northamptonshire and neighboring counties.[103]

---

[96] *Pipe Roll 16 John*, p. 86.

[97] *Feet of Fines for Lincs.*, pp. 171–72, no. 333, fine with William of Weston. Later Simon's son gave this property to the monks of Pipewell, Br. Mus. Add. MS. 37022, f. 152.

[98] Sidney Painter, *The Reign of King John* (Baltimore, 1949), p. 19.

[99] *Complete Peerage*, x, 313; Farrer, *Honors and Knights Fees*, i, 93.

[100] Foss. *Judges*, ii, 437–38.

[101] William Dugdale, *The Baronage of England* (London, 1675–76), ii, 143. John of Pattishall received a summons to Parliament as a baron from Edward III.

[102] *Rot. Lit. Claus.*, i, 200.

[103] C.R. Cheney, "The Twenty-five Barons of Magna Carta", *Bulletin of John Rylands Library*, 50 (1967–68): 303.

Whatever the reason for John's suspicion of Pattishall, it subsided quickly. On 20 May, the king issued a safe-conduct for him, stating, "If it is as the abbot of Woburn said to us on your behalf, then we relax all our wrath and indignation which we had against you."[104] By December 1215, John was returning Simon's property to him.[105] The next spring, in the midst of civil war, Simon was back at his judicial work, for the king appointed him to take an assize at Northampton.[106] Doubtlessly, with the disruption of government work, he had retired to his estates near Northampton.

Since Pattishall's name does not surface on the administrative records after their resumption at the end of the rebellion in 1217, he must have died about the same time that his royal master did. He was buried in Pipewell Abbey, a Cistercian house in Northamptonshire, where Robert of Pattishall – possibly a kinsman – was abbot.[107] Like any good Christian, Simon had already made provision for prayers for his soul, setting aside some property for the purpose: a house and land at Stamford, which he had bought from Deulesaut the Jew.[108] Besides being remembered in the prayers of the monks at Pipewell, Simon was remembered in the mid thirteenth century by the chronicler Matthew Paris. He was remembered not as one of King John's 'evil counselors', as were many of the monarch's *curiales*. Instead, Matthew Paris described him as a faithful and honest man "by whose wisdom all England was at one time ruled," and "who at one time guided the reins of the justices of the whole kingdom."[109]

---

[104] *Rot. Lit. Pat.*, p. 138; *Memoranda Roll 10 John*, p. 141, no. 104.
[105] *Rot. Lit. Claus.*, i, 244.
[106] Ibid., i, 270, 30 Mar. 1216.
[107] *Complete Peerage*, x, 312; for Robert, see *The Heads of Religious Houses in England and Wales 940–1216*, ed. David Knowles, C.N.L. Brooke, Vera London (Cambridge, 1972), p. 139.
[108] BL, Add. MS. 37022, ff. 148, 151d, The Pipewell Cartulary.
[109] *Matthaei Parisiensis Chronica Majora*, ed. H. R. Luard (Rolls Series, London, 1872–84), iii, 296, 542.

12

Roger Huscarl, Professional Lawyer in England and Royal Justice in Ireland, c. 1199–1230

No names of royal justices working in Ireland survive before 1221. Among the names encountered about that time is the Anglo-Scandinavian one of "Huscarl". Roger Huscarl had considerable experience as a lawyer and judge in England under King John. Although his role as one of the earliest royal justices in Ireland has long been recognized, he has only recently been pointed out as a pioneer in the English legal profession, an early professional lawyer (*1*).

Because his surname was unusual in the thirteenth century, it is likely that Roger Huscarl belonged to the family which held three knight's fees of the honor of Wallingford in Berkshire, Oxfordshire, and Surrey in the twelfth and thirteenth centuries. The *cartae baronum* of 1166 show Gilbert Huscarl as the holder of the three fees. By the end of the twelfth century, their holder was Roland Huscarl, whose son Thomas succeeded to them about 1212 (*2*). Roger was possibly Roland's younger brother who went off to London to make his way, since he was without inherited land (*3*). In any case, the connection with Roland Huscarl is clear enough to indicate that Roger, like most of King John's justices, had ties with a rural knightly family (*4*). Richard I granted the honor of Wallingford to his brother Prince John in 1189, and the estate remained with John after his coronation in 1199. Roger Huscarl, then, might appear to be another resident of a royal estate who entered the king's service. There is nothing to connect Roger with King John, however, until long after he had moved to London.

Another set of Huscarls holding land in northwestern Middlesex at Harrow and Wembley confuse the picture: Godfrey Huscarl and his son William (*5*). Added confusion comes from Roger Huscarl's naming his eldest son William also. Godfrey's son William held part of the manor of Wembley of the archbishop of Canterbury, paying £2 15s. annual rent.

(*1*) H. G. Richardson and G. O. Sayles, *The Administration of Ireland, 1172-1377* (Dublin, 1963), pp. 33-34.

(*2*) For an account of the Huscarls and their holdings, see *Victoria Co. Hist., Berks.*, 3: 418; H. E. Salter and A. H. Cooke, eds., *Boarstall Cartulary*, Oxf. Hist. Soc., 88 (1930): 322. Roland Huscarl held the three fees by 1201, *Rot. de Obl. et Fin.*, p. 166; his son Thomas by 1212, *Book of Fees*, 1: 118.

(*3*) Doris M. Stenton, ed., *Rolls of the Justices in Eyre for Yorks. in 3 Hen. III (1218-19)*, Selden Soc., 56 (1937): xxiii.

(*4*) Ralph V. Turner, "The Judges of King John: their background and training", *Speculum*, 51 (1976): 450-51.

(*5*) *Curia Regis Rolls* (hereafter *C.R.R.*), 15: 137, no. 652; *A Calendar of the Feet of Fines for London and Middlesex, Ric. 1-12 Eliz.* (London, 1892-93), pp. 18, 22.

William granted ninety-four acres to the priory of St. Helen, Bishopsgate, in 1236, and one hundred thirty-three acres to the nuns of Kilburn in 1243 (*6*). Perhaps Roger and Godfrey were cousins, or even brothers; no more can be ascertained about their connection.

Roger Huscarl first appears in the *curia regis* rolls as an attorney for several different people coming from two separate sections of the country: some from Suffolk, Essex and Hertfordshire, and others from Somerset and Dorset. His work as an attorney spread over the years from the spring of 1199 to the spring of 1209 (*7*). On the basis of this evidence, H. G. Richardson suggested, "It is just possible that he was in fact a lawyer by profession," a suggestion enthusiastically endorsed by Lady Stenton. She wrote, "There is no doubt that the reign of John saw the emergence of the professional attorney" (*8*). Besides working as an attorney at Westminster, acting as his absent client's *alter ego* in conducting his case, Roger may well have worked as a *narrator* or pleader, one who substituted for parties to suits or their attorneys present in court, speaking in their stead (*9*). Little evidence of the *narratores'* work survives before about 1235, for their appointment was not recorded on the plea rolls as was appointment of an attorney. Neither did the *narratores* have official standing as did attorneys, and their activity is only hinted at with oblique references on the rolls.

Most twelfth- and thirteenth-century knights gained an intimate knowledge of English law through years of attending the courts, local and royal. After all, "suit to court" was traditionally a basic feudal obligation. Sons of knightly families began attending the courts of shire and hundred as boys, accompanying their fathers; and later they were participants, suing in their own right, acting as attorneys for their lords, and serving on juries. As lords of their own lands and stewards or bailiffs of estates, they themselves had to preside over seignorial courts. Some of these men began to gain reputations for their skill in pleading and to serve as pleaders for others in return for grants of land (*10*).

Monasteries in twelfth-century England made a practice of employing one of their knights as a pleader in suits coming before secular courts. As early as the time of the Conqueror, Abingdon Abbey won a suit in county

---

(6) C.R.R., 15: 460, no. 1832; *Victoria Co. Hist., Middlesex*, 4: 207.

(7) He was attorney for six persons, one of them twice, and a surety for another's law, Doris M. Stenton, *Pleas before the King or his Justices, 1198-1212*, Selden Soc., 83 (1966), 3: Appendix, cccxvi-cccxvii.

(8) Richardson, "William of Ely, the King's Treasurer, 1195-1215", *Trans. Royal Hist. Soc.*, 4th ser., 15 (1932): 67; Stenton in *Pleas before the King or his Justices*, 3: xxxvi-xliv. See also C. T. Flower, *Introduction to the Curia Regis Rolls*, Selden Soc., 62 (1943): 405-7.

(9) For one who was both attorney and pleader, see John of Bucuinte, attorney for more than 30 clients from 20 counties, and pleader for abbot of Crowland, Lady Stenton, *Pleas before the King or his Justices*, 3: cccvii-ccxi; and *English Justice between the Conquest and Magna Carta* (Philadelphia, 1964), pp. 194-95.

(10) Robert C. Palmer, "The Origins of the Legal Profession in England", *Irish Jurist*, 11 (1976): 126-35.

court because of its pleaders, or *causidici,* "whose speech no wise man could gainsay" (*11*). The abbot of Battle in a 1167 case had one of his monks and one of his knights speak for him to explain "the whole matter to the king and his justices from the very beginning" (*12*). The chronicler of St. Albans praised a knight who acted as the abbot's legal adviser in a plea at Westminster in the early thirteenth century. The knight is described as *miles eloquentissimus et sapientissimus* and *in placitis civilibus providus et circumspectus* (*13*). No doubt, lay lords imitated the abbots in employing one of their knights, skilled in speaking, as a pleader in the courts. They had the feudal obligation of supporting the suits of their vassals in the public courts, and great lords with holdings in several shires would have found it useful to have specialist-pleaders to assist them. Such knights, knowledgeable in the law, could also have acted as attorneys—substitutes in the lords' own suits, when they found it impossible to be present in court. The *Leges Henrici Primi* and *Glanvill* hint that it was not uncommon for stewards or bailiffs to act as their lords' attorneys (*14*).

Most scholars date the origin of the legal profession around 1200 because they link it with the rise of the royal courts, centered at Westminster. Recently, however, Robert C. Palmer has maintained that professional lawyers were needed in the county and local courts throughout the twelfth century, and that it is only the lack of surviving evidence that prevents us from seeing them earlier. In his view, the greatest significance of the rise of the central law courts for the legal profession is their records, which enable us to see the repetition of attorneys' names on the plea rolls. He writes, "Both for attorneys and for pleaders, it was the provincial courts probably rather more than the king's court which were decisive for generating the legal profession" (*15*).

Roger Huscarl could have been active in legal affairs without being a fulltime lawyer at Westminster; he may have had other employment at the same time. If the London husting, wards and sokes had left records, then we might have evidence of other legal work undertaken by him. Roger did witness a number of charters and grants for the priory of Holy Trinity, Aldgate, after 1197 (*16*). His witnessing might mean only that he was their tenant, but it hints that he was a steward or other lay official of

---

(*11*) *Chronicon Monasterii de Abingdon,* ed. J. Stevenson, Rolls Series (1858), 2: 2.
(*12*) Eleanor Searle, ed. and trans., *The Chronicle of Battle Abbey,* Oxford Medieval Texts (Oxford, 1980), p. 214.
(*13*) *Gesta Abbatum S. Albani,* ed. H. T. Riley, Rolls Series (1867-69), 1: 221, 225-26.
(*14*) *Leges Henrici Primi,* ed. and trans. L. J. Downer (Oxford, 1972), pp. 100-101, cap. 7, 7a; *Glanvill,* ed. and trans. G. D. G. Hall, Medieval Texts (London, 1965), pp. 133, 167, XI, 1; XIII, 33; *Dialogus de Scaccario,* ed. and trans. Charles Johnson, Medieval Classics (London, 1950), pp. 116-117, shows barons represented before the Exchequer panel by their stewards.
(*15*) Palmer, "Origins of Legal Profession", p. 145.
(*16*) Gerald A. J. Hodgett, ed., *Cartulary of Holy Trinity, Aldgate,* London Rec. Soc. Pub'ns., 7 (1971): 208, no. 1020; *Cat. Anc. Deeds,* 1: 207, no. A1760; 216, no. A1817; 2: 3, no. A1835; 10, no. A1883. Later his son was a witness, 2: 98, no. A2592.

the canons. While it may be an exaggeration to label Roger Huscarl a "professional attorney", he clearly was spending enough time at Westminster to attract attention, and he won appointment to his first official post at the end of 1209. He served as William de Nevill's deputy-sheriff in Wiltshire from Christmas 1209 until the Easter Exchequer of 1210 (*17*).

Little is known about the education of laymen in the twelfth and thirteenth centuries. Not until the early thirteenth century at the earliest were there "business schools" for aspiring accountants, attorneys, secretaries, or estate stewards. Yet the *miles literatus* cannot have been so rare as scholars today usually assume that he was. Knights may not have been *literati* in the sense of being learned in classical literature, but many of them had the practical literacy in Latin needed for their work as estate stewards or bailiffs. As H. G. Richardson and G. O. Sayles stated, "We may presume . . . that a layman who exercised an office demanding the use of written instruments was literate" (*18*).

Roger Huscarl first came to the *curia regis* as a justice on 27 October 1210 following King John's return from Ireland. There is no evidence of Roger's activity from the time he became an under-sheriff at the end of 1209 until his appointment to the bench in the autumn of 1210. Perhaps he had accompanied the royal expedition to Ireland and had won John's confidence there. Roger's appointment to the judiciary came more than a year after King John's closing of the court of common pleas at Westminster in order to concentrate all justice at the court *coram rege*. In the years 1209-1214, John relied on a small band of trusted judges following him about the kingdom for all work of royal justice. He could no longer count on clerics to serve him, for many of them left the royal service following his excommunication in 1209 (*19*). No clues in the shape of prominent clients provide a key to the secret of Roger's recruitment for the judiciary. Neither are there other useful clues to explain how he attracted King John's attention, although we can speculate that the king encountered him on his Irish expedition. A crisis caused by a shortage of available clerics forced King John to turn to the group of professional attorneys, essoiners, and pleaders growing up at Westminster to staff his *curia regis*.

John's only justice *coram rege* to come from this group, however, is Roger Huscarl. The others included Simon of Pattishall, a justice with long experience going back to 1190; James of Potterne, who had been on the bench since 1198; and Henry de Pont-Audemer, who first joined the court *coram rege* in 1207. The first two had come to their posts through Geoffrey fitz Peter the justiciar; the third had long been active in the

---

(*17*) *Pipe Roll 12 John*, pp. 76, 82; *Pipe Roll 14 John*, p. 147.
(*18*) H. G. Richardson and G. O. Sayles, *The Governance of Mediaeval England* (Edinburgh, 1963), p. 274. See also Ralph V. Turner, "The *Miles Literatus* in twelfth and thirteenth-century England: How rare a phenomenon?" , above, pp. 119-36.

(*19*) Stenton, *English Justice between the Conquest and Magna Carta*, pp. 97-98.

administration in Normandy before coming to England. Two others sat with the justices *coram rege* with some regularity, though less continuously than the other four: Robert de Aumari, autumn 1210 to autumn 1211; and Jocelin de Stukeley, spring and summer 1213, after the return to Westminster. Others joined the court for brief periods as it travelled about the kingdom, witnessing fines as justices. A particularly large number arrived and departed from the *curia regis* in 1209.

King John's final campaign to recover his continental possessions brought a revival of the Bench in 1214 and 1215 under his new justiciar Peter des Roches, bishop of Winchester. Roger Huscarl was a member of this revived Bench during its brief lifetime. The crisis arising from baronial discontent brought an end to the court's sittings by early May 1215. Two justices, Roger Huscarl and Henry de Pont-Audemer, were among the king's adherents at Runnymede; they took an oath to obey the committee of twenty-five barons (*20*). The royal courts did not revive until 1218 after a new king had been crowned, the rebellion crushed, and the French invaders repelled. Roger Huscarl served Henry III as an itinerant justice on the northwestern circuit of the first general eyre of the new reign, autumn 1218–spring 1219. Then he returned to Westminster for an Easter term that was much shortened because of the length of the eyre.

Roger Huscarl's career under Henry III lay mainly in Ireland, where his judicial experience won him appointment to a post at the side of the justiciar. Roger first went to Ireland sometime after the summer 1219, and he witnessed charters in company with Geoffrey Marsh, the justiciar of Ireland, until 1221 (*21*). Roger returned to England in the autumn of 1221, sent by Geoffrey Marsh, retiring as justiciar, to return custody of Irish lands and castles to Henry III (*22*). He crossed the Irish Sea again in December 1222, sent specifically to assist the new justiciar, Henry of London, archbishop of Dublin, conducting "the king's affairs and pleas" (*23*). No doubt, Roger was sent to Ireland chiefly because of his expertise as a judge, and he continued his judicial work there. The writ authorizing his journey described him as *nuntius* to the archbishop, but not long after his arrival he joined Henry of London in handling an important action. The archbishop seized into the king's hand Walter de Lacy's liberty of Meath because of an unjustified delay in an appeal in the court of his liberty. The seizure is described in an inquisition dating from 1280 as having been made on the advice of Roger Huscarl then justice "of the bench at Dublin", as the justiciar's court is anachronistically called.

(*20*) Matthew Paris, *Chron. Majora*, Rolls Series, 2: 605.
(*21*) *Calendar of Ormond Deeds,* ed. E. Curtis, Irish MSS. Commission (Dublin, 1932-34), 1: 21, no. 40; *Cartulary of Oseney Abbey,* ed. H. E. Salter, Oxf. Hist. Soc. (1929-36), 5: 130, no. 612D; *Chartularies of St. Mary's Abbey, Dublin,* Rolls Series (1884-86), 1: 121.
(*22*) *Pat. Rolls, 1216-1225,* pp. 315-17, 2 Nov. 1221; *Cal. Docs. relating to Ireland,* 1: 155-56, no. 1015.
(*23*) *Rot. Lit. Claus.*, 1: 526b, 527; *Cal. Docs. relating to Ireland,* 1: 163, no. 1067.

This trial took place probably about 1222 *(24)*. Roger was present with William Marshal the Younger, justiciar, his deputy Geoffrey Marsh, Walter de Lacy, Theobald Walter, and other *fideles* for an inquest at Limerick on 22 October 1224, part of what seems to have been a general eyre *(25)*. Roger may have been present for similar inquests at Dublin as part of the same eyre. An undated charter was made at the assizes at Drogheda which were taken "before Roger Huscarl and certain others of the king's faithful" *(26)*. Roger remained in the king's service in Ireland until shortly before his death, which came probably before January 1230 *(27)*.

Roger played a part, then, in the work of the English *curia regis* in the last, difficult years of King John's reign and in pioneering an Irish itinerant judicature, which was just getting underway in the early 1220s. Little evidence for any administrative activity away from the bench by Roger survives; his career indicates the growing specialization and professionalization in early thirteenth-century royal government. Justices were among those King John assigned to make investigations in 1213 into damages to the Church during "the time of discord between the king and the clergy of England". As part of the settlement of the Canterbury succession crisis, John had promised to pay for damages to Church property during the Interdict. Roger Huscarl was a member of a group of three who visited the bishopric of Hereford *(28)*.

With Roger Huscarl, we seem to be approaching more closely the salaried judicial officer. Several instances of grants of money to him for his expenses while on the king's service survive. In October 1212, the king notified the treasurer and chamberlains of 100 shillings of prests to be paid to Roger, and in 1214 he was to be paid twenty shillings *(29)*. Prests were advances to a royal servant, either advances against sums he would later collect in the course of his work or advances to be deducted from future salary payments. In December 1222, Roger received five marks for the expenses of his crossing to Ireland *(30)*. In March 1224, the young Henry III—or rather his counselors—gave Roger as a gift five marks to be paid him out of the tallage of Bristol, a payment which suggests strongly that Roger visited Bristol on the king's business at that time *(31)*. Roger received £20 a year later to be paid either in cash at the Irish Exchequer

---

(24) Cal. Close Rolls, 1279-1288, pp. 55-56; *Cal. Inq. Misc.*, 1: no. 339.
(25) K. W. Nicholls, "Inquisitions of 1224 from the Miscellanea of the Exchequer", *Analecta Hibernica*, 27 (1972): 105, from P.R.O. E163/1/3/mm. 2-6.
(26) Chart. St. Mary's, Dublin, 1: 64-65. For other charters witnessed by Roger in Ireland, see *ibid.*, 1: 56, 60, 62, 64-65, 121; *Calendar of Archbishop Alen's Register, c. 1172-1534*, ed. Charles McNeill, Royal Soc. of Antiquaries of Ire. (Dublin, 1950), p. 45; *Ormond Deeds*, 1: 42, no. 96 (misdated as 1240).
(27) C.R.R., 13: 528, no. 2486.
(28) Rot. Lit. Claus., 1: 164b.
(29) Rot. Lit. Claus., 1: 125b; *Pipe Roll 16 John*, p. 124.
(30) Rot. Lit. Claus., 1: 526b.
(31) Rot. Lit. Claus., 1: 588.

or in land *(32)*. By June 1226, Roger was receiving £25 yearly income for his service to the king in Ireland *(33)*. £25 a year was a substantial salary in the early thirteenth century, for a few years later, when regular payments to royal servants became the rule, 40 marks (or £27) *per annum* was the salary of a senior official "well up towards the top of the scale" *(34)*.

Other signs of favour shown to Huscarl are the routine royal letters of protection issued to royal servants. Roger received letters patent of protection for his voyage to Ireland in December 1222, and later the protection was extended until the end of the king's minority *(35)*. More important as a favour was the postponement while he was in the king's service in Ireland of a debt of eight and a half marks he owed the Jews in 1223, and then the next year the pardon of his debt entirely *(36)*.

Roger Huscarl did secure some grants of land from John and Henry III, although none of startling size. King John rarely gave his servants hereditary holdings, preferring grants that could be withdrawn if they lost his favour. He commanded the sheriff of Kent in 1212 to give Roger seizin of the lands of Roger of Tanton (Stainton?) "for sustaining himself in the lord king's service". This was probably land at Cowstead (in Stockbury), Kent, valued in 1219 at fifteen shillings yearly, though it had risen to a value of a hundred shillings by 1227 *(37)*. Before August 1225 Henry III had given Roger some land of the manor of Balscadden, Ireland, also to hold at bail. Roger was to continue to hold his portion for some time, even though the king gave the bulk of the estate to William Marsh on 28 August 1225 *(38)*. Henry III granted two carucates of the manor to Amaury de St. Amand the next year, on 10 June 1226, but he left the residue to Roger, who was to receive a money-payment from the Irish Exchequer if the income remaining to him from Balscadden failed to provide his £25 yearly salary *(39)*. Amaury de St. Amand had difficulty securing the two carucates, for he found lessees of Roger Huscarl in possession of them. The king issued several mandates to the Irish justiciar, seeking to enforce his grant, but as late as January 1228, Roger's lessee still had seizin *(40)*. Huscarl also had land in the forest of Ross, which William Marshal the younger, justiciar in Ireland, 1224-1226, gave him

---

(32) Rot. Lit. Claus., 2: 32b; *Cal. Docs. relating to Ireland*, 1: 192, no. 1271, 20 librates out of the king's escheats, 22 April 1225; and *Rot. Lit. Claus.*, 2: 40; *Cal. Docs. relating to Ireland*, 1: 196, no. 1295, £20 a year to be paid at the Irish Exchequer, 20 May 1225.
(33) Rot. Lit. Claus., 2: 125; *Cal. Docs. relating to Ireland*, 1: 212, no. 1400.
(34) T. F. T. Plucknett, *Early English Legal Literature* (Cambridge, 1958), p. 44, discussing Bracton's salary in 1240.
(35) Pat. Rolls, 1215-1225, p. 358; *1225-1232*, p. 3; *Cal. Docs. relating to Ireland*, 1: 201, no. 1331.
(36) Exch. L. T. R. Mem. Roll 5: m. 8; *Rot. Lit. Claus.*, 1: 587.
(37) Rot. Lit. Claus., 1: 204b; and 229, 20 Sept. 1215. *Book of Fees*, 1: 269; 2: 1346.
(38) Rot. Lit. Claus., 2: 59b; *Cal. Docs. relating to Ireland*, 1: 199, no. 1320.
(39) Rot. Lit. Claus., 2: 125; *Cal. Docs. relating to Ireland*, 1: 212, no. 1400.
(40) Rot. Lit. Claus., 2: 188b; *Cal. Docs. relating to Ireland*, 1: 230, no. 1523, 4 June 1227; *Close Rolls, 1227-1231*, p. 11, 3 Jan. 1228.

permission to enclose or to do with as he chose, "saving to us the savage beasts" *(41)*.

Roger Huscarl's English lands were centered in southeastern Middlesex, around Stepney, where a final concord as early as 2 John shows him to have had a holding *(42)*. Several lawsuits in the *curia regis* provide some information about his other holdings around Stepney: half a virgate and a messuage at Stepney in contention as early as 1200, warranty of five acres, and a heath in 1204-1205 *(43)*, seven acres claimed as "Wale merse" in Stepney in 1212 *(44)*. In 1219, Roger, his two sons, and others were defendants in an assize of novel disseizin concerning a free tenement at Stepney, but the jurors found that they had not disseized the plaintiffs *(45)*. He claimed seven acres of land at Bruton, Somerset, in 1217-1218, when he made a final concord giving the claimant a sparrow-hawk in return for his quitclaim *(46)*. It seems likely that the land had been a grant for the Montacutes, Somerset landholders who were Roger's clients. Perhaps Roger gave his younger son his Somerset lands, for in 1229 Alexander Huscarl was bringing an assize of novel disseizin for a tenement at Babcary, about ten miles from Bruton *(47)*.

Roger Huscarl does not seem to have speculated in offices and wardships as did some other royal officials in an effort to reap profits. As has been shown, he was undersheriff of Wiltshire for a short while before he joined the bench. Otherwise, he held no public office other than his place at the bench and his multi-purpose post as assistant to the justiciar of Ireland. Roger held only one wardship, custody of William fitz Robert, a Middlesex lad *(48)*. In sum, he does not seem to have improved his position in any striking way through his contacts with the king and the powerful *curiales*.

Roger was certainly no *familiaris regis* dramatically winning an earldom in the manner of a William Marshal or a Geoffrey fitz Peter. Neither did he do as well out of his service to the king as another professional judge, Simon of Pattishall, who was able to increase the size of his landholdings some six-fold during a quarter century of service on the bench *(49)*. Nothing indicates any significant holdings for Roger that would have moved him out of the lower levels of knightly landholders.

Roger Huscarl left two sons, William his elder son and heir and

---

(41) Chart. St. Mary's, Dublin, 2: 157.
(42) Feet of Fines for London and Middlesex, p. 5. He was not a party to the agreement, but his service figured as part of the settlement.
(43) Rot. Curia Regis, 2: 262; *C.R.R.*, 1: 345; 3: 204, 328.
(44) C.R.R., 6: 282, 392, no conclusion recorded.
(45) C.R.R., 8: xi. Plaintiffs were William Blund and his wife.
(46) Pedes Finium for the County of Somerset, ed. Emanuel Green, Somerset Record Soc., 6 (1892): 29. The claimant was Henry de Glanvill with his wife.
(47) Pat. Rolls, 1225-1232, p. 291.
(48) C.R.R., 10: 290.
(49) Ralph V. Turner, "Simon of Pattishall, Northamptonshire Man, Early Common Law Judge", above, pp. 209-12.

another, Alexander, at his death sometime before January 1230. A case before the *curia regis* in Hilary term 1230 makes clear that Roger had died sometime earlier. His son William was seeking half an acre at Stepney, which he maintained his father had claimed by an assize of novel disseizin, but that Roger had died before the assize could be taken (50). It is not known whether Roger returned to England before his death or died in Ireland, although his son's statement about the assize seems to indicate his return to his native land sometime before his death.

(50) *C.R.R.*, 13: 528, no. 2486; 14: 8, no. 49. William was one of twelve knights elected to take a grand assize at Stepney, summer 1239, *C.R.R.*, 16: 198, no. 1045.

13

Changing Perceptions of the New Administrative Class in Anglo-Norman and Angevin England: The *Curiales* and their Conservative Critics

A complaint among twelfth-century English moralists and chroniclers was that monarchs were choosing "men raised from the dust" to be their ministers and counselors instead of members of old noble families. They charged that the king was choosing as his courtiers or *familiares* low-born men—*plebes, ignobiles,* even *rustici* or *servi*—allowing them to usurp places that belonged to the aristocracy. This chorus of complaint began in the time of William the Conqueror's sons. Only then did *nobiles* and *curiales* begin to divide into two distinct groups, and new administrative posts provided opportunities for new men to rise to greater wealth and influence.

The early twelfth-century monastic chronicler, Orderic Vitalis, wrote that William the Conqueror "raised up the lowest of his Norman followers to the greatest riches."[1] Often cited is his complaint about Henry I, "So he pulled down many great men [*illustres*] from positions of eminence.... He ennobled others of base stock [*de ignobili stirpe*] who had served him well, raised them, so to say, from the dust, and heaping all kinds of favors on them, stationed them above earls and famous castellans."[2] The author of the *Gesta Stephani* also complained that Henry I took men of low birth [*ex plebeio genere*], who had entered his service as court pages and enriched them, endowed them with wide estates, and made them his chief officials.[3] Another

---

[1] Orderic Vitalis, *Historia ecclesiastica*, 6 vols., ed. and trans. Marjorie Chibnall (Oxford, 1968–80), 2:261; similarly, of William Rufus, 5:202–3.
[2] Orderic, 6:16.
[3] *Gesta Stephani*, ed. K. R. Potter, Medieval Texts (Edinburgh, 1955), p. 22.

chronicler, Richard of Hexham, made a similar comment, although in admiring rather than condemning language, "He oppressed many nobles because of their faithlessness; he elevated to high honors many commoners [*ignobiles*], whom he found to be upright and loyal to him."[4]

Later in the twelfth century, the chorus grew louder once an administrative or ministerial class reappeared at Henry II's court. Latin writers of moral treatises, letter writers, and poets writing in the vernacular formed a virtual school of court satirists, complaining of *curiales*. An early critic of Henry II's courtiers was Ralph Niger, who wrote that the king brought to England to serve as his officials "bastard serfs and common soldiers of chamber and hall."[5] Later Walter Map charged that the reason for the greater oppressiveness of the clerics among Henry II's royal justices compared to laymen was that they were sons of villeins [*servi vero, quos vocamus rusticos*] who had gone off to the schools, seeking to rise above their proper station.[6] Peter of Blois also complained of the low birth of Henry's judges, writing that *viri nobiles et discreti* resented having their causes judged by commoners, *plebis*.[7] By the end of the century, Gerald of Wales had added his voice, asking of Henry II, "Who behaved more nobly to commoners [*ignobili*] and more ignobly to the aristocracy [*nobilior*]? Who raised the lowly higher or depressed the high so low?"[8] These English writers were not reacting against a literary fiction or conventional portrayal, but against social realities that they perceived as wrongs.[9]

In the late twelfth-century romances, the folly of trusting the lowborn instead of men of good birth was an important motif.[10] The theme of the villein upstart who usurps the place of his betters, gaining admission to a bad prince's councils, was common in vernacular literature.[11]

---

[4] *Chronicles of the reigns of Stephen, Henry II, and Richard I*, ed. Richard Howlett, Rolls Series (London, 1886), 3:140.

[5] *Chronicles of Ralph Niger*, ed. Robert Anstruther, Caxton Society, 13 (London, 1851), p. 167: "servos spurios, caligatos cubiculi mensae."

[6] *De nugis curialium*, ed. and trans. M. R. James, rev. C. N. L. Brooke and R. A. B. Mynors (Oxford, 1983), bk. 1, chap. 10, pp. 12–15.

[7] *Patrologia Latina*, vol. 207, col. 300, epistle 95.

[8] Gerald of Wales, *Topographia Hibernica*, ed. J. F. Dimock, in *Opera*, Rolls Series (London, 1867), 5:199.

[9] C. Stephen Jaeger, *The Origins of Courtliness* (Philadelphia, 1985), p. 55.

[10] Peter S. Noble, "Knights and Burgesses in the Feudal Epic," in *The Ideals and Practice of Medieval Knighthood*, ed. Christopher Harper-Bill and Ruth Harvey (Woodbridge, 1986), p. 110; Georges Duby, *Les trois ordres ou l'imaginaire du féodalism* (Paris, 1978); citations are from the English translation, *The Three Orders* (Chicago, 1980), p. 279.

[11] Georges Duby, "Situation de la noblesse en France au début du XIIIe siècle," *Tijdschrift voor Geschiedenis* 82 (1969): 309–15, translated in *The Chivalrous Society*,

Benedict of Sainte-Maure, author of the *Chronique des ducs de Normandie*, praised Duke Richard for tolerating no villein at his court, but granting access only to sons of knights.[12] No doubt, some of this prejudice is simply due to personal dislike of courtiers, such as John of Salisbury demonstrates in his *Policraticus* and his letters. In the view of some conservative critics, however, new men were taking places close to the king that belonged rightly to the baronage, members of old landed families who exemplified traditional feudal values.

These critics were defending their ideal of a static social order, in which everyone was expected to know his place and to be content to remain in his place. In the Middle Ages, a vision of society arranged according to orders or ranks came naturally. Was not heaven itself arranged according to rank? The medieval church taught that a hierarchically arranged society on earth mirrored the heavenly hierarchy. Since classes and ranks are part of both the divine and natural order of things, all persons should accept their places and do nothing to alter them. To seek to improve one's lot, to be motivated by ambition was a sin, connected to the sins of pride and envy. Clerics devised the doctrine of three distinct social orders, stressing the superiority of clergy and nobility, to keep lowborn people in their places at a time when they were beginning to climb higher. The trifunctional division of society into *oratores, bellatores, laboratores,* first stated in the ninth century, enjoyed a resurgence circa 1175–80 at Henry II's court.[13]

Historians have joined the chorus of cries about new men versus old aristocracy, seeing the conflict as a major aspect of medieval English social and political history. A truism of textbooks is that feudal societies naturally fostered an adversarial relationship between magnates and monarchs, assisted by their lowborn administrators, to whom they turned because such servants' complete dependence upon royal favor made them more loyal than great nobles with castles and large estates. Sir Richard Southern addressed the problem in his 1962 Raleigh lecture on King Henry I. He praised the king for recruiting a corps of qualified and trusted royal servants, new men, and for purchasing their loyalty with royal patronage. Southern recognized that,

---

trans. Cynthia Postan (London, 1977), p. 182. The romance *L'escoufle* depicts an early Norman count aiding the German emperor in ridding himself of serfs to whom he had handed over control of castles and cities and restoring the proper order of things (ed. H. Michelant and Paul Meyer, Société des anciens textes français [Paris, 1894], pp. 45–49).

[12] *Chroniques des ducs de Normandie,* ed. Carin Fahlin, Bibliotheca Ekmaniana Universitatis regalis Upsaliensis, nos. 56, 60 (Uppsala, 1951–54), 2:196–97, line 28,824; Duby, "Situation," p. 182.

[13] Duby, *Three Orders.*

despite the protestations of some hostile writers, none of the administrators promoted by Henry I actually had servile origins but that royal patronage raised middling knights to the position of magnates or obscure clerics to bishoprics.[14]

Judith A. Green has made a quantitative analysis of the royal servants in 1130, and she found that of twenty-five important household officers, eight belonged to great landholding families, seven to lesser landed families, and ten to families that cannot be traced. She finds that of eighteen men gaining substantial property through royal patronage before 1135, six belonged to greater landholding families, and four to lesser ones. Green concludes that Henry I did recruit some new men "of a middle station in society" and raise them up, but she finds "a measure of exaggeration" in both chroniclers' complaints and Southern's congratulations.[15] More recently, Charlotte A. Newman has sought to identify and to trace the new men for the entire reign of Henry I. She finds a somewhat larger number, twenty-four royal servants on whom the king increasingly relied and who had no noticeable standing before 1100.[16] She notes that his reliance upon such men did enable "individuals of lesser status to rise into or within the nobility." She sees few spectacular gains by such men; only six of thirty-eight greater heiresses married new men, and only four of twenty-four newly created baronies went to them. They mostly built up their wealth through slow accumulation of smaller rewards, especially royal exemptions from feudal and public obligations.[17] Emma Mason has given flesh to such figures with an account of the rise of two twelfth-century curial families, the Mauduits and the Beauchamps, to the earldom of Warwick to illustrate use of machinery of royal government to climb to noble status.[18]

Students of Angevin royal administration have found that the family background of *curiales* serving Henry II and his sons was "the lower ranks of the feudal class."[19] Of thirteen chief justiciars from Henry I's to Henry III's time, all but three came from this category, if

---

[14] R. W. Southern, "The Place of Henry I in English History," in *Medieval Humanism and Other Essays* (New York, 1970), pp. 208–28.

[15] Judith A. Green, "The King's Servants," chap. 7 in *The Government of England under Henry I* (Cambridge, 1986), pp. 134–93, and tables 4–5, pp. 284–86.

[16] Charlotte A. Newman, *The Anglo-Norman Nobility in the Reign of Henry I: The Second Generation* (Philadelphia, 1988), app. A, pp. 183, 189.

[17] Ibid., pp. 138–40, 176.

[18] Emma Mason, "Magnates, *curiales* and the Wheel of Fortune," *Anglo-Norman Studies* (formerly *Proceedings of the Battle Conference*) 2 (1979): 131–40.

[19] Charles R. Young, *Hubert Walter* (Durham, N.C., 1967), p. 165.

not from one even lower.[20] My own study of a sample of forty-nine royal justices in the late twelfth to early thirteenth centuries shows the same to be true of these royal servants; almost half came from knightly families with a tradition of service to the king in minor offices. This led me to conclude, "Critics of the royal justices' ambition were simply engaging in hyperbole when they complained of the judges' servile origin."[21] One came from the London patriciate, and possibly one other came from the provincial bourgeoisie.[22] I failed to determine the origin of eleven (22 percent): nine clerics and two laymen. One of the laymen, however, is called *miles* in his earliest appearance in the public records, as witness to a final concord in the Wiltshire county court; and the other began his career in the household of the earls of Oxford, where his brother was the earl's *vadletus*, a household servant who might or might not be of knightly rank.[23]

It is curious that these writers chose to accuse the new administrative class of base birth. How can we explain this accusation, which was clearly false except in the rarest of instances? A major problem is the uncertain status of the knight or *miles* in the centuries before the mid- or late twelfth century, which meant that not all sons of warriors were considered to have been nobly or gently born. The word *chevalier* or *miles* could apply to both nobles of the highest social level and to simple fighting men.

In early feudal society, knights had occupied an intermediate place; above the peasants, but below aristocrats known as *nobiles*, *proceres*, or *optimates*. The aristocracy consisted of hereditary holders of large estates conscious of a distinguished ancestry reaching back to the Carolingian Empire and exercising wide jurisdictional powers. Their adoption of patrilineal patterns of descent for property around the year 1000 strengthened their separate identity. Knights were their military retainers, either landless or holding little land, often of obscure origin, and defined by their military skills rather than by their ancestry or property. Lack of precision in terms used to describe warriors in the post-Conquest period adds to confusion about knightly status. It appears, however, that chroniclers and charter drafters did try to find

---

[20] Robert de Beaumont, earl of Leicester; William de Mandeville, earl of Essex; and Hugh de Puiset, bishop of Durham, are the three aristocrats. Backgrounds of clerics Roger of Salisbury and William Longchamp are obscure; see nn. 73 and 79 below.

[21] Ralph V. Turner, *The English Judiciary in the Age of Glanvill and Bracton* (Cambridge, 1985), p. 293.

[22] Henry of London, a Blund, and Master Ralph of Norwich.

[23] James of Potterne, see Turner, p. 142; Walter of Creeping, ibid., p. 144. Most of the nine clerics can be linked indirectly to knightly families, so that they were at least poor relations, unlikely to have been servile in status.

different terms for enfeoffed knights, landless ones, and more lightly armed military men.[24]

The two levels in feudal society of aristocrats, *nobiles*, and knights, *milites*, were sharply separated before the eleventh century, and perhaps it was not until the late twelfth or early thirteenth centuries that knights came to be considered noble.[25] Eventually, however, "knighthood, so it seemed, absorbed the nobility," as David Bates writes in his study of Normandy before the conquest of England.[26] Aristocrats' military functions gradually took precedence over their older public responsibilities, and as they adopted the warrior ethos of their *milites*, the distinction between the two groups became blurred. The Barnwell chronicler's account of the rebellion against King John illustrates this triumph of the military ethos among England's nobility. He wrote that younger men, sons and nephews of magnates, joined the baronial cause "as though they wanted to make their name through warlike deeds."[27]

Another word denoting rank that underwent changes in meaning is "vavasor," or Latin *vavassor*, derived from *vassus vassorum*. P. R. Coss has recently traced the evolution of the term in England.[28] He found that in twelfth-century France it meant roughly *arrière-vassal*, or tenant of a count or duke. In Normandy, however, the term took on a narrower meaning, and it referred to one whose landholding placed him below a *miles*, one who owed lesser military responsibilities but not

---

[24] For example, Orderic Vitalis (n. 1 above), *pagenses milites*, 6:26–27; *gregarii equites*, 3:108–9. Florence of Worcester, *Chronicon ex chronicis*, ed. Benjamin Thorpe, English Historical Society (London, 1848–49), 1:49, uses *milites gregarii*. Wace, *Le roman du rou*, ed. A. S. Holder, Société des anciens textes français (Paris, 1970–73), 2:123, lines 6,417–22, speaks of *barons, chevaliers, vavasors*, and *soldeiers*.

[25] Joseph R. Strayer, "The Two Levels of Feudalism" in *Life and Thought in the Early Middle Ages*, ed. Robert S. Hoyt (Minneapolis, 1967), pp. 51–65; also Georges Duby, "Une enquête à poursuivre: La noblèsse dans la France médiévale," *Revue Historique* 226 (1961): 1–22. For a survey of the literature, see Joachim Bumke, "On the State of Research into Knighthood," chap. 7 in *The Concept of Knighthood in the Middle Ages* (New York, 1970), translation of *Studien zum Ritterbegriff im 12. und 13. Jahrhundert*. For more recent French research, see Jane Martindale, "The French Aristocracy in the Early Middle Ages: A Reappraisal," *Past and Present*, no. 75 (1977), pp. 5–45; and Constance B. Bouchard, "The Origins of the French Nobility: A Reassessment," *American Historical Review* 86 (1981): 501–32. For German research, see John B. Freed, "Reflections on the Medieval German Nobility," *American Historical Review* 91 (1988): 535–75.

[26] David Bates, *Normandy before 1066* (London, 1982), p. 52.

[27] Walter of Coventry, *Memoriale*, ed. William Stubbs, Rolls Series (London, 1872–73), 2:220.

[28] P. R. Coss, "Literature and Social Terminology: The Vavasour in England," in *Social Relations and Ideas: Essays in Honour of R. H. Hilton*, ed. T. H. Ashton, P. R. Coss, Christopher Dyer, and Joan Thirsk (Cambridge, 1983), pp. 109–50.

servile labor. Early usage in post-Conquest England corresponds to Norman usage, but after the beginning of the twelfth century, its meaning was looser, implying all military tenants below the rank of baron.[29] By the end of the century, its meaning was approaching the French sense of a knight who held land in return for mounted military service and presided over a court with minor jurisdiction. The Latin *vavassor* became less common as the twelfth century progressed, but its Anglo-Norman equivalent grew more common in vernacular literature late in the century and in the early thirteenth century. The Anglo-Norman vernacular word seems to preserve the French sense of *arrière-vassal*.

A number of explanations have been offered for the rising status of knights. One is the increasing cost of horses, armor, and weapons in the twelfth and thirteenth centuries, which made it difficult for many small landholders to perform military service as mounted warriors, raising the status of those who could afford knightly accoutrements.[30] Economic change in the late twelfth century and early thirteenth century led to a crisis for the knightly class with rapid rises in the costs of maintaining a noble standard of living. Contributing to the crisis was the division of feudal landholdings into ever smaller plots with a resulting dissipation of resources and a relative loss of wealth. Exacerbating this situation was the growing wealth of urban merchants, whose rising standard of living menaced the knights' social standing. Fears of slipping down the social scale, fueled by economic crisis, led knights to seek to assert their solidarity with the nobility, as members of a single caste based upon military function.

The role of the troubadours, propagandists for knights of low birth, is significant in proclaiming this solidarity of all members of the knightly class. In an effort to neutralize the inherent conflict between the two groups of aristocrats and their retainers, they maintained that all mounted warriors, no matter what their family background, landed wealth, or lack of land, belonged to a single class of *bellatores,* different in function from clerics and peasants. The romances taught that all fighting men who lived by the chivalric code belonged to a single superior caste, regardless of their possession of land. Scholars of medieval literature debate whether or not the aristocrats or their military retainers led in shaping chivalric ideals and practices. For example, some students of troubadour poetry would argue that the cult of courtly love was devised by the lesser nobility—knights—as a way to

---

[29] F. M. Stenton, *The First Century of English Feudalism, 1066–1166* (Oxford, 1932), p. 16.

[30] Sally Harvey, "The Knight and the Knight's Fee in England," *Past and Present,* no. 49 (November 1970), pp. 31–34, 42.

assert their superiority to the aristocrats. Erich Koehler observed that in the second half of the twelfth century the question of whether the rich and powerful are capable of courtly love was a subject for vigorous arguments among poets.[31]

Also the church, seeking to channel warfare into causes that furthered its goals, encouraged the merger of nobles and knights. It encouraged the concept that all warriors formed an order, a *militia Dei* in the service of Christ, and it sought to redefine the knightly virtues. Preachers warned that a warrior who exploited the church and preyed upon the poor was no true knight, but a robber. The Peace of God movement and especially the crusades helped to propagate the new clerical definition of knighthood.[32]

Two popularizers of this clerical notion of knighthood as an order were Henry II's subjects. John of Salisbury's *Policraticus* sets forth clearly the concept of an "order" of knighthood, a brotherhood of warriors bound to defend the church, the clergy, and the poor.[33] Stephen of Fougères, Henry II's chaplain and later bishop of Rennes, in his *Le Livre des manières*, also depicted knighthood as an order, *[H]aute ordre fut chevalerie*. His work emphasizes more strongly than the *Policraticus* the necessity of good birth for a knight: *Franc hom de franche mère nez, s'a chevalier est ordenez*.[34] Stephen's aim was "to shore up the ramparts that kept upstarts and newly-rich vulgarians

---

[31] Erich Koehler, "Observations historiques et sociologiques sur la poèsie des troubadours," *Cahiers de civilisation médiévale* 7 (1964): 31–32. Compare Ariane Loeb, "La définition et l'affirmation du groupe noble comme enjeu de la poèsie courtoise? Quelques analyses des textes du troubadour Peire Vidal," *Cahiers de civilisation médiévale* 30 (1987): 303–14. She attacks Koehler's article as "largement tributaire d'une vue simplificatrice des théories marxistes." She argues that troubadour poetry was part of a process by which great nobles sought to preserve their privileged position and to impose their values on their knights, the reverse of a process by which the aristocracy accepted knightly values. Jean Flori, "Chevalerie, noblesse et luttes de classes au Moyen Age: À propos d'un ouvrage récent," *Le Moyen Age* 94 (1988): 263–66, maintains that the *nobiles* did not copy the *milites* in formulating the chivalric code, but rather the reverse.

[32] Georges Duby, "Les origines de la chivalerie," in *Ordinamenti militari in occidente nell'alto medioevo, settimane di studio del centro italiano di studi sull'alto medioevo* 15, 2 vols. (Spoleto, 1968), 2:759–60; translated as "The Origins of Knighthood" in *Chivalrous Society* (n. 11 above), pp. 165–67. Also, Sidney Painter, "Religious Chivalry," chap. 3 in *French Chivalry, Chivalric Ideas and Practices in Medieval France* (Baltimore, 1940), pp. 65–94; and Colin Morris, "*Equestris ordo*: Chivalry as a Vocation in the Twelfth Century," in *Religious Movitation: Biographical and Sociological Problems for the Church Historian*, ed. Derek Baker, Studies in Church History (Oxford, 1978), 15:87–96.

[33] *Policraticus*, 2 vols., ed. C. C. J. Webb (Oxford, 1909), 2:8–58; chap. 6; Painter, pp. 65–94.

[34] *Le livre des manières*, ed. J. Kremer (Marburg, 1887), p. 129, lines 585–90.

apart from good society."[35] Hence both churchmen and poets spread the concept of a single knightly order embracing the entire warrior class.

Continental scholars have built the case for this view of change in knights' social standing, basing their conclusions chiefly on French evidence. In Germany, the situation is complicated because many knights were *ministeriales*, who had come from the servile peasantry, and before the thirteenth century, their legal status conflicted with their military obligations and their economic position.[36] Across the Channel in England not so much material has yet been evaluated. Because of the Norman Conquest, almost all invading warriors in England after 1066 were in a sense equals; all owed service to some lord, to the king if to no other. Opportunities for new men to rise to wealth, landholdings, and social position were greater than elsewhere because of the colonial situation.[37] Yet the greatest landholders and occupants of castles, like their Continental counterparts, soon came to claim a proud ancestry, though often of doubtful authenticity, and stood aloof from those they considered inferiors. By the mid-twelfth century, Anglo-Norman families were asserting special prestige because of their ancestors' participation in the 1066 expedition.[38]

Relevant for any application of these views on *nobilis/miles* relations to England is the situation in Normandy before 1066. David Bates's recent book reaches similar conclusions about societal changes there. He finds an ambiguous and vague terminology in Norman charters of the mid-eleventh century. Examples of Carolingian terms to denote the noble elite—*principes, nobiles*—continued to be used, yet the terms were applied in such nonspecific ways that they point to an absence of any strict definition for nobility. At the same time great men did not disdain to be called knights. Eleventh-century documents occasionally use the term *miles* to denote a magnate, although the usual meaning of the word was simply "soldier," little different from the meaning of *vavassor*, as noted above. Nonetheless, aristocratic marriage patterns, in which they limited themselves to a small number of acceptable patterns, indicate that the nobles recognized themselves as a distinct group above and apart from the knights, a lower social group. Bates concludes that nobility and knighthood had not yet fused by

---

[35] Duby, *Three Orders*, p. 285; Painter, pp. 7–73.
[36] Freed (n. 25 above).
[37] J. C. Holt, "Feudal Society and the Family in Early Medieval England: Part 1, The Revolution of 1066," *Transactions of the Royal Historical Society*, 5th ser., 32 (1982): 206.
[38] Holt, pp. 206–7; Mason (n. 18 above), pp. 122–23, 130.

1066; slowly, however, the military ethos of the knights would percolate upward among the aristocracy.[39]

Sally Harvey has turned her attention to post-Conquest England, asking whether knights there were nobles, and her answer is similar to the views of her colleagues on the Continent.[40] She proposes that there were three categories of feudal tenants in the years following the Norman Conquest. First, she finds men of baronial rank who held fees from other magnates; especially common was the lay noble who held land of bishops or abbots in return for knight service. A second category is *milites mediae nobilitatis,* "active knights of good birth holding a manor or two, but . . . often younger sons or brothers of important men, and as a type are in a minority."[41] Third are the *milites gregarii* or *stipendarii,* professional knights or warriors hired by those in the first two categories; they might be household knights or enfeoffed by their lords, but only for small tracts of land. Harvey finds that these third-category knights had low social status and landholdings not much larger than those of well-off peasants. According to her study of the Domesday Book, such knights held about one-and-a-half hides, or a yearly income between 30s. and £2. This would support the costs of his arms and one or two horses but would leave no surplus for social climbing.[42] Marjorie Chibnall recognizes that the households of both the Anglo-Norman monarchs and the great lords included knights serving for cash payment. She finds evidence that these knights were sometimes granted small landholdings to supplement their stipends, as a bonus for good service or for maintenance of a wife and household of their own.[43]

Chibnall's study of the troops in Henry I's household also illustrates the problem of defining knightly status in the Anglo-Norman period. She finds that many of Henry's household knights were "young

---

[39] Bates (n. 26 above), pp. 104–11, 132.

[40] Harvey (n. 30 above).

[41] The phrase is from Guillaume de Poitiers, *Histoire de Guillaume le Conquérant,* ed. Raymonde Foreville (Paris, 1952), p. 232. Guillaume in the same passage mentions *gregarii.*

[42] Harvey, pp. 20–21. Frank Barlow, *William Rufus* (Berkeley, Calif., 1984), p. 163, notes that in most eleventh-century literary texts, *milites* seem to be "little more than common soldiers." R. Allan Brown vigorously disputes Harvey's view: "But it is certain that by the mid-eleventh century Norman knights at least . . . were a military elite, and therefore a social elite." See Brown, "The Status of the Norman Knight," in *War and Government in the Middle Ages,* ed. John Gillingham and J. C. Holt (Cambridge, 1984), p. 30.

[43] Marjorie Chibnall, *Anglo-Norman England, 1066–1166* (Oxford, 1986), pp. 15–16, 32.

men of good, even noble families." Some were landless younger sons, owning only their horses, armor, and weapons, serving for wages, but hoping to win land as reward for their military skills. They were little different in status from others with more modest origins, with barely enough resources to equip themselves as knights.[44] Serving alongside the *milites* were *servientes*, sometimes called *stipendarii*, archers and lightly armed mounted men and the distinction between the two was not always clear since they served together as castle garrisons. In Normandy, the term *stipendarii* may have applied also to the king or duke's household knights.[45]

In Harvey's view, Henry II's early years marked an important stage in the rise in these knights' status.[46] By the end of the twelfth century, the term *miles* or knight had become more a definition of social status than a definition of function, and the number of men to whom the title could be applied fell. Payment of scutage replaced their obligation to appear personally in the king's military force, and, more and more, administrative and judicial tasks in the counties occupied their time. The *Dialogus de Scaccario* speaks of the *dignitas militie*, the honor of knighthood, noting that crown debtors of knightly rank ought not to be confined in prison cells but be kept in free custody within the prison house.[47] The treatise also notes that those who had obtained the *militie cingulum* should have the privilege of keeping their horse when their chattels were sold for debt, "lest a man who is entitled by his rank to ride, should be compelled to go on foot." If he actually practiced the profession of warrior, he should be allowed to keep his armor and other horses as well.[48] This distinction between knighthood as social rank and knighthood as military profession is evident by the end of the thirteenth century. Noël Denholm-Young concluded that by Edward I's time there were no more than 750 actual fighting knights in England. He finds, however, the total number of the knightly class, "that is, including men who should have been knights and were not," to be 9,000.[49] Other studies have found that there must have been no more than 2,000 men of knightly rank at any one time

[44] Marjorie Chibnall, "Mercenaries and the *Familia regis* under Henry I," *History* 62 (1977): 17–18, 22.
[45] Ibid., pp. 18–20.
[46] Harvey, p. 31; Chibnall, *Anglo-Norman England*, p. 220.
[47] *Dialogus de Scaccario*, ed. Charles Johnson, Medieval Texts (Oxford, 1950), p. 117.
[48] Ibid., p. 111.
[49] Noël Denholm-Young, "Feudal Society in the Thirteenth Century: The Knights," *Collected Papers on Medieval Subjects*, new ed. (Cardiff, 1969), pp. 83–88.

during the thirteenth century actively involved in local administration.[50]

Due to the lawyers, a tenurial definition for a knight came to prevail: a holder of a knight's fee, which had its heritability guaranteed by the king's court, and possessor of a court with jurisdiction over peasants, that is, a definition much like the French *arrière-vassal*. The late twelfth-century law book *Glanvill* identifies *miles* with a holder of a knight's fee, *per feodum militare tenens*.[51] These landholders, ancestors of the gentry, had an important role to play in implementing Henry II's legal reforms; they attended the shire courts and provided the *legales milites* who formed the juries in the royal courts. While merely *liberi homines* were suitable for the possessory assizes, *legales milites* were required as jurors in writs for the grand assize and as viewers of essoiners, litigants seeking excuses on account of illness. The term "lawful knights" appears to have indicated men of substance, excluding landless knights.[52] The plea rolls record instances in which men sent to view essoiners were rejected because they were not of knightly rank. The abbot of Chertsey in a 1204 action complained that *quatour liberi homines, qui non fuerunt milites*, had viewed his essoining opponent.[53] In 1220, a Herefordshire knight was barred from serving as one of the four knights sent to view an essoiner because he was "from a household and did not have any land" [*de familia est et non habet terram*].[54] King John occasionally ordered possessory assizes taken by juries of knights instead of ordinary freemen.[55] In cases in which the king's rights were at issue, the justices sometimes instructed the sheriff to select knights as jurors.[56]

---

[50] A recent estimate, found in J. Quick, "The Number and Distribution of Knights in Thirteenth Century England: The Evidence of the Grand Assize Lists," in *Thirteenth Century England, Proceedings of the Newcastle upon Tyne Conference, 1985*, ed. P. R. Coss and S. D. Lloyd (Woodbridge, 1986), p. 119. An older one is found in R. F. Treharne, "The Knights in the Period of Reform and Rebellion, 1258–67: A Critical Phase in the Rise of a New Class," *Bulletin of the Institute of Historical Research* 21 (1946–48): 9.

[51] *Glanvill*, ed. G. D. G. Hall, Medieval Texts (Oxford, 1965), bk. 7, chap. 3, p. 75; bk. 7, chap. 9, p. 82.

[52] Ibid., bk. 2, chaps. 10–11, p. 30; bk. 9, chap. 7, p. 111, grand assize; bk. 1, chap. 19, p. 11, viewers of essoiners; *Bracton*, ed. G. E. Woodbine, trans. S. E. Thorne (New Haven, Conn., 1968–70), 4:57, fol. 331b, grand assize: "quatuor legales milites . . . ad eligendum . . . duodecim de legalioribus militibus"; viewers of essoiners, 4:113, fol. 353. Quick, pp. 115–16.

[53] *Curia Regis Rolls*, Public Record Office (PRO) (London, 1923–), 3:211, Michaelmas 1204. See also 3:201–2, and 1:203: "duo pauperes, non milites venerunt."

[54] *Curia Regis Rolls*, 9:157, Trinity 1220.

[55] For example, *Curia Regis Rolls*, 3:129, 224.

[56] For example, *Curia Regis Rolls*, 1:287, *milites et probos homines*; 6:28, jury discharged and knights ordered summoned to replace them; 9:232, Henry III in 1220.

In the minds of royal judges, then, the term *miles* meant more than a mounted warrior; it meant a landholder who was superior in rank to a *liber homo*. By Henry III's time, landed status had definitely become more significant than military service for defining the *milites*. Henry's acts for "distraint of knighthood" demanded that all freeholders with land worth twenty pounds a year be dubbed knights. The king's motive was not to increase the size of his army but was in part to meet the increasing need for men to serve on grand assizes and to carry out other administrative functions in the counties and partly to gain money by increasing the opportunity for feudal incidents.[57] Such men were bearing the burden of local government, and they were the essential element in the work of the shire courts and the judicial eyres. Some moved from local office or some magnate's service into the central administration.[58] Clearly, the English knight's function was shifting from narrowly military to broader public service.

The term *vavassor* still causes confusion, mainly because of its use in the great thirteenth-century law book, *Bracton*. The author ranked vavasors below barons and above knights. Following his description of barons, he describes vavasors as "men of great dignity"; then he moves on to knights, defining them as "persons chosen for the exercising of military duties."[59] This is confusing because the clause in the 1258 Provisions of Oxford treats the term vavasor as if it meant knights of the country.[60] P. R. Coss proposes a solution to the problem. He suggests that, by the end of the thirteenth century, vavasors could be distinguished from knights by their larger and richer landed estates, for the vavasors were substantial landholders though below baronial rank. Certainly the whole tenor of the Provisions of Oxford article on vavasors as sheriffs is that they should be substantial landholders, rich enough to resist temptation to take bribes. Coss attributes this usage of the word to a growing awareness of distinctions within the group of knights of the counties.[61]

Despite the shared outlook of the entire knightly class, a great distance lay between the magnates holding many knights' fees, their household knights, and knightly tenants, who held a few manors or

---

[57] F. M. Powicke, *The Thirteenth Century*, Oxford History of England, 15 vols. (Oxford, 1953), 4:547; A. L. Poole, *The Obligations of Society in the Twelfth and Thirteenth Centuries* (Oxford, 1946), p. 4.
[58] Treharne, pp. 3–4.
[59] *Bracton*, fol. 5b, 2:32–33.
[60] *Documents of the Baronial Movement of reform and Rebellion, 1258–1267*, ed. R. F. Treharne and I. J. Sanders (Oxford, 1973), pp. 108–9; *English Historical Documents*, vol. 3, *1189–1327*, ed. Harry Rothwell (London, 1975), p. 365.
[61] Coss (n. 28 above).

possibly only one. It is difficult to say when medieval English barons began to consider themselves a hereditary peerage, a distinct class closed off from the rest of the knights, perhaps not before the fourteenth century. Even in Henry I's time, however, magnate families sought to marry within their own ranks, using marriage with noble daughters as a means of maintaining noninheriting younger sons' superior social status.[62] This was less easy for them than for Continental nobles, however, since so many aristocratic English heiresses fell into the king's custody, and he might marry them off to *curiales*. Nobles were experiencing fears by the early thirteenth century that their daughters or widows might be "disparaged," that is, married off to knights who were not their social equals; article 6 of *Magna Carta* aimed to protect them from this possibility.[63] This notion of disparagement shows that great aristocrats did not necessarily feel a sense of solidarity with all knights.

Yet the medieval nobility was always a more fluid group than it cared to admit. Old families died out, and monarchs bestowed their lands and titles on new men, often trusted administrators; these royal servants' sons might prosper and attain baronial rank, or they might fail to make any mark at court and fade from view. Some of the great families of the thirteenth century owed their standing to administrative services that their ancestors had performed for Henry I or Henry II. As soon as a corps of administrators appeared early in the twelfth century, however, earls and barons began to mistrust the *curiales*, who seemed to threaten the bonds of feudal society. Men at the royal court were relying more on personal influence—patronage—than on traditional ties of vassalage cemented by land grants as a path to power and wealth.[64]

Clerical writers' expressions of contempt for *curiales'* lowly origins often disguised other reasons for their disdain for courtiers. The new royal administrators' success in raising royal revenues, often at the church's expense, did not endear them to monastic chroniclers. To the spiritually minded, the careerists at the royal court symbolized a dangerous secular spirit that was spreading in the twelfth and thirteenth centuries.[65] Orderic Vitalis condemned churchmen, "who waited on the royal court out of covetousness for high office, and, to

---

[62] Newman (n. 16 above), p. 127.
[63] William Stubbs, ed., *Select Charters and Other Illustrations of English Constitutional History*, 9th ed. rev. (Oxford, 1913), p. 294.
[64] Mason (n. 18 above), p. 130.
[65] Egbert Türk, *Nugae curialium: Le régne d'Henri II Plantagaenet (1145–1189) et l'éthique politique* (Geneva, 1977), p. 184.

the great discredit of their cloth, shamelessly pandered to the king."[66] Later Ralph Niger complained that Henry II chose his abbots and bishops from "chamber servants and triflers of the hall."[67] Some conservative clerics feared that the royal servants' courtly manners would weaken the knights' manliness and military prowess.[68]

The most spectacular cases of *curiales* coming from unknown families and rising through royal favor to office, power, and riches were clerics. A little more than half the bishops appointed between the reigns of William I and John came from curial backgrounds.[69] The example of their dramatic rise from obscurity must have fed the popular belief that courtiers were sons of serfs. An early example is Ranulf Flambard, "born of poor and obscure parents," son of a village priest from the diocese of Bayeux, who rose to be the right-hand man of King William Rufus in governing England.[70] Orderic Vitalis's disparaging comments on the courtiers of William Rufus, especially Ranulf Flambard, mask his personal distaste for the immoral atmosphere at the royal court.[71] Orderic described Ranulf's early life as "educated from boyhood with base parasites among the hangers-on of the court" and his later life as a royal official as "too addicted to feasts and carousals and lusts; cruel and ambitious, prodigal to his own adherents, but rapacious in seizing the goods of other men."[72] Another cleric of obscure origin who rose dramatically is Roger of Salisbury, head of Henry I's administration. The chonicler William of Newburgh described him as "a poor priest in the suburbs of Caen," and his own grandnephew Richard fitz Neal described him as poor and unknown in his youth, *ignotus non tamen ignobilis*.[73]

Jealousy may have sharpened the pens of some writers. Several critics of Henry II's *curiales* were themselves courtiers disappointed in their careers. They were secular clerics such as Gerald of Wales or Peter of Blois, who had their hopes of elevation to a bishopric dashed and who wished to place blame for their failure on the ambition, av-

---

[66] Orderic Vitalis (n. 1 above), 2:269.
[67] *Chronicles of Ralph Niger* (n. 5 above), pp. 168–69.
[68] Jaeger (n. 9 above), p. 195.
[69] David Walker, "Crown and Episcopacy under the Normans and Angevins," *Anglo-Norman Studies* 5 (1982): 220, 54 percent down to 1216.
[70] Orderic Vitalis, 4:170–73.
[71] Antonia Gransden, *Historical Writing in Medieval England, 550–1307* (Ithaca, N.Y., 1974), pp. 156–57.
[72] Orderic Vitalis, 4:170–73.
[73] William of Newburgh, *Historia rerum anglicarum*, ed. H. C. Hamilton, English Historical Society, 2 vols. (London, 1856), 1:35–36; *Dialogus de Scaccario* (n. 47 above), p. 42.

arice, and syncophancy of their rivals.[74] Hugh de Nonant, bishop of Coventry, disliked intensely William Longchamp, bishop of Ely, whom Richard I left in charge as chancellor and justiciar on his departure on crusade. Hugh wrote a letter, copied in full in Roger of Howden's chronicle, which denounces Longchamp as the grandson of a peasant [*rusticus*], "who being of servile condition in the district of Beauvais, had for his occupation to guide the plow and whip up the oxen; and who at length to gain his liberty fled to the Norman territory."[75] Peter of Blois replied to Hugh de Nonant, complaining of his treatment of Longchamp and accusing him of envy. Peter made no comment on Longchamp's origin, but he did say of Hugh, "England . . . receiving you poor enough, amplified you with mighty honors."[76]

Howden himself wrote of Longchamp, quoting the Roman poet Claudian, "Nothing is more unendurable than a man of low status when he is exalted on high. On every side he strikes, while on every side he fears; against all does he rage, that they may have an idea of his power; nor is there any beast more foul than the rage of a slave let loose against the backs of the free."[77] Gerald of Wales, who also despised Longchamp, borrowed Hugh de Nonant's tale for his denunciation of the chancellor, attributing it to a *clericus sine nomine*.[78] While Longchamp was clearly a *novus homo*, "of relatively humble origin," he was hardly of peasant background.[79] Although it seems likely that many royal clerks whom the Norman and Angevin kings elevated to the episcopate came from lower levels of the knightly class or from prosperous bourgeois families, these few well-known cases may have created an impression that royal offices and favor frequently fell to the lowborn.

---

[74] Türk, p. 188; Jaeger, p. 66.

[75] Louis Boivin-Champeaux, *Notice sur Guillaume de Longchamp, évêque d'Ely, vice-roi d'Angleterre* (Evreux, 1885), pp. 6–9; Roger of Howden, *Chronia*, ed. William Stubbs, Rolls Series (London, 1868–71), 3:142; translation from *English Historical Documents*, vol. 2, *1042–1189*, ed. David C. Douglas and George W. Greenaway (London, 1968), p. 70; William Stubbs, *Historical Introductions to the Rolls Series* (London, 1902), pp. 214–15.

[76] Roger of Howden, 3:150, with translation from *English Historical Documents*, vol. 3 (n. 60 above), pp. 75–77; also *Patrilogiae cursus completus: Patres . . . latinae*, ed. Jacques Paul Migne (Paris, 1844–55), vol. 207, col. 281.

[77] Roger of Howden, 3:72. This passage from Claudian is also quoted by Walter Map, in *De nugis curialium* (n. 6 above), bk. 1, chap. 10, pp. 14–15. For a translation, see *English Historical Documents*, 2:65.

[78] Gerald of Wales, *De vita Galfridi*, ed. J. F. Dimock, in *Opera*, Rolls Series (London, 1873), 4:418.

[79] Stubbs, p. 214; A. L. Poole, *From Domesday Book to Magna Carta*, 2nd ed. (Oxford, 1955), p. 352.

Gerald of Wales was perfectly capable of inventing a noble ancestry for one of Henry II's *curiales* who had befriended him and whom he favored. Walter of Coutances, archbishop of Rouen, remained in Richard I's service, and he succeeded Longchamp in the justiciarship. Gerald gave the archbishop a mythical ancestry more noble than that of mere Normans, tracing his forebears to ancient Trojan heroes who had escaped to Cornwall. In fact, Walter's background was no different from that of most new men; he was descended from a family of minor Cornish knights of probable Norman origin.[80]

Not only clerics, however, could shock their contemporaries by rising from obscurity to highest posts in secular government. Richard de Lucy, Henry II's justiciar until 1179, belonged to the knightly class, but his landed inheritance left him far below baronial rank, "a person of minor consequence."[81] Through his long service to King Stephen and to Henry II, he built up landholdings of baronial scope. Two other justiciars started at the fringes of knightly society but succeeded in becoming earls through service to the king. Geoffrey fitz Peter, son of a royal forester, became justiciar at the end of Richard I's reign and received the title "earl of Essex" from King John. The anonymous minstrel of Béthune described him as *uns sages chevaliers; mais n'estoit nie de grant lineage.*[82] Hubert de Burgh, justiciar during Henry III's early years, used his position to become one of the wealthiest men in the kingdom and earl of Kent. His origins are so obscure that his father's name is nowhere recorded, but his most recent biographer concludes that he belonged to "an ambitious minor gentry family."[83]

Let me suggest that Anglo-Norman and Angevin chroniclers, preachers, and poets relegated the king's *familiares* to a low level because they did not fit their definition of true knights. In the traditionalists' view, only those courtiers who demonstrated chivalric virtues of prowess, loyalty, courtesy, and generosity deserved knightly rank. Instead, the *familiares regis* or *curiales* too often presented

---

[80] Gerald of Wales, *De vita Galfridi*, in *Opera*, 4:408, *Vita Sancti Remigii*, in *Opera*, 7:38. On Walter's career, see Peter A. Poggioli, "From Politician to Prelate: The Career of Walter of Coutances, Archbishop of Rouen, 1184–1207" (Ph.D. diss., Johns Hopkins University, 1984).

[81] Francis West, *The Justiciarship in England, 1066–1232* (Cambridge, 1966), pp. 37–38; W. L. Warren, *Henry II* (Berkeley, Calif., 1973), describes Richard de Lucy's background as "the fairly well-to-do knightly class" (p. 261).

[82] *Histoire des ducs Normandie et rois d'Angleterre*, ed. Francisque Michel, Société de l'histoire de France (Paris, 1840), p. 115.

[83] Michael Weiss, "The Castellan: The Early Career of Hubert de Burgh," *Viator* 5 (1974): 235, n. 1.

qualities that might be more appropriate for bureaucrats or for the bourgeoisie. Writers decried not only their low birth but also their ambition, greed, and sycophancy. Naturally, a central concern for the *curiales* was winning and keeping the king's and other great men's favor, behavior that exposed them to such charges.

Can it be that the critics' labels of commoners, rustics, or villeins were simply their shorthand for someone who did not fit their preconceptions of truly knightly conduct? Men who failed to exemplify the values traditionally associated with the mounted warrior and who instead showed qualities associated with clerics or with merchants could not possibly spring from knightly stock. Vernacular poets often selected the term *vilein* to describe unattractive, boorish types, lacking in chivalric courtesy, sometimes applying it to the bourgeoisie whom they found contemptible on account of their greed.[84] Furthermore, the critics were seeking to tighten the standards for admission to the select circle that enjoyed royal patronage, to shut out as many as possible. High social status was essential to the ideal knight as depicted in early feudal epics and later courtly romances.[85] As Georges Duby writes, "To evoke the peasantry . . . was first of all to issue a reminder that the gateway to the court was shut."[86]

These twelfth-century complaints that royal servants were of villein birth have a parallel with criticisms of civil servants in *ancien-régime* France. Old-school nobles at Versailles resented the influence and power of these new men and also the more modern rational and scientific outlook that they brought to law and government. To blacken the royal servants' reputations, they frequently accused them falsely of bourgeois origins, when in fact a high proportion came from noble families.[87]

Curiales, earning reward through dull work of administration or, as some suspected, through flattery and influence peddling, seemed a

---

[84] Glyn S. Burgess, "Social Status in the *Lais* of Marie de France," in *The Spirit of the Court, Selected Proceedings of the Fourth Congress of the International Courtly Literature Society*, ed. Glyn S. Burgess and Robert A. Taylor (Woodbridge, 1983), p. 69; C. Foulon, "Les tendances aristocratiques dans le roman de Guillaume d'Angleterre," *Romania* 71 (1950): 231.

[85] Sally North, "The Ideal Knight as Presented in Some French Narrative Poems, *c.* 1090–1240: An Outline Sketch," in *The Ideals and Practice of Medieval Knighthood: Papers from the First and Second Strawberry Hill Conferences*, ed. Christopher Harper-Bill and Ruth Harvey (Woodbridge, 1986), pp. 125–26; Burgess, pp. 71–72.

[86] Duby, *Three Orders* (n. 10 above), pp. 278–79.

[87] For example, the personnel of the *Parlements*, about 90 percent of whom had already belonged to the nobility before they bought their offices; see R. C. van Caenegem, *Judges, Legislators and Professors: Chapters in European Legal History* (Cambridge, 1988), p. 184, n. 15.

threat to the military caste's special status. In a feudal society, the time-honored way to satisfy ambition and greed, praised by poets, was warfare, taking plunder and prisoners to ransom. By the time of Henry I, war was less likely to be the route to wealth, but literature kept alive this outmoded code of conduct. The thirteenth-century biography of William Marshal, for example, pictures him devoting his time to war and tournaments. It neglects his activity as royal justice, sheriff, and baron of the Exchequer.[88] As Judith Green has pointed out, the new men condemned by Orderic Vitalis "had not fought their way to the top with the strength of their right arms, but by collecting the king's revenues and administering his justice. . . . It was of course still possible to take up the profession of arms and win wealth in that way, but now there were additional avenues of advancement created by the growth and specialization of government."[89]

The question of new men versus magnates can be approached in another way then, by looking at the role of education and literacy in late twelfth-century government. The magnates were more likely to offer the monarch the older feudal virtues of loyalty to their leige lord and miliary prowess than they were proficiency with letters and numbers. More and more, the king required intimates who were numerate and literate, masters of administrative skills, such as Thomas Becket, who had been a "clerk and accountant" before entering Henry II's service.[90] Although John of Salisbury stressed the *curiales'* rise through flattery, in fact they were winning power because they could apply reason to problems of government. Even in the Anglo-Norman period, the warriors' skills were no longer enough for royal servants. Few of the king's familiars in the early twelfth century had much formal education, but they had prudence or intelligence as well as courage and loyalty.[91]

Recent works by several scholars assert the significance of this connection between reason and learning and a new ministerial class. Michael Clanchy views the two decades on either side of 1200 as a decisive stage for government's growing reliance on written documents for carrying out its work. This steady increase in numbers of documents forced literacy in Latin to spread beyond the few royal clerks and monks who had monopolized reading and writing in the Anglo-Norman period. Royal officials who were not churchmen had to have a

---

[88] Georges Duby, *Guillaume le Maréchal* (Paris, 1984), trans. Richard Howard as *William Marshal: The Flower of Chivalry* (New York, 1986).

[89] Green (n. 15 above), p. 144.

[90] Michael T. Clanchy, "*Moderni* in Education and Government in England," *Speculum* 50 (1975): 681.

[91] Mason (n. 18 above), p. 129.

working knowledge of Latin because their offices required them to use written instruments. Perhaps by 1200, English knights of the counties had achieved "pragmatic literacy," an ability to read such simple Latin writings as a royal writ. In Clanchy's view, the proliferation and preservation of written records by government paved the way for literacy, not the reverse.[92]

Another scholar, Alexander Murray, takes a broader approach to the significance of the revival of schools, arguing that the twelfth-century Renaissance had practical applications. From the end of the tenth century, wider circulation of money in the West gave greater value to men learned in mathematics and logic, and the influence of educated men spread beyond the cloisters and schools to society at large. Princes needed men skilled in mathematics because they, like merchants, had to keep accounts; indeed, because princes' revenues were so much greater, they needed even better accounting techniques. Murray argues that, "more even than commerce, it was government . . . that mainly encouraged the arithmetical mentality."[93]

A third writer, C. Stephen Jaeger, also stresses the significance of education and literacy for straining relations between *curiales* and tradition-minded aristocrats. Instead of seeing bourgeois virtues among the *curiales*, however, he finds qualities like those of Italian Renaissance civic humanists characterizing them. According to Jaeger, the Ottonian court chapel produced educated and cultivated clerics to serve the emperor, best exemplified by his courtier-bishops. These imperial advisers defined themselves not only by their talents, which they placed at the emperor's service, but also by their contrast with the knightly class whom they saw as boorish, rough-cut warriors. At the Ottonian court chapel, an educational program for courtiers was created and taught in cathedral schools, based on "a Christian-humanist ethic of worldly service." This ethic of state service based on classical models passed to the secular clergy of France and England, who taught it to the lay aristocracy, chiefly through the vernacular romances. In the romances chivalry was redefined, with courtesy playing a larger role. Some of the most enthusiastic pupils were found at the court of the counts of Anjou in the twelfth century. According to Jaeger, conservative critics opposed this new ethic, seeing what the *curiales* saw as virtue as vice instead, as "wretched ambitious servility." The conser-

---

[92] Michael T. Clanchy, *From Memory to Written Record, England, 1066-1307* (2nd edn., Oxford, 1993).

[93] Alexander Murray, *Reason and Society in the Middle Ages* (Oxford, 1978), pp. 195-96.

vative clerics saw knightly heroism and manliness, as depicted in early epic poems, being undermined by this new civility.[94] While I tend to doubt that Henry II's courtiers felt much of Renaissance public-spiritedness, Jaeger does clearly depict the new class of professional royal servants as possessing an outlook in conflict with the traditional warrior ethos, and one that alarmed monastic churchmen and warrior aristocrats alike.

Increasingly, rulers valued rational qualities of mind in their servants. Clearly, a need for literate and numerate agents in royal government was arising in the twelfth century, perhaps earlier in England than elsewhere. As Clanchy writes, Henry II and his advisers saw the usefulness of "subtle men, trained to think ingeniously in the schools."[95] They could see at least dimly a connection between knowledge and power; application of reason to governmental processes implies greater control, a means of manipulating people. John W. Baldwin has shown that the Angevin kings made great use in government posts of *magistri*, many of whom had earned degrees in France.[96]

The revolution in government demanded a new kind of royal servant, one beginning to resemble the modern bureaucrat. Evidence for these new officals in England is the spread of practical manuals for instruction of civil servants. Two of the best examples come from the end of Henry II's reign: Richard fitz Neal's *Dialogus de Scaccario* and *Glanvill*. The Angevin monarchs relied less on men with military resources to staff their councils and offices and more on graduates of the schools or men with practical administrative experience, men with financial, legal, and record-keeping skills. It was not so much royal antagonism toward the barons or conscious effort to recruit lowborn men as it was a need for capable operators of complex machinery of government that caused kings to turn to men of obscure origin. This need explains the new men surrounding the monarch. My own recent chronicling of six Angevin royal servants' careers is evidence. All came from minor or middling knightly families, yet all showed administrative ability early on, and by entering the royal administration, they patiently accumulated lands, ending in possession of bishoprics and baronies. They exploited fully the opportunities for patronage offered

---

[94] Jaeger (n. 9 above), passim, esp. pp. 39, 43, 58, 96, 101, 152–53, 173–74, 195–97, 201–7, 222.
[95] Clanchy, "*Moderni* in Education and Government," p. 679.
[96] John W. Baldwin, "*Studium et Regnum:* The Penetration of University Personnel into French and English Administration at the Turn of the Twelfth and Thirteen Centuries," *Revue des études islamiques* 44 (1976): 199–211.

by their positions so close to the center of power. None won the king's attention through exploits on the battlefield.[97]

Young men from lower-ranking knightly families, spurred by the need to support themselves and by ambition to surpass their fathers' social standing, sought an education that would equip them with the needed skills. In an earlier generation the *juvenes,* boisterous younger sons of knights unlikely to inherit a landed estate, had expected to attract attention by their military exploits.[98] But opportunities to win wealth from plunder and ransoms were fading in the last years of the twelfth century. Troubadours sought to persuade the great barons that they had a duty to provide patronage for young knights without landed inheritance or marriage prospects, but that was not a satisfactory remedy for the poverty facing many of them. Landless younger sons had to find some means of supporting themselves and, if possible, improving their situation. Even those young knights who stood to inherit some land found their social status threatened by the inflation that began in the late twelfth century and continued throughout much of the thirteenth century.[99]

Luckily, this crisis facing the knightly class coincided with the governmental revolution that was occurring during the reigns of Henry II and his sons. A generation grew up in the last quarter of the twelfth century who "had learned that the new administrative system could be as interesting as a tournament, and was far more closely related to the problems presented in the managenent of their own estates."[100] By the late twelfth century, administrative offices in the shires, at Westminster on the justiciar's staff, or with the itinerant royal household as members of the *familia regis* were providing opportunities for growing numbers of royal clerks and knights. Government departments were defining their duties more clearly and were adopting the regular procedures that are a characteristic of bureaucratic government. Personnel at the Exchequer and the Bench was becoming more professional, with a growing measure of specialization.

Magnates might wish to share in great decisions of policy, but every day the king had to make decisions on administrative matters;

---

[97] Ralph V. Turner, *Men Raised from the Dust: Administrative Service and Upward Mobility in Angevin England* (Philadelphia, 1988).

[98] Georges Duby, "Dans la France du nord-ouest au XIIe siècle: Les jeunes dans la société aristocratique," *Annales,* vol. 19 (1964), translated in *Chivalrous Society* (n. 11 above) as "Youth in Aristocratic Society," pp. 112–22.

[99] P. R. Coss, "Sir Geoffrey de Langley and the Crisis of the Knightly Class in Thirteenth-Century England," *Past and Present,* no. 68 (August 1975), pp. 22–28.

[100] F. M. Powicke, *Cambridge Medieval History,* 8 vols. (Cambridge 1924–36), 6:219, actually referring to nobles, although his words seem more applicable to knights.

and he decided by discussions with his *familiares* or *curiales*, who were in daily attendance upon him. The barons were too busy supervising their own lands and tenants for constant consultation, but they were often suspicious of those surrounding the king, feeling them to be unworthy of his trust. Worse in their view was the competition for royal patronage that these new men presented. Charlotte Newman's recent work shows how Anglo-Norman nobles of the second generation felt that their status, not their service, entitled them to favors from the king.[101] They joined the chorus of complaints against the supposed upstarts. Suspicions arose among the magnates that lowborn or foreign-born, ambitious, and avaricious *familiares regis* were flattering the monarch with bad advice in exchange for favors.

Such suspicions rose to a peak in the years preceding the rebellion against King John, and a number of chroniclers complained about his promotion of aliens. The Barnwell chronicler wrote of Fawkes de Breauté, one of John's mercenary captains, "King John had raised him with others from being a poor attendant into a knight [*a satellite paupere in militem*], and then had made him the equal of an earl, because of his assiduous obsequiousness."[102] In fact, the chroniclers of John's reign exaggerated the role of aliens, who were never more than a small group, mainly among the king's military captains. Perhaps John's opponents knew the *Bible* of Guiot de Provins, an early thirteenth-century satirical poem, which complained that modern kings, unlike Alexander or Arthur, took counsel with mere soldiers, "cross-bowmen and miners, catapult-machinists and engineers," instead of seeking wise barons' advice.[103] Aliens were simply the easiest objects to attack among the beneficiaries of royal patronage.[104]

Henry III also came under attack for his favoritism toward foreigners, his Savoyard in-laws and his Poitevin half brothers. The major chronicler for Henry III's reign, Matthew Paris, harshly denounced the aliens advising the king, yet he neglected to complain of the low birth of native-born counselors. While he denounced their greed, repeating earlier denunciations of *aulici* and *curiales* who "seek their own profit by fair means and foul," he failed to accuse them of base birth. He accepted their knightly status; for example, his epitaph for Adam fitz William, a royal justice, describes him as a rich knight, "but desirous

---

[101] Newman (n. 16 above), pp. 18, 46, 98.

[102] Walter of Coventry (n. 27 above), 2:253; Gransden (n. 71 above), pp. 334, 344.

[103] John Orr, *Les oeuvres de Guiot de Provins, poète lyrique et satirique* (Manchester, 1915), p. 18, lines 168–76. Orr dates it 1204–9, perhaps 1206 (p. xx).

[104] J. C. Holt, "King John," in *Magna Carta and Medieval Government* (London, 1985), pp. 106–8.

of becoming richer."[105] Doubtless Matthew Paris's failure to condemn royal officials for their servile origins reflects the thirteenth-century character of knights, less warriors than a rural governing class, forerunners of late medieval justices of the peace and early modern gentry. Since they were reading lawbooks and keeping accounts, the line between them and the *curiales* was dimming. They were no longer winning power and prestige from military exploits but from their governmental responsibilities. Perhaps their reading of the romances had taught them something of the civility and courtesy of Jaeger's courtiers. Indeed, some were moving into central government posts from their local offices or estate stewardships.[106]

Resentment of royal servants who demonstrated traits foreign to the feudal nobility had led twelfth-century writers to doubt that they could have possibly sprung from knightly stock. Conservative writers saw the *curiales* demonstrating the concern with orderly procedures and attention to detail of the bureaucracy combined with the ambition and acquisitiveness of the bourgeosie, values alien to the traditions that they treasured.[107] Their protobourgeois outlook had little in common with the chivalric virtues of prowess, honor, and lavish generosity. The chivalrous class looked down on work and those who worked and on money and those who occupied themselves with making money.[108]

Clearly, then, it was largely new men who were staffing the newly created departments of government from Henry I's time, and some did rise to higher rank, winning bishoprics and baronies. Yet they can hardly be described accurately as rustic, servile, or ignoble in origin. All came from the knightly class, although perhaps from its lowest level, from younger sons of poor knights with only one or two knight's fees. Because of this, some genuine confusion about their social stand-

---

[105] *Chronica Majora*, ed. H. R. Luard, Rolls Series (London, 1872–84), 3:388. The king permits "now Poitevins, now Germans, now Provencals, now Romans" to get rich off England. Also *Chronica monasterii S. Albani, gesta Abbatum*, ed. H. T. Riley, Rolls Series (London, 1867–69), 1:306–7, on Adam fitz William. See also his obituary of the sheriff of Northumberland, "a hammer of the poor, and a persecutor of the religious orders, William Heron, a most avaricious man"(*Chronica Majora*, 5:663). Matthew Paris condemned Master Ralph of Norwich's election as archbishop of Dublin because he was "a man wholly secular, and . . . occupied with custody of the Irish treasury by the king's patronage"; he said nothing of his probable bourgeois background (*Chronica Majora*, 5:560).

[106] For example, Robert Carpenter. See Noël Denholm-Young, "Robert Carpenter and the Provisions of Westminster" (n. 49 above), pp. 96–110; C. A. F. Meekings, "More about Robert Carpenter of Hareslade," *Studies in 13th-Century Administration* (London, 1981). See also A. L. Poole, *Obligations of Society* (n. 57 above), pp. 53, 56.

[107] Joel Rosenthal, review of Turner, *The English Judiciary in the Age of Glanvill and Bracton*, in *Medieval Prosopography* 7 (1986): 100.

[108] Foulon (n. 84 above), p. 233.

ing was possible, for the status of the knight—low in the years following the Conquest—was rising throughout the twelfth and thirteenth centuries. Old nobility and fighting men of obscure origins tended to merge into a single military elite. By the mid-thirteenth century, English knights had undergone further change, shedding much of their military tradition and becoming a rural governing class.

The disparaging comments on Anglo-Norman and Angevin royal officials' base birth by conservative critics must be labeled more propaganda than accurate social analysis, an attempt to discredit the new administrators. Nonetheless, these writers' resentment of "new men" does reveal their vague awareness of actual societal change. A class of professional civil servants—protobureaucrats—was arising in the twelfth century that would compete with warriors and aristocrats for royal favors.

Perhaps this propaganda was fueled by a few famous examples of clerics from obscure origins, but at least four other explanations must have played a part. One was conservative clerics' strong resentment of *curiales*' success in advancing in the ecclesiasical hierarchy through service to the monarch in secular government. Another was aristocratic fear of being replaced as the king's natural counselors by professionals of obscure origin and of competing with these new men for patronage. Third, there was the contempt of lesser knights threatened economically by the late twelfth century—represented by the troubadours—for other knights who were surpassing them economically, the growing corps of professional royal servants who were gaining lands and riches, but who failed to fit their definition of worthy followers of the chivalric code. The ambition, greed, miserliness, and lack of martial spirit of Henry I's and Henry II's officials resembled too much qualities of the bourgeoisie. Fourth was the conservatives' fear that the courtier virtues of civility and courtesy, or—expressed in less flattering terms—the fawning and malleability they practiced in order to win a prince's patronage, were spreading among the warrior class, sapping their strength and softening them.

Note

On the vexed question of the status of knights in the Anglo-Norman period, see the recent paper of Donald F. Fleming, "Landholding by *Milites* in Domesday Book: A Revision," *Anglo-Norman Studies*, 13 (1991), pp. 83–98.

14

The Royal Courts Treat Disseizin by the King: John and Henry III, 1199–1240

MEDIEVAL ENGLISH THINKERS' VIEWS OF THE ROYAL POWER sometimes seem contradictory. One of their basic beliefs was that the king was under the law. In the twelfth century, John of Salisbury contrasted the true prince who rules in accordance with the law and the tyrant who is guided only by his despotic will.[1] In the thirteenth century, *Bracton* stressed the ruler's submission to the law when he wrote, "Moreover, the king ought not to be under man but under God and the law, because the law makes the king."[2] Along with these opinions, there was the view that the king was above the law, a view supported by doctrines derived from Roman law and by traditions of theocratic kingship. John of Salisbury could hail the prince as "the likeness on earth of the divine majesty."[3] Also in the twelfth century, the *Dialogus de Scaccario*, attributed to Richard fitz Neal, repeated the old theocratic doctrine that the king was accountable to God alone.[4] And the legal treatise attributed to Glanville cited the Roman Law maxim *quod principi placet legis habet vigorem*.[5]

A king below the law and above it at the same time was not simply a difficulty for political thinkers; it was also a practical problem for many of the king's subjects. The king was "the author of justice," who was chosen "that he might do justice to everyone."[6] Yet he was also a feudal suzerain and a landlord of great personal power. Conflicts could easily arise between the king's interests as a

---

[1] *Policraticus*, ed. C. C. J. Webb (Oxford 1909), v. 2, lib. iv, cap. 1.
[2] *De Legibus et Consuetudinibus Angliae*, ed. G. E. Woodbine (New Haven 1915-42), v. 1, 33, f. 5b.
[3] *Policraticus*, v. 2, 236, lib. iv, cap. 1; v. 2, 74-80, lib. vi, cap. 25-6; v. 2, 345, lib. viii, cap. 17. Bracton too wrote of the king's likeness to Jesus Christ, "whose vice-regent he is on earth," f. 5b-6.
[4] *Dialogus de Scaccario*, ed. and trans. C. Johnson (Edinburgh 1950), *Praefatio*, 1.
[5] *Tractatus de Legibus et Consuetudinibus Regni Anglie qui Glanvilla Vocatur*, ed. and trans. G. D. G. Hall (Edinburgh 1965), *Prologus*, 1.
[6] Bracton, v. 2, 304-6, f. 107.

feudal lord or as a private person and his position as head of the judicial system. The king was a great and sometimes greedy landlord, and he might threaten the lands of others, if he chose.

This conflict can be seen clearly in the time of the Angevin kings. Because early English law was unwritten, it is difficult to declare their acts unlawful, but they were capable of actions going beyond traditional law and custom, so that *malevolentia regis,* the king's personal ill-will, became a familiar hazard to his subjects.[7] Henry II and John made disseizin *per voluntatem regis* into an administrative measure to punish their enemies, to discipline royal servants, and to collect crown debts. The administrative records provide numerous examples of disseizin without judgment.[8] At the same time that these monarchs were taking arbitrary action against some of their subjects, they were giving justice to others in their courts. Under Henry II, the system of writs and assizes began to take shape. Henry II's work in the judicial sphere is well-known, but King John was also active in the courts, although his work there has been overshadowed by the chroniclers' accounts of his cruelty.[9] This meant that the king could be called to play a dual role in his courts: he and his servants were the judges, and at the same time they were questioning his acts. Obviously, the king's dual role posed a dilemma for persons seeking recovery of lands from him.

The political thinkers of the twelfth and thirteenth centuries recognized that the king could do wrong, but they knew that he had no mortal superior who could judge his acts. The problem is summarized well in the *Dialogus de Scaccario,* where it is written, "And although this wealth [of the kings] is not theirs by strict process of law, but proceeds . . . sometimes even from their mere arbitrary power, their subjects have no right to question or condemn their actions."[10] A century later, Bracton wrote in his treatise on English law that the king had a superior in God and the law; but he also wrote, "No one can adjudge an act of the king or his charter, so that the act of the king should be voided."[11] Political thinkers

---

[7] J. E. A. Jolliffe, *Angevin Kingship* (London 1955), chap. IV, "Ira et Malevolentia."

[8] See the references in Jolliffe, *op. cit. supra,* note 7, chaps. III-IV; in J. C. Holt, *Magna Carta* (Cambridge 1965), 116-18; in Barnaby C. Keeney, *Judgment by Peers,* Harvard Historical Monograph Series 20 (Cambridge, Mass., 1949), 61-62; and in Sidney Painter, *The Reign of King John* (Baltimore 1949), chaps. VI-VII.

[9] For a valuable account of the historical interpretations of John through the years, see C. Warren Hollister, "King John and the Historians," 1 *Jl. of British Studies* 1-19 (1961).

[10] *Dialogus de Scaccario, Praefatio,* p. 1.

[11] Bracton, v. 2, 109-110, f. 34.

could solve the problem that a king with a duty to observe the law but with no superior to enforce his observance presented by stating that only a tyrant, not a true king, would refuse to obey the law.[12] And victims of a ruler's arbitrary acts could find consolation in the knowledge that he would have to face divine judgment. But were there no regular instruments to force royal observance of the law? Did the courts offer them any means of gaining relief?

Bracton's treatise presents a good picture of the rules of law which had evolved in the English royal courts by the mid-thirteenth century. *Bracton* stated that the writs and assizes ordinarily available to John's and Henry III's subjects offered no remedy for those with grievances against them. In the section of his treatise considering novel disseizins, he set forth clearly this rule, "But if it is a prince or a king who has no superior except God, there is no remedy against him by assize."[13] This does not mean that there is no remedy at all against the king. Bracton went on to present three possible approaches for those seeking justice:

1.) There was the possibility of a judgment by the earls, barons, and other great men who composed the *magna curia regis*. Bracton pointed to this in two passages. He posed it as a possible remedy without stating his acceptance of it in his section on novel disseizins, and he expressed it more strongly in the passage known as the *addicio de cartis*.[14] Whether this second passage was written by Bracton or was added later by another writer is a matter of scholarly controversy.[15] But whoever the author of the

---

[12] E.g. *Policraticus*, lib. iv, cap. 1; Bracton, *De Legibus*, v. 2, 305, f. 107.

[13] Bracton, v. 3, 43, f. 171b.

[14] Bracton, v. 3, 43, f. 171b, and v. 2, 109-110, f. 34.

[15] C. H. McIlwain, *Constitutionalism: Ancient and Modern*, revised ed. (Ithaca 1947), 60, note 2, 157-58, summarizes current scholarly opinion. Maitland thought it possible that the addition was made after the completion of the treatise by Bracton himself, *Bracton's Note Book* (London 1887), v. 1, introduction, 30-33. H. Kantorowicz, *Bractonian Problems* (Glasgow 1941), 49-52, found "no passage more genuinely Bractonian." H. G. Richardson and G. O. Sayles, *The Governance of Mediaeval England from the Conquest to Magna Carta* (Edinburgh 1963), 145, note 1, see no reason to reject the statement as non-Bractonian. For opposing views, see Woodbine's review of Bractonian problems, 52 *Yale Law Jl.*, 428-44 (1943); Fritz Schulz, "Bracton on Kingship." 60 *Eng. Hist. Rev.* 136-76 (1945); and Gaillard Lapsley, "Bracton and the Authorship of the 'Addicio de Cartis,'" 62 *Eng. Hist. Rev.* 1-19 (1947). Brian Tierney, "Bracton on Government," 38 *Speculum* 113 (1963), refuses to take a stand; he writes, "The point does not seem capable of proof one way or the other."

addicio might be, it has little significance for the work of the courts in the thirteenth century. The common law courts were staffed with professional judges, and they failed to provide the mechanics necessary for judgments by the great men of the kingdom.

2.) A victim might humbly petition the king to right the wrong that he had done. He could not bring a regular action against his sovereign, but he could request that the king allow the courts to hear his complaint. Such petitions were matters of grace that the king was free to accept or reject, but those that he accepted were often heard before the royal justices and were recorded on the plea rolls.[16] By 1270, this procedure was fully developed as the petition of right, but such appeals were frequent even earlier in the thirteenth century.[17]

3.) The third possibility presented by *Bracton* is the most commonly encountered one on the plea rolls. A third-party—the person who carried out the king's command, the one granted the land by the king, or some other royal agent—might be sued. Then the king would be placed in an awkward position, forced either to refuse to right his wrong, openly disobeying the law, or admitting his wrong and correcting it.[18] It is with this third possibility that this paper is concerned.

The first surviving plea rolls date from the reigns of King John and Henry III.[19] These rolls make possible a comparison of *Bracton*'s theories with the practice of the royal courts. The majority of pleas heard in the common law courts were possessory assizes and proprietary actions. Sometimes these suits concerned lands seized by the king, but not all these seizures were unjust or unlawful. Temporary seizure of lands, 'distraint,' was a common means of securing obedience to court orders, and lands could be seized for failure to render

---

[16] H. G. Richardson and G. O. Sayles, *Select Cases of Procedure Without Writ under Henry III*, Seldon Society 60 (London 1941), lxx.

[17] For examples, see Ralph V. Turner, *The King and his Courts: The Role of King John and Henry III in the Administration of Justice* (Ithaca, N.Y., 1968), chap. IV, part 2.

[18] Bracton, v. 3, 43, f. 171b.

[19] The surviving plea rolls are housed at the Public Record Office, London. Publication of them was begun in the nineteenth century with the *Rotuli Curiae Regis*, Record Commission (London 1835), 2 vols., and continues with the *Curia Regis Rolls*, Public Record Office (London 1922 —), 14 vols. to date. The published rolls extend only to 1232, but *Bracton's Note Book*, 3 vols., includes a selection of pleas from 1217 to 1240. In addition, the Selden Society and various local record societies have published excerpts from the rolls of the justices on eyre.

the services by which they were held. Sometimes more arbitrary disseizins could be placed within the letter of the law, particularly the law of the Exchequer.[20] Nevertheless, the phrase "disseizin by the king's will" does occur from time to time on the plea rolls. These disseizins without judgment reached their peak with King John, and they contributed to the barons' discontent which culminated in *Magna Carta,* an attempt to limit the king to procedure *per judicium.* A comparison of pleas from the years of John's reign—before the Charter—with pleas from Henry III's time—after the Charter—should reveal its success in subjecting the king to the law. This period is important for another reason. At this time, the royal courts were tending to "go out of court," to drift away from the king's immediate control and to hand down judgments in his name without his personal supervision. A study of cases indirectly questioning the king's acts should indicate the extent of their autonomy at this time.

Normally freemen whose lands had been recently taken from them unlawfully had recourse to the assize of novel disseizin, but this remedy was not available to those disseized by the king, since no action lay against him. *Bracton* states, "No person is entitled [to a writ of novel disseizin] who has been disseized by the king or his bailiffs in his name, unless the disseizin be evident, in which case the king's will is to be awaited."[21] Elsewhere he stated this in a slightly different way, "But if it be a bailiff or servant acting in the king's name, the assize must be held, but it should not proceed to judgment until the king's will is known."[22]

In any case, land seized by the king rarely remained long in his hand. He usually granted it to another, and the victim might then attempt to bring an assize of novel disseizin against the third party. Technically the assize did not lie against one who had gained the land by a royal grant, for the assize lay only against the disseizor; and it was the king, not the tenant having entry through him, who had made the disseizin. *Bracton* explained:

> If the king has caused a disseizin and has afterwards transferred the property to another, each is the principal disseizor: the king is the first and principal one having done the act; and the other is also a principal because of his entry. And although he is a principal, he should not answer without the king, because he made the disseizin in conjunction with him.[23]

---

[20] Holt, *op. cit. supra,* note 8, chap. IV, "Custom and Law."
[21] Bracton, v. 3, 35, f. 168.
[22] Bracton, v. 3, 43, f. 171b.
[23] Bracton, v. 3, 118, f. 204, and similarly, f. 171b.

In another passage, *Bracton* hinted at a solution, stating, "Indirectly and without a writ, however, the prince may be placed in such a position that he will amend his own act, or the injury will clearly reflect ill upon him."[24] He went on to explain that if an assize were brought against the person who had gained the land through the king, then he would seek the king's warranty. At this stage, the king would be placed in the position of either acknowledging his unlawful action and amending it, or of refusing and placing himself openly in the wrong.

Bracton's author was an able judge, and his treatise was based on a study of cases from the rolls of the royal courts. In his study of cases he would have found some suits that did proceed even though the complainant alleged that he or his ancestor had been disseized by the king. This becomes clear from an examination of the rolls surviving from the reigns of King John and Henry III. The cases from each reign may be divided into two groups for consideration: first, those in which disseizin by an earlier ruler was alleged; and second, those in which disseizin by the reigning monarch was at issue.

There are a few proceedings brought in King John's courts to regain lands seized by his father, Henry II, or his brother, Richard I—a half dozen or so. The courts heard these cases, but John took an interest in them, and his judges were careful to consult him. One of the actions centered on an attempt to recover lands which King Richard had seized from John's allies in his rebellion in 1193-1194. William Bret made fine with King John in 1200 for "such seizin of that land as Robert Bret his father had on the day on which he was disseized of that land and of his other lands." When William went to claim the lands, he found someone else, Geoffrey Mauduit, in possession, and he had to bring an action against him. The royal justices gave William's plea a hearing even though it questioned an act of Richard I. Geoffrey told the justices that the land was rightfully his because, while it was in King Richard's hand, he had purchased a writ for an inquest which had confirmed his right by reason of a debt owed to his uncle.[25] This case placed the royal justices in the awkward position of reversing seizin as commanded by a king, either the reigning monarch or his predecessor, whatever their decision. They postponed judgment until they could hear King John's will.[26] He commanded that the plea be heard before him at a later date.[27] The tenant neither came nor essoined himself on that day, perhaps

---

[24] Bracton, v. 3, 43, f. 171b.
[25] *Curia Regis Rolls*, v. 1, 207-8, 245, Trinity 1200.
[26] *Curia Regis Rolls*, v. 1, 287.
[27] *Curia Regis Rolls*, v. 1, 338, Michaelmas 1200.

knowing what the king's will would be, so that William Bret gained seizin by default.[28]

Also in 1200, another tenant of lands seized following the rebellion of 1193-1194 found himself in litigation with one of John's former allies. The recognitors declared that the tenant had gained possession when the plaintiff was disseized "for service to the lord king," meaning for his support of John in the revolt against Richard.[29] The court clerk left a blank space for John's decision, which was inserted later, "The lord king commands that if he was disseized on that occasion, let him have his seizin." Neither of these cases proves much about redress of grievances against the king, for in both, King John had an obvious interest in reversing his brother's action.

Less than a year later, King John's justices again postponed a case alleging disseizin by one of his predecessors until they could consult him. Aubrey de Vere, earl of Oxford, brought an action to recover a manor. He alleged that his father had held the manor of the abbot of Westminster, but that he had lost it when Henry II had disseized the abbot *per voluntatem*.[30] He asked that a jury recognize whether his father had been disseized unjustly and without judgment, but the justices hesitated to allow such an inquest. They found the earl's writ to be *extra assisam*, and they felt that consultation with the king was necessary. They postponed the case until they could consult King John, but no further reference to the case has survived, so that his pleasure is unknown.

In 1211 Peter fitz Herbert, a prominent royal servant, brought an assize of mort d'ancestor against the abbot of Westminster.[31] He maintained that land in the abbot's possession had been his father's in the time of Henry II before he was disseized *per voluntatem domini regis*. He offered King John two palfreys for an inquest to determine whether his father had been dispossessed by Henry II, as he claimed. When the abbot opposed the inquest and presented charters in support of his claim, Peter promised to add to his fine four Norwegian hawks. King John refused the fine, but nevertheless commanded that an inquest be held.[32] This jury found that Peter's father had been disseized, tactfully stating, "But they do not know in what manner, but they believe by the will of the lord king Henry."[33] The

---

[28] *Curia Regis Rolls*, v. 1, 265-66.
[29] Doris M. Stenton, ed., *Pleas Before the King or His Justices*, 1198-1202. Selden Society 67-68 (London 1948-49), v. 1, 299, no. 3123.
[30] *Curia Regis Rolls*, v. 1, 464-65.
[31] *Curia Regis Rolls*, v. 6, 176-77, Michaelmas 1211.
[32] *Curia Regis Rolls*, v. 6, 287, Easter 1212.
[33] *Curia Regis Rolls*, v. 6, 296, Trinity 1212.

abbot of Westminster responded that he had not placed himself on any jury, and he offered four palfreys to have judgment according to his charters. The conclusion to this case is not recorded, probably because the justices wished to consult the king before pronouncing judgment. A final concord ending another case years later indicates that the abbot of Westminster remained in possession.[34]

Peter fitz Herbert had to offer a large fine for an inquest to prove arbitrary royal action, and in another case one of the parties offered a large fine for a similar inquest. In 1208 an action was brought against Roald fitz Alan, constable of Richmond, forcing him to defend his right to four manors and several knight's fees.[35] He offered the king £100 and two palfreys for an inquest to determine whether Henry II had disseized his grandfather unlawfully of those lands. King John accepted the fine, and the inquest supported Roald's charge that his grandfather had been disseized without judgment.[36] The plea roll records that Roald was careful to state that "He wished the court to know that it [the jury] was not summoned as for a plea," that is, that this was not a proceeding against the king.

These cases indicate that it was possible through a third party action in King John's court to correct unjust or unlawful disseizin by his father and brother. Yet these actions were rare, they were only brought by prominent persons, and they required special attention. The litigants who brought these actions were aware that they were unusual, offering oblations for a hearing; and the justices showed a similar awareness, seeking the king's counsel before pronouncing judgment.

More significant than these proceedings questioning acts of the king's predecessors are those which questioned his own acts. There is little evidence from the plea rolls that persons disseized by King John sought recovery of their lands by bringing actions against third parties. Indeed, in all the records of pleas in John's common law courts there appears only one such case. The presence of this single proceeding is explained by the prominence of the rival claimants: William Marshal, earl of Pembroke, against William de Reviers, earl of Devon, and his wife, the countess of Meulan. Both the earl marshal and the countess sought possession of the manor of Stur-

---

[34] *Curia Regis Rolls*, v. 7, 239, Trinity 1214. Final concord dated 30 Henry III, L. F. Salzmann, ed., *An Abstract of Feet of Fines Relating to the County of Sussex, from 2 Richard I to 33 Henry III*, Sussex Record Society, v. 2 (1903), 114, no. 426.

[35] *Curia Regis Rolls*, v. 5, 147-48, Hilary 1208.

[36] In fact, the loss of the lands was more the result of the anarchy of Stephen's reign than of any positive act of Henry II, Holt, *op. cit. supra*, note 8, 88.

minster in Devonshire, which was in the king's hand.[37] The earl marshal claimed the manor on grounds that the count of Meulan had long ago granted it to him; the countess stated that she had held it, but had been disseized *per preceptum domini regis*.

The case became more complicated when William de Reviers and his wife failed to appear before the justices on the appointed day. William Marshal then sought immediate seizin of the land, but King John was cautious and sought his counselors' advice. They were unwilling to give an opinion and suggested that the action be postponed until "the lord archbishop and other great and wise men of the land" would be present. This is an unusual example of the king's familiar counselors declaring themselves unqualified to advise him, so that the matter had to be postponed for the *magna curia regis*.[38] The plea rolls record no conclusion to this case, but on the date assigned for hearing, there was a great council held at Worcester.[39] Apparently, the countess of Meulan's complaint went unheeded there, for King John issued letters granting the manor of Sturminster to William Marshal.[40]

This survey of actions brought against private persons to regain lands seized by the king reveals only one plea alleging disseizin by John himself, and in that one plea the accusation was made by the wife of a great noble. Of course, there were other ways of approaching the problem. One could go outside the regular processes and petition the king, or one could seek a remedy through the Exchequer, the tribunal for financial matters. But the events of 1215-1216 force the conclusion that there was no effective means of challenging the king's arbitrary acts. *Magna Carta* was an attempt to supply some means. In chapters fifty-two and fifty-six of the Charter, King John promised to restore the lands, castles, privileges, and rights of persons whom he had disseized without judgment. He made a similar promise to the victims of disseizins by his father and brother. These promises were omitted from the versions of the Great Charter issued under Henry III, yet they were still very much in the minds of Henry's subjects. Further, chapter thirty-nine of *Magna Carta* (chapter twenty-nine of the Charter of 1225), the article protecting freemen from

---

[37] *Curia Regis Rolls*, v. 3, 124, Trinity 1204.

[38] *Curia Regis Rolls*, v. 3, 147, postponed to the morrow of Assumption, 16 August 1204.

[39] H. G. Richardson, "The Origins of Parliament," *Trans. Royal Hist. Soc.*, fourth series 11 (1928), 153-54.

[40] 9 Sept. 1204, *Rot. Lit. Pat.*, Record Commission (London 1835), 45; *Rot. Lit. Claus.*, Record Commission (London 1833), v. 1, 7b.

unlawful acts by the king, remained as a warning to Henry against arbitrary measures.

A survey of cases from the courts of Henry III in which royal disseizin was alleged should show how seriously these clauses of the Charter were taken. It is evident that they were taken seriously, for the number of cases in which arbitrary disseizin by one of Henry's predecessors was alleged increased greatly. In addition, the records of these cases contain little to indicate that they presented problems to the justices. A number of cases came into the courts in which arbitrary disseizin by the king's grandfather Henry II was an issue. Sometimes the reasons given for his seizures are bizarre. In a grand assize, jurors found that he had disseized a man because of a quarrel over a sparrow-hawk.[41] Another grand assize gave an even more bizarre reason for disseizin by Henry II; supposedly he disseized a man because he refused to give dinner to a royal huntsman.[42]

Perhaps more significant are the pleas brought before Henry III's courts by persons seeking recovery of lands seized by his father, John. An assize of novel disseizin taken before the itinerant justices in 1221 shows Henry III's court acting to correct arbitrary action by John's chief forester, Hugh de Neville.[43] The jurors state that the complainant had been disseized unjustly and without judgment by the forester's command. The justices adjourned the case to Westminster for judgment on receipt of a writ from Hugh, which informed them that:

> Walter Hose [the complainant] was a malefactor in King John's forest when Hugh was forester, and by the lord king's command, he took that land into the hand of the lord king because bows and arrows and other things contrary to the assize of the forest were found in the house of Hugh Hose, and Hugh and the said Walter his man, withdrew and would not stand to right.

The justices of the bench decided that disseizin for the offense of possessing bows and arrows contrary to the assize of the forest was an arbitrary act. They restored Walter's land to him, and they

---

[41] *Curia Regis Rolls*, v. 9, 332-33, Michaelmas 1220, assize between Geoffrey Goldsmith, complainant, and Ralph Hopeshort, tenant.

[42] *Bracton's Note Book*, v. 2, 586-88, no. 769, Trinity 1233, assize between the prior of Newark and the prior of Sherborne.

[43] Doris M. Stenton, ed., *Rolls of the Justices in Eyre for Gloucester, Warwickshire and Staffordshire*, 1221, 1222, Selden Society 59 (London 1940), 520-21, no. 1188.

amerced Hugh for his part in the disseizin.⁴⁴ The justices' decision in this case is evidence of the effort made during the minority of Henry III to implement the Great Charter and to protect the king's subjects from arbitrary acts.

Another action coming before Henry III's judges involved disseizin by the will of King John. In 1219 the tenant in a plea of land sought to place himself on the grand assize, but the complainant answered that the grand assize ought not to lie.⁴⁵ He explained that he had held the land in question by the right of inheritance until his imprisonment by King John. He had made fine with the king to gain his release from prison, but he had fallen in arrears on his payments, so that the sheriff had seized his land into the king's hand for debt. No jury was called to confirm this story of John's financial dealings, for the two parties settled the dispute by a compromise.

In another case, the knights of a grand assize did affirm that an individual had been unlawfully disseized by John. In 1223 an assize had to rule on the relative claims of two royal officials, William Briwerre and Geoffrey de Lucy, to one carucate of land.⁴⁶ The jury found that Rose, Geoffrey's sister, had granted him the land in question, but that the king had become angered with him and had seized it. Rose then offered the king a fine to have that land back, and it was returned to her; then she granted it to William Briwerre, probably in 1212. It seemed to the jurors that Geoffrey de Lucy had the greater right, since he had been given the land first. However, the justices did not pronounce judgment on the basis of the jurors' statement. Instead, they postponed the case for hearing before the justiciar and the barons of the Exchequer. The fact that the case was removed to the Exchequer might seem to indicate that it was marked for special attention, but Briwerre was a baron of the Exchequer; and by virtue of his position as baron, the Exchequer had jurisdiction over his case.⁴⁷

Another important person, Humphrey, earl of Hereford, claimed that King John had disseized his father "unjustly and

---

⁴⁴ Stenton, *op. cit. supra*, note 43, xlvii.

⁴⁵ *Curia Regis Rolls*, v. 13, x, Trinity 1219; also *Bracton's Note Book*, v. 2, 16, no. 17. The tenant was the son of the sheriff, Reginald de Cornhill.

⁴⁶ *Curia Regis Rolls*, v. 11, 77-78, no. 416, Hilary 1223; also *Bracton's Note Book*, v. 3, 466-67, no. 1593.

⁴⁷ F. M. Powicke, *King Henry III and the Lord Edward* (Oxford 1947), v. 1, 3, 57, 68. Briwerre had been a trusted deputy of King John as well.

without judgment" of a manor.[48] King John had seized the earl's lands in 1213, but he promised to restore them in 1215, and he issued writs commanding their restoration, but in the confusion of the barons' war the writs were never obeyed. This suit was postponed to another date by Henry III's command, but the postponement was not due to Henry's anger at the accusation against his father. Rather it is explained by the tenant's presentation of royal charters and by his plea that he should not be required to respond without the king. The records of these pleas concerning arbitrary disseizin by King John, like the cases treating disseizins by Henry II, indicate that they were heard by the royal justices without undue difficulty.[49]

It seems clear from these cases that an effort was made during Henry III's early years to abide by the principles of the Great Charter, at least to the extent that those disseized by the king's ancestors could seek restoration of their lands in the royal courts. The question does arise concerning the disseizins of Henry III. Did his own victims find a hearing in his courts? Could they bring assizes of novel disseizin against the person to whom the king had granted the land? It has already been shown that *Bracton* discussed the problem of these cases in the section on novel disseizins in the treatise. The assize on novel disseizin did not lie against the tenant because it was not he who had made the disseizin, but the king.[50] But the royal judges did hear these assizes from time to time, handling them in different ways, sometimes dismissing them and sometimes referring them to the king.

The plea rolls dating from Henry's minority offer examples of these assizes of novel disseizin. In 1219 the prior of the Hospitalers' assize brought a reply from the tenant that he held the land in question at the king's command. The sheriff produced a royal writ in support of the tenant's statement. But the prior refused to believe that the writ came from the king's Chancery, and he maintained that if it did, then it was made *contra legem*

---

[48] Unpublished *Curia Regis Roll* 115B, m. 25, no. 1293, 7 Jan. 1235. The earl of Hereford against Hugh Despenser for the manor of Ryhall, Rutland. For another plea in which Humphrey de Bohun sought to recover lands King John had seized from his father, see *Curia Regis Rolls*, v. 12, 528-29, no. 2646, Easter 1226.

[49] For other examples of disseizin by John treated in the courts of Henry III, see *Curia Regis Rolls*, v. 10, 279-80, Trinity 1222; v. 12, 65, no. 356, Hilary 1225.

[50] Bracton, v. 3, 118, f. 204.

terrae et consuetudinem regis.[51] The outcome of the prior's statement is not known, for the plea rolls make no further reference to the case.

In another assize, dating from Henry III's early majority, the tenant produced a royal writ as evidence that the king had granted him possession.[52] The justices, when they saw this proof, decided in his favor and found the plaintiff in mercy. The reason they gave for their judgment was that the tenant did not disseize the plaintiff, since he had entry *per preceptum domini regis*. Bracton knew both of these cases, for he recorded them in his *Note Book*. The judges' dismissal of this second suit is in accord with the teaching in his treatise and with his comment on the first case in the margin of his *Note Book*.

Bracton commented on another case in his *Note Book*, this time an assize of mort d'ancestor, in which the tenant claimed that he held at the king's will.[53] His comment expresses the view that the judges should not dismiss the assize at once, but that they should allow it to proceed, then postpone judgment until they could consult the king. Bracton repeated this suggestion in his treatise, when he discussed assizes of novel disseizin brought against the king's agents.[54] Bracton's suggestion seems to be the solution most often reached by the royal justices in treating these assizes.

Two assizes of novel disseizin concerning parts of the royal demesne illustrate their willingness to hear such cases. One of them came before the intinerant justices in 1221 contesting arbitrary disseizin by one of Henry III's officers.[55] This case is interesting for two reasons: first, the jurors' evidence indicates that the complainant was a villein sokeman on the royal demesne; second, the jurors stated that the man named in the writ did not disseize the complainant, but that it was done arbitrarily by the agent of the king. If the judges had wished, either of these facts would have given them excuses for dismissing the assize.

---

[51] *Curia Regis Rolls*, v. 8, 132-33, Michaelmas term 1219; also *Bracton's Note Book*, v. 2, 68-69, no. 176. The tenant was Adam de Bereville.

[52] *Bracton's Note Book*, v. 2, 329-30, no. 401, Easter 1230, action by Walter de la Grava against Walter de Langford.

[53] *Bracton's Note Book*, v. 3, 595, no. 1766, eyre in Kent 1227. Assize brought by Richard fitz Roger against Joscelin de Oye. The jurors declared in favor of Richard, and the king then gave him seizin.

[54] Bracton, v. 3, p. 43, f. 171b.

[55] Doris M. Stenton, ed., *Rolls of the Justices in Eyre for Lincolnshire (1218-19) and Worcestershire (1221)*, Selden Society 53 (London 1934), 530-31, no. 1061. The official was William de Cantilupe.

Instead, "by counsel of the court," they restored seizin to the tenant. They were careful to safeguard the king's rights by stating that "The king, if he wishes, may deal with him according to the custom of the manor."

A few years later, in 1224, the royal justices reacted differently to an action touching the royal demesne. Richard de Percy, a Yorkshire baron, brought an assize of novel disseizin against a large number of men of a royal manor in Yorkshire.[56] The king's men came and said that the assize should not be taken because the land named in the writ pertained to the royal manor. The judgment was: "And because the manor of Scarborough is demesne of the lord king and he does not wish to admit the assize, it is considered that a perambulation be made between the lord king and Richard by twelve knights." Thus Richard could not bring an assize against the king, but his complaint could be remedied in much the same way.

During Henry III's personal rule, the royal justices continued to allow possessory actions to proceed which indirectly questioned disseizin by the king. In 1235-1236, they heard an assize of novel disseizin against Walter Mauclerc, bishop of Carlisle.[57] Walter had fallen from royal favor in 1233, and he had lost his office as treasurer along with his estates; but his fall did not last long, and he was soon restored to his lands.[58] His bailiff maintained that the land now disputed had been returned to him by a royal writ at the time of his restoration to the king's good graces. Consequently, he did not think that an assize of novel disseizin should lie, since responsibility for the disseizin lay with the king. The judges followed the procedure in this assize of novel disseizin which *Bracton* recommended, that is, taking the verdict of the jurors and then delaying judgment.[59] The jurors found that the bishop had disseized the complainants, although they did not know whether he did so by the king's warrant or not. The justices withheld judgment until the king could give his warranty, if he wished. Henry III did acknowledge that the bishop had seizin through him, and the complainants were unable to regain their land by the assize.

Perhaps most significant of all indirect proceedings against the king are the actions brought by Hubert de Burgh, the former justiciar, in the summer of 1234. Henry III provoked a crisis in

---

[56] *Curia Regis Rolls*, v. 11, 419-80, no. 2414, Michaelmas 1224; also *Bracton's Note Book*, v. 2, 697-98, no. 907.

[57] *Bracton's Note Book*, v. 3, 170-71, no. 1153.

[58] *Dict. Nat. Bio.*, v. 13, 79-80, "Walter Mauclerc."

[59] *Bracton's Note Book*, v. 3, 595, no. 1766.

government by his outlawry of Hubert and of other great men in the kingdom. Once they were outlawed, he seized their lands into his hand. But his acts aroused the opposition of the barons, and they reasserted the principle of *Magna Carta* that the king is subject to the law. Henry's arbitrary acts were checked by the judgment of the *magna curia regis,* representing the incorporate realm, which declared that his outlawry of his enemies was unlawful.

Once Hubert de Burgh's outlawry was revoked, he began proceedings in the royal courts to regain the lands that the king had taken from him.[60] Since these lands had been granted by Henry III to others, Hubert's pleas were not proceedings against the king, but were private pleas against the tenants who had gained entry through the king. Yet the suits were clearly extraordinary actions to cope with an unusual situation, for they were not assizes of novel disseizin, nor were they proprietary actions begun by writ of right. Rather Hubert demanded of the tenants by what right, *quo warranto,* they held his lands.

The king became involved in the actions when one of the tenants, Robert Passelewe, attempted to vouch him to warranty. Robert had been one of Henry's advisers at the time of Hubert's outlawry, but he was now out of favor. The king cannot have been eager to come to the defense of one of his 'evil counselors.' Henry replied to Robert with a strong statement of monarchical supremacy, much like the view of kingship that Bracton expressed later in his treatise:

> And moreover no one who is vouched to warranty concerning any land is bound to respond to that warranty without a summons by writ of the lord king or by the precept of his justices; and the lord king can neither be summoned nor submit to the command of anyone, since he has no superior in the kingdom.[61]

Clearly, the king meant that he was not subject to the jurisdiction of his own courts. Nevertheless, he did acknowledge that he had seized Hubert's lands and granted them to others, although in one case he justified his act by explaining that he had been made to understand by his counselors that he could legally do this, since Hubert had been outlawed. Once the outlawry had

---

[60] *Curia Regis Rolls,* 115B, m. 18, no. 1207; 116B, m. 2d, no. 1895; *Bracton's Note Book,* v. 3, 126-28, no. 1108; 129-30, no. 1111; 156-57, no. 1136; 161, no. 114.

[61] *Curia Regis Rolls,* 115B, m. 6d, no. 1058; also *Bracton's Note Book,* v. 3, 127-28.

been nullified, Hubert had a very strong case, and judgment was given that the king's unlawful grants did not give their holders any rights. The justices restored Hubert's land to him in each case. Perhaps the pleas brought by Hubert de Burgh are the best illustration of *Bracton*'s proposal that proceedings against some third party might be brought which would place the king in such a position that he must acknowledge his unlawful act.

Robert Passelewe's attempt to defend his land against Hubert de Burgh by drawing Henry III into the suit raised a question for the royal justices: could the king be vouched to warranty? Henry clearly stated that he could not be. Many times individuals did call upon King John and Henry III to warrant their charters and grants, but by the time that Bracton composed his treatise the courts were hedging individuals' right to seek the king's warranty. *Bracton* states that the king could not be called to warrant as could an ordinary person, but one who sought the king's warranty could say "with a certain courtliness" *(cum quidam curialitate)* that he could not answer without the king, from whom he held a charter. He added that this should not be allowed unless the royal charter included the king's promise to give warranty.[62] Yet the king's warranty of his charters did not mean that his acts were being judged in his courts, as would his being vouched to warranty. When a tenant's right to his land was challenged in court, he could "vouch to warranty" the person who had granted him his land. This was more serious than simple warranty of a charter, for the grantor then replaced the tenant as the defendant in the suit, and the remainder of the action was conducted in his name. If the grantor lost the suit, causing his tenant to lose the land, then he had to compensate the tenant with other land equal in value to that land lost.[63]

Obviously, if Robert Passelewe had been successful in his attempt to vouch the king to warranty, the suit against him would have been converted into a proceeding against the king. His attempt was not the first time that the royal justices had faced this question. It was raised in an assize of novel disseizin against Robert de Mortimer taken before the itinerant justices in 1219. Robert's bailiff said that the assize ought to be dismissed because his master had seizin of the land from the earl of Surrey at the command of King John.[64] If his statement was true, then the assize of novel disseizin did not apply. The complainant gave a complicated

---

[62] Bracton, v. 4, 197, f. 382b.

[63] F. Pollock and F. W. Maitland, *The History of English Law*, 2d ed. (Cambridge 1898), v. 2, 662-64.

[64] Stenton, *op. cit. supra*, note 55, 132-34, no. 297.

account of his loss of the land during the barons' revolt of 1215-1217, which indicated that Robert had seized the land during the war and had refused to surrender it when peace came. Robert's bailiff did not know how to respond to this account, so he vouched the king to warranty. Nevertheless, the justices proceeded with the assize because, "He had no warranty through the lord king except the letters of the aforesaid earl [William]," and because, "It is not customary for anyone to vouch the king to warranty concerning disseizin." Here the justices seemed to set forth the principle that the king could not be vouched to warranty in cases of novel disseizin.

The justices were still uncertain when the question arose once more in January 1235 in a suit by a chaplain to recover custody of a manor. He complained that he had been disseized *per voluntatem domini regis*, but the current custodian, Gerard Talbot, replied that he held the manor at bail of the king.[65] Gerard called the king to warrant, but because he had no charter or other proof of his grant, King Henry was uncertain whether he ought to warrant him. Actually, Henry did not need to give his warranty, for Gerard was able later to present royal letters in proof of his grant of the custody.[66] The case was postponed until the king's will could be known.[67] His decision is not recorded on the plea rolls, but the patent rolls record a letter indicating that the chaplain recovered custody of the manor.[68]

This survey of pleas brought against third parties by persons who had been disseized by the king reveals several points. The plea rolls for King John's reign indicate that almost never did his victims have recourse to the courts, although in some cases victims of his father or brother brought suits to recover their lands. The records of those cases reveal payments of fines and postponements for consultation with the king. The rolls for Henry III's reign reveal a change. Pleas for recovery of lands seized by his royal predecessors increased, and they proceeded with less difficulty. More important, pleas in which disseizin by Henry himself was an issue were sometimes heard in court, even though the justices knew that the possessory assizes did not lie against the king. Apparently, *Magna Carta's* meaning was understood by the royal justices.

---

[65] *Curia Regis Rolls*, 115B, m. 21, no. 1311.
[66] *Cal. Pat. Rolls*, 1232-1247, Public Record Office (London 1901—), 39, 10 Feb. 1234.
[67] *Curia Regis Rolls*, 115B, m. 8, no. 1466.
[68] *Close Rolls*, 1234-1237, Public Record Office (London 1902—), 294, 27 July 1236.

Yet this does not mean that the justices were willing to pass judgment on their master's acts. They hardly had gained that much autonomy. They would not allow him to be drawn directly into disputes by being vouched to warranty, nor would they pronounce judgment without first knowing his wishes. Yet in many cases they did allow the assize to proceed to the jurors' recognition, even though their statement sometimes amounted to an accusation of unjust or unlawful action by the king, and even though there were technical excuses for dismissing it. To this extent, then, the common law courts provided instruments for the correction of the ruler's wrongful acts. *Bracton*'s doctrine that proceedings could be brought in the common law courts in a way that would place the king in an unpleasant position and that would require him to amend his act was already a reality in the early years of Henry III.

Note

Since this article was first published, HMSO has published three additional volumes of *Curia Regis Rolls* down to the year 1242.

15

Exercise of the King's Will in Inheritance of Baronies: The Example of King John and William Briwerre

By the late twelfth century, the principle that hereditary succession guaranteed title had triumphed in English feudal land law, and this threatened lords' rights to choose their tenants freely.[1] Henry II's assizes were providing mesne tenants with security of tenure. They separated title to a tenement from lordly acceptance of the tenant when the the tenant was a direct descendant of the previous landholder.[2] An undoubted male heir could take possession at once, not waiting for his lord to put him into possession, denying the lord his right to take the land into his hand and hold it until relief was paid.[3]

The new actions available to mesne tenants did not apply to direct tenants of the Crown, however. The Angevin monarchs resisted following rules that their courts were enforcing against other feudal lords in their treatment of their own tenants-in-chief. The king held to the old view that an heir does not succeed to his ancestor's property automatically, but only has a customary claim to be accepted as tenant. As *Glanvill* noted, the king claimed primer seizin, his right to take possession of a barony and to place the heir in possession only once the heir had done homage to him and made arrangements to pay relief.[4]

Although the common law was beginning to draw up careful rules of seniority for heirs and heiresses, the king insisted on playing a part in successions to great lordships with their military and economic resources. What J. C. Holt wrote of inheritance under the Anglo-Normans applies also to the Angevins, "The more distant or debatable the claim, the more substantial would be the overlord's [king's] consent and the more likely would he be concerned with the political impact of the settlement."[5] The king's will, his *benevolentia* or *malevolentia*, were facts of political life, accepted "with a curious equanimity," even seen as

---

[1]Samuel E. Thorne, "English Feudalism and Estates in Land," *Cambridge Law Journal* (1959): 194–209.

[2]Robert C. Palmer, "The Origin of Property in England," *Law and History Review* 3 (1985): 22; also Thorne, "Feudalism and Estates in Land," p. 201.

[3]S. F. C. Milsom, *The Legal Framework of English Feudalism* (Cambridge, 1976), pp. 162–63, 171.

[4]G. D. G. Hall, ed., *Glanvill*, Medieval Texts (Oxford, 1965), 9: 6, p. 110; Milsom, *Legal Framework*, pp. 163–64. Also Scott L. Waugh, *The Lordship of England, Royal Wardships and Marriages in English Society and Politics 1217–1327* (Princeton, 1988), pp. 66–67.

[5]J. C. Holt, "Politics and Property in Early Medieval England," *Past & Present* 57 (1972): 22.

a legitimate aspect of royal government.⁶ A factor in this exercise of the king's will is the contradiction that S. F. C. Milsom noted about twelfth-century feudal courts; the king as lord was party to the suit at the same time that his own court — the *curia regis* — was sitting in judgment.⁷ A claimant challenging a tenant put in seizin by the king could hardly expect an impartial hearing.

Several scholars recently have looked at succession to baronies in the Anglo-Norman period, and they find that most descended with little royal interference. One estimate is 80%, while another found more royal intervention by Henry I: nine baronies without direct male heirs passing to lateral heirs, and six to which lateral heirs failed to succeed.⁸ To my knowledge, however, no one has attempted a similar study for the Angevin period. A look at such inheritances should be instructive. In 1189, England had 202 baronies, including fifteen in the king's hand and fifteen already divided among heirs into thirty-four parts. During the years down to 1237, 167 would change hands, some several times.⁹

The king's action in these successions to great lordships must have resembled the response which great lords themselves had made to disputed successions coming before their own courts before Henry II's new remedies took such cases away from them. Political advantage may have weighed as heavily as legal reasoning in determining succession to a barony or earldom, and magnates suffering the king's ill-will might find themselves in court defending their right to long-held inheritances.¹⁰ W. L. Warren, Henry II's biographer, found it paradoxical that Henry, "who did so much to define and protect the rights of heirs, and to erect the developing principles of succession into rules of law, should have kept the heirs of tenants-in-chief at the mercy of his uncertain pleasure."¹¹

I hope to make a start toward a study of the Angevin kings' role in hereditary succession to great lordships by examining William Briwerre's acquisitions of lands with the support of King John. Like other *familiares regis*, he had royal support in exploiting uncertainties in the land law to expand his holdings.

⁶J. E. A. Jolliffe, *Angevin Kingship* (London, 1955), pp. 56, 95.

⁷Milsom, *Framework*, p. 16; Waugh, *The Lordship of England*, p. 127.

⁸"Politics and Property": p. 30; RaGena De Aragon, "The Growth of Secure Inheritance in Anglo-Norman England," *Journal of Medieval History* 8 (1982): 383. Charlotte A. Newman, *The Anglo-Norman Nobility in the Reign of Henry I: The Second Generation* (Philadelphia, 1988), p. 119.

⁹Based on I. J. Sanders, *English Baronies* (Oxford, 1960). Compare my figures with Charlotte A. Newman's 187 for Henry I's time (*The Anglo-Norman Nobility*, p. 116); or Sidney Painter's 197 baronies in 1199 (*The Reign of King John* [Baltimore, 1949], p. 19); or Scott Waugh for 1200, who calculates 192 separate baronies or portions in 1200 (*Lordship of England*, p. 18, n. 10).

¹⁰E.g. Geoffrey de Say's rivalry with Geoffrey fitz Peter and his son over the Mandeville inheritance. See Ralph V. Turner, *Men Raised from the Dust: Administrative Service and Upward Mobility in Angevin England* (Philadelphia, 1988), pp. 56–58, 67–68.

¹¹W. L. Warren, *Henry II* (Berkeley, Calif., 1973), p. 386. Not all would accept Warren's view, however; see Thomas K. Keefe, "King Henry II and the Earls: The Pipe Roll Evidence," *Albion* 13 (1981): 191–222.

Briwerre began his service to the Angevin monarchy as a local agent for Henry II in the southwest, and he became a *familiaris* of Richard I and John, and a member of young Henry III's regency council. He held a number of shrievalties and was also prominent at Westminster, among the half dozen or so men closest to the center of power in England until his death in 1226.[12] A baron of the Exchequer under Richard I, Briwerre was one of the senior men in royal finances by King John's time, "probably the greatest expert of his day in financial matters."[13] Like other barons of the Exchequer in Richard Lionheart's and King John's time, William Briwerre sat among the royal justices occasionally, chiefly *coram rege*.[14]

Besides being an Exchequer expert, William Briwerre became an expert in acquiring estates, and he accumulated so much land that he ranked among the baronage. Rich reward came from his services to four monarchs; yet he never won the title of earl, as did Geoffrey fitz Peter or Hubert de Burgh, whose careers resemble his. By 1219 Briwerre was assessed scutage on more than sixty knights' fees, holdings sufficient to rank him solidly among the barons. His early career in the southwest enabled him to build up a bloc of holdings there scattered over several shires, centered in Devonshire, but extending into Cornwall, Somerset, and neighboring counties.[15]

William Briwerre was a beneficiary of John's policies which were alienating the king from the old landed families, who felt that John was trampling underfoot their lawful rights of inheritance. In fact, royal interference in succession to baronies was not entirely due to the king's initiative; rather his will often moved in directions inspired by counselors such as Briwerre, who were seeking to expand their possessions. Several uncertain points of law offered opportunity for royal intervention in succession to honors, and some of William Briwerre's acquisitions resulted from such uncertainties: first, succession of females, or partition of fees among co-heirs in default of male heirs; and second, uncertainty about descent when a male died leaving another male claimant, not his eldest son, but a younger son, brother, nephew, or possibly distant cousin.

---

[12]*Chronica Rogeri de Hovedene*, ed. William Stubbs, Rolls Series (London, 1868–71), 3: 6; *Gesta Regis Henrici Secundi Benedicti Abbatis*, ed. William Stubbs, Rolls Series (London, 1867), 2: 101; *The Chronicle of Richard of Devizes*, ed. and trans. John Appleby, Medieval Texts (London, 1963), p. 6.

[13]*Roger Wendover*, 3: 238, 347. Matthew Paris, *Chronica Majora*, ed. H. R. Luard, Rolls Series (London, 1872–84), 2: 635, describes him as *martius et expertus*. J. E. A. Jolliffe, "The Chamber and the castle treasuries under King John," in R. W. Hunt, W. A. Pantin, R. W. Southern, eds., *Studies in Medieval History presented to F. M. Powicke* (Oxford, 1948), p. 131.

[14]See my *Men Raised from the Dust*, pp. 74–75.

[15]Ibid., pp. 80–86.

In a feudal society, where descent by strict male primogeniture was favored, an "heiress was one of the fluid elements in the social structure."[16] Henry I's coronation charter indicates that women were eligible to inherit fiefs in default of males.[17] The rule then was that the entire inheritance went to one daughter's husband, with the lord choosing whichever one he favored. The lord would have preferred, of course, a single heiress and an undivided tenement held by a loyal vassal. Although the eldest daughter and her husband acquired a right recognized by the courts, gradually their moral obligation to share with her sisters also won legal recognition. A specific ruling of Henry I's court, dating c. 1130–35, appears to have introduced the change in custom. An 1145 charter refers to a *statutum decretum* by which daughters were to share in case of no surviving son, and the eldest could not lawfully take her younger sisters' share.[18]

In short, the custom of *parage* described by *Glanvill* developed, by which the eldest daughter's husband did homage to the chief lord for the whole fee, and the younger daughters and their husbands performed their services "by the hand of" the eldest daughter and her husband.[19] S. F. C. Milsom sees the Church's influence in securing acceptance for such a provision, on account of its concern that younger daughters should have adequate marriage-portions.[20] J. C. Holt does not find such lofty motives for the custom of partition. He suggests that *Glanvill*'s rule was not yet the law of the realm, not the only way to settle descent of lands among daughters, only what the author hoped would become the law. Holt points out that the king, landless knights in his service, and younger daughters all benefited from divisions among co-heirs. A 1213 fine was offered for division of land between two sisters "into two equal parts," which is "according to the custom of England." Customary or not, one sister's husband still found it prudent to proffer 500 marks to King John.[21] By 1236, the law for

---

[16]Holt, "Feudal Society and the Family in early Medieval England: IV. The Heiress and the Alien," *Transactions of the Royal Historical Society* 35 (1985): 1 [hereafter cited as *T. R. H. S.*].

[17]William Stubbs, *Select Charters and other Illustrations of English Constitutional History* (9th ed.; Oxford, 1913), p. 118.

[18]Holt, "Feudal Society and the Family: IV," pp. 2–10; F. M. Stenton, *The First Century of English Feudalism 1066–1166* (Oxford, 1932), pp. 37–41.

[19]*Glanvill*, 7: 3, p. 76; *Bracton*, ed. G. E. Woodbine, trans. S. E. Thorne (Cambridge, Mass., 1968–77) f. 66b, 2: 194.

[20]*On the Laws and Customs of England: Essays in Honor of Samuel E. Thorne*, ed. Morris S. Arnold, et al. (Chapel Hill, 1981), pp. 69–78.

[21]*Rotuli de Oblatis et Finibus*, ed. T. Duffus Hardy, Record Commission (London, 1835) [hereafter cited as *Rot. de Obl. et Fin.*], p. 507. Division of the barony of Cavendish, Suff., between two sisters: Mabel, widow of Hugh Bardolf, and Basilia, wife of Hugh de Odingselles. For details, see *Pipe Roll 5 Ric. I*, p. 124; *6 Ric. I*, p. 92; *Pipe Roll 7 John*, pp. 34, 197 (all pipe roll citations are from Pipe Roll Society, London, editions); *Memoranda Roll 1 John*, Pipe Roll Society, n. s. 21 (1943): 54.

tenants-in-chief of the Crown was that all daughters should do homage to the king, all holding in-chief; and Holt cites cases where this rule had been followed earlier, or where equal partition had not been made.[22]

Partition among heiresses may have been the rule by the end of the twelfth century, but it still offered occasion for royal intervention in favor of the king's friends. A recent count of the descent of baronies from 1200–1330, finds sixty-eight (35%) partitioned among heiresses.[23] My own count reveals thirty-eight divided among coheirs between Henry II's death in 1189 and 1237. Although modern genealogical studies often leave an impression of smooth successions, digging beneath the surface can uncover previously undetected royal interventions. An examination of the circumstances indicates some royal intervention in roughly 48% (18/38) of these cases.[24] Rarely would the king be so bold as to ignore entirely an heiress's claim, but he might delay handing over the land, make an unequal distribution, or require a hefty fine.[25] 32% (12/38) of these took place before the death of King John.

In several instances of King John's interference in partition among co-heirs, William Briwerre was a central character. Uncertainties about the law of inheritance, coupled with royal favoritism and heirs' financial difficulties, enabled him to gain possession of some baronial holdings. Perhaps the most blatant example of royal bending of custom concerning coheirs is the case of John de Bidun's sisters. [See App. A] John died sometime before 1185, leaving five sisters as heirs to his honor of Lavendon, Bucks.[26] An entry on the *Memoranda Roll* for John's first year reads, "It is said that five sisters are sharers in the land of John de Bidun and none of them returns John's debt, and it is found on the roll that the same John had several debts."[27] I could find no record of

[22]Holt, "Feudal Society and the Family: IV," pp. 10–11, citing the *Statutum Hiberniae de Coheredibus*. See also *Bracton*, f. 78, 2: 227.

[23]Scott L. Waugh, "Marriage, Class, and Royal Wardship in England under Henry III," *Viator* 16 (1985): 183–85.

[24]Baronies: Benington, 1235; Bulwick, 1215; Burgh by Sands, 1202; Cavendish, 1203; Great Torrington, 1227; earldom of Chester, 1232 and 1237; honor of Leicester, 1204; Odell, 1217; Pleshy, 1190; Southoe, 1219; Stainton la Vale, 1202; and West Dean, 1200/01. Probable baronies: Egremont and Papcastle, 1213; Lavendon, 1185–1204; Hepple, 1198; Odcombe, 1199; Pontefract, 1193; Stogursey, 1224–25.

[25]Geoffrey fitz Peter and his wife Beatrice de Say's agreement with her sister illustrates this royal intervention; see my *Haskins Society Journal* article, "The Mandeville Inheritance, 1189–1236: Its Legal, Political, and Social Context," 1 (1989): 147–72. Also 500 mark fine for one of three sisters' part of the barony of Cavendish, *Pipe Roll 16 John*, p. 113. In 1217 following the death of the lord of Odell, each of his daughters offered £100 as fine and relief for half the barony, *Pipe Roll 2 Hen. III*, p. 63.

[26]*Pipe Roll 30 Hen. II*, p. 108; *Rotuli de Dominabus et Pueris et Puellis*, ed. J. H. Round, Pipe Roll Society, (London, 1913), p. 43, 45; xlii–xliii.

[27]*Memoranda Roll 1 John*, pp. 65–65.

debts on earlier pipe rolls, other than a few pounds for scutages. In April 1204, King John conferred the five and a half fees comprising the honor on William Briwerre with each of the sisters' husbands to hold mediately of him while William held in-chief of the king.[28] Apparently, John de Bidun's unpaid debts gave the king an excuse for doing this. In this and other cases, William Briwerre's financial dealings may form a shadowy background. Briwerre having grown rich from royal favor and lucrative offices, he could well have engaged in a little money-lending. It seems possible that this royal grant cloaks some private arrangement between him and the Bidun sisters for payment of their brother's debts.[29]

Another case by which William Briwerre managed to win a barony was the succession to the honor of Odcombe in Somerset and Devon, which he secured for his eldest son. [See App. B] Walter Brito III died in 1199, leaving as heirs two sisters.[30] The son of one sister, Walter Croc, had his right to half of his uncle's holdings challenged soon afterwards, and he offered a 200 mark fine to have an assize of *mort d'ancestor*. His opponent proffered double that sum to have, instead, an inquest into whether or not his father had been disseized unjustly by King Henry II.[31] The assize went forward, however, and the jurors declared that Walter Brito had died seized of his barony and that Walter Croc was his nearest heir. Somehow Walter was persuaded promptly to surrender his half of the honor to King John for William Briwerre's son, Richard Briwerre, to hold in-chief of the king. William took care to have Walter's concession recorded on the pipe roll.[32] Two years later, Briwerre won the king's consent to take the other half of the honor for his son as part of a 500 mark fine he had proffered for other favors. The husband of Brito's other sister came to the *curia regis* and conceded her half to William.[33] Years afterwards, jurors in an inquisition *post mortem* recalled what they thought had happened, declaring that

---

[28]The five husbands were Henry de Clinton, Miles and Richard de Beauchamp, Geoffrey fitz Geoffrey, and Adulf de Gatesden, *Rot. Lit. Pat.*, p. 41; *Red Book of the Exchequer*, ed. Hubert Hall, Rolls Series (London, 1897), pp. 137, 173. See *Rot. de Obl. et Fin.*, pp. 145, 149, 151, for holdings of the sisters' husbands in 1201.

[29]On Briwerre's wealth, see my *Men Raised from the Dust*, pp. 76–77, 80–85. Another *curialis*, Hugh Bardolf, likely engaged in money-lending (Ralph V. Turner, *The English Judiciary in the Age of Glanvill and Bracton, c. 1179–1240* [Cambridge, 1985], p. 118).

[30]Painter, *King John*, p. 78; Sanders, *English Baronies*, p. 132.

[31]*Pipe Roll 1 John*, pp. 128, 238; *Rot. de Obl. et Fin.*, pp. 10, 23, 171. Apparently John de Montacute, who brought the action, was an under-tenant, *Curia Regis Rolls*, Public Record Office (London, 1923–), 1: 139, Trinity 1200. See a plea of service between John and William Briwerre, *Curia Regis Rolls*, 12: 115, no. 577.

[32]*Pipe Roll 2 John*, pp. 99–100; *Rot. de Obl. et Fin.*, p. 184, part of Briwerre's acquisition of the daughters of Hugh de Morvill.

[33]*Pipe Roll 4 John*, p. 256, Richard de Hescombe.

these lands "had been alienated from their just heirs through the power of Lord William Briwerre the elder."[34]

Whatever jurors of a later generation thought of William's dealings with Walter Croc, the two men remained close, perhaps due to Walter's financial difficulties. Here, too, the explanation for their relationship may be William Briwerre's behind-the-scenes financial dealings. About 1213, Walter granted Briwerre additional land at Draycote, Wilts., in return for a cash payment and service of two knights.[35] Walter Croc seems to have been plagued with debts. In 1220, he sought to escape paying a 135 mark debt to a moneylender by entering a monastic house.[36] At the time Walter took his religious vows, his heir was a brother who renounced the inheritance in favor of his own underage son, whom the king promptly placed in William Briwerre's custody.[37] Had Walter's earlier surrender of his inheritance to Briwerre had also been an attempt to escape creditors?

A wonderfully complicated case is the inheritance of Henry II's justiciar, Richard de Lucy (d. 1179). Uncertainties about succession to his properties continued into Henry III's reign, due to the number of daughters and granddaughters who outlived male heirs, bringing into play the principle of *parage*. [See App. C] William Briwerre became involved in the complexities, seeking to profit from them. Geoffrey de Lucy, eldest son of the justiciar Richard, had predeceased him, and Geoffrey's two sons died in turn without offspring early in Richard I's reign. This left as claimants to the Lucy legacy Geoffrey de Lucy's daughters, Rose and Maud. To complicate matters more, these two sisters had three aunts, daughters of Richard de Lucy whose descendants also claimed portions of the Lucy lands.[38] A further complication was the Lucy family's remarkable lack of imagination in choices of names; the names Rose, Maud, Geoffrey, and Richard recur over and over.

Richard de Lucy had inherited from his father several fees in East Anglia and Kent.[39] The honor of Ongar, his chief holding and *caput* of all his lands, he had created for himself, however. It consisted of some thirty knights' fees,

---

[34]*Calendar of Inquisitions Post Mortem*, Public Record Office (London, 1904–), 1: 191, no. 597, following the death of Joan Briwerre.

[35]P.R.O., DL 42/2, f. 200d.

[36]*Curia Regis Rolls*, 8: 135, Michaelmas 1219; 9: 259, Hilary 1220. His creditor was William de St. Michael. Earlier in 1216, he had lost land because of debts to the Jews (*Rot. Lit. Claus.*, 1: 272b).

[37]*Exc. Rot Fin.*, 1: 41; P.R.O. SC 1/1, no. 184.

[38]See J. H. Round, "The Heirs of Richard de Lucy," *The Genealogist* 15 (1906): 129–33; and "The Honour of Ongar," *Transactions of the Essex Archaeological Society*, n. s. 7 (1900): 142–52.

[39]*Red Book of the Exchequer*, 1: 351–52; 2: 639. His Kent estates included the manor of Lesnes (or Westwood or Erith), half of which he used to endow his abbey of Lesnes.

chiefly in Essex, but with fees as far away as Cornwall. This Lucy barony was carved out of three other honors, not held in-chief of the king.[40] It fell to Richard de Lucy's second son, Godfrey bishop of Winchester, as his nephews' guardian.[41] The picture is clouded, however, since Godfrey held some Lucy lands by his own right of inheritance.[42] Because much of Richard de Lucy's lands consisted of acquisitions, he could have given portions to his younger son and daughters as he chose. Both the *Leges Henrici Primi* and *Glanvill* recognized a landholder's right to grant away his acquired lands as he chose.[43]

In 1194, King Richard I and Godfrey de Lucy quarrelled, and the king disseized the bishop of his guardianship of Ongar. Following her uncle's fall from royal favor, the widowed Rose de Lucy, known by her late husband's toponymic as Rose of Dover, then sought half the honor as her right. She offered the king a £700 fine to have half her grandfather's honor and for freedom to remarry as she pleased.[44] She paid £200 at once, but soon defaulted on her payments and evidently failed to secure seizin. The king then handed part of the honor to Geoffrey de Lascelles, Poitevin husband of Rose's sister, Maud.[45] By 1206, Geoffrey de Lascelles had disappeared from the scene, either dead or returning to the Continent, and custody of Ongar had passed to the justiciar.[46]

Godfrey de Lucy recovered the remaining Lucy lands, for he made a £1000 fine in 1198 to have that part of the Lucy inheritance not included in Rose's fine. Early in John's reign, the bishop of Winchester was holding the Cornwall fees plus land in Essex and the honor of Lesnes, Kent.[46a] His death in 1204 reopened the question of the Lucy inheritance. Lawsuits from early in the reign of Henry III give

---

[40]Round, "Ongar," p. 142, for fees of the honor of Boulogne, of earldoms of Gloucester and Cornwall.

[41]*Pipe Roll 1 Ric. I* (Record Commission edition), p. 20; *Pipe Roll 2 Ric. I* (Pipe Roll Soc.), p. 104; *6 Ric. I*, pp. 24, 28, xxi–xii.

[42]See *Curia Regis Rolls*, 8: 25–26, for a claim that Godfrey had held his father's barony of Lesnes, Kent, by inheritance.

[43]*Leges Henrici Primi*, ed. L. J. Downer (Oxford, 1972), pp. 224, 70, 21: "The first-born son shall have the father's ancestral fee [*feodum*]; the latter shall give any purchases or subsequent acquisitions of his to whomever he prefers" (*Glanvill*, 7: 1, p. 71).

[44]*Pipe Roll 6 Ric. I*, p. 250. She had been married to Fulbert of Dover, baron of Chilham, Kent, Sanders, *English Baronies*, p. 111.

[45]*Pipe Roll 2 Ric. I*, p. 4, Geoffrey de Lascelles and his brother Charles came to England from overseas. *Pipe Roll 7 Ric. I*, p. 217, he has Ongar; also *8 Ric. I*, p. 111; *9 Ric. I*, p. 63; *10 Ric. I*, p. 126; *1 John*, p. 86; *2 John*, p. 37; *3 John*, p. 58; *4 John*, p. 259; *5 John*, p. 123. For honor of Gloucester fees, see *Pipe Roll 1 John*, p. 37; *4 John*, p. 283; *5 John*, p. 83; *6 John*, p. 231; *7 John*, p. 104. For Cornwall fees, see *Pipe Roll 8 Ric. I*, p. 142; *1 John*, p. 186; *5 John*, p. 83; *6 John*, p. 40–41. Pipe rolls for Richard I also mention a William de Lascelles, who held land in Cumberland and of the honor of Peverel of Nottingham.

[46]*Pipe Roll 8 John*, p. 19. Geoffrey de Lascelles disappears from the pipe rolls after this entry. *Victoria County History, Essex* 4: 160, note, suggests that he was killed in the fighting in Normandy.

[46a]*Pipe Roll 10 Ric. I*, p. 26.

different versions of what had happened. In one suit the tenant of Lesnes, grandson of one of Godfrey's sisters, maintained that on the bishop's death that honor had passed to his three sisters to hold *in proparte sororum*, that is, sharing as co-heirs. The claimants, however, held that Godfrey de Lucy had only held the land as custodian for his nieces.[47] In another plea, it was argued that Godfrey had handed over his holdings to Robert fitz Walter, son of his sister Maud—not to be confused with his niece Maud—and to Gilbert de Montfichet, husband of another of his sisters.[48] Following Bishop Godfrey's death, his nephew, Robert fitz Walter, proffered 300 marks for his uncle's lands and for recognition as his heir; and the knight service owed to Godfrey in Cornwall and in Kent went to him.[49]

William Briwerre, however, gained custody of the Ongar lands that the bishop had held before his death.[50] Rose of Dover, upon her uncle's death in 1204, saw an opportunity to revive her struggle for her grandfather's lands, but still widowed, she fell into William Briwerre's custody. He offered King John 800 marks for Rose's custody, for her son's custody, and for the boy's marriage.[51] The next year—1205—Rose remarried without royal permission, and she offered 100 marks and two palfreys to secure her dower lands.[52] Two years later, she offered King John another £100 and paid the balance of her earlier offerings, so that he should return to her and her new husband the Lucy barony which her brothers had once held, and which she claimed by hereditary right. Briwerre was supporting Rose's suit financially, standing behind Rose as a pledge for her new £100 offering, and he witnessed the royal writ to the sheriffs placing her in possession.[53]

Rose and her custodian, William Briwerre, began to cooperate in an attempt to win the Lucy lands still held by her cousin Robert fitz Walter. By now they were connected still more closely, since Briwerre had married one of his daugh-

---

[47]*Curia Regis Rolls*, 8: 25–26.

[48]*Bracton's Note Book*, ed. F. W. Maitland (Cambridge, 1887), 3: no. 1764, dated 1227.

[49]*Pipe Roll 6 John*, p. 34, fine for the bishop's inheritance, but Robert must stand to right in the *curia regis* should anyone wish to plead against him. For other evidence of Robert in possession, see *Rot. Lit. Claus.*, 1: 14; *Red Book of the Exchequer*, 1: 161; 2: 539, *Pipe Roll 13 John*, p. 160, Cornwall, "Heirs of Richard de Lucy owe 20 marks, but Robert fitz Walter is quit by king's writ." Round, *Genealogist*, p. 132, says that Robert was named by Godfrey heir to Diss, Norf.

[50]*Rot. Lit. Claus.*, 1: 8b.

[51]*Rot. de Obl. et Fin.*, p. 229, £800; but pp. 321–22, the fine appears as 800 marks; *Pipe Roll 7 John*, p. 117. Rose's son was Fulbert II de Dover.

[52]*Pipe Roll 7 John*, p. 195; *Rot. de Obl. et Fin.*, pp. 261–62, 267. She married Nicholas fitz Alan. William Briwerre was to have the autumn harvest, however.

[53]*Rot. de Obl. et Fin.*, p. 414.

ters to Rose's son or grandson.[54] Robert fitz Walter's quarrel with King John meant that Rose's prospects improved markedly. In October 1212 the king commanded that all the Lucy lands held by Robert be turned over to William Briwerre, and a month later, the king granted her half the Lucy barony.[55] The day of the royal grant, she and her new husband granted to William Briwerre the service of all her eleven knights in Cornwall, which he was to hold of her.[56] Sidney Painter concluded, "Thus Rose recovered her inheritance at the expense of giving most of it to William Briwerre as a fief."[57]

Usually sons succeeded to their fathers' baronies without difficulty, although they sometimes had to resort to proffers of fines and purchase of political influence to secure what they regarded as their rightful inheritance. The pipe rolls record fines offered the Angevin kings for inheritances, in addition to relief, and reliefs rising far above the customary £100, sometimes even from undoubted sons and heirs.[58] The oblations increased whenever the succession was more complicated than simply from father to eldest son, and whenever any doubt about hereditary right might arise. As Holt wrote, "The more distant the succession the more likely that the claimant would have to pay a heavy *finis terrae* or offer a high price for the good will or arbitration of the king."[59] To illustrate, the period 1189–1237 shows brothers seeking succession to brothers' baronies thirty times, at least eight of whom (26%) had to offer very large fines. Robert de Vere offered 1,000 marks in 1214 for the inheritance of his brother, the earl

---

[54]Sanders, *English Baronies*, p. 111. Young Fulbert d.s.p. *ante* 1212.

[55]*Rot. Lit. Claus.*, 1: 125, 5 Oct.

[56]*Rot. Lit. Claus*, 1: 126b, 127; *Rot. Chart.*, pp. 189, 190; PRO DL10/61, 10/63; DL 42/2, f 225.

[57]Painter, *King John*, p. 76. Suits continued into Henry III's reign over the Lucy lands, as descendants of Richard de Lucy's daughters—Robert fitz Walter, Richard de Montfichet, and Richard de Umfraville—and his son Geoffrey's descendants battled each other. E.g. *Curia Regis Rolls*, 8: 25–26; 9: 277; 11: 77–78, no. 416; 12: 23–24, no. 136; 13: 571, no. 2703; 13: 471–72, no. 2213; 14: 186, no. 919; 14: 435–36, no. 1717; also *Bracton's Note Book*, 2: no. 476; 3: no. 1764.

[58]Painter, *King John*, pp. 219–21. High reliefs continued after John's death; e.g. Nigel II Mowbray paid £500, 1223/24, *Exc. Rot. Fin.*, 1: 113; Henry de Scales owed 190 marks as fine and relief, 1218, *Pipe Roll 2 Henry III*, p. 32.

[59]E.g. Richard de Clifford, a younger son, proffered 300 marks, presumably because his elder brother was outside the kingdom (*Pipe Roll 2 Ric. I*, p. 126). Ralph de Somery offered 400 marks for his uncle Gervase Paynell's barony (*Pipe Roll 10 Ric. I*, p. 122; *1 John*, p. 164). William de Werbirton and Giles de Muncele offered 500 marks for having the inheritance of Juliana, wife of William fitz Aldulf, "whose nearer heirs they are, as they say" (*Pipe Roll 2 John*, p. 206). Robert de Girros offered 20 marks for his inheritance from his aunt, *Pipe Roll 1 John*, p. 75. Five daughters and heirs of Stephen of Turnham offered 20 marks, a palfrey, and promised to pay their father's £100 debt for having his land (*Pipe Roll 16 John*, p. 32). Robert Marmion, a younger son, offered £500 for his father's lands until his elder brother should return to the king's peace; even then he was to retain certain specified manors (*Pipe Roll 2 Henry III*, pp. 54–55). See also Holt, "Politics and Property," p. 24.

of Oxford.⁶⁰ Less clear claims by more distant male kin provided occasion for a more active royal role.⁶¹

William Briwerre benefited from this uncertainty of male succession, just as he had from uncertain female succession. Several times successful male claimants to lands promptly granted part of their newly won estates to Briwerre to hold of them, as Rose of Dover had done. He held several manors as a gift from Fulk Paynell, whose generosity is easily explained.⁶² Fulk had fled England around 1185, forfeiting the barony of Bampton, Devon, which he had purchased with a 1000 mark proffer. William Briwerre had custody of the lands at the time of King John's accession, when Fulk offered another 1,000 marks to recover them.⁶³ No doubt, Fulk's gift was in appreciation for William's political influence and monetary aid. Not only was Briwerre's friendship with the king useful in persuading him to restore Fulk Paynell's lands, but he also lent financial support, providing 220 marks of Fulk's fine.⁶⁴ Another link between William Briwerre and Fulk Paynell was the marriage of one of Briwerre's daughters to Fulk's son.⁶⁵

In 1199, William de Ferrers, earl of Derby, also generously granted William Briwerre the manor of Blisworth, Northants., a dependency of Higham Ferrers that the earl had just received from King John. These estates were part of the honor of Peak, Derbyshire, which Henry Plantagenet had seized from the wicked William Peverel shortly after succeeding to the English throne; Richard Lionheart had granted the honor to his brother, Count John. The earl had a claim because his grandfather, Robert de Ferrers, had once held part of Peak through his marriage to Peverel's daughter and heir. [See App. D] The editor of the

---

⁶⁰*Pipe Roll 16 John*, p. 11. Hugh d'Aubigny proffered 2500 marks for his brother's earldom of Arundel, shortly before he came of age, 1233/34 (P.R.O. C.60/33, m. 11; *Exc. Rot. Fin.*, 1: 250, 399). Also 200 marks for half the barony of Poorstock in 1198 (*Pipe Roll 10 Ric. I*, pp. 218, 221); 300 marks for Sudeley, also in 1198 (*10 Ric. I*, p. 7; *Memoranda Roll 1 John*, p. 39); Hugh de Bolbec offered 200 marks and two palfreys for his brother's barony of Whitchurch, 1205 (*Rot. de Obl. et Fin.*, p. 314); 300 marks and seven palfreys offered for Castle Carey, 1207 (*Pipe Roll 9 John*, p. 605); Warin de Montchesney offered 2000 marks for his inheritance from his brother (*Pipe Roll 16 John*, p. 31). Largest by far is the 10,000 mark fine offered by Nicholas de Stuteville, 1205 (see note 71 below).

⁶¹E.g. contention over Cottingham, see Ralph V. Turner, *The King and his Courts* (Ithaca, N.Y., 1968), pp. 150–61; for Totnes, pp. 160–61; for Trowbridge, pp. 163–64; for Richmond, see James W. Alexander, *Ranulf of Chester, A Relic of the Conquest* (Athens, Ga., 1983), pp. 10, 20.

⁶²*Rot. Chart.*, p. 28; P.R.O. DL. 42/2, f. 217d. For other gifts of Fulk Paynell, see *Cal. Inq. Post. Mort.*, 1: 34, no. 139.

⁶³*Pipe Roll 26 Henry II*, pp. xxvii, 94; *31 Henry II*, pp. xxviii, 164, 182; *10 Richard I*, p. 178; *Rot. de Obl. et Fin.*, pp. 4, 71; Sanders, *Baronies*, p. 5.

⁶⁴*Pipe Roll 6 Ric. I*, pp. 30, 167, 172; *Memoranda Roll 1 John*, p. 73; *Pipe Roll 2 John*, pp. 227, 230, 235.

⁶⁵Sanders, *Baronies*, pp. 5, 123.

Complete Peerage exclaims, "It is astonishing that anyone could ever have had the hardihood to deny that in 1199 the Earl of Derby was the right heir of William Peverel of Nottingham."[66] Following John's coronation, William de Ferrers withdrew his claim against the new king for the honor; and in exchange for a 2000 mark fine, he received Higham Ferrers in compensation.[67] Doubtless, Briwerre won Blisworth as reward for his role in the negotiations.

In 1204 the escheated barony of Burun or Horsley, came to William from King John, although another claimant, Peter de Sandiacre, had held it for several years.[68] Roger de Burun was said to have left a son and heir, but for some unknown reason he failed to succeed to the barony; and the honor had lapsed to the crown in 1194. Peter de Sandiacre had secured the barony in 1198, offering £100, and claiming it as his inheritance. Another party, seeking the property in 1200, brought an assize of mort d'ancestor which was postponed *per preceptum regis* for hearing before the king; but no conclusion is recorded.[69] Peter de Sandiacre was compensated with other land when the king made the grant to William Briwerre, although the king kept for himself Hareston Castle, which he had recently constructed on land lying within the honor.[70]

One case, centering on the Percy honor in Yorkshire, Topcliffe, raised a question of the representative principle similar to the *casus regis*, John's claim to the English Crown versus that of his nephew Arthur of Brittany, that is, the claim of a younger son versus that of his nephew, an elder son's lineal descendant standing as his father's representative. [See App. E] The uncertainties of *casus regis* gave rise to much litigation. As J. C. Holt has written, "Wherever the *casus regis* was replicated, uncle and nephew in knightly and lesser families battled it out in the courts."[71] At the time *Glanvill* was written, c. 1187/89, the law governing descent in such cases was unclear. The author wrote that "a great legal problem [*iuris dubitatio*] arises as to which is to be preferred to the other

---

[66]*Complete Peerage*, 4: 766.

[67]*Complete Peerage*, 4: 765–66; Sanders, *English Baronies*, p. 136; Painter, *King John*, pp. 15–16; *Pipe Roll 1 John*, p. 16; *Rot. de Obl. et Fin.*, p. 3.

[68]William displaced Peter de Sandiacre at Horsley, *Rot. Chart.*, p. 123; *Pipe Roll 6 John*, p. 161; *Pipe Roll 7 John*, p. 232.

[69]*Pipe Roll 10 Ric. I*, p. 118; *Curia Regis Rolls*, 1: 268; Walter Malet brought the assize, paying 20 marks, *Pipe Roll 2 John*, p. 20

[70]*Pipe Roll 6 John*, p. 161; *Pipe Roll 7 John*, p. 232; *Rot. Chart.*, 123; Sanders, *English Baronies*, pp. 122–23; Painter, *King John*, pp. 26, 76–77.

[71]J. C. Holt, "Feudal Society and the Family in early Medieval England: III. Patronage and Politics," *T. R. H. S.* 5th ser. 34 (1984): 20. E.g. Nicholas de Stuteville's 1205 fine of 10,000 marks for his brother William's inheritance, although William left a legitimate son (*Pipe Roll 7 John*, p. 59). For details, see Painter, *King John*, pp. 334–36.

in that succession, namely, whether the son or the grandson." He noted that some favored the younger son, while others felt that the grandson should be preferred to his uncle. The author of *Glanvill* tended toward the latter view, which accorded with strict lineal succession.[72] Until Arthur of Brittany's sister, Eleanor, died in 1241, no English judge could have been expected to follow the representative principle, for he would have been casting doubt on the king's claim to his crown.[73] The justices of John and Henry III avoided giving judgment in such cases, marking them for consultation with the king or his council.[74] The author of *Bracton* seems to have favored the grandchild over the uncle, but dared not say so directly because of the precedent of the *casus regis*. Bracton states that such cases could not proceed to judgment, but must remain in suspense unless the parties could reach agreement.[75]

The Percy inheritance illustrates the problem. [See App. F] In 1175, the honor of Topcliffe had descended to two sisters, Maud and Agnes de Percy. These sisters died early in John's reign within a short time of one another, Agnes apparently first in 1203, and then her sister Maud soon after, in 1204. Since Maud left no children, next in line were her sister Agnes's offspring: a grandson, William III de Percy, son of her deceased elder son; and Richard de Percy, a younger son.[76] William de Percy was a minor in William Briwerre's custody, and the boy was married to one of his daughters. King John, instead of deciding in favor of one or the other claimant, made a division of lands. Probably the king would have preferred to place the entire honor in William Briwerre's custody, but the similarity of Richard de Percy's claim to Topcliffe to his own claim to his throne prevented him.[77] King John commanded that Richard be put in possession of all his mother's lands and all lands that his aunt had held of the earl of Chester in Yorkshire, and that William Briwerre, William de Percy's custodian, should take all Maud's lands except those held of Chester.[78]

This division set in motion a long series of legal actions, partly because of genuine uncertainty over which lands had belonged to which sister, but also

---

[72] *Glanvill*, 7: 3, pp. 77–78.

[73] T. F. T. Plucknett, *A Concise History of the Common Law* (5th ed.; London, 1956), p. 718.

[74] E.g., Doris M. Stenton, ed., *Pleas before the King or his Justices*, 2, Selden Society 68 (1949): 144, no. 528; *Bracton's Note Book*, 3: 595, no. 1766.

[75] *Bracton*, f. 64b, 2: 189; f. 267b, 3: 283–85, f. 267b; 4: 46, f. 327b; 173–74, ff. 374–374b. F. Pollock and F. W. Maitland, *A History of English Law* (Cambridge, 1898), 2: 285.

[76] Sanders, *English Baronies*, p. 148; *Complete Peerage*, 10: 450–53.

[77] J. C. Holt, *The Northerners* (Oxford, 1960), pp. 21–22.

[78] *Rot. Lit. Claus.*, 1: 11b. See also *Pipe Roll 8 John*, p. 196 (1206); *Pipe Roll 9 John*, p. 82 (1207); William Briwerre evidently had control of Agnes' lands, but soon they were in Richard de Percy's hands.

because neither side was willing to accept the division. In 1212, William Briwerre brought suit against Richard de Percy for intruding on his ward's possessions. Richard offered two palfreys for an inquest to declare whether the property in question belonged to his or his nephew's inheritance, but since he could not deny that Briwerre held seizin as William de Percy's guardian, his suit was dismissed without the inquest ever being taken.[79] In 1214, William de Percy brought suit against Richard for five Topcliffe manors, which he claimed he had held while in Briwerre's custody; but the action was also dismissed due to a flaw in the writ. Percy had named among the manors he sought one that he already held.[80]

No doubt, Richard de Percy's dissatisfaction with the division contributed to his role as one of the leaders among the Northerners in the rebellion against King John. William de Percy, on the other hand, saw loyalty to John as the way to win land from his uncle, and he served in the 1214 campaign to Poitou. Richard's role in the baronial rebellion led to seizure of his estates, which were confided to his nephew's custody.[81] Henry III's counselors in May 1217 returned all Richard's land to William de Percy as his right, "inasmuch as he is the nearer heir who is in our service." Once Richard de Percy had returned to the king's service, however, he instituted proceedings to reclaim his possessions.[82] Finally, an agreement was reached in 1218 for apportionment of the lands between uncle and nephew, but that did not end litigation, which dragged on until 1234.[83]

What does this tracing of William Briwerre's acquisitions of estates tell us about law, government, and society in Angevin England? According to one authority, Henry II's reforms concerning landed inheritance had grown out of "immediate political-military problems." The king had wished to reduce his magnates' military strength by making it more likely that their tenants' lands would descend to minor sons, widows, or daughters.[84] No doubt, reducing the military resources of potentially over-mighty aristocrats continued to motivate monarchs. The fate of the earldom of Chester following the deaths of Earl Ranulf III and John the Scot in 1232 and 1237 illustrates well enough such a motive.[85]

[79] *Curia Regis Rolls*, 6: 321.

[80] *Curia Regis Rolls*, 7: 160.

[81] *Rot. Lit. Claus.*, 1: 207, 250, 308; Holt, *Northerners*, p. 67.

[82] *Rot. Lit. Claus.*, 1: 308, 339, 360b.

[83] *Complete Peerage*, 10: 450, note b.

[84] Robert Palmer, "Origins of Property," pp. 16–19.

[85] Richard Eales, "Henry III and the End of the Norman Earldom of Chester," in *Thirteenth Century England, Proceedings of the Newcastle upon Tyne Conference 1985*, ed. P. R. Coss and S. D. Lloyd (Woodbridge, Suff., 1986), pp. 100–12.

Yet royal intervention in baronial successions cannot be separated from the ambition of *curiales* such as William Briwerre. Royal counselors had their own reasons for promoting principles of inheritance similar to those the common law courts were applying, making more likely succession of minors or division among heiresses. Royal patronage in the form of marriages to heiresses provided an easy means for *curiales* and their kinsmen to rise in social rank and wealth, while wardships of minors and marriages to widows with dower estates offered them temporary control of wide lands. The initiative in many instances came from *curiales* and other *familiares regis* in a position to spy disputed inheritances, wardships, and marriages coming available.[86] Not only did royal servants secure lands for themselves, but they used their wealth and influence in support of others' claims. Their financial resources enabled them to support claimants with advances of cash or at least to provide security for their proffers to the king. Successful suitors then rewarded them out of newly won lands, as grants made to William Briwerre show. The ambition of such royal servants as Briwerre alarmed conservative moralists, many aristocrats, and jealous colleagues at court, who saw them as "new men" threatening the traditional social order.[87]

Henry II and his successors certainly insisted on more freedom in determining baronial inheritances than they allowed their barons to exercise in deciding succession to their tenants' holdings. The cases involving William Briwerre are sufficient to show that King John still exercised discretionary power in situations where succession was uncertain, at a time when his royal justices were working out strict rules of hereditary succession that were limiting lords' freedom to pick and choose among heirs. The king might decide to honor his courts' rules or not, depending on what man — or woman — the chances of heredity created as heir, and depending on whether or not it served royal purposes to keep a barony undivided. When lordships descended to daughters, the king usually allowed equal division among them to proceed, although occasionally one daughter's right might be ignored. Division among heiresses proved advantageous both to the monarch and his servants, giving him added lands with which to reward them, while preventing any one of them from getting too powerful. A recent study of succession to baronies under Henry III takes note of his marriages of heiresses to his kin and to foreign friends, and of the concern this caused the baronage.[88] The king had more freedom of action in instances of lateral male heirs, where genuine uncertainty about priority of hereditary right gave scope for royal intervention. The question of descent to a younger son or

---

[86]*English Judiciary*, pp. 52–63; 112–120.

[87]Turner, *Men Raised from the Dust*, pp. 1–13.

[88]Waugh, "Marriage, Class, and Royal Lordship," pp. 199–205.

to the son of a deceased elder son was a confused one, with or without the complications of the *casus regis*.

In such uncertain situations, rights of heirs other than undoubted legitimate sons or daughters were not absolute, and strict hereditary claim alone might not move the king. Financial inducements such as large fines, need for estates with which to reward faithful *curiales*, or political considerations such as preventing a baron from building up his power base weighed more heavily than purely legal factors in deciding such cases. Such judgments were not usually made by the professional justices who presided over the assizes, but were made by a political process, private consultations with intimate counselors, or by a financial process of negotiations at the Exchequer.

The monarch saw uncertainty of succession as an opportunity for patronage, a supply of estates with which to reward royal *familiares*, such as William Briwerre. *Familiares* saw the opportunity first and then persuaded King John to favor their cause. The role of *curiales* as custodians cannot be overlooked, as they proved eager bidders for wardships of minor heirs. William Briwerre played a prominent part in the Rose of Dover and the William de Percy cases because he was their guardian. Neither can their financial resources be overlooked, for royal servants such as Briwerre apparently had available considerable cash, which gave them advantages. They could advance funds to suitors or, at least, stand surety for their proffers to the king; and they expected rewards with grants of land from successful claimants' baronial inheritances.

Old landed families had good reason for their fears that King John was threatening their lawful rights of inheritance. Articles of *Magna Carta* show their efforts at ending his arbitrary seizures of land that they considered their heritage and his exorbitant reliefs for land that they felt to be theirs by hereditary right.[89] The barons had as much to fear from rapacious royal *familiares*. Enjoying easy access to the king, his servants secured custodies of coheirs, either married them or married them off to their sons, and began legal proceedings to add as much of the inheritance as possible to their families' possessions. The aggressiveness at law of such new men as William Briwerre may have contributed to baronial distrust of them as "raised from the dust."

---

[89]*Magna Carta*, articles 2, 3, 39, 52. See Waugh, *The Lordship of England*, pp. 83–84; J. C. Holt, *Magna Carta* (Cambridge, 1965), pp. 115–25, and Appendix IV, pp. 316–37, for text of the Charter.

APPENDIX A
BIDUN

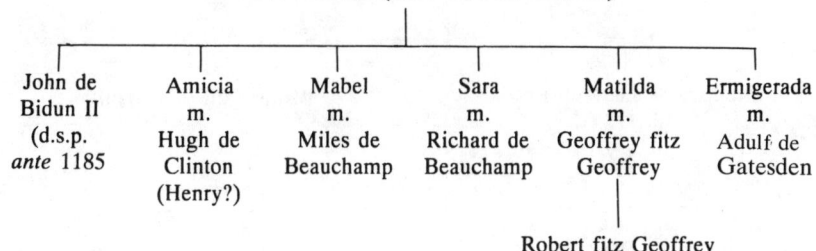

APPENDIX B
ODCOMBE, SOMERSET

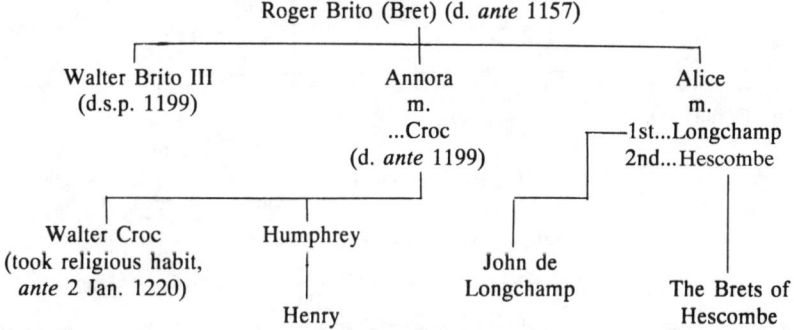

APPENDIX C
THE LUCY INHERITANCE

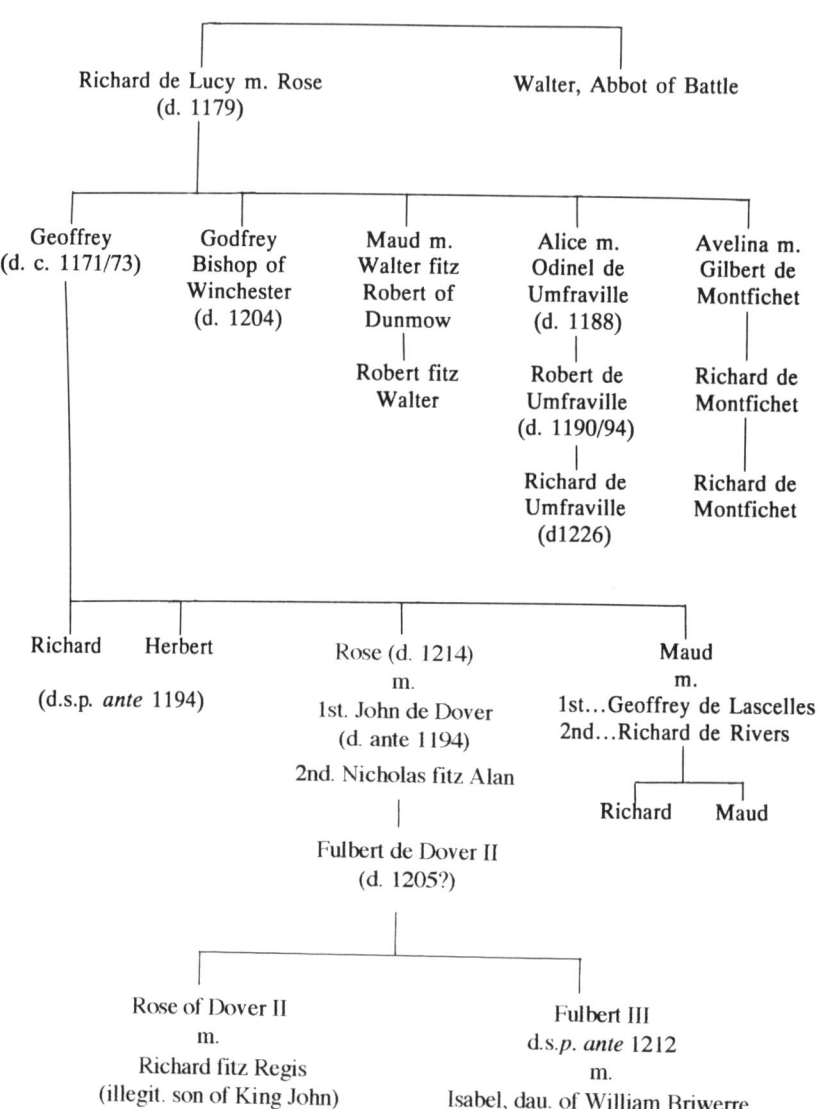

The King's Will in Inheritance of Baronies

APPENDIX D
PEVEREL OF NOTTINGHAM

William II Peverel
(d. *post* 1155)
├── Henry
└── Margaret
    m.
    Robert de Ferrers
    Earl of Derby
    (d. *ante* 1160)
    │
    William de Ferrers
    (d. 1190)
    │
    William de Ferrers
    Earl of Derby
    (d. 1247)

APPENDIX E
THE CASUS REGIS

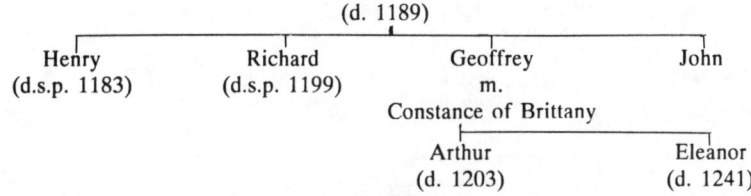

Henry II (d. 1189)
├── Henry (d.s.p. 1183)
├── Richard (d.s.p. 1199)
├── Geoffrey m. Constance of Brittany
│   ├── Arthur (d. 1203)
│   └── Eleanor (d. 1241)
└── John

APPENDIX F
THE PERCIES OF TOPCLIFFE, YORKS.

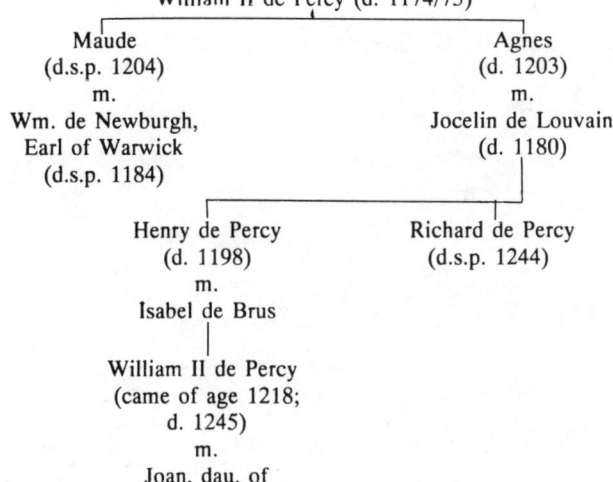

William II de Percy (d. 1174/75)
├── Maude (d.s.p. 1204)
│   m. Wm. de Newburgh, Earl of Warwick (d.s.p. 1184)
└── Agnes (d. 1203)
    m. Jocelin de Louvain (d. 1180)
    ├── Henry de Percy (d. 1198)
    │   m. Isabel de Brus
    │   │
    │   William II de Percy
    │   (came of age 1218; d. 1245)
    │   m. Joan, dau. of William Briwerre
    └── Richard de Percy (d.s.p. 1244)

16

The Mandeville Inheritance, 1189–1236: Its Legal, Political and Social Context

Geoffrey Fitz Peter through his marriage to Beatrice de Say gained the Mandeville honor, catapulting him into the highest levels of the English aristocracy by 1191, and by 1199 securing for him the title of earl of Essex. The honor was one of the richest feudal lordships in late twelfth-century England, consisting of 110 knights' fees in ten counties, one of only three with an annual income of over £500.[1] The story of Geoffrey's acquisition of the Mandeville inheritance and of its fate following his death in 1213 illustrates 'the interplay between inheritance and lordship,' the intertwining of political and legal considerations governing succession to great honors held in-chief of the king.[2] It is, I hope, a very Painteresque topic with its mixture of genealogy, feudal law, politics, and patronage. It brings me back to my doctoral research under Sidney Painter's direction, when I first examined the working of the king's will within the common law courts.

By the late twelfth century, the principle that hereditary succession guaranteed title had triumphed, and this threatened lords' rights to choose freely their tenants.[3] Although the common law was drawing up careful rules of seniority for heirs and heiresses, the descent of the Mandeville lands following William de Mandeville IV's death in 1189 and Geoffrey Fitz Peter's in 1213 illustrates the improbability of strict linear succession. The possibility was always present that the direct patrilinear line would fail and that more distant kin would succeed to the lordship.[4]

The descent of the Mandeville honor touches upon two uncertain points of law: first, the problem of the partition of fees among co-heiresses in case of

---

[1] See my *Men Raised from the Dust* (Philadelphia, 1988), 55–62; see Appendix A and Appendix B, infra, 169–70.

[2] J.C. Holt, 'Feudal Society and the Family in early Medieval England: II. Notions of Patrimony,' *Transactions of the Royal Historical Society* 5th ser. 33 (1983): 207.

[3] Samuel E. Thorne, 'English Feudalism and Estates in Land,' *Cambridge Law Journal* (1959): 194–209.

[4] J.C. Holt, 'Feudal Society and the Family in early Medieval England: III. Patronage and Politics,' *Transactions of the Royal Historical Society* 5th ser. 34 (1984): 15–16; also Scott L. Waugh, 'Marriage, Class, and Royal Lordship in England under Henry III,' *Viator* 16 (1985): 183–85.

default of male heirs; and second, the *casus regis*, or uncertainty about the line of descent when an elder son dies leaving both a child, heir of his body, and a younger brother. While the royal justices may have wanted to spell out strict rules to bind lords in such cases, the king wanted to preserve his own freedom of action. How did royal judges treat these cases, in which the lord was the monarch, greatest of all feudal lords? Or did they have an opportunity to treat them at all?

Clearly, in an uncertain situation such as the death of an earl of Essex, without any son to succeed him and with collateral claimants, both male and female, the king insisted on some say in selection of the heir. The personal tie between lord and tenant, a vital element in feudal landholding earlier, was weakening by the end of the twelfth century and lords were losing control over succession to their tenants' holdings. Henry II's assizes separated title to a tenement from lordly acceptance of the tenant when the tenant was a direct descendant of the previous landholder.[5] The assizes were providing mesne tenants with security of tenure. When there was an undoubted male heir, no lord could take the land into his own hand to hold until relief was paid. The heir could take possession himself without waiting for the lord to put him into possession.[6]

While other lords were losing disciplinary power over their tenants, the power to disseize and disinherit unwelcome claimants to fees, the king insisted on maintaining his own power to regulate succession to earldoms and baronies. J.E.A. Jolliffe wrote that the Angevins 'arrogat[ed] to themselves a discretionary power which they denied their vassals.'[7] The king's will, his *benevolentia* or *malevolentia* were facts of political life, accepted 'with a curious equanimity,' even seen as a legitimate aspect of royal government.[8] The peace settlement between William Longchamp and Count John in 1191, for example, concedes that free tenants should not be disseized at will by royal officers, but it equates disseizin 'by the king's command' with disseizin 'by judgment of the king's court according to lawful customs and assizes of the kingdom.'[9]

The king still regarded a personal relationship with his own tenants-in-chief as essential, and he insisted on some role in choosing the tenant whenever uncertainty of hereditary succession allowed him any choice. The Angevin monarchs resisted following rules that their courts were enforcing against other feudal lords in their treatment of tenants. They held to the old view that the heir does not succeed to his ancestor's property automatically; he only has a customary claim to be accepted as tenant, and the king will only take the

---

[5] Robert C. Palmer, 'The Origin of Property in England,' *Law and History Review* 3 (1985): 22; also Thorne, 'Feudalism and Estates in Land,' 201.

[6] S.F.C. Milsom, *The Legal Framework of English Feudalism* (Cambridge, 1976), 162–63, 171.

[7] Jolliffe, *Angevin Kingship* (London, 1955), 39.

[8] Ibid., 56, 95.

[9] *Memoriale Walteri de Coventria*, ed. William Stubbs, 2 vols., R.S. (London, 1872–73), 1: 463 (hereafter cited as Walter of Coventry).

heir's homage and place him in possession once he accepts him.[10] *Glanvill* noted that when a baron dies, his barony is taken into the king's hand even if the heir is fully of age; and it is not released until the heir has made arrangements for paying whatever relief the king demands.[11] King John sometimes hesitated long before acknowledging a lawful heir's right to his predecessor's property. The Pipe Rolls record many fines offered the Angevin kings for inheritances, in addition to relief, with the offering increasing whenever the succession was more complicated than simply from father to son. Examples are a 400-mark fine by a nephew for a barony in 1199, a 2000-mark fine by a brother for another barony in 1214, and a 2050-mark fine by another brother inheriting an earldom in 1234.[12]

J.C. Holt, RaGena de Aragon, and Charlotte Newman have looked at succession to baronies in the Anglo-Norman period, and they find that most descended without royal interference. De Aragon's estimate is 80%. Charlotte Newman found more royal interference by Henry I: nine baronies without direct male heirs passing to lateral heirs, and six which had lateral heirs failing to pass to them. Scott L. Waugh's study of baronies' descent, 1200–1330, centers more on baronial group and family interests than on royal intervention in hereditary succession.[13] To my knowledge, however, no one has made a study of the king's role in baronial inheritances for the Angevin period. The litigation that arose following the death of William de Mandeville, earl of Essex, and that continued after the death of his successor, Geoffrey Fitz Peter, can be a start. It shows how political circumstances could color legal judgments. Luckily, a chronicle account of the lawsuit survives to supplement the limited evidence of charters, Plea Rolls, and Pipe Rolls.

Geoffrey Fitz Peter was one of Henry II's *curiales* who appeared out of nowhere around 1184. The son of a forester with only one knight's fee, he quickly won several shrievalties and the post of chief royal forester. He belonged to the council left behind to govern England during Richard I's

[10] Milsom, *Legal Framework*, 163–64.

[11] *Glanvill*, ed. G.D.G. Hall, Medieval Texts (Oxford, 1965), 9: 6, p. 110.

[12] E.g. Ralph de Somery offered 400 marks for his uncle Gervase Paynell's barony, *P.R. 10 Richard I*, 122; *P.R. 1 John*, 164. William de Webirton and Giles de Muncele offered 500 marks for having the inheritance of Juliana, wife of William fitz Aldulf, 'whose nearer heirs they are, as they say,' *P.R. 2 John*, 206. Robert de Girros offered twenty marks for his inheritance from his aunt, *P.R. 1 John*, 75. Five daughters and heirs of Stephen of Turnham offered twenty marks, a palfrey, and promised to pay their father's £100 debt for having his land, *P.R. 16 John*, 32. Robert de Vere offered 1,000 marks for the inheritance of his brother, Earl Aubrey de Vere, *P.R. 16 John*, 11. Warin de Montchesney offered 2,000 marks for his inheritance from his brother, *P.R. 16 John*, 31. Hugh d'Aubigny, brother of the late earl of Arundel, made fine with Henry III for 2,050 marks to have his lands shortly before he came of age, P.R.O. C.60/33, m. 11.

[13] J.C. Holt, 'Politics and Property in Early Medieval England,' *Past and Present* 57 (1972): 30; RaGena de Aragon, 'The Growth of Secure Inheritance in Anglo-Norman England,' *Journ. Med. Hist.* 8 (1982): 383; Charlotte A. Newman, *The Anglo-Norman Nobility in the Reign of Henry I: The Second Generation* (Philadelphia, 1988), 119. Scott L. Waugh examines the descent of 195 baronies, 1200–1330, and he finds 43 (22%) descending to single heiresses and 68 (35%) partitioned among heiresses, 'Marriage, Class, and Royal Lordship,' 184–86.

crusade, and he took office as justiciar in 1198, a post he continued to hold until his death in 1213.[14] Geoffrey Fitz Peter shared the ambition of other *curiales*. As Sidney Painter wrote: 'The dearest ambition of most lay servants of the crown was to build up a barony that would enable them and their descendants to take their places among the magnates of the realm.'[15] Royal patronage soon permitted Geoffrey to fulfill that ambition. Sometime before the compilation of the *Rotuli de Dominabus* in 1185, Geoffrey had married one of his wards, a common means for royal servants to rise out of obscurity and obtain new lands and higher social status.[16]

Geoffrey's bride was Beatrice de Say, elder daughter of William de Say (d. 1177). He undoubtedly had Henry II's consent for the marriage, since heiresses were a valued royal resource, an easy means for the king to reward landless knights in his service. Geoffrey's bride was co-heiress with her younger sister to estates in Norfolk, but more important were her connections with the powerful Mandeville family, which would eventually give Geoffrey the earldom of Essex.[17] Geoffrey and his wife did not divide the Say inheritance equally with her sister, Maud, and her husband, William of Buckland; by their final concord of January 1185, Geoffrey and Beatrice gave up only one manor, the service of two tenants, and a promise of land worth £10 from future acquisitions.[18]

In a feudal society, where descent by strict male primogeniture was supposedly the rule, 'The heiress was one of the fluid elements in the social structure.'[19] As early as the time of Henry I's coronation charter, women were eligible for inheritance of fiefs.[20] The rule at that time concerning succession of daughters as heirs evidently was that the entire inheritance went to one daughter, with the lord granting it to the husband of one of the daughters, choosing whichever husband he favored. The lord would prefer, of course, a single heiress and an undivided tenement held by a loyal vassal. Although the eldest daughter and her husband acquired a right which the royal courts recognized, gradually their moral obligation to share with her sisters also won recognition. The change in this custom seems due to a specific ruling of the royal court, dating c. 1130–35. An 1145 charter refers to a *statum decretum* by which the daughters are to

---

[14] For Geoffrey's biography, see chapter 3 of my *Men Raised from the Dust*.
[15] Painter, *The Reign of King John* (Baltimore, 1949), 73.
[16] *Rotuli de Dominabus et Pueris et Puellis*, ed. J.H. Round, P.R.S. 35 (London, 1913), 49–50.
[17] G.E. C(okayne), *The Complete Peerage of England, Scotland, Ireland, Great Britain, and the United Kingdom*, eds. Vicary Gibbs, et. al., new ed., 13 vols. (London, 1910–40), 5: 123.
[18] P.R.O., DL 10/29; *P.R. 10 Richard I*, 139, manor of Bruninton; Richard I's confirmation, 1198, *Ancient Charters, Royal and Private*, ed. J.H. Round, P.R.S. 10 (1888): 108–9, no. 66. The Walden Chronicle states incorrectly that they divided the inheritance equally, *Mon. Angl.*, 4: 145.
[19] Holt, 'Feudal Society and the Family in Early Medieval England: IV. The Heiress and the Alien,' *Trans. Royal Hist. Soc.* 35 (1985): 1.
[20] *Select Charters and other Illustrations of English Constitutional History*, ed. William Stubbs, 9th ed. (Oxford, 1913), 118.

share in case of no surviving son to succeed, and the eldest cannot take her younger sisters' share *nisi vi et iniuria*.[21]

In short, the custom of *parage* described by *Glanvill* developed, by which the husband of the eldest daughter did homage to the chief lord for the whole fee, and the younger daughters and their husbands performed the service through, 'by the hand of,' the eldest daughter and her husband.[22] S.F.C. Milsom likens the manner of the younger daughters' holding to a modern trust or to widow's *maritagium*; that is, the land is the eldest daughter's, but she has a moral obligation to allow her younger sisters a share. And he sees the influence of the Church, eager to see that younger sisters had an adequate marriage-portion, in securing acceptance for such a provision.[23] By the early years of Henry III, younger sisters seeking their rightful share had available that writ *nuper obiit* to initiate an action in the royal courts.[24]

J.C. Holt does not find such lofty motives for the custom of partition among heiresses. He suggests that *Glanvill*'s rule was not yet fixed as the law of the realm at the time of the lawbook's composition, that it was not the only way to settle the descent of land when only daughters survived, but that it was what the author hoped would be the fixed rule. In Holt's view, the king, landless knights in his service, and younger daughters all benefited from division of fees among co-heirs. He points out that by 1236, the law for tenants-in-chief of the crown, at least, was that all daughters did homage to the king, all holding in-chief; and he gives examples of cases where *Glanvill*'s pattern was not followed, where a younger daughter was favored, or where the 1236 rule had been followed earlier.[25] A fine was offered in 1213 seeking division of land 'into two equal parts;' it states that such a partition between two sisters is 'according to the custom of England.' Such a division may have been customary, but one sister's husband still found it prudent to proffer 500 marks to King John. What is interesting in this case is what is left unsaid; the rights of an unmentioned third sister were being ignored.[26] Usually the Plea Rolls use less precise language, referring to a 'reasonable portion.' Does this imply that exactly equal shares were unnecessary?

---

[21] Holt, 'Feudal Society and the Family: IV,' 2–10; F.M. Stenton, *The First Century of English Feudalism, 1066–1166* (Oxford, 1932), 37–41.

[22] *Glanvill*, 7:3, p. 76; *Bracton*, ed. G.E. Woodbine, trans. S.E. Thorne, 4 vols. (Cambridge, Mass., 1968–77) fol. 66b, 2: 194.

[23] *On the Laws and Customs of England: Essays in Honor of Samuel E. Thorne*, ed. Morris S. Arnold, et al. (Chapel Hill, 1981), 69–78 (hereafter cited as *Thorne Festschrift*).

[24] Ibid., 69, 73–74.

[25] Holt, 'Feudal Society and the Family: IV,' 10–11, citing the *Statutum Hiberniae de Coheredibus*. See also *Bracton*, fol. 78, 2: 227.

[26] *Rotuli de Oblatis et Finibus*, ed. T. Duffus Hardy, Record Commission (London, 1835), 507 (hereafter cited as *Rot. de Obl. et Fin.*). Division of the barony of Cavendish, Suff., between two sisters: Mabel, widow of Hugh Bardolf; and Basilia, wife of Hugh de Odingselles. For details, see *P.R. 5 Richard I*, 124; *P.R. 6 Richard I*, 92; *P.R. 7 John*, 34, 197; *Mem. Roll 1 John*, 54: £16 13s. 4d.

Following the death of William de Mandeville in 1189, Geoffrey laid claim to the vast Mandeville honor through his wife's right. The earl had served Henry II as soldier and diplomat, and Richard I had named him co-justiciar on the eve of his departure on crusade; but Mandeville died in November or December 1189, before he could play any role in the absentee government.[27] William left neither children nor surviving brothers, so that his heir was his aunt Beatrice, who had married William de Say. *Glanvill* makes clear the line of succession: 'In default of lineal descendants, then brother or brothers succeed, or, if there are no brothers, sisters are called; if they are already dead their children are called. After these, uncles or their children are called, and lastly aunts or their children.'[28] If the earl's aunt were to be bypassed, then succession would pass to her descendants: her surviving younger son, Geoffrey de Say; or the daughters of her deceased elder son, William de Say II. At this point the succession was uncertain: should it pass to a younger son of the aged Beatrice, or to the representatives of her deceased elder son, his two daughters, one of whom was Beatrice, wife of Geoffrey Fitz Peter?

Of course, feudal law preferred a male heir over a female, even a remote male relative over a nearer female one. As *Bracton* states, 'In the matter of succession the male sex must always be preferred to the female.'[29] But succession to such a significant honor – one of England's greatest – would not remain simply a legal issue. What Holt wrote of inheritance in the Anglo-Norman period applies also to the Angevin kings: 'The more distant or debatable the claim, the more substantial would be the overlord's [king's] consent and the more likely would he be concerned with the political impact of the settlement.'[30] Also royal finances could be a factor, and the successful claimant might be the one who could offer the king the larger fine for his support.[31]

The fullest account of the rivalry between Geoffrey de Say and his neice Beatrice de Say for the Mandeville inheritance is found in the Walden Chronicle, an account strongly biased against Geoffrey Fitz Peter and one that occasionally conflicts with the record evidence. Geoffrey's acquisition of the Mandeville honor brought him patronage of Walden Abbey, and he and the monks soon quarrelled. Geoffrey resented William de Mandeville's deathbed grants to Walden of land and privileges, which embroiled him and the monks in a series of lawsuits lasting until King John's accession.[32] The chronicler wrote that Geoffrey 'took several properties away from us and gave them to his own men

---

[27] For William de Mandeville's death date as 14 Nov. 1189, see Round, *Ancient Charters*, 98.

[28] *Glanvill*, 7:4, p. 79; *Bracton*, fol. 64b, 2: 188–90.

[29] *Bracton*, fol. 65, 2: 190; 191. See a 1220 case where three sisters unsuccessfully defended their right to land from the son of their deceased brother. The justices found that because the boy was *de masculo* he should have the greater right to the land, *Curia Regis Rolls*, Public Record Office, 15 vols. (London, 1923–49), 9: 268–69.

[30] 'Politics and Property,' 22.

[31] Ibid., 24.

[32] Susan Wood, *English Monasteries and their Patrons in the Thirteenth Century* (Oxford, 1955), 167–70.

to hold, and we do not know of any good work to ascribe to him.' The monks also hated Beatrice de Say, source of Geoffrey's power over them; the Walden chronicler labelled her *autrix ... malorum*.[33]

It is little wonder that the Walden monks supported Geoffrey de Say's claim to the Mandeville inheritance. According to the chronicle, Beatrice de Say the elder sought to have her younger son, Geoffrey, 'a great and warlike man,' secure the Mandeville barony as her representative, since she was 'now decrepit and of full days.' She must have realized that no monarch was likely to consider seriously the claims of an elderly widow to a great barony.[34] Mother and son rushed to Richard I at Canterbury shortly before the king sailed from England in December 1189, and Geoffrey gained seizin of the honor, on condition that he pay a fine of 7,000 marks. The prospect of so much money probably moved Richard I much more than the petition of the widowed Beatrice de Say. According to the Walden chronicler, Geoffrey de Say made an initial payment of seventy marks, but was unable to raise the money for a second one; and when payment was demanded from his pledges, neither could they pay. He then, 'not very wise and not wishing to follow the counsel of the wise,' turned over the barony temporarily to William Longchamp, the justiciar, to take its revenues until they generated a sum equivalent to his fine.[35] This account is unsupported by the Pipe Rolls, for the roll of 4 Richard I still records the full debt of 7,000 marks.[36] Geoffrey de Say can have had seizin of the Mandeville honor for only a short time, if he ever fully secured it; the Walden account is contradictory on this. He did hold some part of it long enough, however, to collect an aid from tenants.[37]

When Geoffrey Fitz Peter heard of Geoffrey de Say's difficulties in making his payments, he made a claim to the Mandeville inheritance based upon his wife's right as her deceased father's representative. The law's uncertainty gave an excuse for a consideration of her claim, yet it would be treated in extraordinary ways. Since no writ lay against King Richard I, the chief lord, none of the new actions would be applicable. Neither did an assize of *mort d'ancestor* lie against Geoffrey de Say, the nominal possessor, because the claimant, Geoffey Fitz Peter's wife Beatrice, and the tenant, her uncle Geoffrey de Say, were 'both of the same stock' from which the contested inheritance descended. In *Glanvill's* words, such 'blood relationship stops the assize.'[38] Also the claim of Geoffrey Fitz Peter's wife was bound to receive a sympathetic hearing, since he was one of the *appares* ruling England during the king's

---

[33] *Mon. Angl.*, 6(2): 975.

[34] Ibid., 4: 139–46.

[35] Ibid., 4: 139, 145; *P.R. 2 Richard I*, 111; *P.R. 3 & 4 Richard I*, 171; *P.R. 5 Richard I*, 5 records Geoffrey's debt of 7,000 marks.

[36] *P.R. 3 & 4 Richard I*, 171.

[37] *Mon. Angl.*, 4: 145; *P.R. 2 Richard I*, 2.

[38] *Glanvill*, 13: 3–13, p. 155. Similarly a marginal note in *Bracton's Note Book*, ed. F.W. Maitland, 3 vols. (Cambridge, 1887), 3: 631, no. 1829, 'Note that the assize of death does not lie between those heirs descending from a common stock, namely between uncles and nephews.'

absence, while Geoffrey de Say apparently lacked influential supporters. The entire episode illustrates how a *curialis* could use his influence and knowledge to further his fortunes, taking advantage of powerful friends at court and a knowledge of the workings of the courts and the Exchequer. If Beatrice de Say had not been married to Geoffrey Fitz Peter, her claim would hardly have been treated seriously. In none of these proceedings was anything said of the right of Geoffrey Fitz Peter's sister-in-law and Geoffrey de Say's cousin, Maud de Say.

The case bears some resemblance to the later *casus regis*, the question of John's claim to the English crown *versus* that of his nephew, Arthur of Brittany, or the claim of a younger son *versus* his nephew, an elder son's lineal descendant who stands in his father's stead as his representative. The difference here is that the representatives of the deceased elder son are female not male. At the time *Glanvill* was written, c. 1187/89, the law governing descent in such cases was not yet clear. The author wrote: 'When ... anyone dies leaving a younger son and a grandson born of an eldest son, a great legal problem (*iuris dubitatio*) arises as to which is to be preferred to the other in that succession, namely, whether the son or the grandson.' He noted that some favored the younger son, while others felt that the grandson should be preferred to his uncle. The author of *Glanvill* tended toward the latter view, which accorded with strict linear succession.[39] The author of *Bracton* also seems to have favored the grandson or granddaughter over the uncle, but he dared not say so directly because of the precedent of the *casus regis*; and he hesitated to suggest any legal remedy for them.[40] The uncertainties of *casus regis* gave rise to much litigation; as J.C. Holt has written: 'Whenever the *casus regis* was replicated, uncle and nephew (or sometimes uncle and niece) in knightly and lesser families battled it out in the courts.'[41]

The Walden Chronicle states that Geoffrey Fitz Peter offered a fine that surpassed Geoffrey de Say's offer, but the Pipe Roll records an oblation of only 3,000 marks. Geoffrey's offer for his wife's inheritance was made 'provided that he will be of such service to the lord king that it shall be in the king's pleasure whether he chooses to accept it or not.' Fitz Peter paid at once 900 marks.[42] Richard Lionheart accepted Geoffrey Fitz Peter's fine, and he acknowledged Geoffrey and his wife as *juste et propinquior heredes* in a charter of January 1191, issued in Sicily, where he had stopped en route to the Holy Land.[43]

Beatrice had a younger sister, Maud, married to William de Buckland, with whom the inheritance should have been shared according to *Glanvill*. The lawbook discussed cases in which a tenant left no son, only daughters, but

---

[39] *Glanvill*, 7:3, pp. 77–78.

[40] *Bracton*, fol. 64b, 2: 189; fol. 267b, 3: 283–84; fol. 374b, 4: 173–74; F. Pollock and F.W. Maitland, *A History of English Law*, 2 vols. (Cambridge, 1898), 2: 285.

[41] 'Feudal Society and the Family: III,' 20.

[42] *P.R. 2 Richard I*, 104, 111.

[43] Round, *Ancient Charters*, 97–98, no. 59.

nieces. Their father had died before 1185 without ever having had possession of the earldom. As seen above, according to *Glanvill* in cases in which more than one daughter is heir, the custom of *parage* should prevail: the inheritance to be divided among them, with the chief messuage going to the eldest daughter. The claims of Maud to half the inheritance were ignored however.[44]

The Mandeville honor with its *caput* at Pleshy, Essex, carried with it the title 'Earl of Essex' and the third penny of the county. The income was granted to Geoffrey promptly, but he would have to wait until the accession of King John before winning formally the title of earl.[45] Apparently John girded Geoffrey with the sword of the earldom of Essex on his coronation day as reward for his support for his claim to the crown over Arthur of Brittany.[46]

Geoffrey Fitz Peter paid off the balance of his debt within three years, quickly for a *curialis*, since royal servants in the king's favor frequently left Exchequer debts unpaid for years on end.[47] Evidently Geoffrey wanted nothing to cloud his claim to the Mandeville lands. Even with his royal charter, Geoffrey could never feel entirely secure in his possession of the earldom; and his unclear title gave King John a weapon for keeping him loyal. One of the reasons that Fitz Peter gave for seeking release from his crusading vow c. 1200–2 was his need to protect the inheritance of his young children from powerful enemies.[48] Insecurity of tenure was one of the Angevins' instruments for guaranteeing loyalty and obedience from their servants, and Geoffrey Fitz Peter knew that the dormant De Say claim could be revived whenever the king sanctioned it.[49] Geoffrey de Say may have regretted that he did not follow the king to Marseilles or Messina to argue his case. He did have opportunity to complain to Richard Lionheart about the disposition of the Mandeville inheritance after it was too late, for he was in the king's company a number of times once he returned from the Holy Land. Geoffrey was among those who traveled to the captive king in Germany, accompanying him on his return to England, and he accompanied Richard on his travels about England in April 1194.[50]

A charter that Geoffrey Fitz Peter issued shortly after securing the Mandeville inheritance possibly sheds some additional light on those proceedings. He granted William Pointel, custodian of the Tower of London, custody of a major Mandeville tenement with the right to marry his son to the heiress in return for payment of 100 marks. This same royal agent had been custodian of

---

[44] See supra, n. 18.

[45] *Chronica Rogeri de Hovedene*, ed. William Stubbs, 4 vols., R.S. (London, 1868–71), 4: 90 (hereafter cited as Roger Howden); *P.R. 2 Richard I*, 104.

[46] Francis West, *The Justiciarship in England, 1066–1232* (Cambridge, 1961), 102; Roger Howden, 4: 86–88.

[47] Walter of Coventry, 2: 146.

[48] *The Letters of Innocent III, 1198–1216*, ed. C.R. Cheney and Mary G. Cheney (Oxford, 1967), no. 633.

[49] Jolliffe, *Angevin Kingship*, 70.

[50] *Itinerary of Richard I*, ed. Lionel Landon, P.R.S. n.s. 13 (1935), 80–84, 90–92. He was also with Richard at a great council in Rouen, Oct. 1197, 123.

the earldom of Essex for the justiciar, William Longchamp.[51] Does this transaction represent Geoffrey's pay-off to one of Longchamp's cronies in return for favorable consideration of his claim to the Mandeville honor?[52]

Geoffrey de Say would eventually renew his campaign to win the Mandeville barony, bringing suit in 1212, probably with King John's encouragement as a means of harrassing his justiciar.[53] The suit would not have been brought without royal sanction, for Geoffrey de Say did not enjoy the king's confidence. That very year he was compelled to hand over his son and heir to the king as a hostage.[54] The suit was not heard until 1214 after Geoffrey Fitz Peter's death, when Geoffrey de Say's opponent was yet another Geoffrey, the justiciar's eldest son. This young man linked himself to his mother's distinguished lineage, taking the name Geoffrey de Mandeville (IV). Following his father's death in October 1213, King John installed him with the whole of the Mandeville inheritance and with his father's custodies, although he did not gird the boy with the sword of the earldom of Essex.[55]

This time Geoffrey de Say claimed that he and his mother, Beatrice de Say, had held the lands in the time of Henry II, but young Geoffrey de Mandeville succeeded in securing dismissal of the case on a technicality. He alleged that the original writ was invalid, 'since he [Geoffrey de Say] seeks by his writ against him [Geoffrey de Mandeville] more than he himself [Mandeville] holds;' and the justices agreed that he ought not respond to the writ, although they gave Geoffrey de Say leave to seek another writ, should he wish.[56] Then in July he tried a new route, offering the king an enormous fine of 15,000 marks for recognizing that Richard I had disseized him *voluntarie*.[57] King John had reason to distrust young Geoffrey de Mandeville and to wish to dislodge him from his powerful position as earl of Essex. Geoffrey's father-in-law, Robert Fitz Walter, had conspired against the king and fled to France in 1212, returning in 1213 to find his castles destroyed by the king's command and by 1215 had become one of the leaders of the rebels. The king accepted Geoffrey's de Say's fine and commanded his new justiciar, Peter de Roches, to take counsel with other financial experts about how this 'might be expedited best for us.'[58]

---

[51] Thomas K. Keefe, unpublished paper, 'Two Faces of Indebtedness in Late Twelfth-Century England: Some Observations on the Pipe Roll for 1189–90.'

[52] William Salt Library, MS. S.D. (Pearson), 248; I owe this reference to Thomas K. Keefe.

[53] *Curia Regis Rolls*, 6: 270, Easter term.

[54] *Rotuli Litterarum Clausarum*, ed. T. Duffus Hardy, 2 vols., Record Commission (London, 1833–44), 1: 124, 8 Sept. 1214 (hereafter cited as *Rot. Lit. Claus.*).

[55] *Rot. de Obl. et Fin.*, 502–3; 4 Nov.; *Rotuli Litterarum Patentium*, ed. T. Duffus Hardy, Record Commission (London, 1835), 105 (hereafter cited as *Rot. Lit. Pat.*); Walter of Coventry, 2: 221.

[56] *Curia Regis Rolls*, 7: 110–11. Geoffrey de Say died sometime in 1214, succeeded by his son also named Geoffrey de Say, *Rot. de Obl. et Fin.*, 535.

[57] *Rot. Lit. Claus.*, 1: 168b; 15 July 1214.

[58] *Curia Regis Rolls*, 7: 110–11; also *Rot. Lit. Claus.*, 1: 168b.

Young Geoffrey, wounded in a tournament, died in 1216 without any children as heirs. His younger brother, William de Mandeville, was his heir; and William had to fight off another claim to the inheritance, when Maud de Say, younger sister of Beatrice and aunt of these young Mandevilles, put in a claim for her share. This revived claim to the Mandeville inheritance was before the courts from 1217 to 1219. Maud de Say had received nothing in 1191, when Richard I had ignored *parage* and had granted the entire earldom to Geoffrey Fitz Peter through the right of Maud's sister Beatrice. She came before a great council in August 1217 seeking from William de Mandeville to have her right recognized to her share of the earldom, appointing as her attorney Robert de Ferrers, a brother of Earl William de Ferrers. Robert de Ferrers made homage to Maud that same day in return for her promise that a third of whatever she might gain should go to him and his heirs; in addition, she promised him that she would make no agreement concerning the lands without his counsel and assent.[59]

Robert de Ferrers was in fact Maud de Say's son-in-law. He had offered King John a fine of 500 marks for marrying her daughter and for having lands of the girl's father, William of Buckland, and her inheritance, saving to Maud her reasonable dower and *maritagium*.[60] Obviously, Robert de Ferrers sought the marriage as a means of securing a claim to part of the Mandeville inheritance, and he had come to some agreement with his prospective mother-in-law, who was the key to his claim. Maud de Say's suit against the earl of Essex came before the justices at Westminster in Michaelmas term 1219, only to be postponed until the next term of court, Hilary 1220.[61] At that time Maud was unable to pursue her claim, since the king's council declared that it dared not give judgment concerning royal charters, presumably because the king was a minor. In the autumn of 1220 the case was again postponed, and no conclusion to the case was ever recorded.[62]

In 1227 William de Mandeville also died childless. The two brothers had a third brother, Henry, for whom Geoffrey Fitz Peter had chosen a clerical career, and he failed to succeed to the earldom.[63] This meant that the Mandeville inheritance again passed through the female line to their sister Maud (died 1236), who had married Henry de Bohun, earl of Hereford. The vast Mandeville inheritance then passed to the Bohuns, an old baronial family. Geoffrey Fitz Peter had not succeeded in siring a long-lived dynasty that would celebrate his name for centuries.

---

[59] *Cal. Pat. Rolls, 1216–1225*, 113. For Robert's relationship to the Earl, see *Excerpta e Rotulis Finium*, ed. Charles Roberts, Record Commission (London, 1835–36), 1: 160 (hereafter *Exc. e Rot. Fin.*).

[60] *P.R. 3 Henry III*, 57; *P.R. 4 Henry III*, 6; *Exc. e Rot. Fin.*, 1: 64–65.

[61] *Curia Regis Rolls*, 8: 117.

[62] *Bracton's Note Book*, 2: 6–8, no. 8; *Curia Regis Rolls*, 8: 117, 236; 9: 247. Robert de Ferrers was dead by Jan. 1226, *Exc. e Rot. Fin.*, 1: 136.

[63] *Rot. Lit. Pat.*, 75. King John named him to a prebend at Lincoln in 1207, *Fasti Ecclesiae Anglicanae, 1066–1300*, 3; *Lincoln*, ed. Diana Greenway (London, 1977), 126–27.

The justiciar did have another son by his second wife, John Fitz Geoffrey; but John was ineligible for the Mandeville inheritance, and eligible to inherit only acquisitions his father had made in his lifetime. Distinctions between inheritance and acquired lands go back to the *Leges Henrici Primi*, and *Glanvill* too recognized that a man could give away his acquired lands as he pleased.[64] A younger brother, especially a half-brother, was likely to feel that he was entitled to his father's acquisitions, since only the eldest son could succeed to the patrimony.[65] Geoffrey Fitz Peter had acquired wide lands in addition to the earldom of Essex during his lifetime in royal government, and he had designated some of these for his son by his second wife, most notably the great honor of Berkhamstead.[66]

The tangled succession to the Mandeville earldom shows dramatically the Angevin kings resisting following the rules of inheritance that their judges were laying down for lesser lords. Following William de Mandeville's death in 1189, the male was not preferred; neither was an equal division made between female heirs. To place the story of the Mandeville inheritance in context, it is useful to examine some similar cases from the same period: from Richard I's accession through Henry III's early years. 1237, the date for the division of the earldom of Chester among co-heirs, seems a convenient stopping point. I have found some in which partition among co-heirs was an issue and others centering on the *casus regis*, or principle of representation. Since cases resembling the *casus regis* are less common, let us turn to them first.

In 1193 a situation foreshadowing the later *casus regis* arose on the death of Robert de Lacy, lord of Pontefract, Yorkshire. When he died that year without heirs of his body and without any surviving brothers, the succession could be traced to descendants of an aunt, his father's sister. The nearest male heir was Roger, Constable of Chester, the great-grandson of Robert's aunt.[67] Because Roger feared that his right might not be recognized, his grandmother, who was still living, agreed to release her right to him.[68] A rule that Holt laid down proves true in this instance: 'The more distant the succession the more likely it was that the claimant would have to pay a heavy *finis terrae* or offer a high price for the good will or arbitration of the king.'[69] Roger felt it necessary in

---

[64] *Leges Henrici Primi*, ed. L.J. Downer (Oxford, 1972), 224, 70, 21: 'The first-born son shall have the father's ancestral fee (*feodum*); the latter shall give any purchases or subsequent acquisitions of his to whomever he prefers.' *Glanvill*, 7:1, p. 71.

[65] Holt, 'Feudal Society and the Family: III,' 19.

[66] *Rotuli Chartarum*, ed. T. Duffus Hardy, Record Commission (London, 1837), 151b (hereafter cited as *Rot. Chart.*); *Rot. Lit. Claus.*, 1: 154b; *Rot. Lit. Pat.*, 104.

[67] John T. Appleby, *England without Richard, 1189-1199* (Ithaca, N.Y., 1965), 182-83; I.J. Sanders, *English Baronies* (Oxford, 1960), 138; W.E. Wightman, *The Lacy Family in England and Normandy, 1066-1194* (Oxford, 1964), 86.

[68] *Early Yorkshire Charters*, ed. William Farrer and Charles Travis Clay, Yorkshire Archaelogical Society Record Series and Extra Series, 12 vols. (1914-65), 3: no. 1522.

[69] Holt, 'Politics and Property,' 24.

1195 to offer the king a 3,000-mark fine, which he paid off with remarkable speed.[70] Even so, Richard I kept the castle of Pontefract in his own hand.

Once King John took the crown instead of his nephew Arthur, the royal justices proceeded cautiously in such cases. Fearful of casting a shadow over the royal title, John's and Henry III's judges preferred to adjourn them without judgment. A case that raised questions much like the *casus regis* centers on the Percy honor in Yorkshire, Topcliffe. In 1175 it had descended to two sisters, Maud, wife of the earl of Warwick, and Agnes, married to Jocelin de Louvain. These two sisters died early in John's reign within a short time of one another. Agnes apparently died first in 1203, and her sister Maud's death soon followed in 1204.

Since Maud left no children, next in line for the two sisters' lands were the offspring of Agnes: a grandson, William III de Percy, son of her deceased elder son; and Richard de Percy, a younger son.[71] William was a minor in the custody of William Briwerre, one of King John's *familiares*; he later married the boy to one of his daughters. King John, instead of deciding in favor of one or the other claimant, made a division of lands following the sisters' deaths. Possibly John would have preferred to see the entire honor in the hands of his trusted companion William Briwerre, but the similarity of Richard de Percy's claim to Topcliffe to the king's own claim to his throne protected him, at least partially.[72] The king commanded the sheriff of Yorkshire to put Richard in possession of all his mother's lands and all lands in the shire that his aunt had held of the earldom of Chester, and that he should give William Briwerre, custodian of William de Percy, all Maud's lands except those held of Chester.[73]

This division led to a long series of legal actions, partly because of genuine uncertainty about which lands had belonged to which sister, but also because of both sides' unwillingness to accept the division. In 1212 William Briwerre brought suit against Richard de Percy for intruding on his ward's possessions. Richard offered two palfreys for an inquest to determine whether the property in question belonged to his or his nephew's inheritance, but since he could not deny that Briwerre had seizin as William de Percy's guardian, he lost his suit without the inquest ever being taken.[74] In 1214 William de Percy brought suit against Richard for five of the Percy manors, which he claimed he had held while he was in William Briwerre's custody; but the case was dismissed on a technicality: he had named among the manors he sought one that he already held.[75]

No doubt Richard de Percy's dissatisfaction with the division contributed to his role in the rebellion against King John; he was among its leaders in the

---

[70] *P.R. 7 Richard I*, 98. He was pardoned £88.
[71] Sanders, *Baronies*, 148; *Complete Peerage*, 10: 450–53; see Appendix C, infra, 171.
[72] J.C. Holt, *The Northerners* (Oxford, 1960), 21–22.
[73] *Rot. Lit. Claus.*, 1: 11b. See also *P.R. 8 John*, 196 (1206); *P.R. 9 John*, 82 (1207); William Briwerre evidently had control of Agnes' lands, but soon they were in Richard de Percy's hands.
[74] *Curia Regis Rolls*, 6: 321.
[75] Ibid., 7: 160.

North. William de Percy, on the other hand, saw loyalty to John as the way to win land from his uncle, and in 1214 he served with the king in Poitou.[76] Richard's rebellious conduct led to seizure of his estates, which were confided to the custody of William de Percy.[77] Henry III's counselors in May 1217 returned all Richard's land to William de Percy as his right, 'inasmuch as he is nearer heir who is in our service.' By autumn, however, Richard de Percy had returned to the king's service, and he instituted proceedings to reclaim his possessions.[78] Finally, an agreement was reached in 1218 for apportionment of the lands between uncle and nephew, but that did not end the litigation, which continued until 1234.[79]

If the royal justices should have ruled in favor of a nephew or niece over an uncle, they would have been casting doubt on their king's claim to his crown. To avoid giving judgment in such cases, they often marked them for consultation with the king.[80] Until Arthur of Brittany's sister, Eleanor, died in 1241, no English judge could have been expected to follow the representative principle.[81] *Bracton* states that because of the *casus regis* similar cases could not proceed to judgment, but must remain in suspense unless the parties could reach an agreement.[82]

An Easter term 1235 case before Henry III's justices was similar to the earldom of Essex succession, a dispute between niece and uncle: Maud, daughter of Henry Hose II, versus her uncle, Matthew Hose, who was her father's younger brother.[83] Matthew offered the king 70 marks for having his father's lands, claiming that he was the nearer heir; but his claim was challenged by Maud, seeking 'since she is the daughter of Henry the eldest brother ... such seizin of said lands and tenements of said Henry her grandfather as said Henry her father would have held if he had lived.' She offered the king 1,000 marks to have seizin. Matthew countered by challenging the legitimacy of her birth, questioning her parents' marriage, and restating his offer of 70 marks. The justices at Westminster accepted his smaller fine, and they ruled that he should have his seizin, a contrast with the conclusion in the Mandeville case.

That was not the end of the matter, however, for the Fine Roll for 1235 records that Matthew Hose had fined with the king in April for 600 marks to have seizin of all his father's lands.[84] Evidently Maud had succeeded in having

---

[76] *Rot. Lit. Claus.*, 1: 207.
[77] Ibid., 250, 308; Holt, *Northerners*, 67.
[78] *Rot. Lit. Claus.*, 1: 308, 339, 360b.
[79] *Complete Peerage*, 10: 450, n. b.
[80] E.g., *Pleas before the King or his Justices*, ed. Doris M. Stenton, 2, Selden Society, 68 (1949): 144, no. 528; *Bracton's Note Book*, 3: 595, no. 1766.
[81] T.F.T. Plucknett, *A Concise History of the Common Law*, 5th edn. (London, 1956), 718.
[82] *Bracton*, fol. 267b, 3: 283-85; fol. 327b, 4: 46.
[83] *Curia Regis Rolls*, 15: 361-62, no. 1409; *Exc. e Rot. Fin.*, 1: 278, order to the sheriff of Sussex to take into the king's hand and hold until commanded otherwise, 1 April 1225.
[84] *Exc. e Rot. Fin.*, 1: 279.

some right to some of her grandfather's lands recognized, for in October 1238 Henry III personally ordered Matthew Hose to return to her one carucate in Wiltshire, 'land of which Henry Hose, grandfather of said Maud, whose heir she is, was seized as of fee on the day on which he died ....'[85]

Maud's persistance in her effort to win recognition as heir is remarkable. In early September 1239, she brought another action, seeking three knights' fees at Hastings from Matthew, maintaining once more that she was her grandfather's heir. Matthew raised several extraneous issues to avoid replying to his niece's writ, but without success. Matthew then argued that he had the greatest right because he was the *astrarius*, or hearth-child, the younger son still at home at the time of his father's death. Maud's response was a statement of the representative principle: Henry her father was her grandfather's eldest son and heir, and the lands should descend to her as eldest daughter and heir of her deceased father. At this point Henry III commanded that the case be removed from the justices at Westminster to his court *coram rege*.[86] Unfortunately no conclusion to the case is recorded. Several adjournments of days assigned for taking their chirograph hint, however, that the case was settled by a compromise.[87] Cases that raised the issue of the *casus regis* included then fines by the parties, hesitation by the justices, and frequent intervention by the king.

Cases concerning partition among heiresses were more likely to go forward without difficulty, but they could offer opportunity for royal intervention in order to favor one of the king's friends. I.J. Sanders' compendium of baronies reveals 37 between the accession of Richard I in 1189 and 1237 that required division among co-heirs. Unfortunately, Sanders' recitation of genealogies often leaves an impression of smooth successions, but a glance beneath the surface can reveal previously undetected royal interventions. A far from thorough examination of the circumstances indicates some royal intervention, at least the king's acceptance of a large oblation, in 45% (17 out of 37) of the cases.[88] Thirty-two percent (12 out of 37) of these took place between the deaths of Henry II and John.

In few instances would the king be so bold as Richard I was in the Mandeville case. He would rarely ignore entirely an heiress's claim, but he might delay a long time handing the land over, make an unequal distribution, or require a hefty fine. For example, in 1217 following the death of the lord of Odell, each of his sisters offered £100 as fine and relief for half the barony.[89] Remember that this is after *Magna Carta* had fixed £100 as the proper relief for a whole barony.

---

[85] *CR, 1237–1242*, 148.

[86] *Curia Regis Rolls,* 16: 183–84, no. 959.

[87] Ibid., 16: 267, no. 1410; 304, no. 1572; 356, no. 1762; 359, no. 1779.

[88] Baronies: Bulwick, Burgh by Sands, Cavendish, Great Torrington, earldom of Chester, honor of Leicester, Odell, Pleshy, Southoe, Stainton la Vale, and West Dean. Probable baronies: Egremont and Papcastle, Lavendon, Hepple, Odcombe, Pontefract, Stogursey.

[89] *P.R. 2 Henry III*, 63.

The uncertainties surrounding the Mandeville lands made it possible for Richard I to reward a capable *curialis*, accepting Geoffrey Fitz Peter as heir in preference to Geoffrey de Say, and ignoring any claims of Maud de Say. King John enjoyed Geoffrey's uncertainty of seizin as a means for keeping him dependent, allowing challenges to his claim to surface. Henry III's counselors continued to entertain challenges to the Fitz Peter family's right, yet their rivals, Geoffrey and Maud de Say, never succeeded in making good their claim.

Heritability of baronies by women, coupled with feudal rights of wardship and marriage, gave the monarch a valuable resource for rewarding his *familiares*. Division among heiresses gave him added pieces of land with which to reward his servants, while preventing any one of them from getting too large an amount. A recent study of succession to baronies under Henry III takes note of his use of heiresses for marriages to members of his family and to foreign friends and of the concern this caused the baronage.[90]

Since I find myself now a historian of bureaucrats, royal financial advantage and patronage opportunities come to my mind most readily as reasons for the king's intervention in the succession of honors. I think that the initiative often came from *curiales*. No doubt cutting potentially over-mighty aristocrats down to size, reducing their military resources, sometimes motivated the monarch. A look at the fall of the earldom of Chester into the king's hand following the deaths of Ranulf de Blundeville and John the Scot in 1232 and 1237 illustrates well enough such a motive. A recent study of the litigation following the two earls' deaths concludes, 'The rights of collateral heirs were often regarded as negotiable rather than demonstrable in the thirteenth century ....'[91]

Old landed families had some basis for their fears that the Angevin kings were trampling underfoot their lawful rights of inheritance. They had as much to fear from rapacious royal servants. Enjoying easy access to the king, his *familiares* secured custodies of co-heirs, either married them or married them off to their offspring, and launched lawsuits to add as much of the inheritance as possible to their families' holdings.

Note

For other accounts of the contest between Geoffrey fitz Peter and Geoffrey de Say, see J.C. Holt, 'The *Casus Regis*: The Law and Politics of Succession in the Plantagenet Dominions 1185-1247,' in *Law in Mediaeval Life and Thought*, ed. Edward B. King and Susan J. Ridyard, Sewanee Mediaeval Studies, 5 (University of the South, Sewanee, Tenn., 1990); and Holt, *Magna Carta*, second edition (Cambridge University Press, 1992), chap. 5, 'Justice and Jurisdiction'; also Thomas K. Keefe, 'Counting Those Who Count: A Computer-Assisted Analysis of Charter Witness-Lists and the Itinerant Court in the First Year of the Reign of King Richard I', *Haskins Society Journal*, 1 (1989).

---

[90] Scott L. Waugh, 'Marriage, Class, and Royal Lordship,' 199–205.
[91] Richard Eales, 'Henry III and the End of the Norman Earldom of Chester,' in *Thirteenth-Century England*, Proceedings of the Newcastle upon Tyne Conference, 1985, ed. P.R. Cross and S.D. Lloyd (Woodbridge, Suff., 1986), 100–12.

Appendix A

Genealogical Chart: The Mandevilles

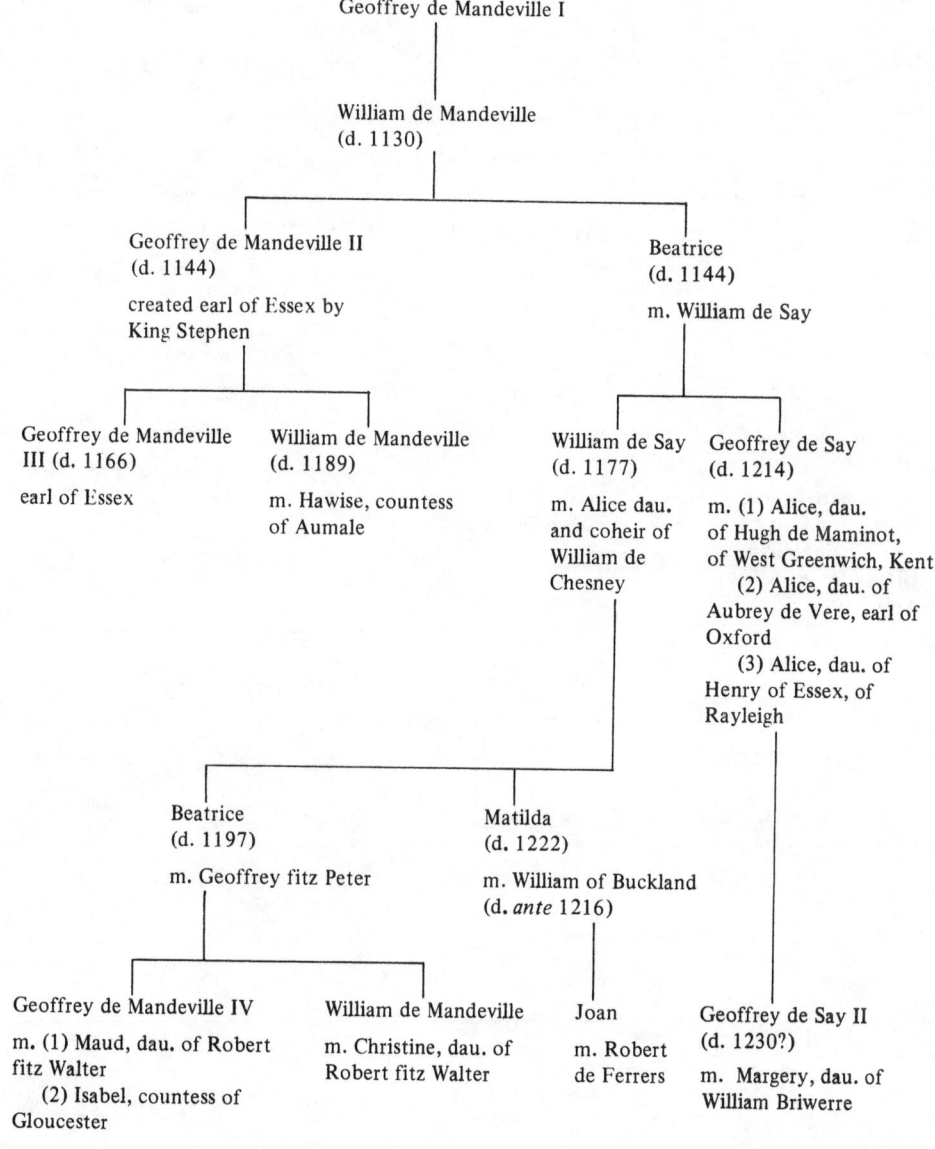

Appendix B

Genealogical Chart: Fitz Peter

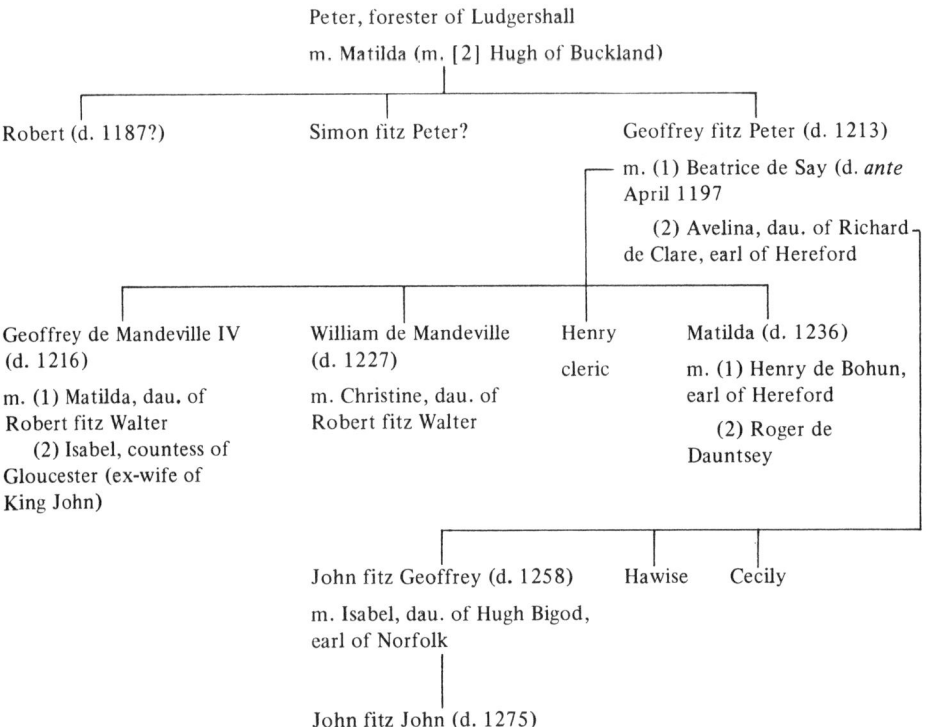

Index

Medieval names are alphabetized by Christian name, modern names by surname.

Abingdon Abbey, Berks., 133, 216-17
Adam de Bereville, 163 n. 52
Adam fitz William, 108 n. 29, 142, n. 25, 146-47, 247, 248 n. 105
Adams, Norma, xv
Adulf de Gatesden, 274 n. 28
Agnes de Percy, w. of William of Newburgh, earl of Warwick, 281, 301
Alexander Huscarl, 222, 223
Alice, dau. of earl Ranulf I of Chester, 128
Amaury de St-Amand, 221
amercements, 116, 189, 205, 208, 261
Amice, countess of Leicester, 124 n. 20
Anglo-Saxon period, x, xi, xii, 8, 9, 14, 24, 42, 47
—, laws, 35-39, 43-44, 45-46, 48, 74-75,
—,—, Wantage Code, 36-37
Anjou, counts of, 244
Arnulf, bp. of Lisieux, 132, 186-87, 195
ars dictaminis, 134
ars notaria, 56-57, 67, 134, 135, 201
Arthur, legendary King of England, xx
—, count of Brittany, 99, 207, 280, 296, 297, 301
Arundel, earldom, 279 n. 60
Assize of Clarendon, 41, 65
Assize of the forest, 260
Assize of Northampton, 13
assizes, grand, 58, 78, 80, 81, 87, 236, 260, 261
—, possessory, xiii, 3, 4-5, 8, 10, 14, 19, 30, 75, 79, 178, 207, 213, 220, 236, 264, 268, 290
—, darrein presentment, 109
—, mort d'ancestor, 4, 207, 257, 263, 274, 280, 295
—, novel disseizin, xii, 4, 9, 41, 60-62, 79, 222, 223, 253, 255-56, 260, 262-67
—, *utrum*, 41
attorneys, lawyers, 89, 125, 132, 178, 184, 216-218
Aubrey de Vere I, earl of Oxford, 128, 257, 278-79, 291 n. 12

Baldwin, archbp. of Canterbury, 164
—, J.W., xviii, xix, xxiv, 80, 245
Bampton, Devon, barony, 279
—, Oxon., church at, 98

Barlings Abbey, Lincs., 145
Barlow, F, xxi
Barnwell chronicler (Walter of Coventry), 230, 247
Bartholomew, bp. of Exeter, 98
Bartlett, R., xviii
Basilia, w. of Hugh de Odingselles, 272 n. 21, 293 n. 26
Bates, D., 230, 233
Battle Abbey, Sussex, 97
Beatrice I de Say, 294, 298
Beatrice II de Say, w. of Geoffrey fitz Peter, xxiv, 144, 273 n. 25, 289, 292, 294-96, 299
Beauchamp family, 228
Beaulieu Abbey, Hants, 146
Bedford Castle, 211
Beech, G., xviii
Benedict, abbot of Peterborough, 52
Benedict of St-Maur, 227
Berkhamstead, honor, 300
Béthune, minstrel of, 241
Biancalana, J., xii
Blackstone, W., 35
blood judgments, 129, 162-63, 167, 171-74, 175, 177-78
Bologna, schools, 53-55, 84-85, 94, 128, 184, 196, 198
Boniface of Savoy, archbp. of Canterbury, 168
Bracton, xiv, 65, 100, 113, 116, 181, 207, 237, 251-56, 262, 264, 266, 268, 281, 296, 302
Bracton's Note Book, 3, 207, 263
Brevarium Alaricanum, 47
Brand, P.A., xiii, xvii
Brian fitz Count, 127
Brooke, C.N.L., 160
Brown, E.A.R., 6
Brunner, H., 35-37, 39-40
Bullington Convent, Lincs., 143 n. 29
Bury St. Edmunds Abbey, Suff., 211
Bushmead Priory, Beds., 211

Caillemar, M., 56
canon law, xiv, xv, 46, 47, 54-55, 60-61, 63, 67, 71, 75, 77, 82-87, 91, 93, 108, 121, 160-64, 171-73, 176, 178, 184, 190, 196

—, Gratian's *Decretum*, 54, 161-62, 171-73
—, inquisitorial procedure, 64-65, 68, 84
canons, regular, 138-39, 142, 143, 148
Cantor, N., 47
Carpenter, D.A., xvii
carucage, 203
casus regis, 14, 99, 207, 280-81, 284, 290, 296, 300-3
Carthusian order, 146
Castle Cary, Somerset, barony, 279 n. 60
castles, custodians, constables, 124, 182, 202, 211
Cavendish, Suff., barony, 272 n. 21, 273 n. 25, 293 n. 26
chamber, royal, 123
—, chamberlains, 123, 130, 220
chancery, royal, 18, 29, 57, 262
—, chancellor, 122, 123, 160, 170-71, 187, 188, 205
charters, 120, 131, 142, 182, 229, 257
—, royal, xx, xxi, xxiv, 6, 24, 32, 96, 114, 181, 182, 186, 188, 208, 210, 262, 266, 272, 292, 296, 299
—, Norman ducal, 39
Cheney, C.R., 54, 57, 64, 164, 212
—, M.G., 9
Chester, earldom, 304
Chetewode Priory, Bucks., 138
Chibnall, M., 234
Chipping Warden, barony, 183
chirograph, *see* final concord
Choques, honor, 211
Christchurch Cathedral, Canterbury, monks of, 148
chroniclers, xix, 20, 90, 104, 106, 109, 118, 125, 137, 146, 182, 203, 217, 225, 229, 238, 247, 252, 291, 294
Cistercian order, 139, 142
Clanchy, M.T., xvi, xvii, xviii, 80, 243-44, 245
coheirs, *see* inheritance
Coke, Edward, 45
combat, trial by, duel, xviii, 80, 81, 172
Constance, w. of Ralph fitz Gilbert, 128
Constitutions of Clarendon, 11, 75, 79, 130, 177, 196
coroner, 23, 131, 181
Coss, P.R., 230, 237
Cottingham, Yorks, barony, 279 n. 61
councils, ecclesiastical, 129, 161-64, 173, 175, 190
—, great, *magna curia regis*, 18-19, 24, 204, 247, 253, 259, 265
—, regency, 27, 109, 115, 271, 282, 291, 299, 302
courtiers, xix-xxii, 10, 23, 51, 58, 81, 88, 95, 103-06, 110, 111, 117, 123, 137-39, 168-69, 173-77, 182, 186, 193, 198, 203-4, 225-29, 238-49, 283-84, 291, 295, 304
courts, ecclesiastical, xiv, xv, xvi, 41, 62-63, 68, 79, 84-87, 118, 121, 161, 189
—, papal *curia*, 118, 170, 186, 209
—, feudal, xi, xii, xiii, xx, 1-4, 6-7, 10, 14, 72, 78, 94, 96, 270
—, Irish, 219-20
—, local, 75, 184, 216
—, London husting, 217
—, royal, *curia regis*
—,—, justices, x, xviii-xix, 2, 3, 8, 10, 13-15, 66-68, 76-77, 173-74, 176-78, 254, 256-57, 259-64, 267-68, 302
—,—,—, clerks of, xv, xxii, 73, 201, 257
—,—, justices, gaol delivery, 109, 177-78
—,—, justices, itinerant, xvi-xvii, 1, 11, 18, 19, 30, 58, 96, 104, 106, 110, 115, 123, 124, 166-67, 169, 176-77, 178, 182-83, 185-186, 188-90, 199, 203-5, 207, 208, 219
—,—, Common Pleas, Bench, xiii, xxii, 17-33, 59, 66, 73, 79, 96, 109, 120, 124-125, 131, 189-90, 199, 203-5, 212, 218-19, 260, 299, 302
—,—, King's Bench, *coram rege*, xiii, 17-33, 109, 117, 164, 204-5, 208-9, 212, 218-19, 271, 303
—, shire, 78, 89, 130, 216
—, venality, corruption of, 103-8, 116-18, 209
Coxford Priory, Norf., 195
Crouch, David, xiii, xxii
curiales, *see* courtiers

Daniel of Morley, 51
David, author of *Life of Henry I*, 128
David, C.W., 125
David of London, Mr. 53
David of Scotland, Earl of Huntingdon, 202
Davy, M.-M., 121
De Aragon, R., 291
debts, action of, 31, 81, 82-83, 101
—, to crown, 12, 21, 203, 209, 210, 235, 252, 261, 273-74, 297
—, to Jews, 202, 221, 275 n. 36

Denholm-Young, N., 235
Deulesaut the Jew, 213
Dialogus de Scaccario, 9, 58, 59, 73, 74, 77, 78, 88, 110, 113, 130, 174, 181, 201, 235, 245, 251, 252
Donahue, C., xv
Dunkeswell Abbey, Devon, 139, 148
Dunstable annals, 107
—, prior, 211
Douglas, D., 40
Downer, L.J., 48
Du Cange, C., 121, 122
Duby, G., 242
duel, *see* combat
Duggan, C., 54

East Rhuddam Priory, Norf., 144, 195
East Tilbury, Essex, pilgrim hostel, 142
Eastbridge, Canterbury, hospital, 141
Eaton Socon, Beds., barony, 211
Edith/Matilda, queen of England, 126
Edmund Rich, archbp. of Canterbury, 106, 166
Eleanor of Brittany, 281, 302
Elias of Dereham, Mr., 147
Elton, G.R., 181
Emma de Cheney, w. of Michael Belet, 193-94
Essex, earldom, xxiv, 289-300
essoin, essoiner, 236, 256
Eustace, bp. of Ely, 190
—, de Fauconberg, bp. of London, 112 n. 54, 147 n. 51
Exchequer, xiii, xxi, xxiii, 18, 22-24, 29, 31, 59, 66, 77, 94, 96, 110, 113, 124, 169, 170, 182, 186, 202-3, 206, 255, 259, 284
—, barons of, 22-24, 120, 124, 131, 189, 192, 203, 243, 261, 271
—, Irish, 220, 221
—, Norman, 194

Faricius, abbot of Abingdon, 41
Fawkes de Breauté, 247
fealty, homage, 2, 3-5, 7, 238, 269, 272-73, 290, 291, 293, 299
feudalism, feudal tenure, x, xi, xii, xxii-xxiii, 3-7, 18, 74, 191, 278, 290-93, 297
—, feudal aid, 295
—, feudal custom, xi, xiv, 2-5, 14, 72, 74, 88, 161, 269, 272-73, 290-91, 294, 300
—, feudal incidents, 5

—, —, escheats, forfeitures, 202, 208, 210, 279, 280
—, —, marriage, 193, 272, 283, 284, 297, 299
—, —, relief, 269, 278, 284, 291, 303
—, —, wardships, xxiv, 13-14, 98-99, 193, 208, 210, 212, 238, 276, 277, 281, 283, 284, 301
final concord, 22, 67, 94, 96, 124, 192, 200, 206, 211, 222, 229, 258, 303
fines, oblations, 31, 116, 202, 203, 206, 257, 258, 267, 272, 273, 274, 276-79, 282, 284, 291, 293, 295, 296, 298, 299, 300-1, 302, 303
Flanagan, M.T., xx
Forde Abbey, Devon, 21
forester, royal, 95, 260, 291
Forville, R., 46
Fotheringay Castle, 202
friars, 139-40
Fulbert III de Dover, 277 n. 51
Fulk de Oiry, 194
Fulk Paynell, 279 & n. 62

Gabel, L., 121
Galbraith, V.H., 120, 125, 127
Geoffrey, count of Perche, 210
—, goldsmith, 260 n. 41
Geoffrey de Lascelles, 276 & nn. 45-46
Geoffrey de Lucy, 98, 261, 275
Geoffrey de Mandeville, 73 n. 6
Geoffrey de Mandeville IV, 298-99
Geoffrey de Say, 270 n. 10, 294-98, 304
Geoffrey de Vinsauf, 134 n. 87
Geoffrey fitz Geoffrey, 274 n. 28
Geoffrey fitz Peter, earl of Essex, xxiv, 13 n. 63, 14 n. 67, 72, 88, 94-95, 96, 112 n. 51, 130, 140 & n. 15, 142, 143-44 & n. 27, 145, 147 n. 50, 191, 201-2, 218, 222, 241, 270 n. 10, 271, 273 n. 25, 276, 289, 291-92, 294-300, 304
Geoffrey Gaimar, 128
Geoffrey le Bel, count of Anjou & Duke of Normandy, 41
Geoffrey Marsh, justiciar of Ireland, 219-20
Geoffrey Mauduit, 256
Geoffrey of Monmouth, 127
Geoffrey Plantagenet, archbp. of York, 160 n. 6, 164 n. 34
Geoffrey Ridel, bp. of Ely, 8 n. 38, 12 n. 57, 13 n. 62, 59, 73 n. 7, 111, 146, 160 n. 6, 181 n. 4, 190

Gerald of Wales, 51, 93, 103 n. 2, 104, 129-29, 139, 170, 226, 239, 240-41
Gerard Pucelle, Mr., 55, 84 n. 81
Gerard Talbot, 267
Gervase of Chichester, 111, 122 n. 10
Gervase of Melkley, 134 n. 87
Gervase of Tilbury, 122 n. 10, 126
Gervase Paynell, 291 n. 12
Gilbert de Glanvill, bp. of Rochester, 147, 187
Gilbert de Montfichet, 277
Gilbert of Preston, 109
Gilbert fitz Baderon, 128
Gilbert Foliot, bp. of London, 52-53, 174, 176, 192-93
Gilbert Huscarl, 215
Gilbertine order, 140
Giles de Muncele, 291 n. 12
Gillingham, John, xxi
Glanvill, ix, xiv, 4, 7, 9, 20-22, 24, 58, 59-60, 62, 63, 64, 71-101, 110, 130, 181, 184, 217, 236, 245, 251, 269, 272, 276, 280-81, 291, 293-97, 300
Guiot de Provins, 247
Godfrey de Insula, 112 n. 51
Godfrey Huscarl, 215
Godfrey de Lucy, bp. of Winchester, iv, 12 & n. 57, 13 n. 63, 14 n. 67, 72, 74, 95-100, 101, 148 n.59, 276-77
Green, J.A., 11, 228, 243
Gundulf, bp. of Rochester, 40-41

Hall, G.D.G., 73, 94, 95, 100
Hareston Castle, 280
Harvey, S., 234-35
Haskins, C.H., 36, 40
Heiser, R.R., xxii
Helmholz, R.H., xv
Henry, son of Geoffrey fitz Peter, 299
Henry de Bohun, Earl of Hereford, 299
Henry de Bracton, 177, 199
Henry de Clinton, 274 n. 28
Henry de Glanvill, 222 n. 46
Henry de Pont-Audemer, 146, 204 n. 37, 218, 219
Henry Hose I & II, 302-3
Henry of Bath, 108
Henry of London, archbp. of Dublin, 112 nn. 51 & 54, 141, 148 n. 59, 219, 229 n. 22
Henry of Northampton, Mr., 97
Henry of Whiston, 112 n. 51

Herbert Losinga, bp. of Norwich, 128
Herbert of Bosham, 196
Hervey Belet, 194-95
Hervey de Glanvill, 88-89
Hilary, bp. of Chichester, 164 n. 34
Hollister, C.W., 123
Holt, J.C., xii, xvi, xxiii, xxiv, 94, 99, 269, 272, 278, 280, 291, 293, 296
Holy Trinity Priory, Aldgate, 145, 217
Honorius, Mr., 68 n. 150
Horsley, Derbys, barony, 280
hospitals, 140-41
household, baronial, 133, 185, 201, 236
—, episcopal, 123, 147, 174, 201
—, royal, 18, 19, 29, 80-81, 91, 110, 164, 169, 175, 181-83, 187, 228, 234-35, 246
—,—, stewards of, 29
Holdsworth, W., 37
Hubert de Burgh, justiciar, 27, 29, 130, 139, 140 n. 33, 147, 149, 241, 264-67, 271
Hubert Walter, archbp. of Canterbury, xiii, xv, 12 n. 57, 13 n. 63, 14, 23, 53, 54, 59, 68, 72, 74, 89, 92-94, 100, 101, 111, 126, 130, 133, 139, 141, 142 n. 25, 147-48, 164-65, 167, 170-71, 182, 189, 201, 259
Hudson, J., xii
Hue de Rutland, 128
Hugh II, abbot of Reading, 92
Hugh Bardolf, 13 nn. 62, 63, 100, 109, 124, 145, 147 n. 51, 204, 274 n. 29
Hugh Barre, 183
Hugh d'Aubigny, 279 n. 60, 291 n. 12
Hugh de Bolbec, 279 n. 60
Hugh de Cressy, 181 n. 4
Hugh de Morvill, 274 n. 32
Hugh de Neville, Chief Forester, 260
Hugh de Nonant, bp. of Coventry, 164, 240
Hugh de Odingselles, 272 n. 21
Hugh de Puiset, bp. of Durham, 181 n. 4, 229 n. 20
Hugh Despenser, 262 n. 48
Hugh Hose, 260-61
Hugh of Avalon, bp. of Lincoln, 97, 164-65, 178
Hugh of Wells, bp. of Lincoln, 115
Hugh Pattishall, bp. of Coventry, 212
Hurnard, N.D., xiv, 38-39, 42
Humphrey de Bohun, earl of Hereford, 261-62 & n. 48

Hyams, P.R., xvi, xvii, xviii, 3, 4

inheritance, laws of, xi, xii, 3-4, 7, 13, 71-72, 94, 98, 101, 269-84, 289-304
—, partition among coheirs, 14, 80, 193-94, 272-74, 275-78, 281, 289-90, 292-99, 303-4
—, see also *casus regis*
inquest; see jury
inquisition *post mortem*, 274
Ireland, xx, 76, 204, 215, 218-20, 221
—, chancellor of, 138
—, chief justiciar, 219-21
Isidore of Seville, 49
Ivo of Cornwall, 97

Jaeger, C.S., xxi, 244-45
James of Potterne, 112 n. 51, 201 n. 17, 204 n. 37, 218, 229 n. 23
James Savage, 147
Jews, 162, 202
—, Exchequer of, 23, 202, 211
Joan Briwerre, 275 n. 34
Jocelin, archdeacon of Chichester, 12 n. 57, 161
Jocelin de Oye, 263 n. 53
Jocelin de Stukeley, 219
Jocelin of Wells, bp. of Bath, 109, 178
John Belet, 194
John Bucuinte, 216 n. 9
John de Bidun, 273
John de Bohun, bp. of Salisbury, 53
John de Mallium, 210
John de Wahull, baron of Odell, 274 n. 25, 303
John fitz Geoffrey, 300
John Gervais, 163
John Kentish, 58 n. 91
John of Alencon, 187
John of Guestling, 112 n. 51
John of Lexington, 108, 123 & n.
John of Oxford, bp. of Norwich, 8 n. 38, 12 n. 57, 13 n. 62, 73 n. 7, 111, 148 n. 59, 190
John of Salisbury, 50, 55, 85, 87, 103-4, 117, 118, 131, 168-69, 227, 232, 243, 251
John of Tynemouth, Mr., 68 n. 150
John the Scot, earl of Chester, 282, 304
Jolliffe, J.E.A., 9, 11, 25, 290
Josce of Wallingford, 210
Joüon des Longrais, F., 60-62
Juliana, w. of William fitz Adulf, 291 n. 12

jury, juries, inquests, xiii, xviii, 1, 7, 10-11, 30, 35-44, 64-65, 66, 83, 206, 222, 236, 257, 263, 282
—, Norman, 35, 39-41
—, of presentment, xiii, xiv, 30, 37-39, 65, 82
—, see also assizes
justices, see courts, royal
justiciar, chief, x, 20, 23, 28-29, 95, 123, 129-30, 170-71, 182, 228-29, 261, 292, 294
—, local, xiv

Kemp, B., 21
Ker, N., 52
Kilburn, Middlesex, convent, 216
Kings of England:
—, Aethelred II, xiv, 36-37
—, Edward I, xvii, 106
—, Henry I, xx, 10, 11, 14, 47, 123, 125-26, 127, 225, 227-28
—, Henry II, xi, xiii, 1-14, 35, 40-44, 58, 62, 65, 77-78, 81, 104, 105, 111, 113, 126, 164, 174, 176, 178, 179, 186-87, 226, 245, 252, 257, 258, 260, 270, 274, 279
—, Henry III, xvii, 27-30, 127, 130, 168, 208-9, 237, 247, 259-61, 262, 264-67
—, John, xxiv, 25-27, 115, 126, 141, 146, 188, 190, 191, 204, 209, 210, 218, 221, 236, 252, 256-59, 261-62, 271-74, 278, 279, 280-84, 290, 298, 299, 301-4
—, Richard I, xix, xxii, 13, 93, 126, 164, 170, 188, 215, 256, 276, 279, 294-97, 301, 303, 304
—, Stephen, x, xii, 6, 50, 126
—, William I, 39, 48
—, William II Rufus, 239
—, Young Henry son of Henry II, 126, 187
kingship, administrative, x, xx, 3, 11-13, 18, 120, 123, 159, 174, 199, 242-45
—, theories, ix, x, xxiii, 5-6, 1-2, 8-9, 12, 78, 114, 141, 174-75, 195-96, 251-53
—, arbitary character, King's will, ix, xxiii, 33, 114, 207, 210, 252-68, 269-70, 274, 278, 280-84, 290, 298
Knights Hospitallers, Templars, 143, 262-63
Koehler, E., 232
Kuttner, S., 54, 86

La Clarté Dieu Abbey, Touraine, 139
Lanfranc, archbp. of Canterbury, 46-47
Lavendon, Bucks., honor, 273
Laxton, honor, 210, 211
Legendre, P., 52
Leges Henrici Primi, 10, 47, 48-49, 217, 276, 300
Leges Willelmi, Leis Willelme, 49
legitimacy, 86
Leiston Abbey, Suff., 139, 275 n. 39
Lesnes, Kent, honor, 276
Lesnes Abbey, Kent, 145, 148
letters of justices, 111, 113-14
Lewes Priory, Sussex, 144 n. 33
Liber Pauperum, 50-51, 85-86
Liber Quadripartitus, 48-49
Liebermann, F., 49
literacy of laity, xviii, 72, 87-88, 91, 119-36, 173, 184, 200-1, 218, 243-44, 248
Lombard law, 46-47
Luke des Roches, 147 n. 50
Lyon, B., 1-2

Mabel, countess of Meulan, w. of William de Reviers, 258-59
Mabel de Limesy, w. of Hugh Bardolf, 272 n. 21, 293 n. 26
Madox, Thomas, 23
magistri, 80, 124, 201, 245
Magna Carta, 30, 103, 115, 238, 255, 259-62, 265, 267, 284, 303
Maitland, F.W., x, xii, 3, 17, 19, 20, 25, 27, 35-37, 41-42, 45, 50, 60, 63, 67, 68, 74, 90-92, 101, 103, 116, 125, 179
Marie de France, 130
Martin, Mr., abbot of Chertsey, 236
Martin of Pattishall, 117, 177 & n. 121, 199, 205, 207
Mason, E., xix, 228
Matthew Paris, 107, 108, 118, 122, 130, 146, 148, 213, 247
Mathew Hose, 301-2
Maud/Matilda, mother of Henry II, 6, 127
—, dau. of Geoffrey de Lucy, 275-77
—, dau. of Henry Hose II, 302-3
—, w. of Henry de Bohun, dau. of Geoffrey fitz Peter, 299
Maud de Cauz, 210
Maud de Percy, w. of Jocelin de Louvain, 281, 301
Maud de Say, w. of William of Buckland, 292, 296-97, 299, 304

Mauduit family, 228
Meath, Ireland, liberty, 219
Meekings, C.A.F., 28, 30, 32, 205
Merton Priory, Surrey, 133
Michael Belet, xix, 13 nn. 61-63, 14 n. 67, 73 n. 6, 100, 112, 144, 181-97
—, Jr., Mr., 112, 192 n. 52, 194
Miles de Beauchamp, 274 n. 28
Milsom, S.F.C., xi-xii, 1-14, 71, 84, 101, 270, 272, 293
Montacute, family, 222
—, John de, 274 n. 31
Mooers, Stephanie, 11
Mottisfont Priory, Hants., 141 n. 22, 146 n. 45
Murray, A., 244

Netley Abbey, Hants., 139
Newark, Surrey, prior of, 260 n. 42
Newman, C.A., xx, 228, 291
Newstead Priory, Notts., 145
Nicholas, archdeacon of Huntingdon, 185
Nicholas de Sigillo, 192 n. 53
Nicholas de Stuteville, 279 n. 60, 280 n. 71
Nicholas fitz Alan, 277 n. 52
Nicholas of Dunstable, Mr., 53-54
Nigel Wireker, 129, 160, 169
Norman conquest, x, 3, 46, 66, 43, 233, 234
Normandy, 25, 26, 35, 39-41, 183, 219, 227, 230, 233
—, customs, laws, 46, 56
Northampton Castle, 202
—, schools, xv, 51, 55, 134, 135
Norwich, school, 128
notaries, 122
—, public, 57, 64

Odcombe, Somerset & Devon, honor, 274
Odell, Beds., barony, 303
Ongar, Essex, honor, 98-99, 275-76
ordeal, xviii, 81, 172
Orderic Vitalis, 47, 128, 225, 238-39
ordines judiciarii, 55-57, 59, 75, 135
Osbert fitz Hervey, 110 n. 162, 107-8, 112 n. 51, 117, 146, 189 n. 38
outlawry, 265
Oxford, schools, xv, 50-51, 55, 72, 85-86, 134

Painter, S. xxiv, 124, 278, 289, 292
Palmer, R.C., xi, 2-3, 5, 8, 12-13, 217
parage; *see* inheritance
Parliament, 116
Patrick, earl of Salisbury, 128
patronage, royal, xix, xx, xxi, xxii, 13-14, 26, 197, 228, 238, 242, 245, 247, 249, 283-84, 292
—, of churches, 143, 192, 211
Paulin Piper, 122
Pavia, 46-47
Peak, Derbys, honor, 279
Peter de Sandiacre, 280
Peter des Rivaux, 27, 29
Peter des Roches, bp. of Winchester, 124, 127, 138, 139, 140 & n. 15, 145 & n. 38, 147, 148, 149, 219, 298
Peter fitz Herbert, 257-58
Peter of Blois, 51-52, 103 n. 2, 105-6, 110-11, 126, 134 n. 87, 166, 174-76, 179, 226, 239, 240
Peter of Cornwall, 97
Peter of Paxton, Mr., 52-53
Peter the Chanter, 129, 171-73
Philip, son of Patrick, earl of Salisbury, 128
Philip II Augustus, king of France, xix
Philip of Aubenay, 127
Philip of Novarra, 133 n. 78
pincerna, butler, 183, 185, 188, 191, 194
pipe rolls, 11, 21, 31, 42, 182, 200, 278, 291, 295
Pipewell Abbey, Northants, 143 n. 29, 213
plea rolls, x, xxii, xxiii, 18, 22, 24, 25, 29, 30, 31, 33, 111, 115, 118, 132, 177, 205-6, 207, 216, 256, 257, 258, 263, 267, 291, 293
Plucknett, T.F.T., 45, 46, 48, 49, 63, 64, 65, 66, 68, 76, 125, 178
Polsloe Convent, Devon, 143 n. 31, 144 n. 35
Pontefract Castle, 301
Popes:
—, Alexander III, 132, 162
—, Innocent III, 142, 162, 170-71
—, Gregory IX, 168
Poorstock, Dorset, barony, 279 n. 60
Powicke, F.M., 103

Prémontré, Abbey, 142 n. 25
Provisions of Oxford, 237

quo warranto proceedings, 265

Ramsey Abbey, Hunts., 43, 106
—, abbot of, 166
Ralf, Ralph de Diceto, dean of St. Paul's, 77, 111, 176, 179
Ralf, Ralph de Haia, 145 n. 38
Ralf, Ralph de Neville, bp. of Chichester, 114, 122, 147
Ralf, Ralph de Somery, 291 n. 12
Ralf, Ralph fitz Gilbert, 128
Ralf, Ralph fitz Stephen, 181 n. 4
Ralf, Ralph Foliot, Mr., 13 n. 63, 23 n. 26, 52, 68, 189 n. 38, 192-93
Ralf, Ralph Hopeshort, 160 n. 41
Ralf, Ralph Niger, 51, 104, 226, 239
Ralf, Ralph of Beauvais, 174 n. 100
Ralf, Ralph of Coggeshall, 107-8, 147
Ralf, Ralph of Stokes, Mr., 112 n. 51, 201 n. 17
Ralf, Ralph of Norwich, Mr., 138, 229 n. 22, 248 n. 105
Ralf, Ralph Tricket, 211
Ranulf, treasurer of Salisbury, 21 & n. 17
Ranulf I, earl of Chester, 128
Ranulf III, earl of Chester, 138, 281, 282, 304
Ranulf de Glanvill, justiciar, 12, 13 nn. 61 & 62, 14 & n. 67, 21, n. 17, 59, 71, 72, 73 n. 6, 74, 88, 90-92, 95, 96, 98, 100, 101, 126, 130, 139, 181 n. 4
Ranulf Flambard, bp. of Durham, 239
Ranulf the Ill-tonsured, 132 n. 77
Rathbone, E., 54, 57, 58
Reedy, W.T., 123
Reading Abbey, 141
Reginald of Cornhill, 131, 147 n. 51, 261 n. 45
retainers, 116, 191
Richard, abbot of Cirencester, 211
Richard, abbot of Woburn, 213
Richard Barre, archdeacon of Ely, xix, 8 n. 38, 13 n. 63, 23 n. 26, 53, 68, 112 n. 51, 182-97
Richard Briwerre, 274

Richard de Anesty, 85, 90, 91, 116 n. 76
Richard de Beauchamp, 274 n. 28
Richard de Hescombe, 274 n. 33
Richard de Lucy, justiciar, 12, 73 n. 6, 95, 97, 98-99, 130, 143, 145, 148, 241, 275-76
Richard de Mores, Morins, *Ricardus Anglicus*, prior of Dunstable, 55, 84 n. 81, 211
Richard de Percy, 264, 281-82, 301-2
Richard de Umfraville, 129
Richard de Wich, bp. of Chichester, 163
Richard fitz Neal, bp. of London, 12 n. 57, 13 n. 63, 58, 68, 73, 88, 110, 112 n. 54, 113, 127, 133, 136, 147 & n. 51, 148 n. 59, 239, 245, 251
Richard fitz Roger, 263 n. 53
Richard Grant, archbp. of Canterbury, 166
Richard Marshal, earl of Pembroke, 29
Richard of Dover, archbp. of Canterbury, 111, 175
Richard of Herriard, 23 n. 26, 112 n. 51, 189 n. 38, 201 n. 17
Richard of Hexham, 226
Richard of Ilchester, bp. of Winchester, 8 n. 38, 12 n. 57, 13 n. 62, 59, 73 n. 7, 111, 141, 142, 181 n. 4, 190
Richard Poor, bp. of Salisbury, 163
Richardson, H.G., 19-20, 21, 24, 26, 38, 40, 42-43, 48-49, 55, 56, 58-59, 60, 62-63, 120, 125, 129, 131, 135, 200, 216, 218
Richmond, Yorks., barony, 279 n. 61
Roald fitz Alan, constable of Richmond, 258
Robert, earl of Gloucester, 126
Robert Bloet, bp. of Lincoln, 127
Robert Carpenter, 248 n. 106
Robert de Aumari, 219
Robert de Beaumont, earl of Leicester, 88, 127, 130, 133, 229 n. 20
Robert de Chesney, bp. of Lincoln, 185
Robert de Condet, 128
Robert de Courson, 129, 171-73
Robert de Ferrers, 279, 299
Robert de Girros, 291 n. 12
Robert de Grandmesnil, 132 n. 77
Robert de Lacy, 300
Robert de Lexington, 28, 117 n. 83, 144 n. 33, 145
Robert de Mortimer, 266-267
Robert de Vere, 278
Robert fitz Hugh, 210-11
Robert fitz Walter, 277-78, 298
Robert Grosseteste, bp. of Lincoln, 106, 129, 163, 166-68, 178
Robert of Pattishall, abbot of Pipewell, 213
Robert of Wheatfield, 100 n. 162
Robert Passelewe, 168, 265-66
Roger, bp. of Salisbury, justiciar, 123, 160, 176, 229 n. 20, 239
Roger, constable of Chester, 300
Roger de Burun, 280
Roger de Condet, 128
Roger fitz Reinfrid, 144 n. 33, 1145
Roger Huscarl, xix, 112 n. 51, 204 n. 37, 215-23
Roger of Howden, 90, 92, 101, 107, 170, 240
Roger of Thirkleby, 109
Roger of Tanton, 221
Roger of Whitchester, 108 n. 29
Roland Huscarl, 215
Roman law, xiv, xv, 12, 33, 45-69, 72, 77, 78, 82-87, 94, 101, 108, 134-135, 171, 183-84, 189, 201, 251
Rose of Dover, dau. of Geoffrey de Lucy, 261, 275-78, 284
Rualon of Avranches, 41
Rufford Abbey, Notts., 144 n. 33, 145

St. Albans Abbey, Herts., 146
St. Bernard of Clairvaux, 161
St. Helen's, Bishopsgate, priory, 216
St. Mary de Pré, Leicester, 145, 148
St. Mary Overy Priory, Southwark, 145
St. Mary's Abbey, Clerkenwell, 144 n. 33
—, Carrow, Norf, 144
St. Osyth's Priory, Essex, 148
St. Paul, 159
St. Thomas' Abbey, Dublin, 141
St. Thomas' Hospital, Southwark, 140 n. 15
Salisbury Castle, 207
Sampson, abbot of Bury St. Edmunds, 93, 190
Saunders, I.J., 303
Sanson de Nantuil, 128

Sayles, G.O., 19-20, 21, 24, 26, 28, 30, 31-32, 38, 40, 42-43, 48-49, 58-59, 60, 62-63, 120, 125, 129, 131, 200, 218
schools, xv, 55-58, 85-86, 133-34, 183, 200, 218, 245
scutage, 185 n. 15, 192, 235, 274
Seffrid the archdeacon, 58 n. 91
Senior, W., 46, 52
sheriffs, xxii, 95, 120, 123, 124, 131, 136, 159, 163, 164, 182, 183, 185-86, 188, 189, 191, 193, 202, 207, 221, 237, 243, 271, 301
—, undersheriffs, 123, 218, 222
Sherborne, Dorset, priory, 260 n. 42
Shouldham Priory, Norf., 140, 143 n. 29, 144, 145
Siffrewast family, 183, 192
Simon de Beauchamp, 221
Simon de Montfort, earl of Leicester, 129
Simon Langton, 122 n. 15
Simon of Pattishall, xix, 112 & n. 51, 143 n. 29, 189 n. 38, 193, 199-213, 218, 222
Simon of Southwell, 53, 68 n. 150
social status, xix, 13, 105, 120, 131, 136, 137-38, 161, 169, 199-200, 209-10, 225-49, 284
—, knights' status, 229-37
—, new men, x, xix, xx, 13, 123, 149, 225-29, 238-43, 247-49, 283
Southern, R.W., xv, 46, 72, 85, 227-28
Spalding Priory, Lincs., 144 n. 33
stannaries, 131
Stein, P., xiv, xv
Stenton, D.M., xi, 25, 31, 38-40, 44, 59, 90, 94, 130, 136, 177, 216
Stenton, F.M., 2, 39, 161
Stephen, bp. of Tournai, 184, 196, 197
Stephen de Fougères, 232-33
Stephen de Segrave, 27, 28, 29, 130, 145, 148
Stephen Langton, archbp. of Canterbury, 52, 163, 171-72
Stephen of Lexington, abbot of Savigny, Normandy, 145
Stephen of Turnham, 291 n. 12
stewards, royal household, 123
—, manorial, 120, 123, 131-32, 184, 216, 264, 267

Stewart-Brown, R., 42
Stubbs, W., 17, 19, 35-37
Sudeley, Gloucs., barony, 279 n. 60
Summerson, H., xvii
Sutherland, D.W., 61-62
Sutton at Hone, Kent, hospital, 140 n. 15

tallage, 203, 220
Theobald, archbp. of Canterbury, 53, 168
Theobald, Walter, 220
Thomas Becket, archbp. of Canterbury, 9, 53, 54, 58, 94, 126, 133, 160, 168, 186, 243
Thomas Huscarl, 215
Thomas of Chobham, 171-74
Thomas of Hurstbourne, Mr., 12 n. 57, 13 n. 63, 111 n. 47, 112 n. 5, 147, 166, 193
Thomas of Marlborough, 52, 53
Thomas of Moulton, 108, 143 n. 29, 144 n. 33
Thomas Wolsey, archbp. of York, 123
Thompson, J.W., 119-20, 125, 127
Thorne, S.E., xii, xiv, 3, 100
Thorney Abbey, Cambs., 43
Topcliffe, Yorks., honor, 280-82, 301
Totnes, Devon, barony, 279 n. 61
Torre Abbey, Devon, 138
Tout, T.F., 20, 119
Tower of London, 297
treasurer, royal, 123, 220
trespass, action of, 32, 62-63
troubadours, 231-32, 246
Trowbridge, Wilts., barony, 279 n. 61

Vacarius, Mr., xv, 50-51, 85-86, 135
Van Caenegem, R.C., x, xi, xii, xiii-xiv, xviii, 6-7, 9, 10, 21, 38, 43-44, 59-60, 62, 63, 65, 68, 83, 124
vavasor, 230-31, 233, 237
Vinogradoff, P., 37-38, 60
Vision of Thurkill, 107-8, 117

Wahull barony, 200
Walden Abbey, Essex, 143-44, 294-95
—, Chronicle, 294-95, 296

Waleran de Meulan, earl of Worcester, 88, 127
Walsingham Priory, Norf., 144 n. 22
Walter, Dominican friar, 147
Walter Brito III, 274
Walter Croc, 274-75
Walter de la Grava, 263 n. 52
Walter de Lacy, 219-20
Walter de Langford, 263 n. 52
Walter de Lucy, abb. of Battle, 89, 217
Walter Espec, 128
Walter Hose, 260
Walter Malet, 280 n. 69
Walter Map, 91, 105, 110,126 n. 32, 129, 226
Walter Martel, xii
Walter Mauclerc, bp. of Carlisle, 264
Walter of Coutances, archbp. of Rouen, 163, 181 n. 4, 241
Walter of Creeping, 112 n. 51, 229 n. 23
Walter of Henley, 132
Walter of Pattishall, 212
Waltham Abbey, Essex, 192
wardrobe, 29
Warin de Montchesney, 279 n. 60, 291 n. 12
Warren, W.L., 270
warranty, voucher of, 33, 89, 192, 256, 265-66, 268
Waugh, S.L., xx, 291
Waverley Abbey, Surrey, 145
West, F.J., 23
Westminster Abbey, abbot of, 142, 257-58
Whitchurch, Bucks., barony, 279 n. 60
William Basset, 13 n. 61, 73 n. 6, 100
William Blund, 22 n. 45
William Bret, 256-57
William Briwerre, xxiv, 14 n. 67, 112 & n. 51, 124, 131, 138, 139, 141 n. 22, 142 n. 25, 143 n. 31, 144 n. 35, 146 & n. 45, 148, 149, 204, 261, 270-84, 301
William de Béthune, 209, 211
William de Braose, 124
William de Cantilupe, 263 n. 55
William de Cheney, 193
William de Ferrers, earl of Derby, 279-80
William de Humez, 181 n. 4
William de Lefremund, 211

William de Mandeville IV, earl of Essex, 130, 229 n. 20, 289, 291, 294
William de Mandeville V, 299
William de Neville, 218
William de Percy III, 281-82, 284, 301-2
William de Ralegh, Raleigh, bp. of Winchester, 28, 29, 100, 101, 108, 112 n. 54, 163-64, 117 & n. 121, 199, 207
William de Reviers, earl of Devon, 258-59
William de St. Michael, 275 n. 36
William de Sainte-Mère-Eglise, bp. of London, 13 n. 63, 23 n. 26, 112 nn. 51 & 54, 148, 189 n. 38
William de Say, 292, 294
William de Stuteville, 280 n. 71
William de Warenne IV, earl of Surrey, 266-67
William de Warenne of Wormegay, 13 n. 66, 138, 144 & n. 33, 145, 189 n. 38
William fitz Ralph, 181 n. 4
William fitz Robert, 222
William Heron, 148 n. 105
William Huscarl, 215, 222
William Longchamp, Longchamps, bp. of Ely, 56, 58, 75, 135, 169, 188, 190, 196, 229 n. 20, 240, 290, 295, 298
William Marsh, 221
William Marshal, earl of Pembroke, xxi, 115, 124, 193, 243, 258-9
William Marshal Jr., justiciar of Ireland, 220, 221
William of Bitton, bp. of Bath, 163
William of Blois, bp. of Worcester, 163
William of Buckland, 293, 296-97, 299
William of Devon, prior of Barnwell, 190
William of Malmesbury, 47, 127, 160
William of London, Mr., 54
William of Poitiers, 46
William of Tyre, 133 n. 78
William of Wrotham, 140 n. 15
William of York, bp. of Salisbury, 28, 112 n. 54, 113, 116, 117, 177 n. 121, 208 n. 62
William Peverel, 279-80
William Pointel, 297-98
wills, testaments, 146-47
Woodbine, G.E., 74, 82, 100

writs, xi, 5, 10-11, 30, 41, 64-65, 74, 76, 89, 101, 131, 167, 192, 209, 257, 262, 263, 267, 282, 295
—, *nuper obiit*, 293
—, of right, 4
—, registers of, 64, 76, 131
Wroxton Priory, Oxon., 195

Zulueta, F. de, xiv, xv.